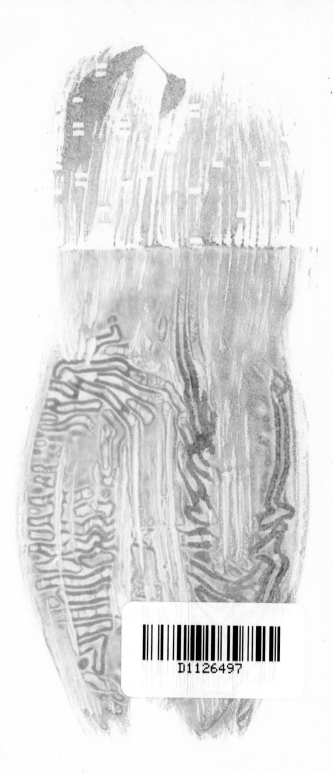

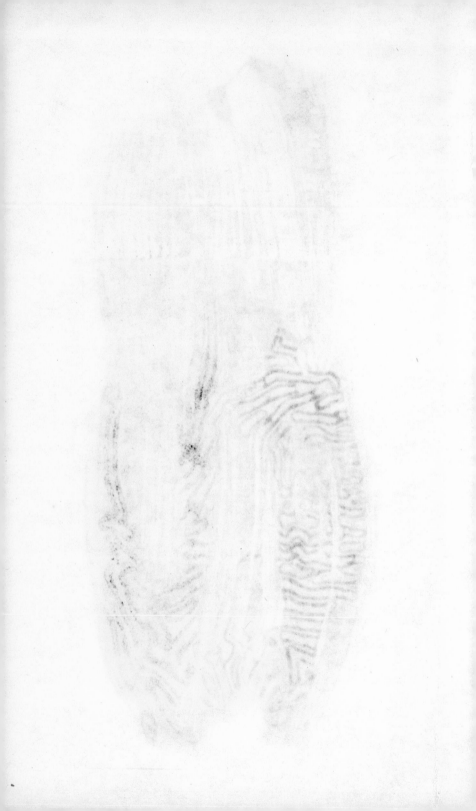

*EVERYWHERE SPOKEN AGAINST*

# EVERYWHERE SPOKEN AGAINST

## Dissent in the Victorian Novel

VALENTINE CUNNINGHAM

CLARENDON PRESS · OXFORD
1975

*Oxford University Press, Ely House, London W.1*

GLASGOW  NEW YORK  TORONTO  MELBOURNE  WELLINGTON
CAPE TOWN  IBADAN  NAIROBI  DAR ES SALAAM  LUSAKA  ADDIS ABABA
DELHI  BOMBAY  CALCUTTA  MADRAS  KARACHI  LAHORE  DACCA
KUALA LUMPUR  SINGAPORE  HONG KONG  TOKYO

ISBN 0 19 812066 4

© *Oxford University Press 1975*

*Printed in Great Britain by
Richard Clay (The Chaucer Press), Ltd., Bungay, Suffolk*

#1916144

May, 1811. But we desire to hear of thee what thou thinkest: for as concerning this sect, we know that everywhere it is spoken against. Acts xxviii.22. H.B.

The first Primitive Methodist class-ticket
Hugh Bourne issued.

*for*
*CAROL*

# PREFACE

To seek to write about nineteenth-century literature or history—unless you have allowed yourself only the most parsimonious of scopes—is to end up feeling inevitably like Canute. You might yourself have paused to put pen to paper, your manuscript is going through the press, but the spate of books and articles keeps coming on! So to write about both literature *and* history—and in this book I've tried to do what is still too rarely done, that is to examine a set of fictional accounts, in this case of religious Nonconformity, within real historical contexts—is to have the usual despairs multiplied. Unavoidably, especially given the wide range of material I tackle here, some important and interesting things have come out simply too late for digestion by my account. I leave historians and literary critics to spot my various cut-off points; otherwise the footnotes will speak for themselves about my literary indebtednesses.

Personal obligations show up, of course, less readily. The possibilities of my topic were first hinted at a long time ago in what I hope wasn't too *insouciant* a moment by Stephen Wall. Rachel Trickett patiently supervised my graduate work in this area. From time to time I have obtained various kinds of valuable advice, help and information from G. S. Haight, John Walsh, Simon Nowell-Smith, Tony Cockshut, Eric Dobson, Michael Turner, Clyde Binfield, and Raphael Samuel (at whose suggestion some of my arguments about the Brontës, *Felix Holt*, and Mark Rutherford were first aired at the Oxford Social History Group and the Ruskin History Workshop). The Fellows of St. John's College, Oxford, kindly elected me to three very enjoyable years as a Junior Research Fellow so that I could finish my work, and they and the Oxford English Faculty have been generous with other financial assistance. I am grateful to Brian Harrison, M. R. Watts, Clyde Binfield, and the (tragically) late A. C. Whitby of BBC's Radio Four for letting me read their theses. The Minister of Lion Walk Congregational Church, Colchester, was generous enough to show me the church records, and the caretaker of Bedford's Bunyan Memorial Church was not only helpful in that way but also gave me some valuable photographs of the portly and notorious Rev. John Jukes. I must thank the staff of Bodley's Upper Reading Room for being, over all the years they have given me their help, unfailingly attentive to even the most out-of-the-way demands. But my greatest and longest standing indebtedness is to John Carey: as my first tutor he set the very first critical example, and later he open-handedly made me all the breaks.

If only, though, one's friends and colleagues were responsible for one's inevitable misjudgements and prejudices. Alas, they are all my own.

*Corpus Christi College, Oxford.*                VALENTINE CUNNINGHAM
*March 1975.*

# CONTENTS

ABBREVIATIONS     xiii

NOTE ON PLACE OF PUBLICATION     xv

NOTE ON EDITIONS OF NOVELS     xv

INTRODUCTION: BACKGROUND INTO
    FOREGROUND     1

I.    OPENNESS     8
    1. Openness versus Illiberalism     8
    2. Dissenting Disabilities and the Novel     18

II.    ALL SORTS AND CONDITIONS     25
    1. The Variety of Dissent     25
    2. The Variety of Dissenting Views on the Novel     48
    3. The Variety of Dissent and the Novel     62

III.    PLACES AND POLITICS     67
    1. The Regionalism of Dissent     67
    2. Dissent and the City     74
    3. Radicalism and Dissent     91

IV.    THE PRESENCE OF DISSENT     106

V.    THE BRONTËS     113

VI.    MRS. GASKELL     127

VII.    GEORGE ELIOT     143
    1. Introductory     143
    2. Adam Bede     147
    3. Felix Holt     171

VIII.    CHARLES DICKENS     190
    1. What Dickens Knew     190
    2. Stereotypes     199
    3. Dickens and the Anti-Dissenting Tradition     215
    4. The Dickens Tradition     225

IX.  MRS. OLIPHANT AND THE TRADITION                231

X.  WAS THERE A REVOLUTION IN TANNER'S
     LANE?                                          249

XI.  THE SENSE OF AN ENDING                         278

     APPENDIX: CHARLOTTE BRONTË'S MS. 'JULIA'       287

     BIBLIOGRAPHICAL NOTES                          293

     INDEX                                          303

# ABBREVIATIONS

| | |
|---|---|
| AYR | All the Year Round |
| BNYPL | Bulletin of the New York Public Library |
| BQ | Baptist Quarterly |
| BQR | British Quarterly Review |
| BST | Brontë Society Transactions |
| BW | British Weekly |
| DNB | Dictionary of National Biography |
| E in C | Essays in Criticism |
| ELT | English Literature in Transition |
| ES | Essays and Studies |
| HW | Household Words |
| JEGPh | Journal of English and Germanic Philology |
| LQR | London Quarterly Review |
| MLQ | Modern Language Quarterly |
| N & Q | Notes and Queries |
| NCF | Nineteenth Century Fiction |
| NOID | New Oxford Illustrated Dickens |
| OED | New Oxford English Dictionary |
| PQ | Philological Quarterly |
| REL | Review of English Literature |
| RES | Review of English Studies |
| SEL | Studies in English Literature |
| SP | Studies in Philology |
| TLS | Times Literary Supplement |
| VS | Victorian Studies |
| WHS Proc. | Proceedings of the Wesley Historical Society |
| WR | Westminster Review |

# NOTE ON PLACE OF PUBLICATION

UNLESS otherwise stated, books are published in London.

# NOTE ON EDITIONS OF NOVELS

UNLESS otherwise stated, quotations from the following authors are taken from these editions:

Brontës: *Life and Works of Charlotte Brontë and Her Sisters*, illustrated edn. (7 Vols., 1872–3); except for *Wuthering Heights, Text, Sources, Criticism*, ed. Thomas Moser (New York, 1962), and *Jane Eyre*, ed. Jane Jack and Margaret Smith (Clarendon edn., Oxford, 1969).

Dickens: *The New Oxford Illustrated Edition* (21 Vols., 1947–58).

Disraeli: *Collected Edition* (10 Vols., 1870–1).

Eliot, George: *Cabinet Edition* (24 Vols., Edinburgh, 1878–[85]).

Gaskell, Mrs.: *The Knutsford Edition*, intro. A. W. Ward (8 vols., 1906).

Hardy: *Wessex Edition* (24 Vols., 1912–31).

Kingsley: *De Luxe Edition* (19 Vols., 1901–3).

Thackeray: *Oxford Edition*, ed. G. Saintsbury (17 Vols., 1908).

White, W. H.: Cheap editions of the novels in single volumes, published by T. Fisher Unwin in the 1890s.

# INTRODUCTION:
## BACKGROUND INTO FOREGROUND

. . . the chief task is the presentation of relevant historical facts which the
reader is not assumed to know.

T. S. Eliot, 'Hamlet and His Problems'

E. M. FORSTER bluntly dismissed the kind of book this one is.
According to his whimsical account in the Introductory Chapter
to *Aspects of the Novel* the English novelists have not only managed the
difficult enough feat of securing a seat in 'a sort of British Museum reading-
room', all together at the same time. They have also succeeded in
shedding every trace of their own particular times and places, and, what's
more, they are apparently content to be writing about nothing very
particular at all. And so, of course, it is the outward and visible sign
of egregious folly in the critic to care about the chronological siting
and the social context of their fictions, and about the specificities and
contingencies of their subject-matter. Concerns like that denote the
pseudo-scholar. And he gets the roughest of handlings:

He classes books before he has understood or read them; that is his first crime.
Classification by chronology. Books written before 1847, books written after it,
books written after or before 1848. The novel in the reign of Queen Anne, the
pre-novel, the ur-novel, the novel of the future. Classification by subject-matter
—sillier still. The literature of Inns, beginning with *Tom Jones*; the literature of
the Women's Movement, beginning with *Shirley*; the literature of Desert Islands,
from *Robinson Crusoe* to *The Blue Lagoon*; the literature of Rogues—dreariest of
all, though the Open Road runs it pretty close; the literature of Sussex (perhaps
the most devoted of the Home Counties); improper books—a serious though
dreadful branch of inquiry, only to be pursued by pseudo-scholars of riper years;
novels relating to industrialism, aviation, chiropody, the weather.

But does this brisk disposing of specificity bear any relevance at all to
Victorian novels as we actually read them? Surely not. Novels—loose,
baggy monsters, mixed media—have had more overt intercourse with
society, with—to borrow the Marxist term—the economic and social
base, than any other literary mode. And in Victorian novels—looser,
baggier, more monstrously spacious, and more mixed, as a rule, than
novels before or since—the bonds of this relationship are that much

more clamorously obvious. And the reader cannot avoid the consequences of a situation in which these novelists at any rate are blissfully
unaware of the supposed autonomy of their art that is sometimes willed
upon them by post-Jamesian criticism. A George Eliot will put her
Methodist aunt into a novel and call her Dinah Morris; a Disraeli will
rehash Blue Books for *Sybil*; and a Mark Rutherford will be so con-
tentedly uncertain about the difference between a history book and his
novel *The Revolution in Tanner's Lane* that Samuel Bamford appears at
one moment as a character in the fiction and at the next is referred to
as an external source of information when the novelist openly inserts
a passage from *Passages in the Life of a Radical*. Neither novelist, nor
publisher, nor any reader, seems to have felt any incongruity about Felix
Holt addressing working men in *Blackwood's Magazine* months after the
novel *Felix Holt* had appeared on the market.

Victorian literature as a whole frequently welcomes clutter. But the
novel, of course, grants house-room to bric-à-brac, to things and
*objets*—tactile, materialistic, solidly *there*—still more generously than
Carlyle's paragraphs and Browning's lines. It has after all more rooms
for lumber, and people and events from life are, like things, liberally
accommodated. This hospitality is often frankly avowed. No Victorian
novelist that I know of would preface his work with such a statement
as the libel laws frequently drive modern novelists to. 'No scene in
these stories is taken from life and all the characters are purely imaginary', plaintively insists (a random case) Maurice Dekobra of his *Stars and
Strips* (1938). Though she might take pains later to rebut all those keen
trackers-down of 'originals' who went and talked with 'Mrs. Poyser', or
winkled out locals willing to testify that Marian Evans had gone around the
village noting down the words of Cousin X and sister-in-law Y or borrowing Aunt Samuel's sermon manuscripts, at the time of writing it George
Eliot freely confided that *Adam Bede* was known to her and to Lewes as
'My Aunt's Story'. And just so did Mrs. Gaskell refer to *Ruth* as her
'Newcastle Story', in token of her basing the Rev. Thurstan Benson on
her guardian William Turner, the Unitarian minister at Newcastle.

Clearly Victorian novelists were not so troubled by the notion of
'originals' for their fictional characters as some of us are. Whenever
the question of 'originals' is mooted, as in a recent discussion in the
*TLS* about Mark Pattison and Casaubon, some voice is bound to be
heard (in this case John Sparrow's) objecting to the very idea.[1] Professor

[1] R. Ellmann, 'Dorothea's Husbands: Some Biographical Speculations', *TLS*, 16 Feb.
1973, 165–8; J. Sparrow, Letter, *TLS*, 16 Mar. 1973, 296.

Ulrich Camillus Knoepflmacher, for instance, makes a habit of complaining of the 'originals'—spotting tendency wherever it manifests itself. He objected vociferously to Gordon Haight's interest in George Eliot's 'originals' in his *Life* of the novelist.[1] Another, still more noted Victorian scholar and critic, the late Geoffrey Tillotson, rebuked G. N. Ray for resurrecting the buried life of Thackeray.[2] These sorts of protest are ones the Victorian novelist might well not have understood: the tactics of the New Criticism, that fascination engendered by symbolism and imagism for the crystalline, bounded literary object, are the kind of dryness they were not prone to.[3] Humphry House's method and assumptions in *The Dickens World* merely accorded with the nature of the material he was handling. Even Mrs. Leavis, who has called his approach 'crass and dangerous' ('ignoring the surely essential and obvious fact that Dickens was a creative artist, [he] treats his novels as accurate or inaccurate sources of facts, implying in Dickens ignorance or dishonesty in the latter case'), finds it handy to make use as occasion serves of House's crassly dangerous data ('research'—House's research no less—'has shown that Chadband's is only a slight caricature of the customary idiom'), and to adopt House's strategy: she uses the life of Matthew Smith to buttress her argument about Arthur Clennam.[4]

It is usually objected—as Mrs. Leavis does—that the novelist transforms the material he recruits from real life, that one must allow for the more or less distorting lens of the imagination, that the novelist builds a more or less self-sustaining fictional world governed by its own rules, that the novel is less a mere reflection of society than a structure of feelings about society. And so on. In relation to the Victorian novel, at least, most of these commonly heard plaints claim too much if they are thought of as putting the whole case. But, of course, even when applied to Victorian fiction, the essence of these claims has a considerable validity. Indeed, it is the fact that fiction transforms reality which makes literary critics at once both more and less than social historians, and that makes historians despair of the kinds of witness about society that the novel bears.

[1] U. C. Knoepflmacher, 'Mr. Haight's George Eliot: "Wahrheit und Dichtung" ' *VS* 12 (June 1969), 422–30.

[2] G. Tillotson, *Thackeray the Novelist* (Cambridge, 1954), Appendix I; G. N. Ray, *The Buried Life: A Study of the Relation between Thackeray's Fiction and His Personal History* (1952).

[3] See Iris Murdoch, 'Against Dryness: A Polemical Sketch', *Encounter*, 16 (Jan. 1961), 16–20.

[4] F. R. and Q. D. Leavis, *Dickens the Novelist* (1970), 177–8, and footnotes 2, p. 38, and 1, p. 137.

What can the historian learn from these novelists...? One would...expect them to be a mine of information for the social historian. Yet in effect they are not, for the factual information they provide about social conditions is highly suspect for the scholar's purposes; it is spotty, impressionistic, and inaccurate. These writers were primarily novelists and artists; their reporting of social conditions is always limited by the background and interests of the writer and, still more important, subordinate to his artistic purpose.[1]

In my experience historians are sometimes too ready—overawed perhaps by myths about the artist as mage and by too mystifying a view of 'artistic purposes', and polite about disciplines not their own—to grant poetic licence to novelists. And literary critics often seem surprisingly willing to condone this awed generosity. But however much licence to distort is conceded to the novelist, his distortions must surely be measured, and some attempt made at gauging his transformations of reality before these can be properly recognized and pronounced on. It is certainly not enough for the critic to announce the inevitability of fictional distortion and then leave it uninspected (which is the astonishing burden of U. C. Knoepflmacher's opening exhortations in *Laughter and Despair*, 1971). That is why I do not apologize for scrutinizing the actual bases of the Victorian novelists' acquaintance with Dissent: their personal knowledge of it, their meetings with it, their families' connections with it, and the actual people and places, preachers and chapels, in their lives.

And there is a duty here to historical truth. Many social historians seem to feel sure the novel is the place for finding the local colour they crave. And, for their part, far more readers and literary critics tend to recruit far too much of their social history from novels. The notable and cautionary case is the late Myron F. Brightfield, who over many years assiduously excerpted illustrations of manners and customs from 1,200 Victorian novels, and built four substantial tomes as a monument to the folly of believing everything the novelists told him.[2] As John Gross has put it, most novelists are 'slippery customers'.[3] And this is especially true when it comes to presenting Dissenters. The novelists frequently have designs on their material, and various kinds of prejudice and antagonism—social, political, religious—help shape the particular picture they grant us. One wants to weigh carefully the evidence they

[1] W. O. Aydelotte, 'The England of Marx and Mill as Reflected in Fiction', *Journal of Economic History*, 8, Supplement (1948), 42–58.

[2] Myron F. Brightfield, *Victorian England in its Novels (1840–1870)* (4 Vols., Los Angeles, Calif., 1968).

[3] John Gross, *The Rise and Fall of the Man of Letters* (1969), 296.

offer, and to help straighten the record—if only a bit. An illustration—though the example is extremer than what most Victorian novels provide—will illuminate the need for checking up on novels. It would be absurd not to mention that something had gone awry with the real historical facts in any discussion of the film, 'based on the life of John Wesley', that Evelyn Waugh describes in *Vile Bodies*. Its action includes Wesley in America being rescued from Red Indians by Lady Huntingdon disguised as a cowboy. The Rector's comment on these sub-Hollywoodian, but doubtless legitimately cinematic, and imaginative and artistically purposeful distortions of the truth, is the right one: 'I had no idea Wesley's life was so full of adventure. I see I must read my Lecky.' A reaction like that would be, I trust, any decent film critic's, and, if a novel were in question, any decent literary critic's too.

Moreover, in the face of the Victorian novel, the historical and biographical inquiry I am about seems not only a useful and necessary critical exercise, but a response to the logic of the case. Johnson remarked about novelists on a famous occasion (*Rambler*, No. 4 (31 March 1750)) that:

They are engaged in portraits of which every one knows the original, and can detect any deviation from exactness of resemblance. Other writings are safe, except from the malice of learning, but these are in danger from every common reader; as the slipper ill executed was censured by a shoemaker who happened to stop in his way at the Venus of Apelles.

And in being, as a body of fiction, perhaps still closer to social actualities than the fictions Johnson knew, the Victorian novel urges upon us all the more the importance of its contingency and of the particularity of its characters. The writers of books like *Seth Bede*, '*The Methody*', and *The Country and Church of the Cheeryble Brothers* have grasped with sure instinct the true nature of the situation: that in regarding the novels' characters as real persons (and I am thinking of John Bayley's discussion in *The Characters of Love*), we are pressed to contemplate their connections with the people they are often based on, to consider the links with *their* character, the events of *their* life, *their* class, and regionality, and religion, and so forth. One discusses real preachers, actual chapels, as one has grown used to discussing strikes in Preston in connection with *Hard Times*. In a sense, 'originals' are what the novel, especially the Victorian novel, is all about.

What is more, of course, an examination of Dissent and Dissenters in Victorian novels is a particularly needful task. The relation of fiction to

Dissent is a zone where, quite simply, misunderstanding and mis-
information have for too long abounded. For example, M. J. Svaglic's
now standard article on 'Religion in the Novels of George Eliot' claims,
with laughable wrongness, that 'Dissent' embraces 'in the popular sense
of the term: Evangelicalism as well as Methodism, Congregationalism,
and so forth'.[1] Not even in a recondite sense has 'Dissent' ever signified
'Evangelicalism'. Though much of it was basically evangelical in theology, Dissent has always been quite distinct from Anglican Evangelicalism,
except in the earliest years of the Methodist revival. Again, in life after
life of the Brontës Winifred Gérin has developed the ludicrous notion
that their Aunt Branwell, an Arminian Methodist doctrinairely opposed
to Calvinism, was a Calvinist imposing Calvinist fears on her charges.
And yet again, ever since Henry James dubbed him so, Silas Marner
has been commonly described as a Methodist, whereas the slightest
acquaintance with church history would reveal that the deacons and
the democratic government of Lantern Yard indicate a congregationalist
group and not a Methodist chapel.[2]

In recent critical debates about the merits or otherwise of the old
and 'new' novel, the renowned contingency of Victorian fiction (what
Virginia Woolf despaired of as 'the laborious process . . . of building up
a model of life from saying how d'you do, and cutting the loaf, and
knocking the cigarette ash into the ash tray, and standing the yellow
bicycle against the wall')[3] has been much adverted to. In a way it is an
extremists' battle: possession of the middle ground is a forlorn business
left to a few patient arbitrators like Malcolm Bradbury in *Possibilities*
(1973). And as the ranks of contenders for and against contingency in
the novel, the cohorts of advocates for the openness or the closedness
of fiction *vis-à-vis* society, flurry to and fro across the critical battlefield,
there is a grave danger that the contingency, the openness, of the
Victorian novel will become not much more than a counter of debate.
Even among its friends—Iris Murdoch and John Bayley, Raymond
Williams and Bernard Bergonzi—and its modest allies like Malcolm
Bradbury, the contingency of Victorian novels seems fated to become
merely a *donnée*, received and noted, but largely unscrutinized in its

---

[1] M. J. Svaglic, 'Religion in the Novels of George Eliot', *JEGPh* 53 (1954), 150.

[2] Henry James, *Atlantic Monthly*, 18 (1866), 479–92, quoted by G. S. Haight (ed.), *A Century of George Eliot Criticism* (paperback edn., 1966), 46; David Cecil, *Early Victorian Novelists* (1934), 308; Joan Bennett, *George Eliot: Her Mind and Her Art* (Cambridge, 1954), 134; R. Speaight, *George Eliot* (1954), 62.

[3] Virginia Woolf, anon. review of D. H. Lawrence, *The Lost Girl*, *TLS*, 2 Dec. 1920, 795.

practical outworkings. But that the kinds and degrees of contingency can go too long unexamined is amply indicated by the continuing neglect of things like Nonconformity in the novel. And there are doubtless other equally large sets of social and religious and political circumstances and ideas and actualities in the Victorian novel that have not been worked over. The gains when long negligence is repaired, and books like Philip Collins's *Dickens and Crime* and *Dickens and Education* appear, are obvious. The trouble is that under the fashionable pressure from post-Robbe-Grillet criticism, assisted by the increasing tendency to New Novel or even so-called 'New-New Novel' practices among western novelists now writing, it would seem not unlikely that criticism might lose interest in the details of the Victorian novel's picture of society and retreat into yet more of the old 'new-critical' chores, or the newer structuralist variants on that tired old theme. Backs, I fear, may be turned on a promising critical patch before it has even begun properly to be dug over. 'This book does not offer moralistic "interpretation" of Dickens's novels or quarry them for social comment', a recent publisher's advertisement prided itself: 'Instead it explores the strange poetry of Dickens' imagination' (as though these things could be that easily separated!). Clearly U. C. Knoepflmacher is not alone in contending 'that the "reality" of any Victorian novel must, first of all, be viewed as an entity in itself, independent of any external historical considerations'.[1] In the face of heresy like that, one must declare boldly that the Victorian novel badly needs a lot more of what E. M. Forster unfairly contemned as pseudo-scholarship.

[1] U. C. Knoepflmacher, *Laughter and Despair: Readings in Ten Novels of the Victorian Era* (Berkeley, Calif., 1971), 6.

# 1. OPENNESS

THE Victorian novel is by no means, then, as self-containing, as bounded, as some critics would wish. And its openness towards (in Lawrence's phrase) its 'circumambient universe' is, as it were, the licence I am assuming for the kind of pursuit I am engaged on here. But this openness, this receptivity, has other aspects, has in fact, as Iris Murdoch has pointed out, an historic connection with liberalism. And that connection I am taking as a basis for my complaints at the unfairness with which Dissent is largely treated by the novelists.

*Openness* is a term much bandied about in modern criticism of the novel. I do not use it in the sense of Alan Friedman in *The Turn of the Novel: The Transition to Modern Fiction* (1966), whose thesis is that the eighteenth- and nineteenth-century novel was a closed form which was transformed in the twentieth century into an open-ended one. Nor do I mean it in the sense of the case Robbe-Grillet puts in his essay 'A Path for the Future Novel' (1956) in *Towards A New Novel* (1962). He desires an infinity of available meanings in fiction, where the characters are 'able to contain a multiplicity of possible interpretations . . . open to every sort of comment to suit every sort of prejudice, whether psychological, psychiatric, religious, or political': in other words, anti-characters. Rather, I use *openness* as Iris Murdoch does in her extremely important articles[1]—which are, of course, intimately related to John Bayley's *The Characters of Love*. In 'The Sublime and the Beautiful Revisited', Miss Murdoch claims that:

A great novelist is essentially tolerant, that is, displays a real apprehension of persons other than the author as having a right to exist and to have a separate mode of being which is important and interesting to themselves. We may decide that 'tolerance' is too mild a word for this capacity at its highest. But 'tolerance' is a word which links nineteenth-century literature with Liberalism.

Later she does indeed go on to suggest that the aptest characterization of this special kind of openness is nothing less than 'love'.

---

[1] 'The Sublime and the Good', *Chicago Review*, 13 (Autumn, 1959), 42–55; 'The Sublime and the Beautiful Revisited', *Yale Review*, 49 (1959–60), 247–71; 'Against Dryness', *Encounter*, 16 (Jan. 1961), 16–20.

This advocacy seems to me absolutely to suit what the novel is and does. To put it briefly and roughly, Defoe wrote a sort of programme for the English novel. The Puritan background, the diary-keeping habit, the practice of daily self-scrutiny before God, provided him, as it were, with some of the novel's most recognizable features, particularly its sense of what would be continuingly important to it: the everyday, the domestic circumstance; the quotidian process, the diurnal round (what happened next); and the ordinary life of ordinary people (the hero as *petit bourgeois* rather than as Aristotelian prince). And underpinning this interest in ordinariness was the Puritan liberalism, the faith in democratic rule and in the priesthood of all believers, the rights of every man to follow his conscience in politics and religion. Paradoxically, of course, this Puritan tradition also bore with it the seeds of its own decay: there was also the fatal commitment to bourgeois values, to middle-class myths and consolations that is so manifest in Defoe's plots. And this bourgeois flavour of the English novel has been continually at odds with the accompanying commitment to ordinariness, to the day-to-day. The one seems to me a closing, illiberal pressure, the other an opening, liberal thrust, and surviving together, as on the whole they have done, they create a continuing tension within individual novels as well as within the historic continuum of the novel. So, given this dialectic, it is not surprising that there should be, on the one hand, illiberality in some novels and, on the other, periodic revolutions, when the novel's closed doors are forced open to welcome some hitherto— or temporarily—despised community, the working class, say, or—in the case I am concerned with—Dissenters.

The Dissenter suffers in Victorian fiction from extensive illiberality at the hands of the novelists who, however, introduce him on such an ample, indeed liberal, scale into their novels. Not surprisingly it is George Eliot—who is really (as Iris Murdoch insists) the only Victorian novelist to come near the great Russians ('especially Tolstoy') in openness—who stands out as a writer who will treat Dissenters with enormous compassion and with a notable measure of fairness. The fact that in the end she does not agree with Christianity is an indication of just how great her openness is. And her compassion, the 'love' in her presentation of a Dorothea or a Casaubon, is undiminished even when she comes to present a Bulstrode.

Elsewhere there is an almost general failure in compassion, sympathy, and tolerance, an absence of the openness that constitutes true greatness in the novel. Chapel-life in the novels is usually presented as being so life-denying, so uniformly dreary, and the members are so unattractive, the preachers so grotesque, that it is difficult on such a showing to see why people bothered to belong. Better informed, or less ill-disposed novelists, however, like George Eliot and Mark Rutherford, or even Mrs. Oliphant, indicate something of the important network of relationships and loyalties, cemented by chapel festivals, anniversaries, mortgages, responsibilities, that being a member of a chapel would involve one in.[1] Where the outsider like Dickens sees only repressive narrowness and gloom, insiders insist on the happiness and joy: 'But the grace of God, the love of Christ were the central themes. These were praised and adored till the chapels were full of happiness. Faces glowed as the people left the little brick chapels, and some of them developed a permanent saintly warmth of expression.'[2]

There is little recognition in the Dickens tradition of any religious spirit or experience that might generate such happiness, little of Beatrice Webb's kind of acknowledgement: that the servant Martha Mills, whose husband, the Baptist local preacher, was pompously Chadbandian, whose theology of atonement, predestination, and eternal punishment was 'primitive if not barbaric', could nevertheless manifestly be filled with the spirit of Christian love.[3]

The common revulsion from the way Nonconformists talk is characteristic of the novelists' failure to be open. Dickens's alienation from the religious content of Nonconformity is indicated by his insistence (with the Trollopes and Thackeray, and after the manner of Sydney Smith) that the intrusion of Biblical language into ordinary speech is impious and leads to canting jargon. The Protestant, evangelical, and characteristically Nonconformist idea that 'familiarity' with the Divine is granted to the most humble, that the assimilation of the Divine into everyday concerns—evident in Herbert's household imagery and Bunyan's metaphors of common life—is actually to be desired as a mark of grace, is completely unknown to him.

According to John Foster (quoted by Humphry House), 'religious cant is often an affected use of the phrases which have been heard as appropriate to evangelical truth; with which phrases the hypocrite has connected no distinct ideas . . .' One agrees with Foster's definition, though *Church Questions*, the game House cites as encouraging cant by

[1] See Robert Currie, *Methodism Divided* (1968), 44–6.
[2] M. K. Ashby, *Joseph Ashby of Tysoe 1859–1919: A Study of English Village Life* (Cambridge, 1961), 81–2. See E. E. Kellett, *As I Remember* (1936), 109 ff.
[3] Beatrice Webb, *My Apprenticeship* (1926), 20–1.

exploring the significance of Biblical metaphors, seems rather calculated to induce an extremely expert acquaintance with Biblical language and meaning. But Foster's is not the charge against Chadband: Dickens is not saying that Chadband has 'no distinct ideas' about the phrases he uses, but that the phrases, meaningful or not to Chadband, are incomprehensible to Jo and other children, and by implication are irrelevant to everybody else.

And, as for that 'coarse familiarity with sacred things which is busy on the lip, and idle in the heart' (1847, *Pickwick* Preface), House's description of Chadbandian cant ('The associations proceed from word to word, ever moving farther from the original point of reference; and a habit of association once formed may proceed in indefinite triumph with no point of reference at all')[1] applies with more point to Dickens's own brand of deathbed rhetoric. Jo's Lord's Prayer and Stephen Blackpool's vision of the star of Bethlehem with Dickens's commentary ('The light is come upon the dark benighted way'; 'The star had shown him where to find the God of the poor; and through humility, and sorrow, and forgiveness, he had gone to his Redeemer's rest')[2] are characteristic Dickensian sentimentalism, based in or connected to no theological or experiential reference-point in the novels and hardly any outside them. One recalls Carlyle's query: 'Is not sentimentalism twin-sister to Cant, if not one and the same with it?'[3] And what novelists lampooned as canting jargon was often a signal of the deepest faith that God was near and knowable: there was no divorce between sacred and secular in the language of Emily Brontë's Joseph ('. . . hor fathur's son gallops dahn t'Broad road, while he flees afore tuh oppen t'pikes') nor in his actions ('. . . he solemnly spread his large Bible on the table, and overlaid it with dirty bank-notes from his pocket-book, the produce of the day's transactions').[4]

The constant reference to Scripture by Dissenters in fact often represented close acquaintance with the text: the allusions were not at all casual, and conveyed precise meanings to those familiar with the context. Biblical authority and parallels for one's own actions were always being sought and found, and the Scriptural reference was thus expressive of Divine guidance and affirmation. For example, Joseph

---

[1] See Humphry House, *The Dickens World* (Oxford paperback issue of 2nd edn., 1960), 116–17.

[2] *Bleak House*, Ch. 47; *Hard Times*, Bk. III, Ch. 6.

[3] *The French Revolution* [1837] (Centenary edn., 3 Vols., 1896), Vol. I, Bk. 2, Ch. 7, p. 55.

[4] *Wuthering Heights*, Chs. 10 and 32.

Arch wore his rough tweed and billycock hat to Westminster; 'like the Shunamitish woman', he said, he would 'live and die' with his brethren. He was recalling, and expecting his readers to take the point, the incident in 2 Kings 4: 13: '. . . wouldest thou be spoken for to the king, or to the captain of the host? And she answered, I dwell among mine own people.' [1] Dinah Morris's description of Loamshire, 'a good land wherein they eat bread without scarceness' (*Adam Bede*, Ch. 8), may be a tedious bit of jargon to the outsider, but to those who recognized the allusion to Canaan, and knew the habit of comparing Christians with Israelites, an exact notion of how Dinah sees the Loamshire–Stonyshire conflict would be conveyed. Loamshire is like Canaan, prosperously flowing with milk and honey; Stonyshire is like the wilderness, a place of toil and hardship. At present she labours in that wilderness: but the time for reward and rest in Canaan will come; Dinah will one day come to dwell in her Canaan, in Loamshire.

John Burnell Payne (grandson of John Dyer, first full-time secretary of the Baptist Missionary Society, and a first cousin once removed of Mary and Rebecca Franklin, George Eliot's Baptist schoolmistresses) who, with his brother Joseph Frank Payne, was frequently entertained by Lewes and George Eliot, noted in his diary her comment on one of his grandfather's diaries:

I have often remarked that people use technical religious language, quotations from the Bible especially, with a certain distinction of taste based on their character and organisation. Your grandfather's sister, Mrs. Franklin (i.e. the wife of Francis Franklin, mother of Mary and Rebecca), was a remarkable instance. Her mind and conversation were impregnated with her impressions of the best religious books and of the Bible, but her quotations were always really significant and appropriate.[2]

In *Adam Bede* (Ch. 5) we can take Joshua Rann's reaction to Will Maskery's Biblical allusions as standing for the obtuse novelists' failure to perceive that the language of Scripture is often, for the evangelical, packed with meaning and relevance to daily life sacramentally viewed.

Yes, sir, but it turns a man's stomach t'hear the Scripture misused i' that way. I know as much o' the words o' the Bible as he does, an' could say the Psalms right through i' my sleep if you was to pinch me; but I know better nor to take

---

[1] *Joseph Arch: the Story of His Life*, by Himself; ed. with preface by the Countess of Warwick (1898), 357–9.

[2] E. A. Payne, 'Gleanings from the Correspondence of George Eliot', *BQ*, N.S. 17 (1957–8), 181.

'em to say my own say wi'. I might as well take the Sacriment-cup home and use it at meals.

Precisely the point!

The novelists' imperception is often undergirded by common snobbery towards Dissent, which is much less excusable than Rann-like blindness. Take tea-meetings. A sort of diluted version of the Methodist Love-Feast, they came to characterize Dissent in our period: 'tea and experience', the Dissenting formula.[1] The grocers had tea before attending Sunday evening chapel, while smarter Anglicans stayed at home for dinner. Wine was superior, tea merely vulgar. How otherwise should Arnold sneer at a 'life of . . . tea meetings'?[2] All the tea in *Pickwick* indicates gluttony, or masks hypocrisy in the form of alcohol.[3] Hardy is rather disparaging: the 'trimmers' in 'The Distracted Preacher' went to chapel 'in the evening or when there was a tea . . .'[4] Even Mrs. Gaskell seemed reluctant about going to a tea-meeting, but she was too sensible to claim any inherent deficiency in the custom: 'As to Congregational tea-parties, I don't precisely see the good they are to effect therefore *I* should not go to them, although I might go to *one* if it gave pleasure to those who did attend them.'[5] Only Mrs. Oliphant, though still wishing us to feel socially superior to Salem tea-meetings, conveys any of their validity for a chapel community, the fellowship they generated. They

. . . were not uncommon occurrences in Salem—tea-meetings which made the little tabernacle festive, in which cakes and oranges were diffused among the pews, and funny speeches made from the little platform underneath the pulpit, which woke the unconsecrated echoes with hearty outbreaks of laughter.[6]

Satire is legitimate, but there is all the difference in the world between Mrs. Gaskell's cook to whom French dishes are unscriptural,[7] or her Jeremiah Dixon ('. . . them Methodees are terrible hands at

[1] 'Tea and Experience', Ch. 9 of C. M. Davies, *Mystic London* (1875), 73–84.

[2] *Culture and Anarchy*, ed. J. Dover Wilson (Cambridge, [1932]; paperback edn., 1963), 58.

[3] Was the 1838 Resolution of Norfolk Primitive Methodists 'that in future the time allowed for tea in any of our tea meetings shall be within reasonable limits' at all related to *Pickwick's* implications, one wonders? Stuart Andrews, *Methodism and Society* (1970), 126.

[4] 'The Distracted Preacher', Ch. 1.

[5] *The Letters of Mrs. Gaskell*, ed. J. A. V. Chapple and A. Pollard (Manchester, 1966), No. 424, p. 549.

[6] *Salem Chapel*, Ch. 1.

[7] *Wives and Daughters*, Ch. 15.

unexpected prayers when one least looks for 'em'),[1] and Dickens's maliciously lampooned Stiggins and Chadband. 'Satire,' Trollope wrote of *The Warden*, 'though it may exaggerate the vice it lashes, is not justified in creating it in order that it may be lashed.   Caricature may too easily become a slander, and satire a libel. I believed in the existence neither of the red-nosed clerical cormorant, nor in that of the venomous assassin of the journals.'[2] The 'sneering little giggle' of the Rev. Mr. Massey, in Lawrence's 'Daughters of the Vicar', is annoying if it is all one hears.

One is not looking, in the name of openness, for advanced theological debate. Newman's *Loss and Gain* is a grim enough warning against trying to incorporate in a novel the sort of theological depth and subtlety that was appropriately informative in the *Apologia*. But one does look, and fairly, for an attempt to understand, to get inside Dissent; for some perception of what it might have meant personally and socially to be a Nonconformist, and not merely in terms of the commonly acknowledged social inferiority, but of the meaningful social touchstones, the reference-points, the boundary posts, the lie of the land. This is not a demand for the novelist's approval, but a complaint against prejudice.

Some novels have a false air of openness. *Shirley* appears to be facing up to narrowness, prejudice, malice wherever they may occur, whether in Barraclough or in the curates; Charlotte lets Helstone put in a grudgingly good word for Dissenters who make converts while the curates gossip over wine, and Shirley attacks the curates' 'small spite against Dissenters', 'their silly narrow jealousies and assumptions' as well as Mr. Yorke's 'strictures on all who differ' from him.[3] But no victim of this critical attention is treated with the intensity of dislike and fear that focuses on Barraclough; and the hero, after all, is the Anglican clergyman, Mr. Hall. Not dissimilarly, in Trollope's *The Vicar of Bullhampton*, where the vicar's prejudices are mildly mocked, or in Dickens's 'George Silverman's Explanation', where the Anglican Lady Fareway is as mercenary and worldly as Hawkyard,[4] the balance is nevertheless weighted more heavily against the sectarians, Puddleham and Hawkyard. Kingsley's concession in *Alton Locke* that Baptist ministers are not all alike falls flat: the writer's energy is more extensively in-

---

[1] *Ruth*, Ch. 16.

[2] *An Autobiography* (2 Vols., 1883), I. 127.

[3] *Shirley*, Chs. 1 and 21.

[4] 'George Silverman's Explanation', *Atlantic Monthly*, Jan.–Mar. 1867, reprinted in *AYR* 19 (1867–8), Nos. 458, 460, 462 (1, 15, 29 Feb. 1868). When I quote from this story it is from *AYR*'s text: the *NOID* text is too different from the original version.

vested in Wigginton than in old, white-haired Bowyer, and nothing, not even the footnote stating that such men are not unique to Baptists, can really compensate for the missionary: 'a squat, red-faced, pig-eyed, low-browed man, with great soft lips that opened back to his very ears: sensuality, conceit, and cunning marked on every feature—an innate vulgarity . . .'[1] Disclaimers, like the *Pickwick* Preface's, that only the 'cant of religion', not religion itself, is under attack, are traditionally followed by an unalleviated examination of the cant, with no glimpse of any alternative, the true religion. A comparison between *Jane Eyre*, and *Pickwick* or Bickerstaffe's *The Hypocrite* (where the character Charlotte urges: 'Let us be careful to distinguish between virtue and the appearance of it'),[2] promptly exposes the irreligious hollowness of Dickens's and Bickerstaffe's claims: Charlotte Brontë actually follows up *her* claim in the Preface to the second edition of her novel ('To pluck the mask from the face of the Pharisee, is not to lift an impious hand to the Crown of Thorns')[3] with credible alternatives to the nasty Brocklehurst.

Mrs. Gaskell, eschewing generalizations on one side or the other, gives us both Benson and Badshaw in *Ruth*, and Ebenezer Holman as well as Brothers Robinson and Hodgson in *Cousin Phillis*. The gains are immediately enormous: Dissenting characters are invested with a particularity they cannot possibly have if they are no more than just further examples of stock hypocrites. Dissenting life is given a new interest, new fictional potential is made available. And because hypocrisy is not, so to say, given, it can actually be investigated. The nuances of Benson's dilemma in *Ruth*—he cannot speak out against Bradshaw's condoning bribery at the election (which is doing evil that good might result) because his own actions in shielding Ruth are precisely of that order— are just not available to Dickens, who tends to write 'hypocrite' and nothing else on his characters' banners. Hardy's *A Laodicean* starts well because the novelist notices good as well as bad factors in Dissent: sweat and social inferiority are not automatically stigmas, and Havill, the deacon and chapel architect who plots against Somerset and is a gobbet from the stock-pot, is balanced by the sincere, and authenticated, minister Woodwell. An aspect of the novel's loss of strength, its degeneration into one of Hardy's worst novels, is that its tools eventually become conventionalized: the Baptists merely morbid, and Woodwell

---

[1] *Alton Locke*, Chs. 1 and 3.
[2] *The Hypocrite* (1769), Act 5, sc. 9.
[3] *Jane Eyre*, xxxi.

a dreary Calvinist who is made to endorse Havill ('a worthy man—the deacon of our chapel').[1] It was obviously hard to keep up the originality of the opening chapters, easier to sail with the prevailing fictional winds.

The better fictional representations of Dissenters are characterized by a refusal to trade in commonplaces, to admit the conventional attitude. They waive the common delusion that anything objectionable cancels out everything valid ('It seem'd, alas! in John's deluded sight, | That all was wrong because not all was right').[2] The point may be exemplified in two of the most convincing portraits of Dissenters in the Victorian novel: William Hale White's (i.e. Mark Rutherford's) Michael Trevanion; and Bulstrode. Trevanion, a Cornish Calvinist, decides he must risk his own salvation to save his son, albeit through lies and slander, from marrying an unbeliever. With 'damnable . . . treasonable fidelity' to God he courts damnation, hoping against hope that God will 'consider him as a sinner for his glory'. He acts out St. Paul's (rhetorically expressed) wish: 'I could wish that myself were accursed from Christ for my brethren, my kinsmen according to the flesh.'[3] Dickens would have derided him as just another hypocrite, antinomian in disposition; but the obsession to know and serve the will of God which results in evil-doing is not strange to the Calvinist mind.[4] Trollope's *John Caldigate* (1879) is likewise a novel of immense power, not least in its presentation of the resonating cruelty of the Low Church Mrs. Bolton in her battle of will with her daughter, whom she keeps prisoner to save her soul from contamination in marriage to the unregenerate, and possibly bigamous, Caldigate. In the case of Bulstrode, the process of his temptation, his accommodation of conscience and scruples to dishonest trading, deception, and robbery, is marvellously revealed: the intricate thicknesses of the web that years of moral evasion have woven, 'padding the moral sensibility'; the yearning for youthfully innocent days as Brother Bulstrode in the Highbury Chapel; the absurd hope that God can be bought off by acts of half-restitution; and finally the bottom of the pit, when he effectively engineers the death of Raffles. This kind of fictional triumph is beyond the scope of a

---

[1] *A Laodicean*, Bk. III, Ch. 11.

[2] George Crabbe, *Tales*, XIX, 'The Convert', lines 312–13: *Poems*, ed. A. W. Ward (3 Vols., Cambridge, 1905–7), II. 260.

[3] *Michael Trevanion*, in *Miriam's Schooling and Other Papers*.

[4] See Richard Wurmbrand, *Soviet Saints* (1968), 23–5, for some cases of Christians murdering their children to save them from atheistic education.

novelist who bestows no second glance on hypocrites. George Eliot does not condone hypocrisy—Will Ladislaw, his mother, and Caleb Garth, are rebuke enough to dishonestly trading Dissenters—but she recognizes its complexity. As she puts it in the epigraph to Chapter 53 of *Middlemarch*: 'It is but a shallow haste which concludeth insincerity from what outsiders call inconsistency—putting a dead mechanism of "ifs" and "therefores" for the living myriad of hidden suckers whereby belief and the conduct are wrought into mutual sustainment.' By recognizing that behaviour like Bulstrode's is never less than human, that his actions spring from morality 'unchecked by the deep-seated habit of direct fellow-feeling with individual fellow-men' (Ch. 61), George Eliot can rope it into the novel for analysis, and can finally and supremely manage that new union of the Bulstrodes in their public shame, penetrate to that eloquent silence of their mutual understanding (Ch. 74).

To make way for her compassionate view of Dissenters, good, like Dinah Morris and Rufus Lyon, or bad, like Bulstrode, George Eliot had to declare against the stock assumptions. Like Mrs. Gaskell, who makes Benson in *Ruth* deformed, gives Holman in *Cousin Phillis* a twang, and then challenges the reader to think less of them for it, George Eliot takes on the tradition. George Whitefield's worth is nothing to do with his squint, and only the spiritually myopic would reject him for it: it is Esther Lyon who covers her father's bust of the Methodist with 'green gauze'. Providence ordained, says Rufus, 'that the good man should squint; and my daughter has not yet learned to bear with this infirmity' (*Felix Holt*, Ch. 5). In presenting Dinah Morris, George Eliot challenges the 'sleek grocer' image of Methodism; and in 'Janet's Repentance' she repudiates the evangelicals' traditional literary image. Dempster's play-bill attacking Mr. Tryan ('Mr. Try-it-on') takes in the whole battery of usual charges, like the 'nasal recitative' and the Company 'warranted to have their *eyes turned up higher*, and the *corners of their mouths turned down lower*, than any other company of Mountebanks in this circuit!' The characters in *The Wolf in Sheep's Clothing; or The Methodist in a Mask* and *The Pulpit Snatcher* were, as we shall see in inspecting the tradition Dickens draws on, old friends. Mr. Boanerges Soft Sawder, Old Ten-per-cent Godly, Dr. Feedemup, Mr. Lime-Twig Lady-winner, Miss Piety Bait-the-hook; Messrs. Saintly Smooth-Face, Worming Sneaker, All-grace No-works, Elect-and-Chosen Apewell, Malevolent Prayerful, Foist-himself-everywhere: their lineage was long and respectably un-respectable. And they would not do: 'This satire, though it presents the keenest edge of Milby wit, does not strike you as lacerating, I imagine. But hatred is like fire—it makes even light rubbish deadly.'[1]

George Eliot earned her right to Bulstrode. And when William Hale White follows her (John Broad was 'not a hypocrite, that is to say, not an ordinary novel or stage hypocrite. There is no such thing as a human being simply hypocritical or simply sincere')[2] the pat nature of the observation indicates not only how readily available to later writers was the zone she strenuously staked out for herself, but also how much her moral authority in possessing that zone, the right to judge her hypocrite—which Hale White does not markedly possess—had been purchased by the effort of clearing away the light, but deadly, traditional rubbish.[3]

## 2. DISSENTING DISABILITIES AND THE NOVEL

He was by no means surprised that such errors should have been committed. Many of their ministers were not often in the same rank of life as the clergy of the Established Church.

> Bishop Samuel Wilberforce in the Lords (1854), charging Dissenters with mendacious exaggeration in their 1851 Census returns.

I have no hesitation about saying that I am an enemy to the Establishment, and I do not see that a Churchman need hesitate to say that he is enemy to Dissent.

Thomas Binney

The failure of many Victorian novelists to be open towards Dissent can be seen as an analogue of the social and political disabilities Dissenters were forced to suffer. Churchmen continued throughout the nineteenth century and beyond to despise Dissenters: the Anglican Jews wanted few dealings with the Dissenting Samaritans. Novelists did not exaggerate when they presented the great social gulf that lay between Church and Chapel. To remain a Dissenter was to lose caste, as Paula Power of Hardy's *A Laodicean* knows. The world of Salem Chapel was one of which, truly, Anglicans had 'no conception'. When Lord Rose-

---

[1] 'Janet's Repentance', Ch. 9.

[2] *The Revolution in Tanner's Lane*, Ch. 17.

[3] *BQR* 10 (1849), 118–38, review of *Coningsby* (5th edn., 1849), (attributed to George Henry Lewes, by *New Cambridge Bibliography*, III [1969], col. 775): 'In the great "Rigby" days, it was a moot point whether a political adversary were better crushed by the accusation of atheistical principles, or of having pimples on his face; and no logic seemed so conclusive as that which, insinuating that a man lived unhappily with his wife, or that a woman wore a wig, proved triumphantly that a poem must be worthless, and that an argument was false. This evil has happily cured itself. We have revolted against such literature as worthy only of the kennel.' (pp. 130–1).

bery heard Spurgeon preach in 1873 he glimpsed for the first time a world 'as completely unknown to the world in which I live as if it did not exist'.[1] Edmund Gosse's short novel *The Unequal Yoke* is precisely about that social gulf. And if Malcolm Kingsley Macmillan was right in his report on this fiction, which Gosse offered anonymously to Macmillan's (the writer was 'evidently penetrated through and through with the bitterness of nonconformity . . .'),[2] Gosse did have an insider's experience of life among the Plymouth Brethren to support his novel's insights into Dissent's status as an out-group.

Charles Booth collected testimony at the end of the nineteenth century that showed Anglican snobbery persisting. A Congregationalist minister found it difficult to work on Charity Committees because of 'frequently offensive behaviour' by the clergy: 'I do not like,' he added, 'being patronised by some boy, merely because he has "orders" on which I, certainly, lay little store.'[3]

Reciprocal defiance was natural, and resentment was common: why should an often inferior Oxford degree 'confer a cachet of distinction' on the Anglican clergy?[4] No wonder Trollope's Primitive Methodists were *naturally* rancorous towards the Church of England.[5] (Had Trollope one wonders, seen, before he wrote his novel about Anglican hostility to a Primitive Methodist chapel, a story featured in the *Illustrated London News* (5 October 1861) about a Suffolk Primitive Methodist chapel moved wholesale after a neighbouring Anglican 'villa' owner won his case about the interference with his light? 'The animus of the Church party was notorious, and it had won the day.')[6]

Most Anglicans were content that Dissenters should go on suffering their traditional civil disabilities: these were part of the penalty for dissenting from the State Church. Until 1 March 1837, Dissenting chapels could not be registered for marriage, and Dissenters had to be

---

[1] Brian Harrison, ' "A World of Which We Had No Conception" ' *VS* 13 (1969–70), 143.

[2] Simon Nowell-Smith (ed.), *Letters to Macmillan* (1967), 208.

[3] Charles Booth, *Life and Labour of the People in London*, ser. iii: *Religious Influences* (7 Vols., 1902), VII. 418–20.

[4] E. E. Kellett, op. cit., 222.

[5] *The Vicar of Bullhampton*, Ch. 36: Mr. Fenwick 'plumed himself on the way in which he had continued to clip the claws with which nature had provided the Methodist minister'.

[6] H. B. Kendall, *The Origin and History of the Primitive Methodist Church* (2 Vols., [1906]), II. 246–7; 'Removal of a Chapel at Melton', *Illustrated London News*, 39 (5 Oct., 1861). 358. Kendall dates the removal in 1862: perhaps misled by the fact (which he notes) that the Primitive Methodist Conference recorded payment of £280 solicitors' fees in the Minutes of 1862.

married at Church; not until the 1880 Burial Bill became law were
Dissenters entitled to perform their own burial rites in parish church-
yards.[1] Church Rates were a running sore of discontent, not remedied
until 1868. John Oakley, the 'poor bloke's parson', and Dean of Manchester, excused John Bright's Dissenting bitterness:

> But if any are tempted to judge hardly Mr. Bright's judgements of the Church
> of England, let him try to realise what it was to be born a Dissenting parishioner
> of Rochdale in 1811—and remember that the boy and lad saw the annual seizure
> of his father's goods for Church rates; sometimes in circumstances of which
> perhaps the less said the better,—and at the instance for some years of the Vicar,
> who as a clerical magistrate, is said to have ordered the Riot Act to be read at
> Peterloo . . . and who is credibly reported to have firmly interdicted all men-
> tion of Religion in his Vicarage-house! [2]

John Clifford's father, a Chartist lace-worker, once took his son to
Nottingham market-place to watch the sale of the goods of Samuel Fox,
a Quaker, distrained for non-payment of Church Rate. And when
Clifford was leading the passive resistance to the 1902 Education Act,
which Nonconformity construed as yet another attempt by the Church
of England to undercut Dissenters in education, he recalled that boy-
hood sight: '. . . an argument far more powerful than the eloquence
of all the preachers in Nottinghamshire in favour of disestablishment
and disendowment'. In 1922 this radical Nonconformist die-hard made
his fifty-seventh court appearance for non-payment of the education
rate.[3]

Education was one of the bitterest zones of conflict, where the
Church of England, in 1902 as in 1843, sought advantage by law over
Dissent. The secure Anglican grip on Oxford and Cambridge was only
very gradually loosened: even Gladstone's Universities Test Act (1871)
recognized the special position of the Church of England, and it was not
until 1915 in Cambridge, and 1920 in Oxford, that the B.D. and D.D.
were opened to non-Anglicans. The first Dissenting Professor of
Divinity at an ancient university was C. H. Dodd at Cambridge, and

---

[1] O. Chadwick, *The Victorian Church* (2 Vols., 1966–70), I. 143–5; II. 202–6.

[2] *The Mid-Lent Gospel: A Sermon, Preached in Manchester Cathedral . . . March 31st, 1889
. . . the Day Following the Burial of the Late Rt. Hon. John Bright, MP*, by John Oakley, D.D.
(Manchester, 1889), 16. See entry for Oakley in *DNB*. For W. R. Hay, Vicar of Rochdale,
see Rev. Canon F. R. Raines, *The Vicars of Rochdale*, ed. H. H. Howorth (2 Vols., The
Chetham Society Publications, Manchester, 1883).

[3] M. R. Watts, 'John Clifford and Radical Nonconformity 1836–1923' (Oxford D.Phil.
thesis, 1966), 2, 351, 487. Cf. Kingsley Martin, *Father Figures* (Penguin edn., 1969), 41–2,
for Martin's father's passive resistance.

that was not until 1935. When Arnold was Oxford's Professor of Poetry, and bringing out *Culture and Anarchy*, Dissenters were still excluded from fellowships and from university government.[1] It was easy enough to attack Dissent from what was still an Anglican vantage point. The Oxford Arnold loved, and which served symbolically as the focus of his social and literary values, was the one Tom Brown matriculated in: at the Senate House, 'they went through the usual forms of subscribing to the articles, and otherwise testifying their loyalty to the established order of things . . .'[2] Dissenters knew the appropriate reply to Arnoldian charges of cultural deficiency:

If Nonconformists are narrow and inadequate in their ideal of human perfection —if they do not attach sufficient importance to culture and poetry—it ill becomes an Oxford Professor, lecturing at Oxford, to tax them with their deficiency. For two hundred years they have been shut out from that University by the exclusive and jealous spirit of the Establishment, and from whatever sweetness and light it is supposed to diffuse. Why select the victims of its meanness and intolerance as an illustration of one-sidedness, when the cruel monopolist to whose injustice it should be attributed is suffered to escape? Why ridicule the stunted proportions and deformities which have been the result of hard usage, and not rather denounce the narrow and inadequate ideal of the Establishment which deliberately and persistently inflicted them? Man of culture and poetry as Mr. Matthew Arnold is, he has not showed himself free from the vice of the system in connection with which he was trained.

As a matter of fact Dissenters are in some senses less narrow and parochial than the Establishment:

We have not asked to shut any one out of the Universities, nor insisted upon sectarian education, nor desired to compel others to support our religious organisations, nor been jealous of the intrusion of other than our own clergy into parochial burying places, nor cast contempt upon other's right to teach Christianity, nor advocated tests, nor infringed upon the sacredness of social life. We have left these things to the Establishment. . . . 'Sweetness and light', forsooth. . . .[3]

Lecturing at Bradford on Cromwell in January 1867, Goldwyn Smith noted that Cromwell as Chancellor of Oxford had been no enemy of culture, but a fosterer of learning: and he 'imposed no tests. (cheers)'.[4]

[1] Chadwick, op. cit., I. 480–1; II. 443–53. See also A. I. Tillyard, *A History of University Reform: From AD 1800 to the Present Time* (Cambridge, 1913).
[2] Thomas Hughes, *Tom Brown at Oxford* (3 Vols., Cambridge, 1861), Vol. I, 'Introductory' chapter.
[3] 'Mr. Matthew Arnold on the *Nonconformist*', *Nonconformist*, 27 (10 July, 1867), 557–8.
[4] *Bradford Observer*, 24 Jan 1867 (a contribution to the *Past and Present* Oxford project on *19th Century Cromwell*': manuscript documents in my possession).

In this atmosphere, where Dissent was considered second-class religion, and Dissenters made to be second-class citizens, it was all too easy for Anglican authors to share a general dislike, even fear, of Nonconformity. Writers in retreat from Calvinism, or upset by puritanism or evangelicalism, found a ready target in an already socially victimized Nonconformity. Anti-evangelical Anglicans like Mrs. Trollope or Thackeray even regard Low Churchmen as quasi-Dissenters: for them Dissent is not only bad *per se* as a schismatic force in the land, but also undesirable because it can have a dangerous appeal to Evangelical Anglicans, diluting their prime Anglican allegiances. Hence, it is under pressure from his Evangelical sisters that Trollope's Marquis of Trowbridge unites with Puddleham against the Broad Church vicar; and the young Pitt Crawley rebelliously patronizes an Independent meeting-house in his uncle the Rector's parish (*Vanity Fair*, Ch. 9). Mrs. Trollope writes not only for non-Dissenters, but for untainted Anglicans: extempore, evangelical-style prayer 'is an abomination to those who have preserved their right to sit within the sacred pale of our established church; and . . . it is among such that I wish to find my readers . . .'[1]

Nonconformists were aware that the novel was often against them. In 1848 Merle d'Aubigné wondered if Puritanism had not been exterminated in England 'under the influence of national developments, and the sneer of the novelists?'[2] In 1899 J. T. Forbes concluded that the 'place to find Dissent truly pictured is in the pages of the historian and the thinker': 'Even in fiction of the introspective order, whose interest centres in moral and religious problems, Dissent is either slightly dealt with or dealt with in an alien spirit.'[3] Continuous maltreatment was wearing, as a passage about Kingsley in *The Life of Hugh Price Hughes* indicates: Kingsley's

. . . support of that 'act of insane and diabolical folly', the Crimean War, his daring to go and welcome 'that scoundrel Eyre' after his return from Jamaica, and last but not least his presentations of Dissent in *Alton Locke* were unforgivable. . . . He said once that he thought Kingsley ought to reappear in some visible form and apologise to humanity for his presentation of Nonconformity in *Alton Locke*, erase it if need be, so that generations of the refined might not grow up with those vulgar and untrue conceptions of Nonconformity. . . . He knew . . . that artists of all kinds had thrown a glamour over that portion of

---

[1] *The Vicar of Wrexhill* (3 Vols., 1837), I, Ch. 13.

[2] *Germany, England and Scotland* (1848), 89; quoted by I. H. Murray, *The Forgotten Spurgeon* (1966), 31.

[3] Rev. J. T. Forbes, 'Dissent in Fiction and History', *Puritan* (1899), 134, 140.

Christ's Church which was High Anglican or Roman, and that the Evangelistic portion, representing for the most part the poor and the humble, had been very badly and unfairly treated at their hands.[1]

It was the quality of the alternative—in Kingsley's case, jingoism instead of Baptists—that appalled Dissenters. They asked whether the quality of life offered by the 'natural man' as a replacement for the self-conscious, 'reflective' ideals of Nonconformity meant a gain of any kind.[2] Were *Household Words'* John Opus and his family's beer and tea on Sunday a substitute of any merit at all for *righteousness*, even when that had to be sought in 'an ugly little brick church'?

. . . in sober earnest, does Mr Dickens believe in this Greenwich tea-garden?—is it so much more satisfactory than the little Bethel? In this nineteenth century, with all our boasts and our enlightenment, are a pipe and a pint of beer the utmost delights which Mr Dickens can offer, in his day of leisure, to the working man? The waiter, in his white apron, with his tray of glasses—is he a better influence than the poor preacher? And the beer stains on the table in the arbour, and the long pipes, and the talk—are these things more good, more beautiful, more improving for the little Opuses, than even the miseries of church-going?[3]

In this context, where D. H. Lawrence's Lewis speaks for all too large a consensus ('I don't know what sort of things I believe in: only I know it's not what the chapel-folks believe in'),[4] contempt is implicit in the novelists' carelessness about mere accuracy in their presentation of Nonformists. When even the better novelists in this respect, like George Eliot and Mark Rutherford, exempted by Dissenting opinion from the general charges about fictional antagonism and distortion,[5] manipulate their material to make their cases, sins of omission or commission by the well-known opponents of Dissent are not surprising.

We will see how precision about Joseph's religion in *Wuthering Heights* was, as it were, beyond Emily Brontë's notice, and how Kingsley seemed scarcely apologetic about a possible major confusion in his *Two Years Ago* between the Bryanites and the Wesleyans: it was unpleasant if he had destroyed the reputation of one Methodist sect instead of another, but this was only privately to be conceded to his Methodist friend Dr. Rigg. These cases are not isolated. Of so little concern to

---

[1] *The Life of Hugh Price Hughes*, by his Daughter (1904), 95.

[2] *Letters of Principal James Denney to W. Robertson Nicoll 1893–1917* (1920), 191–2.

[3] [Mrs. Oliphant], 'Charles Dickens', *Blackwood's Magazine*, 77 (Apr. 1855), 466.

[4] *St. Mawr* (Penguin edn., 1969), 112.

[5] J. T. Forbes, op. cit.: 'With the exception of "Mark Rutherford" . . .' (p. 134); Rufus Lyon: 'one of the finest and best pictures of a Dissenter in all fiction' (pp. 137–8).

Trollope in *The Vicar of Bullhampton* was Nonconformist detail, that the builder from Salisbury who builds the Puddlehamite chapel is now a Baptist (Ch. 36), now a 'regular Wesleyan' (Ch. 55). And in case the Methodists do not have elders—but without bothering to check—he makes the Rev. Henry Fitzackerley Chamberlaine add an ironic rider when he refers to 'the chapel trustees, the elders of the congregation,— if there be any elders' (Ch. 56). Hardy is unfairly careless in his hand-ling of Methodists: in Alec D'Urberville's wild oscillations; or when he attaches his grandfather's smuggling activities ('While supervising the church music . . .') to the Methodists of 'The Distracted Preacher'. Evelyn Hardy missed the point, which was not that Hardy's note about his grandfather 'reiterates the connection between ecclesiastical and illegal occupations, the background for the tale', but that Hardy felt Methodism to be the appropriate dumping ground for religious hypocri-sies of that order.[1] Ironically, of course, for Hardy's story, no smuggler might remain a member of Wesley's societies.

[1] Evelyn Hardy (ed.), *Thomas Hardy's Notebooks* (1955), 35–6.

# II. ALL SORTS AND CONDITIONS

## I. THE VARIETY OF DISSENT

Set up for yourself, my dear sir—set up for yourself; form a new denomination,
sixpence will do it. . . .                              *Loss and Gain*, Pt. III, Ch. 8

What place of Worship do you go to—the Quakers the Moravians, the Unitarians
or the Methodists—[?]
   John Keats, Letter to George and Georgiana Keats (14 Feb.–3 May, 1819)

'T H E number of dissenters is rapidly increasing; sects are multiplying
    infinitely', Lord Radnor informed de Tocqueville in 1833.[1] And
varieties of sects continued to multiply, markedly, if not infinitely.
According to the lists in *Whitaker's Almanack*, 101 different names of
places of worship were lodged with the Registrar-General in 1869; in
1890 there were 244. So 'Dissent' is a portmanteau term, covering, but
not masking, kaleidoscopic shifts and varieties. Increase in Dissent
reflected an expanding population's religious needs: there soon was, if
it did not exist already, something for everyone:

> 'Sects in Religion?'—Yes, of every race
> We nurse some portion in our favour'd place;
> Not one warm preacher of one growing sect
> Can say our Borough treats him with neglect;
> Frequent as fashions they with us appear,
> And you might ask, 'how think we for the year?'
> They come to us as riders in a trade,
> And with much art exhibit and persuade.[2]

Old Dissent—Quakers, Independents [i.e. Congregationalists],
Baptists, and Presbyterians/Unitarians—continued into the Victorian
era, the first three parties revivified by the Evangelical Revival which,
beginning in the mid-eighteenth century, most notably generated
Methodism.[3] Methodist groups proliferated: Methodism, which Crabbe

---

[1] Alexis de Tocqueville, *Journeys to England and Ireland*, trans. George Lawrence and
K. P. Mayer; ed. J. P. Mayer (1958), 57.

[2] George Crabbe, *The Borough*, Letter IV, 'Sects and Professions in Religion', lines 1–8:
*Poems*, I. 314.

[3] R. W. Dale, *The Old Evangelicalism and the New* (1889), 6 ff.; R. W. Dale, *History
of English Congregationalism*, ed. A. W. W. Dale (1907), 583 ff.; R. T. Jones, *Congregationalism in England 1662–1962* (1962), 148 ff.; E. Halévy, *England in 1815* (2nd English
edn., 1949), 417 ff.; E. Isichei, *Victorian Quakers* (Oxford, 1970), 3 ff.

called 'spiritual influenza', was catching.[1] Alexander Kilham's Methodist New Connexion emerged as early as 1797. Thereafter secessions, expulsions, re-groupings, abortive new departures, were common: for example, the Leeds 'Revivalist' Methodists (1803); the Manchester/ Warrington area discontents who formed the Independent Methodists (1805–6) and because of Quaker elements were known as Singing Quakers; the Band Room Methodists (1806) in the Manchester area. The first Camp Meeting was held on Mow Cop in 1807, and in 1812 Hugh Bourne and William Clowes adopted the name Primitive Methodists. Their followers were dubbed 'Ranters' for singing through the streets of Belper. Several similar movements emerged about this time, including James Crawfoot's Delamere Forest 'Mystic' or 'Magic' Methodists, the Bryanites or Bible Christians in Devon (O'Bryan and James Thorne assumed the name Bible Christians in 1815), and in Bristol the Tent Methodists (1820). The most important Methodist secession group, the most serious rival of Wesleyanism, was of course Primitive Methodism. In 1873 a Reverend Guttery from Wolverhampton claimed that 'Once in every six hours the pearly gates of heaven are thrown back for a Primitive Methodist to pass behind them.'[2] But Methodist schism continued: in 1827, unwilling to accept the Wesleyan Conference's decision over an organ, Leeds Methodists formed the Protestant Methodists; in 1832 the Arminian, or Derby Faith Methodists, seceded at Derby over a point of doctrine. The first Assembly of the Wesleyan (Methodist) Association was held in 1836, and the Arminian Methodists, the Independent Methodists of Scarborough, and the Protestant Methodists joined it in the following year. In 1838 the Independent Wesleyans of North Wales, and in 1839 the Scottish United Methodist Churches, followed suit. Teetotal Methodists seceded in Cornwall in 1842. The early 1850s saw mass expulsion and

---

[1] Crabbe's Preface to *The Borough: Poems* I. 271. For accounts of Methodist divisions a useful book is A. W. Harrison, B. A. Barker, G. G. Hornby, E. T. Davies, *The Methodist Church: Its Origins, Divisions, and Reunion* (1932). Robert Currie, *Methodism Divided: A Study in the Sociology of Ecumenicalism* (1968), Appendix I, conveniently lists dates of secessions, etc. See also: John Walford, *Memoirs of the Life and Labours of the Late Venerable Hugh Bourne*, ed. W. Antliff (2 Vols., 1855–6); H. B. Kendall, op. cit.; J. T. Wilkinson, *Hugh Bourne 1772–1852* (1952); Thomas Shaw, *The Bible Christians 1815–1907* (1965); E. Langton, 'James Crawfoot: the Forest Mystic', *WHS Proc.* 30 (1955), 12–15; Samuel Coley, *The Life of the Rev. Thomas Collins* (2nd edn., 1896); A. W. Harrison, 'The Arminian Methodists', *WHS Proc.* 23 (1941–2), 25–6 (and note by F.F.B., 27–8); O. A. Beckerlegge, *The United Methodist Free Churches: A Study in Freedom* (1957); W. H. Jones, *History of the Wesleyan Reform Union* (1952).

[2] C. M. Davies, 'Tabernacle Ranters', *Unorthodox London* (1873), 78.

secession from Wesleyanism when dissatisfaction with the authoritarian Conference boiled over: a majority of the new Reformers joined forces with the Wesleyan Association to form the United Methodist Free Churches (1857). A minority of left-over Reformers created the Wesleyan Reform Union in 1859.

Schism is a witness to the vigour of sectarianism: the life-blood of Dissent is dissent. Many a 'Persuasion' was indeed, in Dickens's phrase, a Doubly Seceding Little Emmanuel.[1] The Methodist sector was particularly lively. About 1809, Methodists in the Rochdale and Rossendale areas went over to Unitarianism.[2] In 1841 Joseph Barker seceded from the Methodist New Connexion, forming his group of (in 1846) about 200 Christian Brethren chapels, which he took over to the Unitarians.[3] William Booth, first a Wesleyan, then a New Connexion preacher, seceded in 1861, eventually to create the Salvation Army as a continuator of Wesley's mission to the poor.[4] Wesley's doctrine of Christian Perfection generated the Salvation Army's stress on Sanctification, and later-Victorian and twentieth-century Holiness movements. Holiness was no merely sectarian property, as the interdenominational Keswick Convention (founded 1875) indicates,[5] but it produced sectarian effects: *Whitaker's Almanack* (1890) lists a Holiness Army. Imitations of the Salvation Army were, of course, numerous: the Blue Ribbon and White Ribbon Gospel Armies, Methodist Army, King's Own Army, and so on. There was even a Salvation Navy. More directly Methodist-derived groups were the Essex Peculiar People, formed by ex-Wesleyan shoemaker James Banyard, advocating prayer, not medicine, for the sick (and strongly attacked in *Household Words*),[6] and the

[1] 'The Haunted House', *NOID, Christmas Stories* (1956), 232.

[2] H. L. Short, in C. G. Bolam, J. Goring, H. L. Short, R. Thomas, *The English Presbyterians: From Elizabeth Puritanism to Modern Unitarianism* (1968), 247.

[3] Joseph Lawson, *Letters to the Young on Progress in Pudsey During the Last Sixty Years* (Stanningley, 1887), 76 ff.; *The Life of Joseph Barker*, written by Himself, ed. by his nephew, J. T. Barker (1880).

[4] Harold Begbie, *The Life of William Booth* (2 Vols., Abridged, 1926), I. 248–54.

[5] See T. R. Warburton, 'Organisation and Change in a British Holiness Movement', in *Patterns of Sectarianism*, ed. B. R. Wilson (1967), 106 ff., and L. E. Elliott-Binns, *Religion in the Victorian Era* (1936), 223.

[6] Rev. C. B. Herbert, 'An Essex Revival', *Essex Review*, 4 (1895), 37–41; 'Volunteer Apostles', *HW* 5 (5 June, 1852), 261–2. William Howitt is listed in the Contributors' Book as the author. On the evidence of his support for poor preachers (*The Rural Life of England*, ([1838]; 2nd edn., 1840), 563 ff., 567–9) this surprises one, though clearly he could have shifted his attitude between 1838 and 1852. The tone of the article, however, is extremely Dickensian: the name Goosetrap Witness for Banyard, and the child's-eye-view hint at his interference at least. It was not unusual for Dickens to intervene in and

Walworth Jumpers, the sort of group Dickens certainly had in mind
when he put Melchisedech Howler's corybantic mangle-breakers into
*Dombey and Son*: a group of 'Bible Christians', led by a prophetess, and
meeting under an arch of the London, Chatham, and Dover Railway.[1]
*Whitaker's* (1890) also throws in, for good measure, Benevolent, Free,
and New Methodist groups.

The Methodist family of churches was the most significant and most
diversified Dissenting group, but there were other families. Among
Baptists divisions usually hinged on the Calvinist heritage.[2] The main
body of Particular Baptists became more open, less Calvinist, at the
end of the eighteenth century, under the influence of Robert Hall and
Andrew Fuller, who were, effectively, responding to the evangelistic
challenge of Methodist Arminianism. A New Connexion of General
Baptists was formed in 1770 by Dan Taylor, Yorkshire coal-miner and
Methodist preacher: Baptist in practice, Arminian in theology. The
older General Baptist churches had drifted into Socinianism and
Unitarianism in the eighteenth century. At the opposite theological
extreme the Strict and Particular Baptists retreated into their High
Calvinist Zoar Chapels (Zoar, their favourite name for a chapel, meaning
'Little': the place Lot escaped to from Sodom) led by William Gadsby
(1773–1844), son of a roadmender, and himself a ribbon-weaver from
Nuneaton. In Zoar they nourished themselves on the ultra-jargonistic
*Earthen Vessel* and turned their backs on the world.[3] In 1829 the regional
Suffolk and Norfolk New Association of Strict Baptists was formed to
combat Fullerism, Open Communion, and 'general Redemption'. The
Scotch Baptists, a development from the eighteenth-century Sande-
manians, spread down from Scotland and got as far as Wales: David
Lloyd George's grandfather was the Scotch Baptist minister at Berea
Church, Criccieth. The old Seventh-Day Baptists managed, if only just,
to survive into Victorian times: when C. M. Davies visited the 'only
congregation in London', in Mill Yard, Goodman's Fields, Whitechapel,
it consisted of six men, five women, and three children.

---

collaborate on other people's contributions to his paper. See also, for the Peculiars, James
Thomson's 'Law v. Gospel': 'And then we have that narrow sect /Of most Peculiar
People', *The City of Dreadful Night and Other Poems*, ed. B. Dobell (2 Vols., 1895), II. 91.

[1] C. M. Davies, 'The Walworth Jumpers', *Unorthodox London* (1873), 89–99.

[2] For Baptists see: A. C. Underwood, *A History of the English Baptists* (1947); E. A.
Payne, *The Baptist Union: A Short History* (1958); and C. M. Davies, 'Saturday with the
Seventh-Day Baptists', *Unorthodox London* (1873), 227–37.

[3] Thackeray held up *The Earthen Vessel* for specific scorn: G. N. Ray (ed.), *The Letters
and Private Papers of William Makepeace Thackeray* (4 Vols., 1945–6), IV. 129.

In 1836 extreme evangelical Quakers seceded in Manchester. The movement was short-lived, but some of these 'Beaconites' joined the contemporary, and much more durable, Plymouth Brethren movement.[1] The Brethren had emerged in the late 1820s; they had no professional ministers and drew discontents from all sides. Their leaders were a clutch of ex-Anglican ministers, peers, military men, scholars, and gentlemen, but they recruited from Dissent as well. For example, they incorporated a block secession of Methodist New Connexion chapels in Yorkshire and Lancashire (1841–3). By 1845 the Brethren were already irradicably split in two, the Open Brethren being excommunicated by J. N. Darby's Exclusive party. The Exclusives continued to fragment, and by the end of the century there were numerous splinters. The Open Brethren, perhaps because their system of local autonomy contains and legitimates diversity, on the whole avoided major divisions.

The Brethren were a strongly Adventist group, and shared this emphasis with the Irvingite, Catholic Apostolic Church. There were definite connections between the two: for example, the Albury Conferences on prophecy (begun in 1826), which were focuses of early Irvingite interest, were replicated in Ireland at Lady Powerscourt's seat, where Irvingites and Brethren participated. The Brethren were deeply stamped with the Second Adventism of the Irish conferences, but came to repudiate any link with Irvingism: they were as shocked by Irvingite *glossalalia* as Carlyle and his wife.[2] Brethren reliance for ministry on the leading of the Spirit is not dissimilar to the Irvingite search for Apostolic inspiration, but the Brethren never went so far as to claim Speaking in Tongues.[3]

[1] For the Plymouth Brethren see W. Blair Neatby, *A History of the Plymouth Brethren* (1901), 323, and the essays in B. R. Wilson (ed.) *Patterns of Sectarianism* (1966). Other histories of the Brethren are H. H. Rowdon, *The Origins of the Brethren, 1825–1850* (1967), and F. R. Coad, *A History of the Brethren Movement: Its Origins, its Worldwide Development and its Significance for the Present Day* (Exeter, 1968). For a charting of Exclusive divisions, see Napoleon Noel. *The History of the Brethren*, ed. W. F. Knapp (2 Vols., Denver, Colorado, 1936).

[2] W. B. Neatby, op. cit., 38–9; Mrs. E. Trotter, *Undertones of the Nineteenth Century* (1905), 28; F. R. Coad, 'Prophetic Developments: With Particular Reference to the Early Brethren Movement', *Christian Brethren Research Fellowship Occasional Paper*, 2 (1966), 21 ff.; T. C. F. Stunt, 'Irvingite Pentecostalism and the Early Brethren', *Christian Brethren Research Fellowship Journal*, No. 10 (Dec. 1965), 40–8, and his note, ibid., No. 12 (May 1966), 21; H. H. Rowdon, op. cit., 1 ff.; J. A. Froude, *Thomas Carlyle: A History of the First Forty Years of His Life 1795–1835* (2 Vols., 1882), II. 213–14, 218–19. And cf. J. N. Darby, *Irvingism: its root principle examined in the light of scripture* (1895).

[3] See Edward Irving, 'Facts Connected with Recent Manifestations of Spiritual Gifts', *Fraser's Magazine*, 4 (Jan. 1832), 759. For an account of Irving and the revival he was

The Brethren were a more coherent expression of an extensive movement in the period, the search for primitive Christian simplicity. The names lodged with the Registrar-General bear witness to the aim: Believers in Christ; Believers meeting in the name of the Lord Jesus Christ; Christian Brethren; Free Christians; Free Evangelical Christians; Primitive Congregation; Primitive Free Church. Such groups, like branches of better-known sects in embryonic stages, met in private houses, hired halls, upper rooms:

> . . . the sect
> He call'd a church, 'twas precious and elect;
> Yet the seed fell not in the richest soil,
> For few disciples paid the preacher's toil;
> All in an attic-room were wont to meet,
> These few disciples at their pastor's feet.[1]

An irate attack on Dissenting statistics in 1879 marvellously reveals the extent of this sort of activity. Many so-called chapels, it is alleged, are only rooms and houses: 'A dwelling-house in the occupation of John Poor, Labourer'; 'Nos. 75 and 76 Railway Arches, under Eastern Counties Railway, North Street, Bethnal Green'; 'Cottage owned by John Evans, Labourer'; 'Brill Ragged School'; 'Building in the occupation of Hezekiah Ketchmaid'; 'Room over a stable, Hoyle Mill'; 'Chamber of a building in the occupation of Abraham Sykes, coal-miner, Littletown, Liversedge'. And many more.[2]

Dickens strongly disapproved of such freelance goings-on, as Brothers Gimblett and Hawkyard, Chadband, Howler, and Stiggins witness. George Eliot treated them severely but not contemptuously in *Silas Marner*. Silas Hocking went much further and strongly approved of the work Joe Wrag did in his cottage tea-meetings for the neighbours.[3] At any rate the novelists could not ignore the phenomenon; indeed, one of them, George Macdonald, was part of it. When the deacons of Trinity Congregational Church, Arundel, drove him from the pastorate, he rented a room in Renshaw Street, Manchester (1854) where he could preach freely.[4] Mrs. Gaskell's friend of Lower Mosley

---

associated with, see A. L. Drummond, *Edward Irving and His Circle: Including Some Considerations of the 'Tongues' Movement in the Light of Modern Psychology* (1938).

[1] Crabbe, *Tales*, XIV, 'The Struggles of Conscience', lines 18–23: *Poems*, II. 186.

[2] '*Nonconformist Chapels*'. *What Are They?: Half-Hours with the Registrar-General, Disclosing Extraordinary Facts and Figures Illustrative of the Utterly Misleading Character of Nonconformist Statistics Respecting Them*, by 'Investigator' (1879).

[3] Silas Hocking, *Her Benny: A Story of Street Life* (1879), Ch. 16.

[4] Greville Macdonald, *George Macdonald and His Wife* (1924), 177–83; 191–214.

Street Sunday School, Travers Madge, left the Unitarian ministry and in 1859 organized meetings in a room in Crown Street, Hulme. His biographer, in a very important passage, notes the analogy with Lantern Yard:

Religious life in our great cities takes more varied forms than most people are aware of. Not even the divergent types of the Anglican church, with the varieties of Baptist and Independent Nonconformity, and the multiform sections of the great Methodist family, can satisfy the restless individuality of the human soul. New offshoots from existing religious communities are growing up every year, which never find any place in the formal catalogue of sects. Probably there is no large town but has, here and there in its great wilderness of absorbed and busy life, some half dozen of these little sporadic churches, that, mostly in little upper rooms in back streets, are carrying on their humble work and worship, and aiming at something nearer to their ideal of what a church of Christ should be, than their members have been able to find in the larger ecclesiasticisms of the religious world. The little sketch of 'The Church of God in Lantern Yard' which forms one of the quaintest parts of George Eliot's story of humble life, 'Silas Marner', is true, almost to the letter, of humble religious communities, which may be met with by the curious in such matters in London, or Manchester, or Liverpool. Some of these have come out from existing churches, because they can find none rigid enough in Calvinistic doctrine or Puritan discipline; others, in search of simpler, homelier, religious communion, and greater scope for evangelistic work; others again, from love of doctrinal freedom and dislike of sectarianism.

Such a little church of humble, earnest folk, was there in 1859, meeting in a room in Crown Street, in Hulme, one of those densely-populated suburbs which have sprung up about Manchester during the last quarter of a century. Here, a few tradespeople and a goodly number of working-folk met together, Sunday by Sunday, carrying on a Sunday school, and holding religious services and prayer meetings. Not bound together by any rigid orthodoxy, and eschewing any sectarian name, they were what would ordinarily be called strongly evangelical. Some of them had come from the Plymouth Brethren, some had been Baptists, some Independents, a good many Methodists. A few were old friends of Travers's at Lower Mosley Street, who like him, partly by his influence, had become dissatisfied with Unitarianism. They had no minister;—if they had any strong cardinal dogma, it was perhaps dislike of what they called the 'one-man system'. As near as might be, they conformed to the habits of the early church; and when they came together, every one had 'a psalm, a doctrine, a tongue, an interpretation'; and so, striving to edify each other, they lived an obscure, but simple, happy, useful, religious life.[1]

[1] Brooke Herford, *Travers Madge: A Memoir* (1867), 137–38. Cf. the review of *Silas Marner* in *Nonconformist*, 21 (24 Apr. 1861), 336–7: 'We will not challenge the religion of

This zone obviously merges at one end into the rationalist and heterodox sectarianism that lay beyond Unitarianism: the Humanitarians, Secularists, Theistic Church, as well as the Positivists, the Christadelphians, Swedenborgians, British Israelites, and Spiritualists of all sorts—like the Exeter Free Spiritual Research Society and the Halifax Psychological Society.[1] At the other it embraces more orthodox efforts, in country as well as town, at evangelistic implantation of sects, at the stage when a new local group of dissidents is not yet able to afford its own chapel, and so meets in temporary premises. Different inhabitants could pass through some halls: 'The Hall where the Independent Religious Reformers gather, situated at No. 14, Newman Street, Oxford Street, is, unless I greatly err, the same as that occupied by the followers of Edward Irving before they migrated to the more ambitious "Catholic Apostolic Church" in Gordon Square.'[2]

As the hired hall was a common stage of sectarian urban expansion, so the cottage meeting was a usual early phase in the village missions of the Primitive Methodists. Cottage meetings, 'though largely unrecorded and unremembered, seem to have been strangely widespread in the rural and industrial villages of nineteenth-century England'.[3] Not totally unrecorded and unremembered: Flora Thompson, for example, gives a fine account of Methodist Sunday evening meetings in North Oxfordshire cottages.[4]

The sectarian kaleidoscope was in a constant state of movement. Sometimes the cottage meeting developed into a fully fledged chapel, just as the hired hall could be the prelude to more permanent premises. But not always: in Shropshire, for example, cottage meetings rarely progressed beyond that phase.[5] Likewise, as the mission could develop

----

the poor as depicted here, as too exceptional; for the author could hardly mean it to be taken as representative: but we fear some will think it more than occasional material for fiction, for the very reason that it is handled reverently and tenderly; and so we venture to remark that neither the creed and practice of "the Church in Lantern-yard", nor the simple moral theology of Raveloe, is a *type* of the beliefs and intelligence of the religious poor, in city or village, any time these hundred years.'

[1] All from the *Whitaker's Almanack* (1890) list.

[2] C. M. Davies, *Heterodox London* (2 Vols., 1874), I. 21.

[3] 'Parish by Parish. The Place of the Victoria County Histories in the Revolution in Historical Method', *TLS*, 13 Mar. 1969, 270.

[4] Flora Thompson, *From Lark Rise to Candleford: A Trilogy* (World's Classics, 1965), 233 ff.

[5] 'Parish by Parish', *TLS*, 13 Mar. 1969, 270.

into the sect, so the sect could develop into the denomination. However, again, not always. H. Richard Niebuhr's famous thesis, that a sect develops classically into a denomination in three generations, is not necessarily always borne out: Bryan Wilson has shown how, for example, the Exclusive Brethren's continuing sectarianism emphatically counters it.[1]

Some sects prospered: perhaps Wesleyanism was the clearest nineteenth-century example of a sect's *embourgeoisement*. In 1831, Brunswick Chapel, Leeds, was providing separate entrances for the rich and the poor.[2] Complaints about strangers being turned out of half-empty pews in the Wesleyan Chapel, Truro, reached the *British Weekly* in 1890.[3] According to A. L. Rowse's not unbiased account, the Cornish Wesleyan Chapel was the 'temple of the worship of money and success' for 'the most businesslike and the most moneyed'.[4] This later-Victorian 'mahogany age'[5] of Wesleyanism paralleled the prosperity Congregationalism enjoyed after the 1862 Bicentenary of Black Bartholomew's Day, a High Noon of Liberalism and of chapels like red-brick Gothic cathedrals.[6] It was offensive to Christians who yearned for primitive simplicity, like Philip Gosse, who returned with distress to British Wesleyanism after his American experiences of it: 'The large and fine Wesleyan chapels of Liverpool, the fashionable attire of the audiences, and the studied refinement of the discourses, so thoroughly out of keeping with my own fresh and ardent feelings, distress me. I mourn over the degeneracy of Methodism.' So he joined with the Brethren 'who met to break bread at Ellis's Room', Hackney.[7]

Some sects and denominations declined:

[1] B. R. Wilson, 'The Exclusive Brethren: A Case Study in the Evolution of a Sectarian Ideology', *Patterns of Sectarianism*, 334–5.

[2] C. M. Elliott, 'The Social and Economic History of the Principal Protestant Denominations in Leeds, 1760–1844' (D.Phil. thesis, Oxford, 1962), 232.

[3] *BW* 9 (30 Oct. 1890), 5.

[4] A. L. Rowse, *A Cornish Childhood* ([Grey Arrow] paperback edn., 1962), 134–5.

[5] A. W. Harrison *et al.*, *The Methodist Church*, 68 ff.

[6] J. C. G. Binfield, 'Nonconformity in the Eastern Counties 1840–1885: With Reference to its Social Background' (Ph.D. thesis, Cambridge, 1965), 197 ff.

[7] Edmund Gosse, *Life of Philip Henry Gosse* (1890), 153, 378. It has been pointed out that, whereas Edmund Gosse suggests his father's allegiance to the Brethren only after the return to Britain from Jamaica (1847), P. H. Gosse actually associated with them in the early 1840s before he went abroad for his second spell: Robert Boyd, 'Philip Henry Gosse, 1810–1888', *Christian Brethren Research Fellowship Broadsheet*, No. 2 (Mar.–Apr. 1969), 4–5. Some of the evidence is a manuscript account of his father by P. H. Gosse: Raymond Lister, *Thomas Gosse: A Biographical Sketch of an Itinerant Miniature Painter of the Early Nineteenth Century* (Cambridge, 1953), 15–16.

> This I perceive, that, when a sect grows old,
> Converts are few, and the converted cold:
> First comes the hot-bed heat, and, while it glows,
> The plants spring up, and each with vigour grows;
> Then comes the cooler day, and, though awhile
> The verdure prospers and the blossoms smile,
> Yet poor the fruit, and form'd by long delay,
> Nor will the profits for the culture pay;
> The skilful gard'ner then no longer stops,
> But turns to other beds for bearing crops.[1]

The Unitarians failed to expand in the nineteenth century: the Quakers expanded comparatively little and tended to be suspicious of converts.[2] The Irvingites rose and fell, and had declined emphatically by the early twentieth century: Gavin Maxwell describes the pathos of aged choirs, empty churches, ancient ministers, with the occasional tongues and prophecy as ironic reminders of the glory that was past.[3] Novelists like George Eliot, William Hale White, and Thomas Hardy were, as we shall see, very interested in the decline of evangelicalism and Dissent. Revivals, too, fascinated the novelists.

The 1859 Revival in Ireland signalled, according to J. Edwin Orr, a Second Evangelical Revival to match the eighteenth-century awakening: an era of Spurgeon and the Salvation Army, of Moody and Sankey, of Missions and Lord Shaftesbury.[4] Atheists, like John Chapman, were expectably antagonistic. Prominent among the conditions for revival, Chapman claimed, were ignorance and illiteracy, and emotionalism triumphing over intellect. He stressed the contagious phenomena of revivalism—convulsions, jumping, jerks, cryings out. Protestant Dissenters, he observed, were very liable to insanity.[5] His discussion chimed in with that in *All the Year Round*: 'Disease combined with Ignorance' generates Eastern Religious hysteria, witchcraft, American and Irish revivalism.[6] For its part the *Saturday Review* was attracted by charges of sexual immorality in the Belfast revivals.[7] And to Mrs.

[1] Crabbe, *The Borough*, Letter IV, lines 158–67: *Poems*, I. 318.

[2] E. Isichei, *Victorian Quakers*, 131.

[3] Gavin Maxwell, *The House of Elrig* (1965), 6–24; see also, for Irvingites, Sir Herbert Maxwell, *Evening Memories* (1932), 9–11; 227–9.

[4] See J. Edwin Orr, *The Second Evangelical Awakening* (1949), and G. Kitson Clark, *The Making of Victorian England* (paperback edn., 1968), 187–90.

[5] John Chapman, *Christian Revivals: Their History and Natural History* (1860). (Reprinted from *WR*, Jan. 1860.)

[6] 'Hysteria and Devotion', *AYR* 2 (5 Nov. 1859), 31–5.

[7] M. M. Bevington, *The Saturday Review 1855–1868: Representative Educated Opinion in Victorian England* (New York, 1951), 87.

Trollope's eyes there was as much sex as hysteria in Camp Meeting revivalism: being 'sick with horror' at an Indiana Camp Meeting did not hamper her noticing 'the insidious lips' of the preachers approaching 'the cheeks of the unhappy girls', or the young man's arm 'encircling the neck of a young girl'. In fact, she did not 'believe that such a scene could have been acted in the presence of Englishmen without instant punishment being inflicted'.[1] We have no record of Dickens's reactions at the time, but he did claim to have 'beheld religious scenes myself in some of our populous towns which can hardly be surpassed by an American camp-meeting'.[2] His hostile interest in revival phenomena is, however, clear. George Silverman's conversion 'would involve the rolling of several Brothers and Sisters on the floor, declaring that they felt all their sins in a heap on their left side, weighing so many pounds avoirdupoise—as I knew from what I had seen of those repulsive mysteries . . .'[3] Among Chadband's many crimes is revivalism: the 'fermentable sinners', like Mrs. Snagsby, must be made to ferment. She becomes, under the influence of his preaching, 'a prey to spasms; not an unresisting prey, but a crying and a tearing one, so that Cook's Court reechoes with her shrieks. Finally, becoming cataleptic, she has to be carried up the narrow staircase like a grand piano.'[4] Part of Timothy Sparks's case against sabbatarianism is that this violent sort of result is striven for by sabbatarian preachers in chapels on Sundays:

. . . working himself up to a pitch of enthusiasm amounting almost to frenzy, he denounces sabbath-breakers with the direst vengeance of offended Heaven. He stretches his body half out of the pulpit, thrusts forth his arms with frantic gestures, and blasphemously calls upon The Deity to visit with eternal torments, those who turn aside from the word, as interpreted and preached by—himself. A low moaning is heard, the women rock their bodies to and fro, and wring their hands; the preacher's fervour increases, the perspiration starts upon his brow, his face is flushed, and he clenches his hands convulsively, as he draws a hideous and appalling picture of the horrors preparing for the wicked in a future state. A great excitement is visible among his hearers, a scream is heard, and some young girl falls senseless on the floor. There is a momentary rustle, but it is only

[1] Mrs. Trollope, *Domestic Manners of the Americans* (2 Vols., 1832), I. 236; 242–3. The *American Quarterly Review* supported her case against this '*maladie du pays*' (Sept. 1832); the *North American Review* (Jan. 1833) defended the good character of Methodists and the conduct of Camp Meetings: *American Criticisms of Mrs. Trollope's 'Domestic Manners of the Americans'* (1833), 14, 42–3.
[2] *American Notes for General Circulation* (2 Vols., 1842); NOID, *American Notes and Pictures from Italy* (1957), Ch. 18, 249.
[3] 'George Silverman's Explanation', Ch. 6.
[4] *Bleak House*, Ch. 25.

for a moment—all eyes are turned towards the preacher. He pauses, passes his handkerchief across his face, and looks complacently round. His voice resumes its natural tone, as with mock humility he offers up a thanksgiving for having been successful in his efforts, and having been permitted to rescue one sinner from the path of evil. He sinks back into his seat, exhausted with the violence of his ravings; the girl is removed, a hymn is sung, a petition for some measure for securing the better observance of the sabbath, which has been prepared by the good man, is read; and his worshipping admirers, struggle who shall be the first to sign it.[1]

Kingsley's ferocity against the Cornish Methodist preachers who, in *Two Years Ago*, exploit a plague of cholera to create a revival, is sterner than Dickens's against the sabbatarian. Creating fear of Hell increases susceptibility to the disease. The Major reacts as Mrs. Trollope's Englishman was to: with his 'martial stateliness' he easily winkles the preacher and congregation out of the 'Meeting house' (which Methodists actually always called 'Preaching Houses'), calls on the men and 'modest married women' to share his protest against the preacher and the 'shameless hussies who like to go into fits at his feet',[2] challenges the preacher's theology of God the Judge ('devil's doctrines'), proves him a coward (he hides among the women from the manly Major and takes refuge in canting jargon), and finally asks God to judge between them. Rather unfairly, not to say surprisingly after the Major's aspersions about 'devil's doctrines', God supports Kingsley and the Major, and the preacher dies, almost immediately, of cholera. It was perhaps somewhat less than manly of Kingsley himself to exaggerate his case by suggesting that the preachers encouraged revival for money; and to sink to mere caricature by making the Bryanite preacher oppose the Rev. Frank Headley's advocacy of sanitary measures as German rationalism's undermining of God's purposes, and by having a rival Dissenter, a 'fanatic on the teetotal question', condemn the vicar for thus supporting drunkenness, since cholera is caused by intemperance.[3] 'Every anecdote and fact' was true, Kingsley claimed. But, under pressure from his Wesleyan reviewer, Dr. J. H. Rigg,[4] he had to

[1] Timothy Sparks [Charles Dickens], *Sunday Under Three Heads. As it is; As Sabbath Bills would make it; As it might be made* (1836), 9–10.

[2] Kingsley stops short before that awful result: 'In another minute there would have been (as there have been ere now) four or five young girls raving and tossing upon the floor, in mad terror and excitement . . . ' (Ch. 17). He thus titillates without committing himself to particular charges which might be taken up by reviewers more friendly to Methodism, and without being explicitly offensive to the puritan reader.

[3] *Two Years Ago*, Chs. 14, 16, 17.

[4] See *LQR*, 8 (1857), 1–49; and 8 (1857), 276–8.

concede that his accuracy did not even extend to getting the evil-doers' denomination right: could it be (he asked in a letter which included a serious warning to Rigg against 'venting a falsehood and a slander' against Hare, Maurice, and himself, by calling them Rationalists), that he had been mistaken: '. . . were the good folks of ——, where all these facts occurred, not Brianites after all, but Wesleyans?'[1] (The historian of North Devon Methodism, assuming on slight evidence that Aberalva is meant for Clovelly, points out, for what it is worth, that there were actually no Bryanites in Clovelly.)[2]

George Eliot was much more serious in her presentation of conversion phenomena. The onlooking stranger in *Adam Bede* (Ch. 2) wonders whether Dinah will be able to rouse her audience's 'more violent emotions . . . a necessary seal of her vocation as a Methodist preacher'. Popular expectation runs in the same direction: 'Are ye coom t'help groon? They say folks allays groon when they're hearkenin' to th'Methodys . . .' Chad Cranage means to groan; his daughter, however, cannot help her response. And Bessy Cranage's reduction to terrified sobbing and to wrenching off her ear-rings is good because it is presented partly from Dinah Morris's point of view (Bessy's 'evident vanity' touched her with pity) and done with a sociologist's or natural historian's objectivity. George Eliot's conclusion, that such conversions are short lived—Bessy falls away and takes to her ear-rings again (Ch. 25)—is Chapman's, some of the Wesleyans', and Hardy's.[3] But to make the comparison with Hardy's casual handling of Alec D'Urberville, who when he again meets Tess abandons his Methodism as suddenly as he took it up, thus indicating that such vehement Christianity is merely the sublimation of sexual urges, is to underline George Eliot's high seriousness. She eschewed any facile condemnation of the revival style, too readily available to novelists as to Methodist Conferences[4] and Churchmen:

---

[1] *Charles Kingsley: His Letters and Memories of His Life*, ed. by his wife (2 Vols., 1877), II. 22. The BQR reviewer was annoyed: 'Mr. Kingsley's description of the Brianite, or local Methodist preachers, we conceive to be as gross a violation of taste as it is utterly false in fact.' *BQR* 25 (1857), 416.

[2] J. G. H[ayman], *History of Methodism in North Devon* (1871), 70.

[3] '. . . the intense religious fervour of the present time will die out, and a large proportion of the new converts will fall away.' Chapman, *Christian Revivals*, 51. And see, e.g., review of Francis Truscott's *Revivals of Religion Vindicated*, *Methodist Magazine*, ser. iii, Vol. 3 (1824), pp. 821–2.

[4] e.g. the 1862 Conference of the Methodist New Connexion censured Booth's Cornish revival; and the 1862 Primitive Methodist Conference disapproved of employing 'Revivalists so-called'. J. E. Orr, *The Second Evangelical Awakening*, 116.

And now a new and noisy set—
The Army of Salvation—
Our equal-minded justice fret
With constant botheration:
For sometimes they obstruct the way,
And sometimes cause a riot;
Too much of zeal—too much, we say,
Why can't the fools keep quiet?

The dean and canons in their stalls
Are placid as stalled cattle,
And never rush out from St Paul's
To give the devil battle.
In streets and lanes to brawl and fight
Is far too low and rowdy;
No, if he wants a spar, invite
Him home to Mrs Proudie.[1]

The variations in religious styles reflected the variations of religious taste in the period, and in Dissent there was almost certainly an even greater range than in the Anglican communion. The almost bewildering variety of choice created notable oscillators. Like Thomas Cooper, who successively sampled Primitive Methodism, Congregationalism, and the Parish Church, became a Wesleyan local preacher, then a Chartist agitator and lecturer on Strauss. Brought back to Christianity partly through the influence of Kingsley, he eschewed Wesleyanism, United Free Methodism, and a Scripture readership offered by Dr. Hook of Leeds, and became a General Baptist and a lecturer on Christian evidences.[2] Or like Joseph Barker, son of a soldier converted to Methodism, who joined the Methodist New Connexion and became a teetotal lecturer. Influenced by Plymouth Brethren and Quaker ideas, he was expelled from the New Connexion and took his 'Barkerite' group with him; he became a Unitarian, and 'gradually slid' down the incline from 'the almost Christian doctrine of Carpenter and Channing' to 'the principles of Paine and Voltaire'; he had a period as a Chartist, but ended his days with a return to orthodoxy, and became finally a Primitive Methodist preacher.[3] There was a tendency among the more educated Dissenters to drift into a form of Unitarianism: for Noncon-formists like William Hale White, as for Anglicans like George Eliot,

[1] James Thomson, 'Law v. Gospel': *Poems*, II. 91–2.
[2] *The Life of Thomas Cooper*, written by Himself (1872).
[3] *The Life of Joseph Barker*.

Unitarianism was a last halt on the way to a region beyond Christianity; for some, like Basil Martin, it was the last fingerhold to which they could cling while honestly remaining in Dissent.[1] The attraction of the Church of England for the affluent and social-climbing is well known. That upward shift was as common as Anglican conversion to Puseyism or Rome. Hardy's *A Laodicean* spells it out tediously, but Paula Power's dilemma about whether to become a Baptist like her father, and opt for the railway and telegraph age, or to choose tradition, an ancient name in marriage, and Anglicanism, to go with her castle, is real enough, and Hardy leaves it unresolved. At a lower social level the dilemma is reduced satirically to a matter of almost mere caprice by the village landlord:

> . . . I was a Methodist once—ay, for a length of time. 'Twas owing to my taking a house next door to a chapel; so that what with hearing the organ bizz like a bee through the wall, and what with finding it saved umbrellas on wet Zundays, I went over to that faith for two years—though I believe I dropped money by it— I wouldn't be the man to say so if I hadn't. Howsomever, when I moved into this house I turned back again to my old religion. Faith, I don't zee much difference: be you one, or be you t'other, you've got to get your living.[2]

Within Dissent there were broad options in matters of polity and practice. On the one hand, the Congregational polity characterized freelance groups and the Plymouth Brethren as well as the Baptists and Independents; on the other hand, Methodism was mainly Connexional, the daughter-groups offering more democratic variants of Wesleyanism's rigidly authoritarian Connexionalism.[3] Baptizers of adults (all the Baptist groups, and the Plymouth Brethren) vied with paedobaptists (Congregationalists and Methodists), and some people were not too concerned either way—there were chapels like William Hale White's at Bedford which combined Baptists and Congregationalists and therefore modes of baptism, and the Salvation Army entirely abandoned the sacraments of Baptism and the Eucharist.[4] Recruiters, who included most evangelicals, particularly the successful Methodist and Methodist-influenced groups, predominated over non-recruiters. Even the unorthodox and the anti-orthodox strained after converts; the Victorian religious

---

[1] Kingsley Martin, *Father Figures* (1966), Chs. 1 and 2.

[2] *A Laodicean*, Bk. I, Ch. 4.

[3] Wesleyanism only conceded lay representation in Conference in 1878: E. R. Taylor, *Methodism and Politics 1791–1851* (Cambridge, 1935), 111. Taylor's account of the democratic pressures on Wesleyanism and its gradual democratization is extremely valuable.

[4] See, e.g., B. R. Wilson, *Religious Sects: A Sociological Study* (1970), 60–4.

market-place was a babel of clamouring voices. Not all the voices were
heeded, though, and the evangelizing Unitarians for example made little
headway.[1] But non-recruiters—as the Quakers, with their hereditary
suspicion of converts, probably were—were exceedingly rare.

One could choose between cool, decorous worship and wilder,
revivalist services. Joseph Lawson contrasted the calm and dignity of
Moravian worship at Fulneck with a Pudsey Methodist revival:

We thought also, and said, that the Moravian style of worshipping appeared as if
its adherents were 'paid by the day', and therefore took matters easy, while that
of the Methodists seemed as if they were 'paid by the piece', and hence the zeal,
hurry and bustle displayed by the latter in their meetings and around the penitent
forms.[2]

Lawrence made the same sort of contrast in 'Hymns in a Man's Life'
between Congregationalism and Primitive Methodism.[3] The Bible
Christians produced the corybantic Billy Bray.[4] Men like Henry
Higginson, the Roving Ranter, who once leapt excitedly through the
pulpit floor at Quarry Street Primitive Methodist Chapel, Bilston,[5] or
Elijah Cadman, who kicked the pulpit's front panel down the aisle at
Grandborough Primitive Methodist chapel, were welcome, and became
legendary, preachers. Cadman's feat (and foot) are celebrated by a
brass tablet and a framed narrative fixed to the chapel wall:

I was telling the Congregation that, after the Devil ventured his last Temptation,
Jesus ordered him off, and gave him a kick that sent him howling through the air.
My foot, being in harmony with my Subject, gave such a kick as to send the front
Panel of the Pulpit flying down the aisle, whereupon some of the Members shouted
'Glory'.

The early Salvationists carried on this ranting tradition: Elijah Cadman
became one of Booth's Commissioners. They horrified the decorous
with their novelty attractions: to Music-Hall tunes, brass bands,
clapping, handkerchief-waving,[6] they added Music-Hall turns. Their
posters might announce:

---

[1] The aggressive Unitarians were those of the British and Foreign Unitarian Association.
See *Catalogue of Books and Tracts Sold at the Book-Room of the British & Foreign Unitarian
Association* (Oct. 1892): copies in the Bodleian Library, John Johnson collection.

[2] Joseph Lawson, *Progress in Pudsey* (1887), 95–6.

[3] *Evening News* (13 oct. 1928), reprinted in *Phoenix II*, ed. W. Roberts and H. T.
Moore (1968) and in *Selected Literary Criticism*, ed. A. Beal (paperback edn., 1967), 6–11.

[4] F. W. Bourne, *The King's Son: or a 'Memoir' of Billy Bray* (1871).

[5] Michael and Jon Raven, *Folk Out of Focus: Folklore and Songs of the Black Country* (Wolverhampton, 1965), 27–8.

[6] Chadwick, *Victorian Church*, II. 292.

Salvation Army, Harwich, Public Hall, Sunday next, Captain Tom Payne, accompanied by Lieutenant W. Whitley, and the Hallelujah Poet, and others, will fight the devil. Subjects for the day: 11.0 am: Lessons from a preacher who came from hell. 3.0 pm: Popping the question, and a few hints to young ladies. 6.30 pm: Fearful battle; Tom Payne will fight the devil on the platform with cords and cut-rope. . . .[1]

Quaker services were renowned for quietness: the Primitive Methodists were more truly the descendants of George Fox when it came to exuberant movings of the Spirit. Charlotte Brontë indicates the intensity of the Briar Chapel Wesleyans' service (*Shirley*, Ch. 9) with an ironic reference to Quakers: '. . . a hymn of a most extraordinary description, such as a very Quaker might feel himself moved by the Spirit to dance to, roused cheerily all the echoes of the vicinage'. Unitarian worship easily lent itself to charges that it was rational and cold. 'All is dry, intellectual, critical, logical. The head is the master of the heart . . .' alleged the anonymous Physiologist of the sects, who perhaps knew of Dickens's forties' flirtation with Unitarianism: 'The immobile, immovable, unemotional Dombey is a fine specimen of the Unitarian proper, and the original of that unlovable personage must have been a member of this sect.'[2] Dickens would not have been best pleased: he approved highly of Unitarians and little of the stiff-necked Dombey. Almost as little as of ranters: in fact exuberance is a sure characteristic of religionists Dickens dislikes: Melchisedech Howler's jumpers, or the brethren of Hawkyard's little assembly who are always ready with a responsive 'That's it', or Chadband's dupes.

One could attend Dissenting services primarily to 'sit under' the preacher: the reason why Hale White joined the 'intelligent' congregation which attended Caleb Morris's chapel in Fetter Lane,[3] and thousands, like A. L. Rowse's aunt and uncle, included an obligatory pilgrimage to Spurgeon's Tabernacle in a trip to the metropolis.[4] On

---

[1] *BW* 9 (11 Dec. 1890), 102.

[2] *The Physiology of the Sects* (1874), 150, 157.

[3] For Caleb Morris, see [James Grant], *The Metropolitan Pulpit; or Sketches of the most Popular Preachers in London* (2 Vols., 1839), II. 197–206.

[4] A. L. Rowse, *A Cornish Childhood*, 58. Cf. the Scot who declared he 'dinna want to die until he gang to London to see Madame Tussaud's and hear Mr Spurgeon': Patricia S. Kruppa, Review of Spurgeon and Moody Literature, *VS* 7 (June 1964), 393. Prints of Spurgeon, 'solid as to the flesh, not to say even something gross', and 'looming heavily', are to be purchased in Carlisle or Wigton: Dickens and Wilkie Collins, 'The Lazy Tour of Two Idle Apprentices', Chs. 1, 2: *NOID, Christmas Stories*, 663–758. Lupex, in Trollope's *The Small House at Allington*, II, ch. 47, would have become famous himself, he

the other hand, one might attend because one could contribute something more than one's presence. Some sects invited high levels of
participation from their members. Hymn-singing was, of course, the
commonest form of audience involvement, entered into fervently and
notably by the Methodists. We have seen that the Lancashire Independent Methodists were known as 'Singing Quakers', and that the
Primitives were nicknamed 'Ranters' for singing in the streets. Given
such a heritage it was only to be expected that music should play so
important a rôle in the Salvation Army's strategy. The Evangelical
Revival had been an affair of song. Dicky Burdsall, the Yorkshire local
preacher, was converted one Christmas-tide after hearing William
Grimshaw preach in a barn at Bingley: he 'trembled so much with the
cold that I thought it would be impossible for me to bear it long', but
when Grimshaw arrived, 'buttoned up from the storm', and gave out
a hymn, 'the people sang like thunder'.[1] Joseph Barker remembered
his father singing 'many and many a time' at the jenny: 'My God! I
know, I feel thee mine . . .' Perhaps it helped to appreciate the worth
of Nonconformist singing if one had some training in it. Amelia Barr
the novelist, daughter of a Methodist minister, returned from America
to Bradford (1888): '. . . I went to an intense Methodist service and
heard a thousand Yorkshire men and women sing "There is a Land of
pure delight", and "Lo, He comes with clouds descending!" as I shall
never again hear them . . .'

There is doubtless an organ and a choir now, and the preacher will have been to
a Theological Institute, and perhaps be not only 'Reverend' but have some mystic
letters after his name, and the congregation will be more polished, and the
precepts of gentility will now be a religious obligation. And I am afraid it is not
genteel now, to be anxious about your soul—especially in public. But I thank
God that I spent that Sunday in Yorkshire. . . .[2]

But an outsider was not necessarily unappreciative. At Spurgeon's
Tabernacle, C. M. Davies noted, the hymns were 'sung—of course, in
unison—by the whole congregation, without accompaniment of any
kind, one man standing behind Mr. Spurgeon to give the pitch . . . and

---

claims, had he been able to paint somebody famous, like 'Lord Derby, or Mr. Spurgeon'.
As one of the most famous men of his day Spurgeon got into *Eminent Persons: Biographies
Reprinted from 'The Times'* (6 Vols., 1892–7), V. 203–10 (Obituary, Monday, 1 Feb. 1892).
    [1] Autobiography of Dicky Burdsall, quoted in Frank Baker, *William Grimshaw 1708–1763*
(1963), 106–7.
    [2] Amelia E. Barr, *All the Days of My Life: An Autobiography. The Red Leaves of a Human
Heart* (New York, 1913), 415–16.

one cannot fail to be struck with the effect of these simple tunes sung by so vast a body of voices.'[1] It is the fervent singing at the Baptist chapel that attracts the attention of Hardy's George Somerset, and helps redefine his initial repugnance for the ugly red brick and plate glass: '. . . in the heaving of that tune [New Sabbath] there was an earnestness that made him thoughtful, and the shine of those windows he had characterized as ugly reminded him of the shining of the good deed in a naughty world.'[2] George Eliot and Mrs. Gaskell (hardly outsiders) became sentimental over Nonconformists' singing; and they both chose for it nostalgic, open-air settings. The stranger in *Adam Bede* rides away at the end of Ch. 2, 'while Dinah said, "Let us sing a little, dear friends"; and as he was still winding down the slope, the voices of the Methodists reached him, rising and falling in that strange blending of exultation and sadness which belongs to the cadence of a hymn.' The tone of this passage is akin to that in Part I of *Cousin Phillis*, where Ebenezer Holman, at the end of the day's farming, leads his men in a psalm: ' "Come all harmonious tongues", to be sung to "Mount Ephraim" tune.' Dickens, however, professed to hear with different ears: Hawkyard's service 'closed with a hymn, in which the Brothers unanimously roared, and the Sisters unanimously shrieked, at me, that I by wiles of wordly gain was mock'd, and they on waters of sweet love were rock'd; that I with Mammon struggled in the dark, while they were floating in a second Ark.' For Alton Locke the 'bawling' at the Baptist church contrasts unfavourably with Lillian's sweet singing.[3]

Higher levels of participation than merely singing were, however, often required of Dissenters. In the face of increased ministerial professionalism, theological training, and university education, lay-preachers persisted strongly. At the end of the century, for example, the number of Baptist lay-preachers was rising faster than the number of Baptist ministers, and 47,781 Dissenting lay-preachers were claimed in 1899.[4] The notable success of Methodism, and especially Primitive Methodism, among the proletariat was clearly related to the opportunities it granted for lay activities. The Independent Methodists had no separate, salaried ministers. Breakaway Methodist sects like the Primitives and Bible

[1] *Unorthodox London*, 67.

[2] *A Laodicean*, Bk. I, Chs. 1 and 2.

[3] Charles Kingsley, *Alton Locke, Tailor and Poet: An Autobiography* (1850; revised edn., 1862), Ch. 14.

[4] Chadwick, *Victorian Church*, II. 256; Rev. Charles Herbert, 'Free Church Progress', *Puritan* (1899), 344–5.

Christians sanctioned even the women preachers Wesleyanism banned
in 1803: the reason for George Eliot's Aunt Samuel's association with
Hugh Bourne and the Arminian Methodists of Derby. The Quakers and
the Plymouth Brethren likewise eschewed clerical functionaries and
existed solely for the laity. Verity Hawkyard, dry-salter, 'was a
prominent member of some obscure denomination or congregation,
every member of which held forth to the rest when so inclined, and
among whom he was called Brother Hawkyard'. And Dickens parodies
this insistent laicism in Hawkyard's prayer for Silverman:

The now-opening career of this our unawakened Brother might lead to his
becoming a minister of what was called The Church. That was what *he* looked
to. The Church. Not the chapel, Lord. The Church. No rectors, no vicars, no
archdeacons, no bishops, no archbishops, in the chapel; but, O Lord, many such
in the Church!

Lay participation can always create absurdity—ungrammatical,
simple, or garbled language in sermons or prayers is often ridiculous.[1]
But the tone was not always what William Hale White alleged (about
Congregationalists, in a passage E. P. Thompson uses, a bit unfairly, to
beat the Wesleyans with): '. . . and then ensued a kind of dialogue with
God, very much resembling the speeches which in later years I have
heard in the House of Commons from the movers and seconders of
addresses to the Crown at the opening of Parliament.'[2] Much more
vitally, God could also be, as it were, welcomed into the democratic
circle of worshippers. Flora Thompson tells how the Methodists would
relate, in prayer, the week's news to God ('As thou knowest, Lord'):
God was for them less 'the Crown' than a superior kind of villager.[3]

In Dissenting theology the notable divisions were, among the orthodox, between Calvinists and Arminians, and, as the period advanced,

[1] ' "Stir us up", he cried with uplifted hands. "We've been setting so long at ease in
Zion that we've got stiff in the joints. We want ilin' we do, Oh Lord, 'ile us, 'ile us with
the Isle of Patmos." ' Silas Hocking, *My Book of Memory: A String of Reminiscences and
Reflections* (1923), 36. One prayer-leader 'could scarce ever utter a sentence that had any
sense in it. He would pray for God to bless our iniquities, and to fill our transgressions
with His Holy Spirit, that they might run like oil from vessel to vessel, refreshed with new
wine.' *The Life of Joseph Barker*, 49–50.

[2] *The Autobiography of Mark Rutherford, Dissenting Minister*, Ch. 1; E. P. Thompson, *The
Making of the English Working Class* (revised edn., Penguin, 1968), 385.

[3] Flora Thompson, *From Lark Rise to Candleford*, 235. Hardy put it less kindly through
Coggan: 'Not but that chapel-members be clever chaps enough in their way. They can
lift up beautiful prayers out of their own heads, all about their families and shipwrecks in
the newspaper.' *Far from the Madding Crowd*, Ch. 42.

between liberals and non-liberals. Hyper-Calvinism was maintained through the period by the Strict Baptists. Alton Locke's mother, brought up an Independent, became a Baptist: 'She considered the Baptists, as I do, as the only sect who thoroughly embody the Calvinistic doctrines' (Ch. 1). But among Calvinists in general the century saw a gradual erosion of the intensity of adherence to the basic points.[1] In 1815 the Baptist Union was designated 'The General Meeting of the Particular (or Calvinistic) Baptist Denomination'; in 1832, the re-organized Union redefined itself merely as a union of Baptist ministers and churches 'who agree in the sentiments usually denominated evangelical'. The pressures of eighteenth-century evangelicalism had generated Fullerism as they had Dan Taylor. Congregationalism also felt the challenge of evangelistic situations:

At home in their study, they might be unable to resist the proof that when the evangelist John wrote that 'God so loved the world that he gave His only begotten Son', he really meant that 'God so loved the *Church* that He gave His only begotten Son'; but in the pulpit they pleaded with men as if they believed that the text was true as it stood.

And, gradually, specifically Calvinist propositions disappeared: 'The doctrines of Election, and a limited Atonement, were mentioned very occasionally, or dropped altogether. They were not denied—they might be true—but they had no real relation to the life and works of the children of the Revival.'[2]

The continuing challenges of evangelism put further pressures on Calvinism: I. H. Murray blames Moody's 'simple gospel' for 'the prevalence of an evangelism non-doctrinal in type' in the '70s and '80s.[3] Even Spurgeon himself, who commanded by then a fairly isolated Calvinist eminence (in 1873 he challenged R. W. Dale's claim that 'Calvinism would be almost obsolete among Baptists were it not still maintained by the powerful influence of Mr. Spurgeon'; in 1881 he did not refute Dale's repeated charge), was influenced. It was certainly

[1] Total Depravity, Unconditional Election, Limited Atonement, Irresistible Grace, Perseverance of the Saints (for the mnemonic, TULIP, see Peter de Vries's story, 'Tulip', in *Without a Stitch in Time* (1974)).

[2] R. W. Dale, *History of English Congregationalism*, ed. A. W. W. Dale (1907), 587. See also R. T. Jones, *Congregationalism in England 1661–1962* (1962), 168 ff. For the rise of Moderate Calvinism among the Baptists, see O. C. Robison, 'Particular Baptists in England, 1760–1820' (D.Phil. thesis, Oxford, 1963).

[3] I. H. Murray, *The Forgotten Spurgeon* (1966), 180–1; 187–8. I. H. Murray is useful on the growth of theological liberalism in the period. So also are R. T. Jones, *Congregationalism in England*; E. A. Payne, *The Baptist Union: A Short History*; and W. B. Glover, *Evangelical Nonconformity and Higher Criticism in the Nineteenth Century* (1954).

a modified Calvinism that allowed him impishly to pray 'Lord hasten to
bring in all Thine elect, and then elect some more.' His own conversion
really confirms Dale's point: son and grandson of Congregationalist
pastors, weaned on Calvinism, he was yet spiritually unawakened until
he heard the barely articulate preacher in Artillery Street Primitive
Methodist Chapel, Colchester.[1] A certain grafting on to the inherited
Calvinism of an evangelistic intensity perhaps more characteristic of
Arminians was inevitable.

   Calvinism did not altogether die, but it was knocked hard as part of
the orthodoxy that became increasingly unfashionable among Victorian
theologians and preachers. In 1873 the Baptist Union made public its
doubt about the 'evangelical' declaration of 1832, and revised it to
accommodate freer thinkers: the Union's statement of faith now read
that '. . . in this Union it is fully recognised that every separate church
has liberty to interpret and administer the laws of Christ, and that the
immersion of believers is the only Christian baptism.' The doctrine of
eternal punishment was replaced by theories of annihilation (R. W.
Dale was one prominent convert to Edward White's school), or by
universalism. The traditional Puritan forensic theory of the Atonement
was revised by Dale and James Baldwin Brown. Scientific discoveries
and textual criticism were gradually accommodated by the liberals.
The Congregationalist *Rivulet* controversy (1855–6) over the orthodoxy
of T. T. Lynch's volume of hymns; the debate (1856–7) over Samuel
Davidson, tutor at the Lancashire Independent College, and his views
on the Pentateuch; the Leicester Conference of Congregationalists
(October 1877), where a paper on 'The Relations of Theology to
Religion' generated wide discussion; the Baptist 'Down Grade' debate,
when Spurgeon resigned from the Baptist Union because it resisted a
precise, theologically evangelical declaration of faith, were less straws
in the wind than debris from an explosion that had already occurred.

   The problems of theological liberalism seemed at the time com-
moner in Dissent than elsewhere in Christendom. Movements founded
on the Word's authority rather than the Church's felt instantly any
impugning of the authenticity of Scripture—and Anglicans jeered that
Spurgeon's Down Grade 'jeremiad' was 'the death-song of a little
human system which has had its day and must soon cease to be'.[2] But

---

[1] E. W. Bacon, *Spurgeon: Heir of the Puritans* (1967), 1–24.
[2] *Church Times*, 12 Aug. 1887, quoted in M. R. Watts, 'John Clifford and Radical Nonconformity 1836–1923' (D.Phil. thesis, Oxford, 1966), 128. *John Bull* anticipated the
'Decomposition of Dissent'; ibid., 166.

liberalism was not evenly spread. Among the orthodox groups it made most rapid headway among Congregationalists, followed by the Baptists. The Methodists lagged behind. The theological revolution began with pastors rather than with people: significantly its most vehement opponents were among the period's most popular preachers—Canon Liddon, Spurgeon, Joseph Parker ('I am jealous lest the Bible should in any sense be made a priest's book'),[1] and the most demotic groups tended to be the most conservative. C. M. Davies was impressed by Kelly's assaults on Colenso in an Exclusive Brethren Bible Lecture at Islington,[2] but the local preacher might well not even have heard of Colenso. A. S. Peake was something of a Primitive Methodist *rara avis*.[3]

One reason offered for the comparatively slow impact of liberalism on Methodism is that its Arminianism cushioned it against the consternation generated elsewhere by the decline of Calvinism. Against the insistence of Calvinism on a limited atonement, the Methodist (unless he were an adherent of Whitefield's or the Countess of Huntingdon's Calvinistic Methodism) sang with Charles Wesley that 'For all my Lord was crucified, For all, for all my Saviour died!'[4] Silas Hocking, a United Methodist Free Churches minister, might be expected to get this theological point right, and in *Her Benny*[5] Joe Wrag, the nightwatchman, is rescued from years of Calvinist-inspired gloom by Nell's retailing what she has heard of the Arminian gospel for the *whosoever* in a (presumably) Methodist chapel. Curiously, though, this major distinction is sometimes blurred by other novelists. Though Alec D'Urberville's Methodism is noted by Hardy (he was 'strangely accoutred as the Methodist'), he preaches the wrong theology. He is an 'extremest antinomian', his doctrine 'a vehement form of the views of Angel's father', and *he* is an extreme Evangelical Anglican Calvinist ('His creed of determinism was such that it almost amounted to a vice . . .').[6]

---

[1] Chadwick, *Victorian Church*, II. 106; Joseph Parker, in *None Like It: a Plea for the Old Sword* (1893), quoted by W. B. Glover, op. cit., 230.

[2] C. M. Davies, *Unorthodox London*, 180.

[3] A. S. Peake (1865–1929), theologian and Biblical scholar; educated at St. John's College, Oxford; a Fellow of Merton; appointed tutor (1892) at Hartley Primitive Methodist College, Manchester, though a known liberal. *DNB*; O. Chadwick, *Victorian Church*, II. 104–5.

[4] Stanza 7 of 'Let earth and heaven agree': No. 33 in *A Collection of Hymns for the Use of the People Called Methodists* (new edn., 1797).

[5] First published in 12 parts in the *United Methodist Free Churches Magazine*, 22 (1879).

[6] *Tess of the D'Urbervilles*, Chs. 25, 44, 45.

## 2. THE VARIETY OF DISSENTING VIEWS ON THE NOVEL

It is a prevalent and unexamined assumption that novelists were against
Dissent because Dissent was uniformly against the novel. But in the
matter of literature, as in theology, there was among Dissenters both
synchronic variety and diachronic change: the attitude towards the
wider culture varied between individuals and groups, and changed as
the nineteenth century grew older. Generalizations about Nonconformist attitudes to fiction are not hard to come by, but they tend to
friability. A pattern of liberalization can be traced, as Trollope, for
example, recognized. He had written *Rachel Ray* for Norman Macleod's
*Good Words* at the editor's suggestion (1863), but publication was
halted because of the dancing in an early chapter. By the time he was
writing his *Autobiography* (in 1876) even the Presbyterians, said
Trollope, would not object to that:

> It has not only come to pass that a special provision of them [novels] has to be
> made for the godly, but that the provision so made must now include books
> which a few years since the godly would have thought to be profane. It was this
> necessity which, a few years since, induced the editor of *Good Words* to apply to
> me for a novel,—which, indeed, when supplied was rejected, but which now,
> probably, owing to further changes in the same direction, would have been
> accepted.[1]

But liberalization did not proceed uniformly; it was not sudden nor
universal; and the newer sects such as the Irvingites and the Brethren,
as well as strict evangelicals elsewhere, continued to abhor the novel.
Again, the stereotype of Unitarian liberalism and culture can be jolted
by the fact that even at William Gaskell's Cross Street Chapel, Manchester, there were novel-readers ready, on moral grounds, to burn
*Ruth*, and that William Gaskell would not allow his own children to
read it.[2] Or again, even the inoffensive Scott was not universally
pleasing. John Angell James 'could not endure fiction', and his son
knew him to have read only one novel apart from *Uncle Tom's Cabin*:
*Rob Roy*.[3] This concession to Scott was common among evangelicals:
Aunt Branwell's gift to her nieces and nephew of Scott's *Tales of a*

---

[1] Anthony Trollope, *An Autobiography* (2 Vols., Edinburgh, 1883), I. 248–50, II. 31–2.
(He began Ch. 3 in Jan. 1876, and finished the account in Apr. 1876: Henry M. Trollope,
Preface, ibid., I. vii.)

[2] *The Letters of Mrs. Gaskell*, No. 150, p. 223, and No. 148, p. 221.

[3] T. S. James, 'Home Life', Appendix to R. W. Dale, *Life and Letters of John Angell James*
(new edn., 1862), 382.

*Grandfather* (in 1828) indicates its extent.[1] Early initiation into Scott
('. . . and before I was twelve I had read at least half of the romances
of the great Wizard of the North') generated Joseph Hocking's ambition
to be a writer.[2] But rejection of Scott does occur, albeit among the
strictest evangelicals only: Mrs. Philip Gosse, or the Rev. Carus Wilson.[3]
For all their fragility, however, some generalizations can be attempted.

The puritan rejection of worldly stimuli of the imagination derived
from the theological belief that the imagination and the senses of the
regenerate are to be devoted wholly to God:

There is a change made on the *body*, and the members thereof, in respect of their
use: they are *consecrated* to the Lord. Even *the body is—for the Lord*, I. Cor. vi.
13. It is *the temple of the Holy Ghost*, ver. 19. The members thereof, that were
formerly *instruments of unrighteousness unto sin*, become *instruments of righteousness
unto God*, Rom. vi. 13. Servants to righteousness unto holiness, ver. 19. *The eye*,
that conveyed sinful imaginations into the heart, is under a covenant, *Job* xxxi. 1.
to do so no more; but to serve the soul in viewing the works, and reading the
word of God. *The ear*, that had often been death's porter to let in sin, is turned
to be the gate of life, by which the word of life enters the soul. *The tongue*,
that set on fire the whole course of nature, is restored to the office it was designed for by the Creator; namely, to be an instrument of glorifying him, and
setting forth his praise. In a word, the whole man is for God, in soul and body,
which by this blessed change [regeneration] are made his.[4]

To the evangelical fiction was intrusive, upsetting a whole-hearted
contemplation of God, distracting readers from prayer and Bible-
reading, '. . . a kind of Devil's Bible, whose meretricious attractions
waged an unholy competition against the reading of God's word. Where
novel-reading comes in Bible-reading goes out was a belief, which,
after all, has much to justify it in the experience of mankind.'[5] In 1881
John Stoughton, who never visisted a theatre after his conversion,
lamented the changes that had occurred in the domestic habits of
Congregationalists:

---

[1] W. Gérin, *Charlotte Brontë: The Evolution of Genius* (Oxford, 1967), 28. Presumably the
gift was the first series of the *Tales* (3 Vols., Edinburgh, 1828 [for 1827]).

[2] Joseph Hocking, 'My beginnings in literature', *Puritan* (1899), 901.

[3] W. Gérin, op. cit., 12. For other readers and non-readers of Scott, see R. T. Jones,
*Congregationalism in England 1662–1962* (1962), 232 and footnote 6, and cf. Trollope, 'On
English Prose Fiction as a Rational Amusement', *Four Lectures*, ed. M. L. Parrish (1938),
14.

[4] Thomas Boston, *Human Nature in Its Fourfold Estate* (12th edn., Edinburgh, 1761),
170–1.

[5] W. T. Stead, quoted by Amy Cruse, *The Victorians and their Books* (1937), 67.

. . . whereas family and private reading was very select, very limited, now with us, as with others, it has become very general, very broad, very 'promiscuous'. Fiction, once even condemned, then only suspected and looked at askance, is now devoured. The most sensational are admitted, discussed, perhaps by some excused, if not praised. Opinions altogether tabooed or unknown are now brought under the notice of young people in periodicals lying on many a drawing-room table. With this freedom in reading, there is often united a freedom in reference to amusements; places of entertainment are frequented, and modes of diversion are common, such as were unknown to families amongst us two genera-tions ago. Moreover, a style of living obtains in contrast with the domestic arrangements and expenses of the old time. Conformity to fashion in some of its excesses may be seen in furniture, dinner, and dress amongst people of different religious circles. . . . And may I be permitted to remark that I have noticed in families I have visited of late years a more frequent omission of domestic evening prayer than used to be the case.[1]

'The Worldliness of family life must entail spiritual loss': [2] it was this connection which led the evangelical and sectarian to close the flood-gates against the tide of the century's fiction. Not all, of course. Joseph Parker, a conservative evangelical and 'the greatest Congregationalist preacher in London', wrote novels and lost Spurgeon's friendship in their feud over his theatre-attendance.[3] And Joshua Taylor, member of the Kilhamite New Connexion when, if *Shirley* is to be believed, its revivalist fervour had by no means cooled, used to lend Charlotte Brontë novels, forty at a time, 'clever wicked sophisticated and immoral'.[4] But Spurgeon's repugnance for fiction was more characteristic of conservative attitudes than Parker's approval. He and his magazine *The Sword and The Trowel* regarded fiction-reading as evidence of the 'Down Grade': [5]

Our Puritan forefathers were strong men, because they lived on the Scriptures. None stood against them in their day, for they fed on good meat, whereas their degenerate children are far too fond of unwholesome food. The chaff of

---

[1] John Stoughton, *Reminiscences of Congregationalism Fifty Years Ago* (1881), 77–8; R. T. Jones, op. cit., 231.

[2] John Stoughton, op. cit., 88.

[3] W. B. Glover, op. cit., 165, 182, 244–5.

[4] W. Gérin, *Charlotte Brontë*, 168.

[5] See, e.g., J. H. Norton, 'Worldly Amusements for Professors of Religion; Or, Where will you draw the line?', *Sword and Trowel*, 23 (1887), 629–32; G. H. Pike, 'Good and Bad Reading—An Alarming Outlook', ibid., 24 (1888), 582–5; 'The "Down-Grade" and the "Up-Grade"; or, The Power of Truth', ibid., 24 (1888), 413–20, particularly 415.

fiction, and the bran of the Quarterlies, are poor substitutes for the old corn of Scripture.[1]

And the sects kept up this sort of resistance to fiction, and some still do: it is often one of the tests by which the standard of 'personal perfection' characteristically demanded by religious sects is measured.[2] Edward Irving preached in 1825 against 'idolatries of profane poets, and fictitious novelists, and meagre sentimentalists, who are Satan's prophets'.[3] At the end of his first article in *Fraser's Magazine* about the recent outbreaks of *charismata* Irving did not veil his contempt for his readers:

This is a riddle to the shallow men whom I am writing to. I leave them a month to discover it. But not one in a thousand will give it as much time as children do to a guess by the fireside. For the men of this generation are but impatient overgrown children. Why then write to them at all? In order to rebuke them, and haply to win some stragglers from the reading mob back again to the proper occupation of man, which is, to think and act, to meditate and contemplate. Reading, and writing, and casting accounts, are doing more to unman mankind than many—than almost all other causes. The only book worth reading is the Bible; and that can be read only with the honest heart, which almost all other books do tend to take away.[4]

J. N. Darby, a founder of the Brethren, likewise eschewed all 'science, knowledge, art, history,—except so far as any of these things might be made useful tools for immediate spiritual results', and tried to dissuade Francis Newman from all 'voluntary' reading except the Bible.[5] Edmund Gosse's ignorance of fiction, on his Open Brethren mother's insistence that 'to compose fictitious narrative of any kind, was a sin', is famous.[6] The testimony of a Polly S—— shows the pietism of Plymouth Brethren sectarianism continuing after most Dissenting denominations had succumed to fiction:

I can never forget the 5th November, 1895, in that lonely country kitchen in Brookmount, when the Lord Jesus convinced me of what I was, I knew His Holy Spirit was striving with me. I had a novel in my hand reading it and the

[1] Quoted in I. H. Murray, *The Forgotten Spurgeon* (1966), 10.

[2] For sect-characteristics, see: B. R. Wilson, 'An Analysis of Sect Development', *Patterns of Sectarianism* (ed. B. R. Wilson, 1967), 22–45; and B. R. Wilson, *Religion in Secular Society* (1966), Pt. IV, 'The Sectarian and Denominational Alternative'.

[3] Mrs. Oliphant, *The Life of Edward Irving* (2 Vols., 1862), I. 274.

[4] Edward Irving, 'Facts Connected with Recent Manifestations of Spiritual Gifts', *Fraser's Magazine*, 4 (Jan. 1832), 761.

[5] F. W. Newman, *Phases of Faith; or, Passages from the History of My Creed* (1850), 28, 37.

[6] *Father and Son* (Windmill Library edn., 1929), 21.

Bible at the other side, but when the Lord took hold of me I threw the novel away. . . .[1]

Edwin Muir's mother could not understand his immediate resort to *Les Misérables* after a profession of faith at a revivalist mission in about 1901.[2] George Moore's making Plymouth Brethren (in *Esther Waters*) spokesmen for the moralistic opposition to novels in the nineties was absolutely right.

There is some link between a ministry to working men and opposition to fiction. Suspicion of learning and secular reading is easier when the preacher or the congregation is ill-educated, and easiest of all when both are unlearned. Significantly, though Wesley ministered to the poor, he was himself an Oxford graduate, and in fact abridged Henry Brooke's *Fool of Quality; or, The History of Henry Earl of Moreland* for Methodist readers in 1781, apparently with the author's approval. It was said the 'generality' of Methodists did not care for it.[3] Joseph Lawson remembered when Pudsey Wesleyans discouraged learning and boasted of reading only 'One Book'.[4] In that phase Wesley's descendants lacked education. Kingsley's Grace Harvey, the 'Brianite', prudish and philistine, is ashamed to have read *The Fool of Quality* ('a foolish romance book').[5]

Openness to fiction is characteristic of the denominational phase, when a sect's members have grown socially more respectable and its ministers have become more educated and professionalized. Primitive Methodists and Baptists, with their relatively high density of lay preachers and working-class members, generated the least number of Nonconformist literary men. Kingsley rightly had Alton Locke's Baptist mother forbid him any reading but *Pilgrim's Progress* and the Bible.[6] Literary culture was not only diverting, it was too élitist and precious for the Million. The Congregationalist J. Campbell vigorously denounced the *British Quarterly Review*, whose contents even Matthew

---

[1] David Rea, *Trophies of Grace: A Collection of Over 500 Authentic Testimonies Given at Different Times During Revival Meetings Held in Ireland, Scotland, and England* (Glasgow, n.d.), 162.

[2] Edwin Muir, *An Autobiography* (1954; paperback edn., 1964), 85–7.

[3] Rev. Richard Green, *The Works of John and Charles Wesley: A Bibliography* (1896), 209; A. L. Drummond, *The Churches in English Fiction* (Leicester, 1950), 235.

[4] Joseph Lawson, *Progress in Pudsey* (1887), 71.

[5] *Two Years Ago*, Ch. 15. Mellot has often 'fancied that I should edit a corrected edition of it'. Kingsley wrote a Biographical Preface to 'A New and Revised Edition' (2 Vols., 1859).

[6] *Alton Locke*, Chs. 1 and 2.

Arnold found it in him to praise:[1] 'half-crown Monthlies and six-shilling Quarterlies' symbolized the retreat of more cultured and leisured Congregationalists from a ministry to the people:

Neglect what you may, remember the Millions! . . . Six-shilling Quarterlies belong to the reign which gloried in castled waggons, drawn by twelve horses, and moving at the dignified pace of twelve miles a day; half-crown Monthlies are of a species with the handsome English stagecoach, driving at twelve miles an hour—good things, *inside*, for people possessing wealth and leisure; but Cheap Periodicals belong to the age of the Railway! Every man, then, to his taste; Gothic things for Gothic men; but light postage, quick transit, cheap Bibles, and cheap Periodicals for the Millions of England![2]

And Campbell's *Christian Witness* deplored novel-reading in the 1840s: D'Aubigné's *History of the Reformation*, it asserted, was 'worth ten times as much as the whole of Bulwer's trash'. Meanwhile, in May 1845, the *BQR* was carrying a genial review of Bulwer's novels.[3]

There is other evidence to link demotic religion with a ban on fiction. For example, G. W. M. Reynolds's *Teetotaler* (1840–1) soon folded; its aim of inculcating 'the principles of Teetotalism through the medium of amusing fictions as much as through dry essays or lectures' displeased the serious Dissenting working-men who would rather read the future travel-agent Thomas Cook's *National Temperance Magazine*—which sternly attacked fictional 'trash' and 'sugar plums'.[4] But the link cannot be pressed too far. Not only working men abhorred fiction: Quakers, for example, were not at all a working-class sect, but their dominant evangelical party opposed novel-reading in some cases as late as 1880,[5] and the Plymouth Brethren embraced many educated men. And, on the other hand, by no means all the Dissenting radicals, whose interests were emphatically directed towards the working class, despised worldly culture. Arnold himself paid tribute to Edward Miall, editor of *The Nonconformist*, as a man 'of character and culture too'.[6] And the radical

[1] See *Letters of Matthew Arnold 1848–1888*, ed. G. W. E. Russell (2 Vols., 1895), I. 310, for his astonishment over 'Matthew Arnold, Poet and Essayist', *BQR* 42 (Oct. 1865), 243–69. Also: R. V. Osbourn, '*The British Quarterly Review*', *RES*, N.S. 1 (1950), 147–52.

[2] Quoted in A. Peel, *These Hundred Years: A History of the Congregational Union of England and Wales 1831–1931* (1931), 138–9.

[3] R. T. Jones, op. cit., 232.

[4] B. Harrison, ' "A World of Which We Had No Conception". Liberalism and the English Temperance Press: 1830–1872', *VS* 13 (1969–70), 148–9.

[5] E. Isichei, op. cit., 153–6.

[6] *A French Eton*, Arnold's Prose Works, ed. R. H. Super, Vol. II, *Democratic Education* (Ann Arbor, 1962), 323.

John Clifford was that rarity, a Baptist novelist[1] (though it is perhaps
not insignificant that Charles Booth exempted Clifford's Westbourne
Grove Chapel from the claim that north of the Thames Baptist chapels
were 'always of rather a lower class than those of the Congregationalists,
and in most cases include a considerable contingent from the working-
classes'[2]).

   Prejudice against fiction was, of course, not unique to Dissent: for
example, Kingsley told Arnold after reading *Culture and Anarchy* that
he had been born 'a barbarian, and bred a Hebrew of the Hebrews'.[3]
And for many it was not their Dissent but natural disinclination
that kept them from novels. Others, noted the *Eclectic Review*,
were less evangelically antagonistic than just too busy for culture:

Our best and most thoughtful tradesmen and manufacturers are too busy for any
reading except that which they feel to be necessary for the strength of their
personal religious life. Their leisure hours are largely given to the maintenance
of our philanthropic and religious societies . . . they give their strength to
business and public duties, not to books.[4]

(This consideration did not, however, prevent the *Eclectic* from review-
ing novels, and books by Huxley, Lyell, and Renan.)

   The evangelical non-readers of novels did not, of course, go without
imaginative sustenance: elsewhere they might find it readily enough, in
emotional engagement with the life and death of Christ and with the
lives of Biblical characters—whose names they gave to their children,
and whose exploits were often on their lips. The imagery of the
Authorized Version, of *Pilgrim's Progress*, of hymns, filled their minds
and coloured their language. Like the Gosses, they might discover
imaginative surrogates for novels in the study of prophecy: political
events could become absorbingly compelling signals of the imminent
Second Advent.[5] In fact the universe need not be grey and flat, its
people outlined in low relief, but, rather, a vivid arena of cosmic
struggle between the forces of Satan and of God—a struggle in which
the individual's imaginative participation was continually invited:

---

   [1] M. R. Watts, 'John Clifford and Radical Nonconformity 1836–1923' (D.Phil. thesis,
Oxford, 1966), 42.
   [2] Charles Booth, *Life and Labour of the People in London*, ser. iii (1902), Vol. VII, p. 123.
   [3] *Charles Kingsley: His Letters and Memories of His Life*, II. 338.
   [4] *Eclectic Review* (1857), quoted by A. C. Whitby, 'Matthew Arnold and the Nonconformists' (B.Litt. thesis, Oxford, 1954), 256–7.
   [5] Edmund Gosse, *Life of Philip Henry Gosse* (1890), 219; Anon., 'A Plymouth Brother',
*BW* 9 (15 Jan. 1891), 189; Gosse, *Father and Son*, 67 ff.

I dreamed I was in Yorkshire, going from Gomersal-Hill-Top to Cleckheaton; and about the middle of the lane, I thought I saw Satan coming to meet me in the shape of a tall, black man, and the hair of his head like snakes . . . But I went on, ript open my clothes, and shewed him my naked breast, saying, 'See, here is the blood of Christ.' Then I thought he fled from me as fast as a hare could run.[1]

John Nelson was an extraordinary man, and, doubtless, had extra-ordinary dreams. Others only got as far as seeing the Antichrist in Napoleon III, or, like Philip Gosse, the Rapture of the Saints presaged by the Chartist petition. But their mental life could hardly be accused of dullness. Besides theological books, travels, lives, there were tracts to be read, or even written. 'Miss Andrews and I went to meeting,' noted little Edmund Gosse in his first diary on 13 September 1857, 'Papa did not but wrote two tracts.' [2] Mrs. Gosse's besetting sin was her 'longing to invent stories': she sublimated it in writing tracts.[3] Spurgeon's colporteurs worked to effect a similar substitution of religious for non-religious stories, as a Mr. Turner's report from Newton Abbot shows:

Called at a house on the 25th inst. The servant came to the door. I asked if I could sell her a book, to which she replied, 'I don't read the class of books you sell. I read nothing but novels.' I entreated her to give them up if she valued her character. I told her of others they had ruined. To which she said, 'I fear they will ruin me; they make me feel anything but serious.' She then told me of a young woman, now lost to all respectable society, who attributes her present condition to the reading of novels. I again entreated her, for the sake of her precious soul, to give them up. I then sold her 'The Orphans of Glen Elder'. She promised, God helping her, she would never read another novel.[4]

Liberalization was not, then, universal, but it was gradual. It can be seen as part of a general softening among the Dissenting groups, not only in theology:

[1] John Nelson's 'Journal', quoted by E. P. Thompson, op. cit., 43.

[2] Edmund Gosse's Letts Diary (1857): MS. in Brotherton Library, Leeds. His mother's Diary (21 Feb. 1855) contains prayers about her 'book on education' (Emily Gosse, *Abraham and His Children: or parental duties illustrated by Scriptural examples* (1855)): 'Bless the parents and teachers who read my book. may it save souls. may it help to train little ones for thy service. Guide us where to give it. and when. May it be favourably reviewed. May it come to a second edition' (MS. in Brotherton Library). Writers of Gospel litera-ture had the usual authorial ambitions.

[3] Gosse, *Father and Son*, 21–3.

[4] 'PERILS OF NOVEL READING', 'The Twenty-First Annual Report of the Metro-politan Tabernacle Colportage Association, 1887', *Sword and Trowel*, 24 (1888), 393. [Margaret Murray Robertson], *The Orphans of Glen Elder: A Tale of Scottish Life* [?1868], was, of course, a piece of religious fiction, published by the Religious Tract Society.

Chapels are now more inviting. . . . Whereas at the time we refer to the idea of a religious society having a cricket or football club would have been looked upon as from the devil; and the idea of 'Wesleyan Harriers' would have been voted down without a dissentient, as being very awful and wicked indeed.[1]

Paradoxically, the years of Dissenting liberalization were the years when the Nonconformist Conscience itched worst: a sort of guilty public assertion of moral stringency precisely when domestic sanctions were being eroded. The consistent unworldliness of the sects was preferable to this. Drunk with the sight of power, as Gordon Rupp puts it,[2] Nonconformity 'stooped to employ such boastings as the Gentiles use': 'Sir Charles Dilke defied the Nonconformist conscience and is a political outcast today. Parnel [sic] despised the Nonconformist conscience and he destroyed himself and his party. Lord Rosebery ignored the Non-conformist Conscience for a racehorse, and the world sees the result', crowed the *Methodist Times* (1896).

And, when fiction was admitted, it often had to accord, as Trollope found, with the petty standards of the Conscience. In an editorial, 'What are your children reading?', the *Puritan* urged Christian parents to 'awake to the awful results which follow the perusal of pernicious literature, the sight of disgusting pictures, and repress such sources of national demoralisation by supporting wholesome magazines and literature.'[3] The moral hollowness of the Conscience is exposed by that invoking of *national* demoralization: Thomas Boston and Philip Gosse were much more concerned about their own demoralization. The vain attempt to impose moral restraints on the nation could not, and did not, last.

For all the puritans' caveats fiction did find its way in. Scott, as we have seen, was one of the earliest novelists to be condoned. After 1852, though, it was *Uncle Tom's Cabin* which did most to initiate Dissenters into fiction. John Angell James read it, if only 'not as a tale'; it was Joseph Hocking's first novel; it was, according to Nassau Senior, the only novel exempted in mid-century by Dissenters; and Quakers attributed their gradual acceptance of novel-reading to its influence.[4] Other

[1] Joseph Lawson, *Progress in Pudsey*, 73

[2] G. Rupp, 'Evangelicalism of the Nonconformists', *Ideas and Beliefs of the Victorians: A Historic Revaluation of the Victorian Age* (New York, paperback edn., 1966), 111–12.

[3] *Puritan* (1899), 251.

[4] R. W. Dale, *Life and Letters of John Angell James* (new edn., 1862), Appendix, 382; Joseph Hocking, 'My beginnings in literature', *Puritan* (1899), 901; Nassau Senior, *Essays on Fiction* (1864), quoted by K. Tillotson, *Novels of the Eighteen-Forties* (Oxford, paperback edn., 1962), 18; E. Isichei, op. cit., 156. Hostile though she is to novels, Bennett's Mrs. Baines accepts *Uncle Tom's Cabin: The Old Wives' Tale*, Bk. I, Ch. 5.

improving fiction, like anti-Catholic novels, obviously also helped pave
the way: a considerable proportion of the Braintree and Coggeshall
Congregationalist Book Clubs' stock was material like Jemima Thompson's *The Female Jesuit* (1851), *A Sequel to The Female Jesuit* (1852), and
so on. (Jemima Thompson was wife of a Congregationalist minister, the
Rev. Samuel Luke, and author also of 'I think when I read that sweet
story of old'.)[1]

The revolution occurred first among the young—their elders found
adapting to fiction difficult. Silas Hocking lost caste with some of the
older members of his United Methodist Free Church, Burnley, when
he published *Alec Green* (1879) in the Burnley *Advertiser*. One old man,
indeed, having eschewed novels all his life, had so little conception of
fiction, but such faith in his pastor's veracity, that he thought the story
true: he suggested Alec Green be invited to speak at a fund-raising
meeting for missionaries.[2] And one suspects too that the urge to read
novels would arise more readily among women, who had, after all,
fewer business distractions to occupy them: the daughters of Wesleyan
ministers make up a significantly large proportion of nineteenth-century
Nonconformist novelists.

The sects accepted fiction as they turned into denominations—
becoming *embourgeoisés*, prizing learning as much as, or more than,
mere fervour in their ministers—or as stringent evangelicalism softened.
A sure sign of fiction's acceptance is the emergence of actual Nonconformist novelists, and this does seem to be related to the varying
rate of the different groups' liberalization and/or *embourgeoisement*. The
Unitarians, no longer evangelical or opposing the wider culture on
sectarian grounds, and setting a high premium on secular learning, led
the way, and Unitarian novelists emerged early in the nineteenth
century. Harriet Martineau, from a notably liberal family, published
*Principle and Practice* in 1827. If, as many suggestions would imply,
William Harrison Ainsworth came from Unitarian stock, then he
preceded her, and was the first Dissenting novelist known to me in
the nineteenth century, with *December Tales* (1823).[3] Unitarianism

[1] *Minute Book* of the Coggeshall Book Club (2 Vols., 1859–61); *Minutes* of the Braintree
Social Book Society (1838–61), quoted by J. C. G. Binfield, thesis cit., 67–72. See Note
on Jemima Luke in *Baptist Magazine* 79 (Feb. 1867), 88–9.

[2] Silas K. Hocking, *My Book of Memory* (1923), 67–72.

[3] H. L. Short, ex-Principal of Manchester College, Oxford, thinks Ainsworth's Unitarianism very probable: Ainsworth was a Unitarian family name. Descent from Henry Ainsworth
the Brownist has been suggested and denied. Ainsworth's mother descended from one of the
ejected of 1662, and was daughter of Ralph Harrison, a Unitarian, and pastor of Cross Street

found nothing incongruous in Mrs. Gaskell's actually writing fiction, nor in Dickens's attendance at a Unitarian chapel.

The Congregationalists tended to see themselves as predominantly middle-class, their mission as 'neither to the very rich nor to the very poor but to that great middle section of the community'.[1] By 1852 the *Nonconformist* (its editor the ex-Congregationalist pastor Miall) was assuming that its readers read novels: 'We suppose there are few, except the conscientious people who refrain altogether from reading fiction, who have not dwelt with eager earnestness and throbbing delight on the glorious pages of "Jane Eyre". . . .'[2] The *Nonconformist*, like its predominantly Congregationalist but politically more moderate contemporary the *British Quarterly Review*, carried as serious and sensible reviews of fiction (as well as of other literature) as any Victorian periodical. The *BQR* was founded in 1845 by Dr. Robert Vaughan, President of the Lancashire Independent College—who moved in Mrs. Gaskell's social milieu—in protest over the *Eclectic Review*'s support of Miall's policies.[3] What was observed of the *Eclectic*, however, applied to the *BQR* and perhaps also to the *Nonconformist*: 'Dr. J. Pye Smith very truly stated, some time ago, that "The Eclectic Review", contains articles which, if they appeared in "The Edinburgh" or "Quarterly" Reviews, would produce a sensation in the literary world.' But, 'Having always identified itself with the cause of Dissent, its circulation is chiefly among the Dissenters.'[4] We have already noted the sensation a *BQR* review made with Arnold. Nor was the *BQR*, so to say, 'done in a corner': in 1846 Vaughan was Chairman of the Congregational Union.[5] His *Review* stood for a broad span of Congregationalist taste, particularly among long-established Independents. The Braintree Social Book Society was founded in 1838, the Coggeshall Book Club in 1849, and their records indicate that these Congregationalists were reading novels

---

Chapel, Manchester (1771–1810); Forster, a Unitarian, was introduced to Dickens by Ainsworth. Frederick Boase, *Modern English Biography*, 'William Harrison Ainsworth'; *DNB*, 'Ralph Harrison (1748–1810)'; 'Memoir of W. Harrison Ainsworth Esq.', *The Mirror of Literature, Amusement, and Instruction*, N.S. 1 (1842), v–xvi; John Evans, 'The Early Life of William Harrison Ainsworth', *Manchester Quarterly*, 1 (1882), 136–55; Edgar Johnson, *Charles Dickens: His Tragedy and Triumph* (2 Vols., 1953), I. 186.

[1] Asa Briggs, *The Age of Improvement, 1738–1867* (1967 impression), 467, quoting Thomas Binney. See also, Charles Booth, op. cit., ser. iii (1902), Vol. VII, p. 112.

[2] Notice of a reprint edn. of *Shirley*, *Nonconformist*, 12 (1852), 992.

[3] Chapple and Pollard, *Letters of Mrs. Gaskell*, Nos. 175, pp. 260–1, and 575a, pp. 936–8; R. V. Osbourn, 'The British Quarterly Review', *RES*, N.S. 1 (1950), 147–52.

[4] [James Grant], *The Great Metropolis* (2 Vols., 1836), II. 310–11.

[5] A. Peel, *A Hundred Eminent Congregationalists, 1530–1924* (1927), 86.

by George Eliot, the Brontës, Kingsley, Dickens, Trollope, and Thackeray, as well as *Lavengro*, *Tom Brown's Schooldays*, *Eric*, and Harriet Beecher Stowe's *The Minister's Wooing*, as soon as they were published.[1] The Congregationalist Charles Edward Mudie opened his store in 1840: his Library would be 'Select', but novels would be its 'staff and stay'. Similarly, W. H. Smith (he was brought up a Wesleyan) and his railway bookstalls (started in 1846) thrived on yellow-backs.[2]

Not surprisingly, then, Congregationalist novelists emerged soon after the Unitarian. Sarah Stickney, a Quaker turned Independent, who married (1837) William Ellis, chief foreign secretary of the London Missionary Society, was probably first, with *Pictures of Private Life* (1833). She prefaced the *Pictures* with 'An Apology for Fiction': '. . . as a member of a religious society, whose sentiments are openly and professedly at variance with works of this description, I would not willingly oppose the peculiarities of many whom I regard with gratitude, esteem, and admiration, without offering in my own vindication some remarks . . .'[3] William Brighty Rands (1823–82), sometime Independent preacher, wrote poems, fairy-tales, a great many journalistic pieces, and novels—beginning anonymously with *The Frost Upon the Pane; a Christmas Story* (1854). His *Henry Holbeach, Student in Life and Philosophy: a Narrative and a Discussion*, by 'Henry Holbeach' (1865) tells how the deacons at the Little Meeting in fenland Graveley came to accept fiction.[4] Henry Robert Reynolds, a co-editor of the *BQR* (1866–74), and his brother John Russell Reynolds, published their *Yes and No* anonymously in 1860.[5] George Macdonald, sometime Congregationalist minister, started his career as a novelist (as opposed to his efforts as a teller of fairy-stories) with *David Elginbrod* (1863), and Joseph Parker's novels began with *Springdale Abbey: Extracts from the Diaries and Letters of an English Preacher* (1868). Parker, twice Chairman of the Congrega-

---

[1] J. C. G. Binfield, thesis cit., 370.

[2] Amy Cruse, op. cit., 312–13, 335–6.

[3] *DNB*; Sarah Stickney, *Pictures of Private Life* (2nd edn., 1833), [v].

[4] *DNB;* and A. L. Drummond, *The Churches in English Fiction* (Leicester, 1950), 256–7. See also, George Eliot's letter to S. S. Hennell (21 Sept. 1857): 'Mr. Rands writes like a sensible tasteful man, whose good opinion must be valuable to you, such a man as one might expect in the author of the "Reading Raids" and "Tangled Talk". We are glad to know who wrote those pleasant papers, the solitary things one could read in Tait. Mr. Lewes used to notice them with admiration in old days, when he wrote the Literary Summary for the Leader.' (Her reference is to the series by Rands in *Tait's Edinburgh Magazine*.) G. S. Haight (ed.), *The George Eliot Letters* (6 Vols., 1954–6), II. 382, and footnote 8.

[5] A. Peel, op. cit., 126.

tional Union, in 1884 and 1901, actually encouraged Mrs. Pearl Craigie ('John Oliver Hobbes') in her literary career. Her Congregationalist parents attended Parker's City Temple, he was a close family friend, and accepted stories from her at the age of 9 (i.e. in 1876) for his newspaper the *Fountain*. (In 1892 she became a Roman Catholic.)[1]

Congregationalists liberalized in advance of Baptists and Methodists. In 1874 the Physiologist of the sects could claim that while Independent life had become 'much broader, more liberal, and, in religious phraseology, more "worldly" than it used to be', 'Your true Baptist is still a denouncer of the play-house, an opponent of the ball-room, and not friendly to novel-reading', and the Methodists fiercely anathematized 'worldly vanities'.[2] But the Baptist resistance was already cracking: in 1874 John Clifford published *George Mostyn: the Story of a Young Pilgrim Warrior*. It had already appeared as 'Familiar Talks with Young Christians' in the *General Baptist Magazine* (1872). The Methodists were, by the seventies, in the last phases of resistance. In 1867 the *Methodist New Connexion Magazine* could still bring itself to sneer that novel-reading 'feeds the passions and pollutes the heart', and it was still claiming in 1871 that all 'the proprieties would be shocked' if it published fiction. To the *Wesleyan Methodist Magazine* (1866) the 'so-called "religious" novel' was 'the most offensive to correct taste', and in 1873 it was still boasting that it published no novels. But in 1877 it began *The Deformed Duchess of Ferrara: an Episode in the History of the Reformation*. The *Bible Christian Magazine*, which spoke for a later and perhaps slightly less cooled-down sect, did not serialize its first novel until 1884. But the *Primitive Methodist Magazine* and the *Methodist New Connexion Magazine* were welcoming fiction by 1877–8.[3] The *United Methodist Free Churches' Magazine* published *Her Benny* in 1879, its first novel, and Silas Hocking's second. Its editor feared an adverse reaction, did not get it, and instead recruited young readers.[4] The last two decades of the century produced a rash of Methodist novelists, mostly, as one might expect of the older sect, Wesleyans.[5] Ellen Thorneycroft Fowler was the daughter of Henry Fowler, the Wesleyan M.P., and granddaughter of a Wesleyan minister. Mrs. Adeline Sergeant, Elizabeth Sophia Fletcher (Mrs.

[1] *DNB* (the entry for Pearl Craigie erroneously labels Parker a Baptist); A. L. Drummond, op. cit., 275–7.

[2] *The Physiology of the Sects* (1874), 83, 92, 120–1.

[3] Robert Currie, *Methodism Divided* (1968), 133–6.

[4] Silas Hocking, *My Book of Memory* (1923), 80–2.

[5] Howard Cameron, 'Free Church Links with Literature', *Puritan* (1899), 10–16 gives a useful list of names.

Robert Watson), and Amelia E. Barr were all daughters of Wesleyan ministers. The Wesleyan Conference Office (the Wesleyan publishing concern) brought out Mrs. Watson's first novel, *Building Her House* (*A Religious Tale*) (1881), and Amelia Barr's *The Hallam Succession: A Tale of Methodist Life in Two Counties* (1885).[1] The latter bears the imprint of T. Woolmer: Theophilus Woolmer, Wesleyan Book Steward from 1879 to 1896, who was responsible for publishing many Methodist novelists at the end of the century.[2] Annie Keeling's first novel, *The Oakhurst Chronicles: a tale of the times of Wesley*, came out in 1883. The Wesleyan Rev. William James Dawson's first novel was *The Redemption of Edward Strachan: A Social History* (1891). His son, Coningsby William Dawson, published novels in the 1920s and '30s. And the father also published sermons, poetry, and literary criticism, some of it in collaboration with his son.[3] The novels of the Cornish Wesleyan minister Mark Guy Pearse developed in the 1870s from the same sort of matrix: his early work includes a *Life of Billy Bray* and temperance tracts. Frederick R. Smith ('John Ackworth'), another Wesleyan preacher–novelist, began with *Clogshop Chronicles* (1896). Joseph Hocking, Silas's brother, started a prolific career with *Harry Penhale: the trial of his faith* (1887). It was just as well that the *New Connexion Magazine* felt able to approve the trend in 1877: 'The new phase which Methodism is putting on with regard to its recognition of general literature, and its appreciation of some of its more attractive forms, we contemplate without disapproval and without alarm.'[4]

The new phase did not begin unopposed, of course. Samuel Ramsbottom could muster supporters for his view that 'For a preacher of the Gospel of Jesus Christ to be a novelist, be he lay or cleric, in my judgement is an abomination of abominations.' He had 'no sympathy with such a representative of Jesus Christ' as Joseph Hocking.[5] But by

---

[1] Amelia E. Barr, *All the Days of My Life* (New York, 1913), 385, 490. She also claimed the Wesleyans published *The Lost Silver of Briffault* (1886), but the Methodist Archives and Research Centre has no record of it, and the BM Catalogue gives Hodder & Stoughton as publisher.

[2] 'Theophilus Woolmer', Obituary notice, *Wesleyan Conference Minutes* (1897), 27–9.

[3] BM Catalogue; and Silas Hocking, *My Book of Memory*, 117–18.

[4] Quoted by Robert Currie, op. cit., 136.

[5] Samuel Ramsbottom, *Who's Right? or, Samuel Ramsbottom and the Editor of the 'Sunday Chronicle' on Novel-Writing Preachers, with other Topics, Personal and Otherwise* (Manchester, 1895), 7, 29. Ramsbottom was the author of similar tracts like *Christ or the Theatre— Which?* and *The Diamond Ring: or Novels and Novel Writing*. The titles of these anti-fiction tracts are of course not unlike the titles of Victorian novels. The same is noticeable about the presentation of other anti-novel literature: it is imbued with the spirit of what it attacks.

the end of the century cultural interest and activity had been on the whole legitimated for Nonconformists. The Rev. Dr. John Watson, minister of the Presbyterian Church of England in Liverpool, and as 'Ian Maclaren' a novelist as well, was elected President of the National Free Church Council in 1907. Silas Hocking served as a lay member of the same Council. Maclaren was discovered and promoted by William Robertson Nicoll, Nonconformist man of letters and editor of the *Expositor*, the *Bookman*, and the *British Weekly*, in the latter of which Maclaren's first fiction, later part of *Beside the Bonnie Brier Bush* (1894), was published (2 November 1893). Nicoll founded the *British Weekly* in November 1886: '. . . I thought that much more might be done in the way of uniting religion with literature, believing that Nonconformists had too long behaved as exiles from the world of culture.' He was at the centre of the Nonconformist literary world. S. R. Crockett, the Free Church of Scotland minister (author of *The Stickit Minister*, 1893), was another of his discoveries. Annie S. Swan, brought up in the Morisonian Evangelical Union,[1] and, not unnaturally, favourably disposed to Congregationalism (she attended Parker's City Temple and became a close friend of his) was also published by Nicoll. He created the *Woman at Home* (1893), known popularly as *Annie Swan's Magazine*, as a vehicle for her, and she wrote for the *British Weekly* as 'David Lyall'.

The *British Weekly* symbolized the cultural liberation: '. . . it has done great things,' rejoiced the *Puritan* in 1899, 'in uniting Nonconformity and culture; indeed, it is due in no mean degree to the *British Weekly* that Nonconformists are no longer looked upon as without the pale of serious thought and literature.'[2]

### 3. THE VARIETY OF DISSENT AND THE NOVEL

We have insisted on the synchronic variety and the diachronic change in Dissent in our period. All too often, however, Victorian novels tend to stress only certain aspects, at the expense of presenting Dissent as a diversity of phenomena. Wild preachers, hectic worship, and revivalism preponderate against the cooler beauties of holiness; the violence,

[1] James Morison (1816–93), expelled from the presbyterian and calvinist United Seccession Church for arminian-type views created the Evangelical Union, Congregationalist in polity, in 1843. In 1897 most of his churches joined the Congregational Union of Scotland. F. L. Cross and E. A. Livingstone (ed.), *Oxford Dictionary of the Christian Church* (2nd edn., 1974), 940–41, 486–7.

[2] Silas Hocking, op. cit., 189–90; W. R. Nicoll, '*Ian Maclaren*': *Life of the Rev. John Watson DD* (1908); 'The British Weekly', *Puritan* (1899), 286–9; *DNB*, 'Sir William Robertson Nicoll, 1851–1923'; T. H. Darlow, *William Robertson Nicoll: Life and Letters* (1925); Annie S. Swan, *My Life: An Autobiography* (1934).

bellowing, and enthusiastic extravagance of Branderham, Barraclough, Hawkyard, and Kingsley's 'Brianites' crop up much more frequently than the more decorous Dissent of *Ruth* and *Cousin Phillis*. The general judgement seems consonant with Crabbe's: 'Yet none the cool and prudent teacher prize.'[1] The hypocrite—Stiggins, Chadband, Alec D'Urberville, John Broad, and so on and on—tends to overshadow any true goodness: it is rare to find true virtue balanced against the harsh and hypocritical as it is in *Ruth*. The narrowness and philistinism of Mrs. Locke, Hawkyard, and Snale the Draper usually predominate over culture: Holman and his daughter (Cousin Phillis) are rarities. Liberal views of eternal punishment, or more gentle ideas about a God of love, tend to get obscured in the hail of preacherly denouncings, the fervently hell-fire doctrines of Kingsley's, or Dickens's, or the Brontës' ministers. The quieter tones of Dinah Morris or Thurstan Benson are simply drowned by the din. Theologically, as we have noted, the novelists can be unsubtle, even to the extent of confusing Arminianism with Calvinism. No Arminian ever confused himself with a Calvinist: a Methodist proof-reader is even alleged to have changed all the 'Calvinism' in Amelia Barr's novel about the Free Kirk Secession, *A Sister to Esau* (1891), into 'Methodism', presumably Arminianism.[2] (A difficult task one might suppose, and the story sounds apocryphal, but it does illustrate the point.)

Of all the available varieties of possible Dissenting subjects, Methodism enjoys by far the highest incidence in the Victorian novel. This is presumably related to Methodism's numerical predominance in Nonconformity, but also—though it is not entirely fair on Methodism to suggest it—to the fact that if one wanted to charge Dissent as a whole with being hectic, narrow, ill-educated, and so on, one could find those things as readily, if not more readily, in some form of Methodism as elsewhere. Methodism also had the disadvantage of being among the least respectable forms of religious life: it took a George Eliot to cut through all that easy scorn. It is interesting to note, by contrast, how relatively absent the Quakers are, and how generally approved of when they do appear. This, for its part, is more than a mere reflection of their fewness, their lack of numerical menace. Thackeray is perhaps unique in his disrespect, in *The Newcomes*, for Miss Hobson's Quaker banking connections. But then, Thackeray instinctively produced in the presence of evangelicalism—whether Quaker or no—the usual tracts for washer-

---

[1] *The Borough*, Letter IV, line 20: *Poems*, I. 314.
[2] Amelia E. Barr, *All the Days of My Life*, 428–9.

women, and his customary Catholic/Hebrew/black converts, bawling preachers, florid prayers, and well-fed unction.[1] Elsewhere, when they do appear, Quakers are handled respectfully. In *Sylvia's Lovers* Quaker peacefulness, order, and cleanliness are thoroughly approved of. We are introduced to a philanthropic Quaker silk-manufacturer whose good name, when it is threatened, is apparently cleared, and Philip Hepburn's judgement ('. . . they're all on 'em right-down good folk') is the novel's.[2] According to Stangrave in *Two Years Ago*, the élitist Calvinists have done nothing about American slavery: the battle has been left to the egalitarian Quakers, who believe there is 'a divine light and voice in every man'.[3] Dinah Morris's Quaker style is approved of, and when Mrs. Bulstrode in her humiliation puts on the Quaker-like clothes of 'an early Methodist' it is a sign of something important learned, a moral education undergone.[4] The Quaker reputation for benevolence, philanthropy, gravity, and tranquillity made for high public regard: novelists could not extensively or plausibly fault them.[5] And so, quietly to ignore that people like Quakers were Dissenters as much as, if not more so than, Methodists, made it easier to fall in step with so many novels '. . . which stow away the ardour of the seraph and the wisdom of the cherub beneath a clergyman's silk waistcoat, lodge the attributes of Belial or of Moloch in the breast of the Papist, and make a canting vulgar hypocrite of every Dissenter.'[6]

The more aware novelists do, however, point out the theological and social variety in the Dissenting spectrum. Zachariah Coleman in *The Revolution in Tanner's Lane* hears a Manchester Methodist preacher graphically apply Hebrews 6:4–6 to the salvation of a soul: now safe on the Rock of Ages, now slipping away into the Devil's hands. Zachariah is made to reflect that that theology is 'Arminian in the extreme'; the Calvinist Mr. Bradshaw had 'boldly declared' the text had 'nothing to do with the elect'.[7] Adam Bede, aged, and apparently wise, is made to express disgust at the Arminian–Calvinist controversy ('The Wesleyans, you know, are strong Arminians . . .'): when a

---

[1] *The Newcomes: Memoirs of a Most Respectable Family*, Ch. 2.

[2] Mrs. Gaskell, *Sylvia's Lovers*, Chs. 7, 14, 17–19, 32.

[3] *Two Years Ago*, Ch. 23. The *BQR*, 25 (1857), 418, pointed out that in England calvinistic evangelicals were as strongly abolitionist as Quakers.

[4] *Middlemarch*, Ch. 74. Amelia Barr published *Friend Olivia* (1890), as a tribute to her mother's family—among Fox's first converts. Amelia Barr, op. cit., 417–18.

[5] E. Isichei, *Victorian Quakers*, 282–6 (she includes some adverse voices too); Chadwick, *Victorian Church*, I. 423; L. E. Elliott-Binns, *Religion in the Victorian Era* (1936), 52–3.

[6] *BQR* 25 (1857), 415.

[7] *The Revolution in Tanner's Lane*, Ch. 9.

Treddleston class leader told him the devil was using his 'pride and
conceit as a weapon to war against the simplicity o' the truth' Adam
had given up exposing what George Eliot thought was the illogic of
Arminianism, and ceased his youthful controversialism:

I began to see as all this weighing and sifting what this text means and that text
means, and whether folks are saved all by God's grace, or whether there goes an
ounce o' their own will to't, was no part o' real religion at all.[1]

In Cowfold,

There were three chapels; one *the* chapel, orthodox, Independent, holding
about seven hundred persons . . . the second Wesleyan, new, stuccoed, with
grained doors and cast-iron railing; the third, strict Baptist, ultra-Calvinistic,
Antinomian according to the other sects, dark, down an alley, mean, surrounded
by a small, long-grassed graveyard, and named ZOAR in large letters over the
long window in front.

The middle class of Cowfold was largely Independent, except for the
Brewer who went to the Wesleyan Chapel ('half-Church, and, above
all, Tory'); the young ladies from the school and old Mr. and Mrs.
Murston were the strength of the Church, with the doctor and landlord
of the 'Angel' professing allegiance; and the Zoar minister was poor,
his wife plain, and his congregation 'about fifty sullen, half stupid,
wholly ignorant people'. Hale White's eye is hard, but his outline is
about right.[2]

And, while it must have been difficult for anyone to avoid noticing
it, only the more honest novelists admit that Dissent is changing and
developing. George Eliot is, of course, extremely interested in all
kinds of social change, and might be expected to dwell on the differences between primitive and mid-century Methodism, as she does in
*Adam Bede* (Seth and Dinah were 'not indeed of that modern type which
reads quarterly reviews and attends in chapels with pillared porticoes'[3]).
Mrs. Oliphant enjoys being able to point up the ironic contasts between
the worlds of *Salem Chapel* (1863) and of *Phoebe, Junior* (1876), between
the narrow, provincial life of the Tozers and the cultural and worldly
aspirations of their niece from the prosperous city chapel. But Dickens
merely shifted his attack slightly, and silently. Gissing pointed out that
the treatment of Stiggins would not do in 1853, though Dickens got
away in the 1830s with all that pugilistic violence left over from the

[1] *Adam Bede*, Ch. 17. See letter to S. S. Hennell (7 Oct. 1859), *GE Letters*, III. 175.
[2] *The Revolution in Tanner's Lane*, Ch. 16.
[3] *Adam Bede*, Ch. 3.

eighteenth century.[1] Dissent had become more respectable and powerful, at least in some quarters, and Chadband, for all the savagery of the
portrait, is no Stiggins. Kingsley eschewed even silent emendation, and
never wrote a novel that conveyed the juster ideas about Dissent which
closer acquaintance forced on him. His friend, the Methodist Dr. Rigg,
was not an illiterate Bible Christian: but *Two Years Ago* remained
Kingsley's final fictional indictment of Methodism.[2]

[1] George Gissing, *Charles Dickens: A Critical Study* (1898), 117.

[2] '. . . in his later years, he came to have more knowledge and juster views as to
Dissent, even of the stronger types, and was much more wise and liberal in his judgement
than he had been at one time. . . .' J. H. Rigg, *Modern Anglican Theology* (3rd edn., 1880),
102.

# III. PLACES AND POLITICS

Provincial. Of a province, away from the centre of things, limited in vision and scope.

William Golding, *The Spire*, Ch. 10

I F Culture meant the 'tone of the centre', and specifically of London, then most Dissenters could be written off, as Arnold did write them off, as uncultured: for Dissent was most strong in the provinces, in the North and in Wales. Inevitably it was the *Nonconformist* which defended the provinces against the charge of 'Provinciality': 'Partial knowledge and incomplete culture are ceasing to depend at all closely on any insurmountable local disadvantage.'[1] In the conflict of North and South, Dissent tended to be aligned with the North, the Church of England with the South. The 1851 Census revealed a majority of Dissenters in Halifax, Huddersfield, Manchester, Bolton, Newcastle-upon-Tyne, Hull, Birmingham: in Bradford (assuming each attendance as one person) 12 per cent of the population went to Church, 27 per cent to Chapel; in Leeds 15 per cent went to Church, 31 per cent to Chapel.[2] Dissent followed manufactures and grew with the growth of industry in the manufacturing towns.[3]

The Congregationalist Edward Baines, editor of the *Leeds Mercury* and Member of Parliament for Leeds from 1859 to 1874, reveals this North–South religious polarity in his protests over Sir James Graham's 1843 proposals for education.[4] In a lively defence of Dissent and the northern towns he accuses Graham's Factory Bill of being part of a plot to undermine Dissent's hold on the North. The Children's Employment Commission (1842) had presented a deliberately pessimistic case, 'to

---

[1] Leader on 'Provinciality', *Nonconformist*, 25 (18 Jan. 1865), 52. Arnold was flattered by the attention: see *Letters*, I. 246 (to his mother, 21 Jan. 1865).

[2] Chadwick, *Victorian Church*, I. 368–9.

[3] e.g., J. D. Marshall, *Furness and the Industrial Revolution: An Economic History of Furness (1711–1900) and The Town of Barrow (1757–1897)* (Barrow in Furness, 1958), 331; T. C. Barker and J. R. Harris, *A Merseyside Town in the Industrial Revolution: St. Helens 1750–1900* (Liverpool, 1954), 420–4.

[4] *The Social, Educational, and Religious State of the Manufacturing Districts; with Statistical Returns of the Means of Education and Religious Instruction in the Manufacturing Districts of Yorkshire, Lancashire, and Cheshire; in Two Letters to the Right Hon. Sir Robert Peel, Bart.* (2nd edn., 1843; New Impression, 1969).

bring home *a full budget'* against voluntary and Dissenting attempts at
education; Ashley, an Anglican and a rural Member, in his speech at
the end of which Graham's Bill was presented, had in turn selected the
Commission's blacker evidence; in the subsequent uproar an Anglican
quarterly review had called Leeds 'this modern Sodom'. Baines had not
failed to perceive

. . . that a spirit of High Church bigotry was greedily swallowing and eagerly
propagating whatever reflected on the districts where other denominations of
Christians considerably exceed the Established Church in numbers,—that great
principles of truth, liberty, and religion were involved,— . . . that one of the
first-fruits of these false views, operating with this spirit of bigotry, was already
seen in the Bill of Sir James Graham, which is the greatest outrage on Civil and
Religious Liberty attempted in modern times. . . .

He fears it may be said 'that in the South of England there is a general
impression that the Manufacturing Districts are scenes of vice, ignorance, sedition, irreligion, cruelty, and wretchedness . . .' He admits

. . . that the Manufacturing Districts have a repulsive exterior. The smoke hangs
over them,—their noisy, bustling, and dirty streets,—the large proportion of
the working classes seen there, many of whom have their persons and clothes
blackened with their occupations,—the hum and buzz of machinery in the factories,—the flaming of furnaces,—the rude earnestness of the 'unwashed
artificers',—and their provincial dialect,—are little calculated to gratify 'ears
polite', or to please the eye accustomed to parks and green fields.

But, more than this,

. . . there is a taint upon the Manufacturing Districts which soils and mars
every thing,—which makes their education to be worthless, their religion
dangerous, and all their good to be evil spoken of,—and which . . . causes you
to bring in Church Endowment Bills, and Sir James Graham Factory Education
Bills. That taint is *Dissent*.[1]

The novelists rightly associated Dissent with the North. Disraeli's
Tadpole 'was coquetting with a manufacturing town and a large con-
stituency, where he was to succeed by the aid of the Wesleyans, of
which pious body he had suddenly become a fervent admirer'.[2] Dinah
Morris knows that in 'the great towns, like Leeds' Methodism prospers:

---

[1] For the way in which partisans could read the evidence diversely, see G. F. A. Best,
'The Religious Difficulties of National Education in England, 1800–1870', *Cambridge
Historical Journal*, 12 (1956), 155–73.

[2] *Coningsby, or The New Generation*, Bk. II, Ch. 2.

It's wonderful how rich is the harvest of souls up those high-walled streets, where you seemed to walk as in a prison-yard, and the ear is deafened with the sounds of worldly toil. I think maybe it is because the promise is sweeter when this life is so dark and weary, and the soul gets more hungry when the body is ill at ease.

There is a 'strange deadness to the Word' in Loamshire; the stranger at Dinah's preaching knows that 'Methodists can seldom lay much hold on' farmers: Snowfield, in Stonyshire, with its cotton-mill, is much more promising soil.[1]

One could find many a Lantern Yard in the northern manufacturing towns, where Dissent flourished in all the diversity to which Coke-town's 'eighteen denominations' bore witness. Industrialists in the novels are often Dissenters: like John Power the Baptist railway builder in *A Laodicean* ('Miss Power—Miss Steam-Power she ought to be called'),[2] or Copperhead the railway magnate in *Phoebe, Junior*. Chad-band is represented appropriately as a factory: he eats to keep his Oil-Mills going, grinds oil with the palms of his hands, and likes to get up steam when he preaches. In fact, he perspires so much that a pall of 'smoke' hangs over his head: he is a Northern Town in miniature.[3]

Dissent's geographical distribution was not, then, uniform.[4] George Eliot's masterly survey, as she conducts the reader of *Felix Holt* on a coach journey through the Midlands, indicates the connection between the incidence of Dissent and specific locales: the absence of hand-looms and mines saves the agricultural labourers from Dissent; coal-pits, hand-looms, the 'breath of the manufacturing town', spawn Dissenting chapels as they do 'riots and trades-union meetings'. And 'In these midland districts the traveller passed rapidly from one phase of English life to another . . .'[5]

The 1851 census showed a majority of Dissenting church attenders

[1] *Adam Bede*, Chs. 2 and 8.

[2] *A Laodicean*, Bk. II, Ch. 4.

[3] *Bleak House*, Chs. 19, 25, 54.

[4] My sources for 1851 are Horace Mann's results, *Census (1851): Religious Worship (England and Wales)*, Parliamentary Papers, 1852–3, LXXXIX. 1; and A. C. Whitby, 'Matthew Arnold and the Nonconformists' (B.Litt. thesis, Oxford, 1954), which provides perhaps the best and most useful breakdown of the available information and statistics. Also useful: K. S. Inglis, 'Patterns of Religious Worship in 1851', *Journal of Ecclesiastical History*, 11 (1960), 74–86; E. J. Hobsbawm, 'Methodism and the Threat of Revolution in Britain', *Labouring Men: Studies in the History of Labour* (1964), 23–33; W. S. F. Pickering, 'The 1851 religious census—a useless experiment?', *British Journal of Sociology*, 18 (1967), 382–407; Geoffrey Best, *Mid-Victorian Britain 1851–1875* (1971), 180–2.

[5] *Felix Holt, The Radical*, 'Introduction'. Cf. Lowick village in *Middlemarch*, Ch. 9: 'no looms here, no Dissent'.

in many major town districts, in the 67 major cities and boroughs taken as a whole, in Wales, and in ten English Counties: Bedford, Chester, Cornwall, Derbyshire, Durham, Lancashire, Monmouth, Northumberland, Nottinghamshire, and Yorkshire. Dissent was thus dominant in all the mining counties, in three of the five main manufacturing counties (the exceptions were Staffordshire and Warwickshire), in Derbyshire and Nottinghamshire (partly mining and partly agricultural), and in only one agricultural county (Bedfordshire). The Church of England had a majority in 26 counties: 21 agricultural, and only five containing industry. It was weakest in Cornwall, in Wales, Durham, Northumberland, Yorkshire, Lancashire, and Cheshire.

Of the Methodist groups, the Wesleyans were mainly urban, and concentrated in industrial towns, until the late-nineteenth century. The Wesleyans were, however, three times as strong in Cornwall as elsewhere. They were strongest where the Church of England was weakest, and vice versa: because Wesley had deliberately sought those places where the Church of England was deficient through absentee clergy or bad organization—in old, hopelessly large parishes, or where churches had become isolated from the people because of population movements. 7 per cent of Wesleyan sittings were in Cornwall; 12·7 per cent in Cornwall, Devon, and Somerset; and 48·7 per cent in Lincolnshire, Staffordshire, Nottinghamshire, Derbyshire, Yorkshire, Durham, Lancashire, Chester, and North Wales.[1] Breakaway Methodists tended to be strong in the traditional Wesleyan areas. The Bible Christians had 75 per cent of their strength in Cornwall, Devon, Kent, Somerset, and Hampshire. The main weight of the New Connexion Methodists was in Staffordshire, Derbyshire, Cornwall; they were also strong in Lancashire, where Wesleyanism was below strength. The Primitive Methodists were strongest in Yorkshire, Durham, the North Midlands, Staffordshire, Leicestershire, Cheshire, Northumberland, and Westmorland. By 1851 their characteristic rural strength had already emerged: they were numerous in Worcestershire and Shopshire (a strongly Anglican agricultural county). The Wesleyan Reform Union (1859) was largely a Yorkshire sect, centred in Sheffield.[2]

[1] See also: John Walsh, 'Methodism at the end of the 18th century', in R. Davies and G. Rupp (eds.), *A History of the Methodist Church in Great Britain*, I (1965), 278; Maldwyn Edwards, *After Wesley: A Study of the Social and Political Influence of Methodism in the Middle Period (1791–1849)* (1935), 144–7, and, in Davies and Rupp, 'John Wesley', 58–9; R. F. Wearmouth, *Methodism and the Working-Class Movements of England 1800–1850* (1937), 13.

[2] E. R. Wickham, *Church and People in an Industrial City* (1957), 130.

The Unitarians were strongest in Warwickshire, Worcestershire, Cheshire, and Lancashire, and tended to be well represented in the vicinity of the great cities of Manchester and Birmingham: they were in fact four times as strong in Warwickshire, especially in and about Birmingham, as elsewhere.

The Baptists and Independents continued to be concentrated, as they had been for 200 years, in the Home and Eastern Counties: Bedfordshire—Bunyan country—was the only largely agricultural county in which Dissent predominated. And so E. R. Conder, chairman of the Congregational Union, could say at the Ipswich Autumn Meetings (1873):

Those of us who dwell in the crowded hives of industry, where the two great magicians, Coal and Cotton, weave their dusky spells . . . may well experience, in visiting this part of England (some of us for the first time) somewhat of the feeling which our brethren of the United States express in paying their first visit to the 'old country'.[1]

21·4 per cent of Congregationalist strength was in Surrey, Middlesex, Hertfordshire, Essex, Suffolk: 15·5 per cent in Wales and Monmouth.

The Baptists had 25·2 per cent of their people in the 'London area' (Berkshire, Hertfordshire, Buckinghamshire, Northamptonshire, Huntingdon, Bedfordshire, Cambridgeshire, Suffolk); 7·6 per cent in Wiltshire and Gloucestershire, and 16·7 per cent in Wales. In other words, 49·5 per cent of all Baptists were in these eleven southern counties and Wales. One notes also their comparative strength in, for example, Berkshire, which was an agricultural county and one of the Church of England's strongest. The Baptists fell away significantly as one went northwards to Nottinghamshire and Lancashire; they were very weak in Lincolnshire, Cheshire, Derbyshire, the East and North Ridings of Yorkshire, and all the extreme northern counties. But their strength in the South continued well after 1851: London had Spurgeon of course, and Charles Booth could comment that 'the Baptist Churches are a great spiritual force in London'.[2] In suburban London they had 'some resounding successes' at the end of the century: the Peckham Rye Tabernacle (founded 1895) had over 1,000 members, and the South London Tabernacle leapt from 661 members in 1886 to 1,615 in 1902–3.[3] Independents were more evenly spread than Baptists: they

[1] *Congregational Year Book* (1874), 64, quoted by Binfield, thesis cit., 4.

[2] Charles Booth, op. cit., ser. iii, Vol. 7, p. 128.

[3] H. J. Dyos, *Victorian Suburb: A Study of the Growth of Camberwell* (Leicester, 1961), 159. See also, A. C. Underwood, *A History of the English Baptists* (1947), 186. The 1902–3

were weakest in Herefordshire and Lincolnshire and in the northern-most counties.

The names of sects, as we have seen, often evinced their regionality: like the Derby Faith Methodists, the Essex Peculiars, the Suffolk and Norfolk New Association of Strict Baptists, or the Plymouth Brethren. The Brethren were emphatically regional: in the 1830s and '40s they were concentrated in the West Country, especially at Bristol and Plymouth. The Salvation Army developed out of Booth's East End missions and was, like Wesleyanism, mainly an urban force, which developed significant strength in the traditional Methodist areas. It tended, though, to have success in reaching working men in the larger towns where the Primitive Methodist were less successful than in smaller urban, mining, and manufacturing areas.[1]

In general, Dissent was associated with areas where the authority of landowners and parsons was not strong. This was obviously the case in the great towns; while

Outside the towns, Dissent was most usually associated either with large parishes, where settlement was dispersed and many inhabitants lived far away from the parish church; or else with parishes where there were many small local proprietors instead of one or two large landowners in control of the parish. For these reasons Dissent tended to find a foothold in areas like the Lincolnshire fenland and the Yorkshire dales, or in woodland territories like the Weald of Kent. In the smaller parishes, by contrast, and in those where land was concentrated in the hands of one or two proprietors, or settlement nucleated in a single village under the eye of squire or parson, nonconformity was relatively rare.[2]

Hereditary tenant-farmers like the Poysers (' "Nay," said Mr. Poyser. . . "It's on'y tradesfolks as turn Methodists; you niver knew a farmer bitten wi' them maggots" ') became Methodists less readily than 'the craftsmen, artisans, freeholders, and yeomanry', i.e. men like

---

Daily News census showed Baptists as the strongest Nonconformist group in Inner London: and they had only slightly less members in Outer London than Methodists (all groups). In South London they were the most prosperous Dissenting group. See discussion and tables, P. d'A. Jones, *The Christian Socialist Revival 1877–1914; Religion, Class and Social Conscience in Late-Victorian England* (Princeton, 1968), 64, 65, 67, 71.

[1] P. Robertson, 'The Salvation Army: the Persistence of Sectarianism', *Patterns of Sectarianism*, 91–2.

[2] 'Parish by Parish: The Place of the Victoria County Histories in the Revolution in Historical Method', *TLS*, 13 Mar. 1969, 270. See also Bernard Reaney, *The Class Struggle in 19th Century Oxfordshire: The Social and Communal Background to the Otmoor Disturbances of 1830 to 1835* (Ruskin History Workshop Pamphlet No. 3, Oxford, 1970), 8–9.

Seth Bede and Will Maskery.[1] It took more than ordinary tenacity for farm-labourers to join the Methodists and forgo the vicar's coals and soup, as well as risk eviction.[2] Trollope makes comedy in *The Vicar of Bullhampton* by having the family of the Primitive Methodist preacher lose its vicarage cabbages because of the squabble of church and chapel. In real life that might mean serious hardship for the little Puddlehams.

The implications for the novel of Dissent's regionalism are important. It means that the place of a novelist's birth or upbringing will dictate the kind of experience of Dissent he has, or its absence. The Brontës in Haworth inevitably knew a lot about Yorkshire Methodism. Mrs. Gaskell, a Unitarian who grew up in Cheshire and lived in Lancashire, was very aware of Methodism and Unitarianism.[3] A Dorset man like Hardy was on the periphery of the Methodist heartland of Devon/Somerset/Cornwall. And Dissenting novelists often come, predictably, from the concentrated Nonconformist regions: Mrs. Gaskell, Manchester Unitarian; William Hale White, Bedford Congregationalist; Amelia Barr, born in Lancashire of Methodist parents and passing early years in Yorkshire and Cornwall; Mark Guy Pearse, a Cornish Wesleyan; and so on. We have seen already that Dissenting interest in fiction is characteristic of a settled denominationalism, and the Dissenting novelist is more likely to emerge from an established Nonconformist family and a traditional Dissenting region, where sectarian and evangelical fervour has had time to cool somewhat or even to disappear.

Of course, living in a Dissenting area did not necessarily mean a developed capacity for understanding the phenomenon. Charles Kingsley was born in Devon (1819), and though the family moved away it did return to Clovelly in 1830. Thereafter, until 1836 when the father moved to St. Luke's, Chelsea, Charles was never far from the West Country: at a private tutor's in Clifton, Bristol, and at Helston Grammar School in Cornwall. But the experience was almost entirely Anglican—tutor and school were Church of England—and his parents were unevangelical at that.[4] And though holidays were later spent at Clovelly, and he met Methodists, his understanding remained fairly

---

[1] Maldwyn Edwards, in Davies and Rupp, op. cit., 58; *Adam Bede*, Ch. 18.

[2] *Joseph Arch: The Story of His Life*, by Himself, ed. the Countess of Warwick (1898), 21–2.

[3] She is proclaimed as a Lancashire novelist by John Mortimer, 'Lancashire Novelists: Mrs. Gaskell', *Manchester Quarterly*, 21 (July 1902), 195–228.

[4] *Charles Kingsley: Letters and Memories of his Life*, I. 3–39.

external.[1] Tregarva of *Yeast* may be regarded as a sort of tribute to Wesleyanism: but Kingsley's sympathy and understanding did not, as we have seen, extend at all to detail ('were the good folks of —— . . . not Brianites after all, but Wesleyans?'[2]).

Some form of Dissent is frequently part of the 'genius of place' that Kathleen Tillotson has discussed: the 'closer localisation and a more lively regionalism' of the Victorian novel.[3] Regional characters and events could, depending on the region, as it were command the inclusion of Dissent: Baptists in London (*Alton Locke*; Edmund Gosse's *The Unequal Yoke*); Congregationalists in Bedford (the Cowfold of *The Revolution in Tanner's Lane*); Methodists in Yorkshire (*Shirley*), in Yorkshire and the Midlands (*Adam Bede*), in the West Country (*Two Years Ago*; *Yeast*—where Tregarva the Methodist is an ex-tin-miner from Cornwall; Hardy's *Tess*, and 'The Distracted Preacher'); Plymouth Brethren in the West Country (Esther Waters comes from Barnstaple); Salvationists in London (*Esther Waters*); Dissenters in general in the north (*Mary Barton*, *North and South*, *Hard Times*). The regionalism of the later Dissenting novel is, if anything, even more marked: in Silas Hocking's *Tales of A Tin Mine* (1898); John Ackworth's *Clog Shop Chronicles* (1896); Ramsay Guthrie's *The Canny Folks O' Coal-Vale* (1910); and the novels, repeatedly set in the West Country, of Joseph Hocking, and of Mark Guy Pearse.

2. DISSENT AND THE CITY

What a wondrous town is Cottonborough! How vast—how populous—how ugly—how sombre! . . .
    I passed through the far-spreading suburbs, consisting for the most part of long rows of mean-looking habitations of red brick. . . . I passed by many public houses; several Methodist chapels. . . .
                    W. Harrison Ainsworth, *Mervyn Clitheroe* (1858), Bk. I, Ch. 8.

Browning cannot, presumably, have been unaware of what he was doing when he had that member of Zion Chapel Meeting in 'Christmas Eve' show off his bad complexion:

> The man with the handkerchief, untied it,
> Showed us a horrible wen inside it.

---

[1] C. K. to J. M. Ludlow (18 Aug. 1849), from Clovelly: R. B. Martin, 'An Edition of the Correspondence and Private Papers of Charles Kingsley, 1819–1856' (B.Litt. thesis, Oxford, 1950), 164–5; also see 168–70 (Letter to Mrs. Kingsley, Aug. 1849).

[2] *Letters and Memories*, II. 22.

[3] *Novels of the Eighteen-Forties*, 88–91.

London was also a wen, of course, 'the great wen of all', as Cobbett described it. And in Browning's poem the 'horrible wen' is made to accompany—and, it is implied, fittingly—the monstrous wen of the city. Dissent, city religion—its congregations drawn from the 'certain squalid knot of alleys, / Where the town's bad blood once slept corruptly'—is presented as being as disfigured as the city was disfiguring. A wen, in fact, in the wen. For while Loamshire may have been held by the Church of England—a common assumption of Anglican writers in the 1840s and '50s was that the country vicar was the typical clergymen—the towns of Stonyshire had already been occupied by Dissent. Anglicans only later woke up to the fact that the city was the significant zone of nineteenth-century social and political action: Dissenters were already concerned in the '40s with the problem of attracting the workers to chapel.[1] Gaskell published figures in 1833 to show the Dissenting ascendancy in manufacturing counties and the Anglican strength in the agricultural.[2] In 1851 Anglicans were little more than half as strong in towns as in the country; their urban weakness became really significant in towns with a population of over 50,000. Of the smaller Dissenting groups the Unitarians, Quakers, and Moravians had the highest proportion of their membership in towns: only the Roman Catholics had a better proportion. Of the Big Three Dissenting denominations, the Congregationalists had the greatest proportion of their seats in urban areas (particularly in towns over 50,000); the Baptists had only a slightly lower percentage of their seats in urban areas (with relatively more in towns under 50,000); and the Wesleyans had a slightly smaller proportion of seats in towns (with their most substantial accommodation in towns of 20–100,000). In the 1881 survey of cities, the Dissenting attendance was higher than the Anglican in all the large northern towns except perhaps Manchester and Liverpool.[3]

Sectarian groups were spawned in the cities: whether Walworth

[1] Chadwick, *Victorian Church*, II. 171–6. Edward Miall's *The British Churches in Relation to the British People* (1849) arose out of Miall's response to concern about working-class 'indifference' in the Congregational Union (Preface, iii–iv). Disappointingly, there is no section of *The Victorian City: Images and Realities*, ed. H. J. Dyos and Michael Wolff (2 Vols., 1973), devoted to Dissent in the city, though incidental evidence of its presence and importance is occasionally afforded. See e.g. Paul Thompson's chapter 'Voices from Within', in Vol. I (pp. 59–80).

[2] P. Gaskell, *The Manufacturing Population of England, Its Moral, Social, and Physical Conditions, and the changes which have arisen from the use of steam machinery; With an Examination of Infant Labour* (1833), 233–4.

[3] Chadwick, *Victorian Church*, II. 229; A. C. Whitby, thesis cit., 87.

Jumpers or freelance meetings of the sort Travers Madge joined. Dissent garnered a ready harvest among the migrant workers who had left 'the old steadying community obligations' and were free of religious restriction.[1] In the same freedom of the city Davies later found the fruitful material for his *Unorthodox*, *Heterodox*, and *Mystic London*: where Methodists had reaped, the Christadelphians, Mormons, Spiritualists were gleaning close behind.[2] Carlyle seems to have linked Irvingism and other forms of second adventism with urban, Cockney ignorance.[3] Migrant Nonconformists, like Bible Christians from the West Country, or Welsh Methodists, brought their regional sectarianism with them to the cities.[4]

The repeal of the Test and Corporation Acts in 1828, with the Municipal Corporation Reform Bill (1835), inaugurated a period when Dissenting confidence in the city could be almost unbounded.[5] It was the Congregationalist Robert Vaughan who coined the phrase 'the age of great cities': 'Our age,' he asserted, 'is pre-eminently the age of great cities. . . .'[6]

Dissent was felt by the urban liberal bourgeoisie to speak for the great cities. The newly founded *North of England Magazine*, published in Manchester 'to represent the feelings, and advocate the interests of the Manufacturing and Commercial classes', reviewed Vaughan approvingly: where the *Quarterly* or the *Athenaeum* might decry great cities, 'We agree with Dr. Vaughan. . . .'[7] Vaughan's book, 'among the very first works to give urban development an historical dimension', was 'a testament of hope in the possibilities of urban progress'.[8] Edward Baines was not unique in speaking for the industrial town: 'The strain

---

[1] W. J. Warner, *The Wesleyan Movement in the Industrial Revolution* (New York, 1967), 166.

[2] C. M. Davies, *Unorthodox London: or, Phases of Religious Life in the Metropolis* (1873); *Unorthodox London*, ser. ii (2nd edn., 1875); *Heterodox London: or, Phases of Free Thought in the Metropolis* (2 Vols., 1874); *Mystic London: or, Phases of Occult Life in the Metropolis* (1875).

[3] J. A. Froude, *Thomas Carlyle: First Forty Years*, II. 227.

[4] Thomas Shaw, *The Bible Christians 1815–1907* (1956), 58–60; Charles Booth, op cit., ser. iii, Vol. 7, pp. 141–3; J. D. Marshall, *Furness and the Industrial Revolution*, 331.

[5] Chadwick, I. 108–12.

[6] Robert Vaughan, *The Age of Great Cities: Or, Modern Society Viewed in Its Relation to Intelligence, Morals, and Religion* (1843), 1; Asa Briggs, *Victorian Cities* (Penguin edn., 1968), 72.

[7] *North of England Magazine*, 1 (1842), 1; 2 (1843), 446–7.

[8] H. J. Dyos, 'Agenda for Urban Historians', *The Study of Urban History*, ed. H. J. Dyos (1968), 3.

of adulation of industry and commerce is a recurrent theme in Independent literature.' And elsewhere.[1]

This middle-class optimism was not unjustified, given the prominence of Dissenters in local affairs. If Saltaire and Bournville were not achieveable everywhere, the liberal bourgeois civilization of urban Dissenters was nevertheless asserted with significant result in many of the great towns. The organs of middle-class city opinion were securely lodged in Dissenting hands: newspapers like the *Sheffield Independent*; the *Leeds Mercury*; the *Manchester Times*; the *Manchester Guardian*—initially very liberal and always pro-Dissent, founded (1821) and first edited by John Edward Taylor, a Trustee of Cross Street Chapel, who was succeeded by his son Russell Scott Taylor, a member of the same chapel (a cousin of C. P. Scott).[2] The *Birmingham Journal* and *Aris's Birmingham Gazette* were on the Dissenting side.[3] Unitarian and Quaker mayors became a byword: in Leicester (labelled 'the metropolis of Dissent' by the *Leicester Chronicle* in 1848) the Unitarian Chapel, which supplied the first five mayors, was allegedly known as the 'mare's nest'; seven of Birmingham's nineteenth-century mayors were Quakers; the first mayor of Manchester, Thomas Potter, who served two terms of office, and was father of Sir John Potter (three times mayor) was a Trustee of Cross Street Unitarian Chapel; the third mayor of Liverpool, the first of Derby, the second of Leeds, the third of Birmingham, were also Unitarians.[4] The first mayors of reformed Norwich and Colchester were Independents, the second reform mayor of Cambridge a Baptist; between 1835 and 1885 the Congregationalists provided six mayors and thirty-five aldermen and councillors for Colchester, and in Wisbech six mayors had Dissenting connections (mainly Baptist).[5] In Sheffield, where the majority of professing Christians were Nonconformists, the Upper (Unitarian) Chapel had in 1870 Aldermen and Town Councillors

[1] C. M. Elliott, 'The Social and Economic History of the principal Protestant Denominations in Leeds, 1760–1844' (D.Phil. thesis, Oxford, 1962), 490; Asa Briggs, op. cit., 67–8.

[2] Richard Wade, *The Rise of Nonconformity in Manchester: With a Brief Sketch of the History of Cross Street Chapel* (Manchester, 1880), 61, 63; J. L. Hammond, *C. P. Scott of The Manchester Guardian* (1934), 26–30; Katherine Chorley, *Manchester Made Them* (1950), 52.

[3] R. G. Cowherd, *The Politics of English Dissent: The Religious Aspects of Liberal and Humanitarian Reform Movements from 1815 to 1848* (New York, 1956; 1959), 71; Donald Read, *Press and People, 1790–1850: Opinion in Three English Cities* (1961), passim.

[4] A. T. Patterson, *Radical Leicester: A History of Leicester 1780–1850* (Leicester, 1954), 247; Asa Briggs, op. cit., 202; R. Wade, op. cit., 60–61; G. Kitson Clark, op. cit., 161. R. V. Holt, *The Unitarian Contribution to Social Progress in England* (1938), 23, lists the Unitarian mayors.

[5] J. C. G. Binfield, thesis cit., 84, 93, 457–60.

as well as local 'literati' in its congregation.[1] Dissenters quickly established themselves in local affairs in the developing areas.[2]

Professor Briggs has written of Birmingham: 'Dale once described Birmingham as "a great village". So in a sense it was. Many of the important decisions about city life were taken by a small knot of Nonconformist families, who knew each other well, frequently intermarried, and continued until the middle of the twentieth century to dominate local social life.' The Unitarian Church of the Messiah (opened 1862) was 'more than the centre of a small sect: it was a cultural and intellectual centre of a whole society, a place where ideas about society were openly and critically discussed.' 'Where Unitarianism was weak in the nineteenth century, Liberalism lacked a social cutting edge.' And what was true of the Birmingham of George Dawson and Charles Vince, of H. W. Crosskey and R. W. Dale, and their developed Civic Gospel of the sixties,[3] held good elsewhere: in Liverpool, for example, and, emphatically of course, in Mrs. Gaskell's Manchester.[4]

If the 'essence and core of the town—business, shopkeeping, and craftsmanship' were Liberal, Dissent, led by its ministers, was of that essence: 'No other occupation was so partisan, so militant, so unfloating, as the Dissenting ministers. They were a sort of Communist hard core to the Popular Front. . . . Moreover, clerical militancy was as great in Manchester (1839) as in rural areas like Suffolk or in the old country towns.'[5] And on the whole the record was good in matters like waterworks, town planning, parks, and libraries. The *Nonconformist* could sneer from London at salvation by 'parks, museums and well-ventilated houses' instead of by 'civil rights',[6] but in general the Dissenting and urban bourgeoisie was in the van in both respects. Sewers and watersupplies were the local corollaries of national demands for Parliamentary reform, repeal of the Corn Laws, and repeal of the Church Rates. The great cities were the focuses of progressive reformism: the Seven Men of Manchester initiated the Anti Corn Law agitation, the Seven Men of Preston the Temperance movement; the Church Rate struggle

---

[1] E. R. Wickham, op. cit., 137–8; Mary Walton, *Sheffield: Its Story and Its Achievements* (Sheffield, 1948), 219–21.

[2] J. D. Marshall, *Furness and the Industrial Revolution*, 331.

[3] Asa Briggs, *Victorian Cities*, 202, 204.

[4] For Liverpool, see R. V. Holt, op. cit.; and Anne Holt, *A Ministry to the Poor: Being the History of the Liverpool Domestic Mission Society, 1836–1936* (Liverpool, 1936).

[5] J. R. Vincent, *Pollbooks: How the Victorians Voted* (Cambridge, 1967), 14–15, 18.

[6] Asa Briggs, op. cit., 372.

was notably vociferous in Birmingham, Manchester, Leeds, and
Sheffield; Edward Miall, founder and editor of the *Nonconformist* was a
Congregationalist from Leicester; and so on. The question Carlyle
heard the Manchester operatives asking ('What do you mean to do with
us?')[1] was the question the great cities posed to the nation. They were
the heart of the Condition-of-England problem, but they were also
where the cutting edge of democratic progress was honed. And in its
own way the Dissenting urban bourgeoisie shared Marx's confidence
(when he acclaimed the Labour Parliament, held in Manchester in 1854)
that the future, as well as the present, lay with the men of Manchester.[2]

Reaction came from the countryside, the zone of the Church of
England and the Tories. Disraeli defined a Tory leader's task as the
upholding of 'the aristocratic settlement of this country', the preserva-
tion of the hierarchical world of a Trollopian county. His image of this
desideratum must have been much like his own Buckinghamshire, with
Lord Lieutenant, Bishop, country members, and a few great landowning
peers, based on a wealthy residential Tory squirearchy and together
comprising a force to counter the 'Whig grandees and their unholy
alliance with the "men of the North who thought that they were to
govern England' ''.[3] Most radical social and political change meant the
victory of town over country, of Dissent over Church:

. . . rent of land believes in the State Church, profit is a dissenter by birth. The
repeal of the Corn Laws of 1846 merely recognized an already accomplished
fact, a change long since enacted in the elements of British society, *viz.*, the
subordination of the landed interest under the moneyed interest, of property
under commerce, of agriculture under manufacturing industry, of the country
under the city.[4]

Mrs. Gaskell, whose very titles insist that she began as the novelist
of Manchester,[5] put her finger on this confrontation, and, in *My Lady
Ludlow*, presented the new urban and Dissenting aristocracy in the
ascendant. Lady Ludlow's rural and Anglican pride is eventually made
to given in to the parvenu farmer, Brooke, the Baptist Baker from

---

[1] 'Manchester Insurrection', *Past and Present* [1843] (Centenary edn., 1897), Bk. I,
Ch. 3, p. 17.
[2] Letter published in the *People's Paper* (18 Mar. 1854): John Saville, *Ernest Jones:
Chartist* (1952), 274–5 (Appendix V).
[3] Robert Blake, *Disraeli* (paperback edn., 1969), 278–80.
[4] Karl Marx, *New York Daily Tribune* (21 Aug. 1852), in *Karl Marx and Friedrich Engels on
Britain* (2nd edn., Moscow, 1962), 352–3.
[5] *Life in Manchester*, by Cotton Mather Mills (1847); *Mary Barton: A Tale of Manchester
Life* (1848); 'The Manchester Marriage', *HW* (Christmas Number, 1858).

Birmingham. Hardy establishes the same antithesis in *A Laodicean*: for
Paula to renege on the Dissent of her father, and marry a de Stancy, is
to forsake progress and modernity, the telegraph and the steam-train,
for a romantic but medieval past, and the Church of England.

Of course, as we shall see, Mrs. Gaskell took her novels out of
Manchester, away from urban Dissent, into a world not yet transformed
utterly by steam-power. George Eliot likewise took Silas Marner away
from the city and sectarianism, in an ironically inverted *Pilgrim's
Progress* (Marner even carries a burden on his back: his weaver's stock-
in-trade) to the Wordsworthian world of Dolly Winthrop—innocent
of chapels as she is of cities.[1] Mark Rutherford found, however, that
Wordsworth was no consolation for the loss of Dissent for those who
actually had to remain in the city:

It was now very difficult for me, except at rare opportunities, to leave London,
and it was necessary for me, therefore, to understand that all that was essential
for me was obtainable there, even though I should never see anything more than
was to be seen in journeying through the High Street, Camden Town, Totten-
ham Court Road, the Seven Dials, and Whitehall. I should have been guilty of
a simple surrender to despair if I had not forced myself to make this discovery. I cannot help saying, with all my love for the literature of my own day,
that it has an evil side to it which none know except the millions of sensitive
persons who are condemned to exist in great towns. It might be imagined from
much of this literature that true humanity and a belief in God are the offspring
of the hills or the ocean; and by implication, if not expressly, the vast multitudes who hardly ever see the hills or the ocean must be without a religion.
The long poems which turn altogether upon scenery . . . and the passionate
devotion to it which they breathe, may perhaps do good in keeping alive in the
hearts of men a determination to preserve air, earth, and water from pollution;
but speaking from experience as a Londoner, I can testify that they are most
depressing, and I would counsel everybody whose position is what mine was to
avoid these books. . . .[2]

Eventually, of course, the city ran away from Dissent: the confidence
was quite short lived. Even the most extreme voluntaryists came by
1870 to perceive that their efforts at education, for example, were not
adequate, and that nationalization must replace *laissez-faire*. The problem, particularly of the expanding group of workers and of the poor

[1] Almost exactly a year before writing *Silas Marner*, which she was engaged on in
November 1860, George Eliot was 'reading old Bunyan again after the long lapse of years'
and was 'profoundly struck with the true genius manifested in the simple rhythmic style':
'Autograph Journal 1854–61' (MS. in Beinecke Library, Yale), 25 Nov. 1859.

[2] *Mark Rutherford's Deliverance*, Ch. 1.

who were untouched by chapel or church (a problem adverted to by
Horace Mann, and familiarized to us by Charles Booth, Wickham, and
Inglis) was soon brought clearly into focus.[1] As Meacham has pointed
out, the chart illustrating William Booth's social scheme in *In Darkest
England and the Way Out* shows that the city is the dark sea of need from
which souls must be rescued: the 'way out' is rural settlement.[2] But
the Salvation Army did not act out all the symbolic implications of its
chart by deserting the city. And Dissenters as a whole, alerted by the
bitter cry of the outcast to the fact that the attempt to mould the city
in the liberal Nonconformist image had failed—and most evidently in
London, where Nonconformity had not had the strength or the
political power it enjoyed in the more northern cities—responded
zestfully. Poorer sects like the Primitive Methodists and the Brethren,
who had anyway none of the illusions about, or faith in, urban progress
that the local government bonanza might have given other denominations, presumably needed little education in the needs of the cities.
And the Salvation Army had developed precisely to meet urban problems. But the response by the more respectable and bourgeois groups
to the Congregationalist pamphlet *The Bitter Cry of Outcast London* (1883)
was enormous.[3] Basil Martin was one Congregationalist who went to
work in the East London slums in consequence; the pamphlet effectively
made John Clifford a Socialist.[4] The surge of endeavour in the latter
part of the century, the City Missions, the Forward Movements, the
Central Halls, the missions for workers, the Pleasant Sunday Afternoons,
all the attempts of Nonconformity to break out of respectability and
through to the working classes, signify Dissent's never willingly
abandoning the city to paganism.[5] There were some individual successes
(for example, the 2,000 or so attenders at A. S. O. Birch's Workmen's
Mission in Sheffield in 1893), but they were not general: with all their
effort the churches as a whole were only managing to keep up, they

[1] Charles Booth, op. cit.; E. R. Wickham, op. cit.; K. S. Inglis, *Churches and the
Working Classes in Victorian England* (1963).

[2] Standish Meacham, 'The Church in the Victorian City', *VS* 11 (1967–8), 375.

[3] *The Bitter Cry*: sponsored by the Congregational Union. Rev. Andrew Mearns, a
secretary of the Union, did the fieldwork, assisted by Rev. James Munro; the writing was
done by Rev. W. C. Preston, Congregationalist Minister. Peter d'A. Jones, *The Christian
Socialist Revival*, 414–15; W. H. Chaloner, Letter in *TLS*, 5 Mar. 1971, 271.

[4] Kingsley Martin, *Father Figures*, 33–4; M. R. Watts, thesis cit., 95 ff.

[5] Henry Pelling, *The Origins of the Labour Party* (2nd edn., Oxford, 1965), 126–30;
E. R. Wickham, op. cit., 157–8; Charles Booth, op. cit., ser. iii, Vol. 7, pp. 132–4;
Kathleen Heasman, *Evangelicals in Action: An Appraisal of their Social Work in the Victorian
Era* (1962), 48–68.

were not going forward. It has been shown that the battle in the cities
was being lost by 1881.[1]

One can observe the shift in attitude from mid-century confidence in
the city's, so to say, going right for Dissent to the later view of the
city as the zone for energetic salvage efforts, by comparing two passages
of comment. Thomas Guthrie (1803–73), one of the Free Church of
Scotland seceders, a teetotaller, labelled by Samuel Smiles as the
'Apostle of the ragged school movement' in Edinburgh, declared for
the city—despite its known 'curses'—in *The City, its Sins and its
Sorrows* (1857):

Yet I bless God for cities. The world had not been what it is without them. The
disciples were commanded to 'begin at Jerusalem', and Paul threw himself into
the cities of the ancient world, as offering the most commanding positions of
influence. Cities have been as lamps of light along the pathway of humanity and
religion. . . . Cities, indeed, have been the cradles of human liberty. They have
been the radiating, active centres of almost all church and state reformation.
The highest humanity has been developed in cities. Somehow or other, amid
their crowding and confinement, the human mind finds its fullest freest expansion. . . . And if . . . you find in the city the most daring and active wickedness, you find there also, boldly confronting it, the most active, diligent, warm-
hearted, self-denying and devoted Christians.

The tone is still recognizably the confident one of a mid-century
Dissenter, soon to be shaken by the overwhelming evidence, important
among which was Mayhew's *London Labour and the London Poor*. The
Rev. William Tuckniss, in his Introduction to Mayhew's fourth
volume ('The Agencies at Present in Operation within the Metropolis
for the Suppression of Vice and Crime'), quoted this passage as a
prelude to his own comments, the later attitude. London, greatest of
cities, is

. . . in fact the great arena of conflict between the powers of darkness and the
ministry of heaven. Here, within the area of our metropolis, the real struggle is
maintained between the two antagonistic principles of good and evil. It is here
that they join issue in the most deadly proximity, and struggle for the vantage-
ground.

Here legions of crime and legions of vices unite and form an almost impene-
trable phalanx, while the strong man armed enjoys his goods in peace—no, not
in peace, for here too the banner of the cross is most firmly planted, and Christianity wins its freshest laurels. Here is the stronghold, the occupation of which
by the everlasting gospel, has given vigour, support, and consistency to the

---

[1] G. Kitson Clark, op. cit., 191–3.

religion of the world. Here is concentrated that fervent and apostolic piety that has made itself felt to the remotest corner of the earth; and here is the nucleus of missionary enterprise, and the radiating centre of benevolence.

Tuckniss lists God's urban 'agencies': British and Foreign Bible Society, Theatre Services, London City Mission, Ragged School Union, National Temperance Society, United Kingdom Alliance.[1] In a way, then, it was still possible for Dissenting evangelistic and social work to be sustained by a kind of recension of the old confidence. 'Shake this great city' they prayed at a lunchtime prayer meeting for Moody and Sankey.[2] But the fact that Tuckniss's 'agencies' are interdenominational and supported by Anglicans as well as Dissenters betrays the recognized magnitude of the urban problem: London at least, and in time Nonconformists knew it was true also of other cities, could not be shaken or shaped by Dissent alone.

The critical truism that the novel is a city animal has recently been challenged and modified.[3] But it is observable that in the mid-nineteenth century, when Dissenting confidence in the city was, most justifiably, at its peak, fictional concentration was sharply focused on the city, and hence, as part of the package, on Nonconformity. If Victorian novels are inevitably about cities, they are also inevitably about Dissenters.

Even for a Mrs. Gaskell there was much to learn about 'the romance in the lives of some of those who elbowed me daily in the busy streets of the town in which I resided'. She, Disraeli, Dickens, were in their novels 'social explorers', penetrating the horrifying regions of the North on behalf of southern readers, and the zones of the poor on behalf of middle-class readers.[4] Awareness of the fact of the northern industrial towns had much to do with generating the enormously creative early Victorian period of the novel: the Victorian novel matured on social problems.

Outsiders naturally had more capacity than the city-dwellers—the space between their own homes and the northern cities perhaps—for

---

[1] Henry Mayhew, *London Labour and the London Poor* (4 Vols., reprint of the 1861–2 edn., New York, 1968), IV. xiv–xv.

[2] C. M. Davies, *Unorthodox London*, ser. ii (2nd edn., 1875), 71–2.

[3] J. H. Raleigh, 'The Novel and the City', *VS* 11 (1967–8), 291–328. Cf. Alexander Welsh, 'Satire and History: the City of Dickens', ibid., 379–400, and Clough: 'The true and lawful haunts of the poetic powers' are 'in the blank and desolate streets, and upon the solitary bridges of the midnight city. . . .' (Quoted by Q. D. Leavis in F. R. and Q. D. Leavis, *Dickens the Novelist* (1970), 175.)

[4] Mrs. Gaskell, Preface to *Mary Barton*; Asa Briggs, *Victorian Cities*, 98–101.

developed horror and shock over industrial red brick. The journey
north was traumatic, for Dickens and Ruskin, as later for Orwell on
his way to Wigan Pier. In 1835 de Tocqueville beheld Manchester:

> Thirty or forty factories rise on top of the hills. . . . Their six stories tower
> up. . . . Amid this noisome labyrinth, this great, sombre stretch of brickwork,
> from time to time one is astonished at the sight of fine stone buildings with
> Corinthian columns. It might be a medieval town with the marvels of the nine-
> teenth century in the middle of it. . . .[1]

This shock over the external appearance of Manchester is akin to
Dickens's over Coketown; and the contrast between the brickwork of
the nineteenth century and the 'fine stone' glories of past styles was,
of course, also made by Pugin in his famous paired and contrasted
engravings. And what is significant for us is that for Pugin the difference
between the 'Catholic Town in 1440' and 'The Same Town in 1840'
is not only that between stone and brick, between the civilization of the
cathedral and abbey and that of the factory/warehouse/ironworks/gas-
works/jail/lunatic asylum, but it is also the contrast between All Saints,
St. John's, St. Botolph's, and the rest, and Mr. Evans's Chapel, the
Baptist, Unitarian, and Wesleyan Centenary Chapels, and the Quakers
Meeting House.[2] Distaste for the urban architecture of red brick coincides with distaste for the Dissenters who worship in chapels built
of it. Horror at the city is one with horror at Dissenters who proliferate
there.

The equation and the prejudice were common. According to Thomas
Arnold, the Parish Church 'should, if possible, be the only place of
public worship'; it has a unique 'sacredness':

> Nor is it a light thing in the judgements of those who understand the ennobling
> effects of a quick perception of what is beautiful and venerable, that some of the
> most perfect specimens of architecture in existence should no longer be con-
> nected, in any man's mind, with the bitterness of sectarian hostility; that none
> should be forced to associate, with their most solemn and dearest recollections,
> such utter coarseness and deformity as characterize the great proportion of the
> Dissenting Chapels throughout England.[3]

Red Brick chapels were the outward and visible signs of mental and
spiritual ugliness. Arnold's famous purple patch about the last enchant-

---

[1] 2 July 1835. Alexis de Tocqueville, *Journeys to England*, (1958), 106.

[2] A. Welby Pugin, *Contrasts: Or, A Parallel Between The Noble Edifices of the Middle Ages,
And Corresponding Buildings of the Present Day; Shewing the Present Decay of Taste* (2nd edn.,
1841).

[3] Thomas Arnold, *Principles of Church Reform* (1833), 69–70.

ments of the Middle Ages implicitly indicts the middle class for building in the red brick of the nineteenth century instead of going in for white stone and dreaming medieval spires, and it manifests relief that Dissenters are still second-class citizens at Oxford and that the industrial North is far away. Dickens's preference in *The Old Curiosity Shop* for the musty village church Nell enters, as opposed to the nightmarish industrial landscape and the urban poor's Dissenting chapels she passed on her pilgrimage, or for the village church and benevolent cricket-loving parson in *Sunday Under Three Heads* against the 'pious warehouses' of Coketown red brick and the Brick Lane Branch of the United Grand Ebenezer Temperance Association in *Pickwick*, sets him in the same Pugin–Arnold tradition. John Lucas misses the point when he claims that the satire on Little Bethel is 'random':[1] Nonconformity is an integral part of the city that is rejected in Dickens's fiction for the sentimental 'Cockney pastoral' world. The attempt at the end of *Barnaby Rudge* (Ch. 77) to assimilate the City of London into the natural order notably excludes Dissent: only 'the spires of city churches and the great cathedral dome' rise 'up beyond the prison, into the blue sky, and clad in the colour of light summer clouds. . . .'

Dickens was not alone among the novelists. *The Vicar of Bullhampton* conducts a good deal of its comic business in architectural terms: the much dwelt-on contrast between the 'yellow-gray' church, with its Norman door, its 'Early English windows in the aisle, and a perfection of perpendicular architecture in the chancel', and the jerry-built Primitive Methodist chapel, of 'staring brick'. Trollope is, of course, ambivalent: he laughs at the vicar and his wife for becoming quite ill at this neighbouring example of Nonconformist bad taste, but insists on their antipathy to an extent that hints at more than a mite of agreement:

It was acknowledged that it was ugly, misplaced, uncomfortable, detestable to the eye, and ear, and general feeling,—except in so far as it might suit the wants of people who were not sufficiently educated to enjoy the higher tone, and more elaborate language of the Church of England services. It was thus that they spoke to each other, quite in an aesthetic manner.

Trollope manages to make the point, while striving to indicate by its tone, that of course *he* finds this sort of prejudice a subject only for mockery.[2] Dickens evinced no such hesitation, and it is noteworthy

---

[1] John Lucas, *The Melancholy Man* (1970), 74, 78–91. It is also wrong to claim (ibid., 91), that 'the Nubbles family are not put under any great pressure by the force of the city world. . . .' Dickens presumably conceived of Little Bethel as city-pressure.

[2] *The Vicar of Bullhampton*, Chs. 1, 34, 60, etc.

that at the (notoriously softened-up) end of *Dombey*, when he relents enough to allow Melchisedech Howler to conduct the only Dissenting wedding in the *œuvre*, he has transferred him to a 'neat whitewashed' chapel: offensive red brick, signal of the entirely damned, is not mentioned.

Sometimes the cheapness and nastiness of chapels is modified by some other factor. Briar Chapel in *Shirley* is 'large, new, raw', but it is brightly lit and, if you like that sort of thing, the singing in it is cheerful and energetic. The conventicles of Marney, in *Sybil*, are described almost fondly by Disraeli:

. . . little plain buildings of pale brick, with the names painted on them of Sion, Bethel, Bethesda; names of a distant land, and the language of a persecuted and ancient race; yet such is the mysterious power of their divine quality, breathing consolation in the nineteenth century to the harassed forms and the harrowed souls of a Saxon peasantry. (Bk. II, Ch. 3)

The brick is pale, and less offensive, because the chapel names happen to assert one of Disraeli's pet themes, the Jewish origins of Christianity. Mere gentiles, like Trollope's Fenwicks, took offence at just this feature of chapels: '. . . with those horrid words,—"New Salem, 186–" legibly inscribed on a visible stone inserted above the door-way. . . . We all know the abominable adjuncts of a new building. . . .' (*The Vicar of Bullhampton*, Ch. 36).

The more open novels and novelists challenge the prejudice. George Eliot gently ridicules the inadequately 'vague idea' held by Milby 'gentility' ('Janet's Repentance', Ch. 2) that the 'salient points' of the creed of the Salem Chapel Independents 'were prayer without book, red brick, and hypocrisy'. She aptly recognized in *Adam Bede* (Ch. 3) that Corinthian porticoes could symbolize in Methodism a change for the worse. And Hardy energetically takes on the whole set of Pugin-esque–Arnoldian assumptions in *A Laodicean*. Paula Power's dilemma is to be torn between, as it were, the Hebraism of a Baptist father, and the Hellenistic escape from that world, and the dilemma is represented as a choice between opposing architectural styles: Baptist Chapel or medieval castle.

One of the rivals for Paula Power's hand is the architect George Somerset. The novel opens with him stumbling across a new Baptist chapel in a field after he has spent a day sketching ancient churches. 'Shade of Pugin, what a monstrosity!' he exclaims on first sight, for the chapel is a sort of combination of pious warehouse and fairy palace:

The building was, in short, a recently-erected chapel of red brick, with pseudo-classic ornamentation, and the white regular joints of mortar could be seen streaking its surface in geometrical oppressiveness from top to bottom. The roof was of blue slate, clean as a table, and unbroken from gable to gable; the windows were glazed with sheets of plate glass, a temporary iron stove-pipe passing out near one of these, and running up to the heights of the ridge, where it was finished by a covering like a parachute. . . .

But—and here the tradition is turned about—Somerset finds it not unauthentic:

The chapel had neither beauty, quaintness, nor congeniality to recommend it: the dissimilitude between the new utilitarianism of the place and the scenes of venerable Gothic art which had occupied his daylight hours could not well be excluded. But Somerset . . . was an instrument of no narrow gamut; he had a key for other touches than the purely aesthetic, even on such an excursion as this. His mind was arrested by the intense and busy energy which must needs belong to an assembly that required such a glare of light to do its religion by; in the heaving of that tune [New Sabbath] there was an earnestness which made him thoughtful, and the shine of those windows he had characterized as ugly reminded him of the good deed in a naughty world. The chapel and its shabby plot of ground, from which the herbage was all trodden away by busy feet, had a living human interest that the numerous minsters and churches knee-deep in fresh green grass, visited by him during the foregoing week, had often lacked. (Bk. I, Ch. 2)

The distinction of the passage is that Hardy has rebutted any external, superficial judgement: he is prepared to look inside and think about the baptismal service going on within and the congregation of 'respectably dressed working people, whose faces and forms were worn and con-torted by years of dreary toil'.

It is now, of course, easier to feel like Hardy than like Dickens about Victorian red brick chapels. In fact, John Betjeman has effectively demonstrated that the chapel, to which the members all might contri-bute labour, materials, money, 'the true architecture of the people', a 'true vernacular', was the nineteenth century's nearest equivalent to the medieval cathedral.[1] Shade of Pugin, indeed!

Revulsion from red brick was usually an alien's reaction, and directed to the surface only of a city and chapel. Insiders, or writers like George Eliot and Hardy who could by an effort of sympathy perceive that there

---

[1] John Betjeman, 'Nonconformist Architecture', *Architectural Review*, 88 (1940), 161–74. Reprinted in *First and Last Loves* (paperback edn., 1969), 90–119. See also Kenneth Lindley, *Chapels and Meeting Houses* (1969).

was an inside, found appreciation easier. The 'Member of the Manchester Athenaeum' who translated Faucher's *Manchester in 1844* added
'copious notes' including one on Dissenting architecture:

The architectural character of the Dissenting places of worship, affords curious
instances of perverted taste and of inconsistency with the principles maintained
by the old non-conformists. Many of the Independent and Baptist chapels have
exchanged the plain meeting-house of the last century for imitations of Gothic
architecture, and diminutive Grecian porticoes—even the Quakers have been
infected with the prevailing fashion; and although their consciences refuse the
ordinary nomenclature of the days and months, yet the Spirit moves them in a
building, so heathen by its architecture, that Jupiter or Bacchus would not be
disgraced by it. The Scotch Presbyterians are building a stone Gothic temple in
Oxford road, which would almost make John Knox turn in his grave with dis-
may—and to complete the character of the town for architectural taste and consistency, the Unitarians have built for themselves a handsome Roman Catholic
chapel decorated with the architectural symbols of the Trinity!

Meanwhile the Methodists, and the writer approves of them for it,
'have adhered to plain and commodious brick structures for their
chapels'.[1]

While Dickens might write complainingly from Preston about the
Bull Hotel ('old, grubby, smoky, mean, intensely formal red brick
house . . .'), Harriet Martineau could praise a factory chimney in
Coventry, 'straight, tall and handsome, in its way, with its inlaying of
coloured bricks, towering before us. . . .'[2] And perhaps it was humane
objections to the injustices of the factory system, which its spokesmen
like Harriet Martineau defended, that made writers like Dickens suspicious of every part of the Dissent/industrial-town/millocracy alliance.
Dissenting chapels in the North symbolized the inhumanity of Dissenting
mill-owners who evaded or attacked the Factory Acts. Admirers of red
brick and defenders of industrialism like Harriet Martineau also
defended this evasion.

Opposition to Factory Acts was the most substantial blind-spot, the

[1] Léon Faucher, *Manchester in 1844: Its Present Condition and Future Prospects* (1844), 25–6,
footnote 8.
[2] Forster, *Life of Dickens*, ed. J. W. T. Ley (1928), 567. H. Martineau, 'Rainbow
Making', *HW* 4 (1852), 485–90, quoted by K. J. Fielding and Anne Smith, '*Hard Times*
and the Factory Controversy: Dickens vs. Harriet Martineau', *NCF* 24 (1969–70), 419.
See Harriet Martineau, *The Factory Controversy: A Warning Against Meddling Legislation*,
issued by the National Association of Factory Occupiers, 13 Corporation Street, Manchester (Manchester, 1855). Dickens and H. Morley, in their reply, 'Our Wicked Mis-
Statements', *HW* 13 (19 Jan. 1856), suggested that this was the work of a *Lancashire* rather
than a National Association.

major flaw in the liberal–bourgeois record.[1] It looked very like self-
interest: the manufacturers stood to gain from lower wages by repeal
of the Corn Laws, and they supported repeal; they would lose money
by reducing working hours, employing children for less hours, fencing
machinery, and they opposed factory reform. The doctrine of *laissez-
faire* coincided nicely, as Engels pointed out, with the self-interest of 'a
class which boasts of philanthropy and self-sacrifice, while its one object
is to fill its purse *à tout prix*'.[2] The Leeds Independents very strongly
opposed the Factory Acts and the Ten Hours movement, attacked
Michael Sadler's evidence, and defended child-labour.[3] John Bright and
Edmund Ashworth tried to circumvent the Ten Hours Act in their
factories by a shift system; Joseph Pease, another Quaker, opposed
reform while an M.P. (1833–41).[4] Dissenters and manufacturers
helped keep reformers out of industrial seats: Michael Sadler lost at
Leeds (1832) and Huddersfield (1834), Richard Oastler at Huddersfield
(1837).[5] Monckton Milnes's Dissenting constituents at Pontefract
disapproved of his supporting Lord Shaftesbury.[6] The Oldham Pollbook
for 1847, when the Unitarian reformer Fielden was unseated after the
passing of the Ten Hours Act, has in its Preface the indignant note:

We the Committee of Working Men beg to call the especial attention of the
Factory Workers and the Public of Oldham to this Fact, that nearly all the Mill
Owners and Manufacturers (about 200) in the Borough voted against Mr.
Fielden, a significant proof as to whether it was 'Dictation' or the Ten Hours
Bill which has called forth this vengeance.

The attention of the Industrious Classes and Public of this Borough is also
drawn to the conduct of the Religious, Dissenting, and Nonconforming part of
the Electors, in splitting their votes between Fox and Duncuft, one of whom,
as a Churchman . . .[7]

On the other hand, Factory Reform was supported by Anglicans.
Marx may have been right about the 'motive, that has so suddenly

---

[1] For the story of factory reform see J. T. Ward, *The Factory Movement 1830–1855* (1962),
*passim*, and W. D. Grampp, *The Manchester School of Economics* (Stanford, 1960), 85–91.

[2] F. Engels, *The Condition of the Working-Class in England in 1844* (1968 reprint of F. K.
Wischnewetsky's 1892 translation), 167, 276.

[3] C. M. Elliott, thesis cit., 491–2.

[4] E. Isichei, *Victorian Quakers*, 246–8; Asa Briggs, 'Quaker Questions' (Review of
Isichei), *Listener*, 83 (23 Apr. 1970), 552–3.

[5] *DNB;* 'Alfred' [Samuel Kydd], *The History of The Factory Movement* (2 Vols., 1857), I.
324; John Vincent, *Pollbooks*, 111–13.

[6] James Pope-Hennessey, *Monckton Milnes: The Years of Promise 1809–1851* (1949), 187.

[7] Vincent, *Pollbooks*, 156.

metamorphosed the gentlemen of the Established Church, into as many knights-errant of labor's rights, and so fervent knights too':

They are not only laying in a stock of popularity for the rainy days of approaching democracy, they are not only conscious that the Established Church is essentially an aristocratic institution, which must either stand or fall with the landed Oligarchy—there is something more. The men of the Manchester School are Anti-State Churchmen, they are Dissenters, they are, above all, so highly enamored of the £13,000,000 annually abstracted from their pockets by the State Church in England and Wales alone, that they are resolved to bring about a separation between those profane millions and the holy orders, the better to qualify the latter for heaven. The reverend gentlemen, therefore, are struggling *pro aris et focis*. . . .[1]

This polarization of Church and Dissent on the Factory issue was not absolute (Fielden was a Unitarian, Joseph Brotherton a Bible Christian), but Dissenters on Shaftesbury's side were few.[2] What George Lansbury wrote later, applied to Dissenting mill-owners unfriendly to factory legislation:

. . . there comes to my mind the picture of a very wealthy man I know well. He gives most generously of his wealth to the chapels of the domination of which he is a member. Away from business he is a generous, open-hearted man, full of good works, but in his business he is mean—mean in paying his men; mean in his dealings with others; always ready and on the alert to overreach his fellows. This man is typical of thousands of members of our churches and chapels. The workman is constantly asking of what use can be such people's faith, and gifts to the poor, if the only effect is to make a man the greater part of his life a mean, grasping sort of person, who salves his conscience and makes his future safe in heaven by giving back a small portion of the proceeds of his meanness to the poor.[3]

Against this background, the immense courage of Mrs. Gaskell in writing *Mary Barton* and contending with the pressures from her class and chapel at which we shall later look more closely—pressures that

---

[1] *New York Daily Tribune* (15 Mar. 1853), in *Karl Marx and Friedrich Engels on Britain*, 383–4.

[2] *DNB; Speeches of the Earl of Shaftesbury, KG: Upon Subjects Having Relation Chiefly to the Claims and Interests of the Labouring Class* (1868), vi.

[3] George Lansbury in *Christianity and the Working Classes*, ed. George Haw (1906), 164–5. Cf. E. P. Thompson, op. cit., 380–4, where the complexities of attitude on both sides, Anglican and Nonconformist, are insisted on. See also, W. O. Aydelotte, 'The Conservative and Radical Interpretations of Early Victorian Social Legislation', *VS* 11 (1967–8), 225–36.

made her balance the mill-owners' account in *North and South*—
becomes clearer.

## 3. RADICALISM AND DISSENT

When you say 'preaching', do you mean religious preaching?—*Quasi* religion,
giving out a text and shouting from it.

He took a text and preached the same as itinerant preachers do, but in so
doing I have no doubt he appealed to their feelings, and working people are very
excitable, and when their feelings were up they would say 'Let us join the
union'.

> Evidence to Royal Commission on Trades Unions (1867–9) about
> the tactics of William Brown, Methodist New Connexion preacher
> and miners' union agitator.

. . . many of us can remember country districts in which the great mass of the
people were christianised by illiterate Methodist and Independent ministers,
while the influence of the parish clergyman among the poor did not extend
much beyond a few old women in scarlet cloaks, and a few exceptional church-
going labourers.

George Eliot, 'The Natural History of German Life'.

If the contempt of Dickens for the religious bodies of Coketown were
based on the perception that the millocratic crimes attacked in *Household Words* were often committed by the pillars of Dissenting chapels,
then it would perhaps be fairly based. Nonetheless the radical disposition
of Dissent cannot lightly be disposed of. Nonconformity was radical
*per se*. As Coleridge expressed it in the first number of the *Watchman* (1
March 1796): '. . . the very act of dissenting from established opinions
must generate habits precursive to the love of freedom.' The Protestant
tradition insisted on personal and religious freedom; the congregationalist system was democratic: a manifestation, like sectarianism itself, of
the priesthood of all believers.[1] And where the potentially élitist
theology of the Calvinists and the authoritarianism of Wesley's Connexionalism might seem to make against democracy, congregationalist
polity on the one hand, and Arminian theology on the other, produced
counter-pressure instead for democracy. The millocracy might oppose
factory reform but it sought repeal of the Corn Laws and Church Rates,
disestablishment, and wider enfranchisement. The shopocracy might
create a stifling respectability in a chapel, and even be intolerant towards

[1] See Albert Peel, *The Christian Basis of Democracy* (1943).

the insurgent unionist, or the great unwashed, but the grocer always
voted Liberal.[1]

Irradical elements were, of course, widely diffused. The Wesleyan
Conference, especially under Jabez Bunting, was notoriously loyalist
and anti-democratic,[2] though the growth of Tractarianism had the
effect of frightening Wesleyans away from the Church of England and
Toryism towards the Liberal/Dissenting fold. Bunting's no-politics rule,
which favoured, as it always does, conservative attitudes, was even
officially shared by the breakaway groups. Methodist radicals were
constantly expelled.[3] Pudsey chapels were closed to republican and
teetotal speakers.[4] Chartists were resisted by Hugh Bourne of the
Primitive Methodists and by Congregationalists, as well as by Wesleyans.
Miall's Anti-State-Church movement displeased many of his fellow-
Congregationalists.[5] The 'little capitalist and deacon' could prevent his
minister expressing sympathy for Arch's Agricultural Labourers' Union;
the Congregationalist farmer and deacon who would not allow George
Edwards time off even for breakfast could probably be found replicated
many times over.[6] Arch's name was hissed at the 1876 Conference of
the General Baptist New Connexion, and only John Clifford supported
the new Union.[7] A coal-merchant walked out of Basil Martin's Independent chapel, never to return, when Martin preached about living-
wages (thus jeopardizing his own living-wage).[8]

But on the other hand there was a strong radical element in Non-
conformity. Middle-class radicalism was robustly widespread: Edward
Miall, the *Nonconformist*, and the Liberation Society; John Clifford;
Silas Hocking; Basil Martin; J. P. Mursell, Miall's *aide*, who led the
Leicester Baptists as the 'shock troops of local Radicalism'; W. T.
Henderson, pastor of Bridge Street Baptist Chapel, Banbury; John
Bright; Joseph Sturge, Quaker leader of the Complete Suffrage Union;

[1] Vincent, *Pollbooks*, 15–16.

[2] E. P. Thompson, op. cit., 387–91, 399–400, 433–6, etc. See John Kent, *Jabez
Bunting: the Last Wesleyan: A Study in the Methodist Ministry after the Death of John Wesley* (1955).

[3] John Kent, *The Age of Disunity* (1966), 127–45; E. R. Taylor, *Methodism and Politics
1791–1851* (Cambridge, 1935), *passim*.

[4] Joseph Lawson, *Progress in Pudsey* (1887), 110 ff.

[5] H. B. Kendall, op. cit., I. 338–9; R. T. Jones, op. cit., 210, 217.

[6] Joseph Arch: *The Story of His Life*, 266; George Edwards, *From Crow-Scaring to
Westminster* (1922), 41.

[7] M. R. Watts, thesis cit., 49 ff.

[8] Kingsley Martin, *Father Figures*, 12–13. For discussion of this problem, see K. S.
Inglis, 'English Nonconformity and Social Reform, 1880–1900', *Past and Present*, No. 13
(1958), 73–88.

William Jackson, the Baptist pastor who spent eighteen months in prison for incitement to riot and armed rebellion.[1] The list could be extended. The politics of these men were rooted in the Dissenting grievances (about Church Rates, disestablishment, the Universities, and so on) and merged into Liberalism and its demands, but in addition there was specific sympathy for the poor and the working man. And some Nonconformist groups in particular had the poor always with them. Admittedly, the poor might be conspicuously absent from most Unitarian chapels, the Quaker aristocracy was embarrassed by its Adult School fringe, and the Voluntary system was deemed to favour the better-off subscribers. Admittedly, also, Irvingite apocalypticism seemed to appeal to aristocrats and gentlemen,[2] and the Plymouth Brethren system encouraged articulate gentlemen. But the poorer classes found the Baptists, breakaway Methodists like the Primitives, the General Baptists, and (depending on the location and therefore on the social composition of the individual chapel) some Congregationalist chapels and Brethren assemblies congenial and welcoming.[3] And, as Coleridge, again, put it, 'men can hardly apply themselves with such perseverant zeal to the instruction and comforting of the poor, without feeling affection for them; and these feelings of love must necessarily lead to a blameless indignation against the authors of their complicated miseries'.[4] Significantly, the *Baptist Magazine* supported the Ten Hours Bill (while Baptist manufacturers evaded the law), and the poorer and more radical Methodists of Leeds openly supported Sadler's candidacy (1831), while the Wesleyan preachers opposed it.[5]

The humbler sects and chapels provided not only religion *for*, but *of*, the poor.[6] Men like Joseph Arch, the tramping champion hedge-cutter, could become local preachers in Primitive Methodism.[7] Dan Taylor, founder of the General Baptist New Connexion, was a collier, and not only dug the stone himself for his chapel at Wadsworth, but

[1] A. T. Patterson, *Radical Leicester* (1954), 231; B. S. Trinder, 'The Radical Baptists', *Cake and Cockhorse*, 2 (Jan. 1965), 179–92; H. U. Faulkner, *Chartism and the Churches* (*Columbia Univ. Studies in History, Economics and Public Law*, Vol. 73, No. 3; New York, 1916), 101–4.

[2] See Gavin Maxwell and Sir Herbert Maxwell, op. cit., and William Howitt, *The Rural Life of England* (2nd edn., 1840), 566–7.

[3] See Henry Pelling, 'Religion and the Nineteenth-Century British Working-Class', *Past and Present*, No. 27 (Apr. 1964), 128–33.

[4] *The Watchman*, ed. Lewis Patten, *Collected Works of S. T. Coleridge*, Vol. 2 (1970), 13.

[5] C. M. Elliott, thesis cit., 477–8, 502–3.

[6] E. P. Thompson, op. cit., 41.

[7] *Joseph Arch*, 48–50.

carried the pulpit to it on his back.[1] When Thomas Cooper returned to Christianity he became a General Baptist.[2] William Gadsby, the illiterate Strict Baptist, conducted a notable ministry to the poor in Back Lane Chapel, Manchester (1805–44).[3] William Howitt observed that open-air preachers tended to be poor men preaching to 'them who are too indifferent, or too shabby, to come into a respectable place of worship'.[4]

In this zone of Nonconformity the interests of the chapel coincided with the interests of the poor, and poor men found avenues of self-improvement in a context of acceptance. Gipsy Rodney Smith was confirmed in his new-found Christian faith by the fact that the old man who knelt with him at the penitent rail in the Primitive Methodist Chapel, Fitzroy Street, Cambridge (17 November 1876), was prepared to acknowledge him in public the next day. Gipsy Smith's tribute to him is a tribute to this whole tradition of Nonconformist ministry for and of the poor:

I never saw him again. But when I reach the glory land, I will find out that dear old man, and while angels shout and applaud, and the multitudes who have been brought to Christ through the gipsy boy sing for joy, I will thank that grand old saint for his shake of the hand and for his 'God bless you!' For he made me feel that somebody outside the tent really cared for a gipsy boy's soul.[5]

Joseph Barker, whose soldier–father taught himself to read and write in order to be able to write to tell his wife of his conversion, was further educated by Methodist preachers; George Edwards was compelled to educate himself out of illiteracy so he could function as a Methodist preacher; for Thomas Cooper too, Nonconformity was a stimulus to education; V. S. Pritchett's grandfather, a bricklayer, became a Congregationalist minister.[6] And though respectability might lurk at the end of this particular road, it began in the gift of self-respect:

And when I found myself noticed and cared for by him [Joseph Hill, a Methodist schoolmaster and preacher who taught Barker Latin at 6 a.m. and helped him with his preaching], and even treated with brotherly respect, it made me feel I

[1] A. C. Underwood, op. cit., 152.
[2] *The Life of Thomas Cooper*, by Himself (1872), 381.
[3] A. C. Underwood, op. cit., 185–6.
[4] W. Howitt, *Rural Life of England*, 563–5.
[5] *Gipsy Smith: His Life and Work*, by Himself (49th Thousand, 1904), 71–4.
[6] *The Life of Joseph Barker*, 13 ff., 69 ff.; George Edwards, op. cit., 31 ff.; *The Life of Thomas Cooper*, 50–1; V. S. Pritchett, *A Cab at the Door, An Autobiography: Early Years* (1968; Penguin edn., 1970), 10–11.

can scarcely tell how. I felt as if I had risen from the rank of nothingness to that of being: I felt as if I really was a man, or destined to be one, and as if the world had not been made in vain. I felt as if I had been an outcast from the world before, an outcast from the world of thoughtful, intellectual, honourable men, and as if I was now admitted within its circle. It was, in fact, a new era in my history. . . .[1]

It was revolutionary enough that fighting and drunkenness among miners should be countered: work-discipline it may inadvertently have been, but civilization, and even (as John Chapman conceded) revivalism, were far better than brutishness.[2] 'If Methodism,' Coleridge noted, 'produce sobriety and domestic habits among the lower classes, it makes them susceptible of liberty.'[3] 'Methodism took the "nobodies", and made the most humble and helpless "somebody".'[4] And even if (as must have been the case with most Methodists) the convert became respectably quietist and a man after Jabez Bunting's own heart, the gospel that sought out the poor, and the change of heart, the religious vision, which gave the suffering and the down-trodden poor—like Mrs. Gaskell's Methodists Davenport and Bessy Higgins—a hope of heaven, were inherently revolutionary. Engels complained about workers brutishly acquiescing in the bourgeoisie's religion of subservience, and some left-wing historians, following Cobbett, have regarded Methodism as a side-tracking hindrance to revolution, a sublimation in religion of urgent political and social pressures ('psychic masturbation' no less).[5] But Beatrice Webb recognized how radical a provision the life of the chapel and the hope of heaven were as resting-places 'to the worn-out or failed lives'.[6] The deep congeniality of Davenport's quietism to Mrs. Gaskell, and the way Barton's unionism and Chartism are made totally antithetical to Davenport's 'resignation to God's will', which

---

[1] *The Life of Joseph Barker*, 73. For some of the kinds of 'common man' who shaped and were shaped by various branches of Methodism, see Henry Allen Wedgwood, *People of the Potteries* (reprint, Bath, 1970).

[2] J. L. and Barbara Hammond, *The Town Labourer: The New Civilization* (1917), 53, footnote 1; W. J. Warner, *The Wesleyan Movement in the Industrial Revolution* (New York, 1967), 166 ff.; Sidney Webb, *The Story of the Durham Miners (1662–1921)* (1921), 21–4; E. R. Taylor, *Methodism and Politics*, 57; John Chapman, *Christian Revivals*, 52; E. P. Thompson, op. cit., Ch. 11, 'The Transforming Power of The Cross, I: Moral Machinery'.

[3] *The Watchman*, ed. cit., 13.

[4] R. F. Wearmouth, *The Social and Political Influence of Methodism in the Twentieth Century* (1957), 247, quoting Jack Lawson.

[5] Engels, op. cit., 118–19, 238–9; E. P. Thompson, op. cit., Ch. II; G. D. H. Cole and Raymond Postgate, *The Common People 1746–1946* (paperback edn., 1968), 270; J. L. and Barbara Hammond, *The Town Labourer*, 281–2.

[6] Beatrice Webb, *My Apprenticeship* (1926), 170.

they would 'taint' (Preface), may indicate just how much the middle class wanted this work of Methodism to continue. The 'Spirit of Christ', which *Mary Barton* would encourage in the poor, is illustrated by Davenport's meekness; John Barton's youthful 'Gospel-days' were perverted into violent unionism (Ch. 35); and Higgins in *North and South* turns from agitation to encouraging his son to recite Methodist hymns (Ch. 41). Nevertheless, the essentially radical character of a gospel for the poor, which brings hope and comfort that are more immediately available than the amelioration political activists promise, should be clear enough. It was presumably the spirit of this implicit radicalism which made Bunting's task difficult and which inspired democratic rebellion against the Conference at the Wesleyan grass-roots. And it helps explain the hold that officially undemocratic Wesleyanism kept on the towns of England.[1]

And, of course, Methodists, even Wesleyans, were not all submissively quietist. Sects like the Primitives have been called 'organisations of potential cadres' of trade unions.[2] Beatrice Webb observed the democracy of the chapel at work in Bacup:

Each chapel, even of the same denomination, manages its own affairs; and there are monthly meetings of all the members (male and female) to discuss questions of expenditure, etc. In fact each chapel is a self-governing community. . . .

One cannot help feeling what an excellent thing these dissenting organisations have been for educating this class for self-government.[3]

Methodism provided many radicals and unionists with training in leadership, with initiation into the necessary style of a popular movement, with a sharp rhetoric of right against wrong, of light against darkness. Chartists and unionists imitated Methodist organization; Primitive Methodists borrowed Chartist songs, as Chartists borrowed Methodist hymns, camp meetings, and singing processions. The unionist on Monday was the preacher on Sunday, deploying the same sort of Biblical language, and talking often to the same people. Agricultural and mining unions were notably led by Primitive Methodist preachers, and campaigns for the union could be conducted like religious revivals, with preaching from Biblical texts, prayers, and hymns.[4]

---

[1] K. S. Inglis, 'Patterns of Religious Worship in 1851', *Journal of Ecclesiastical History*, 11 (1960), 86.

[2] E. J. Hobsbawm and George Rudé, *Captain Swing* (1969), 294.

[3] Beatrice Webb, op. cit., 161.

[4] J. E. Williams, *The Derbyshire Miners* (1962), 76–8, 120–1, 216–17, 467; Henry Pelling, *A History of British Trade Unionism* (Pelican revised edn., 1969), 45; Sidney Webb,

The interaction between Nonconformity and radical political move-ments was widespread. In Leicestershire, Suffolk, Wales, and Yorkshire, Primitive Methodists, Baptists, and Congregationalists figured promin-ently in Chartism, and men like Joseph Rayner Stephens (expelled from Wesleyanism), and John Skevington and Joseph Capper, the Primitive Methodists, brought into their Chartism the democracy of their Gospel.[1] The breakaway Methodists stood for freedom and democratic government against the authoritarianism of the Wesleyan Conference. They continued to assert the rights of women preachers.[2] It was not accidental that democratic pressures came to a head in Methodism at times of country-wide, even European, unrest; it was not merely co-incidental that the New Connexion (1797) was labelled Tom Paine Methodism, or that Wesleyanism's greatest losses came immediately after 1848, when over 100,000 members departed, disenchanted with Bunting's papal supremacy.[3] E. P. Thompson and E. J. Hobsbawm have both pointed out the close connection between some periods of revival and of political unrest. They disagree over the precise nature of the link: and indeed some revivals occurred in the aftermath of political upheaval, in the trough of failure, and provide evidence for Thompson's thesis about the 'chiliasm of despair'; and some preceded political un-rest (e.g. four days before the Pentridge uprising, 1817, a Nottingham-shire informer anxiously reported Ranters' gatherings to Sidmouth) and ran parallel with it, seeming to confirm Hobsbawm's theory that Methodism advanced when Radicalism advanced.[4] Certainly, in the

---

*The Story of the Durham Miners*, 21–4; *Joseph Arch*, xi–xii, 176; R. F. Wearmouth, *Methodism and the Working-Class Movements of England, 1800–1850* (1937), 103, 122; E. P. Thompson, op. cit., 388; H. B. Kendall, op. cit., I. 333–6; E. Welbourne, *The Miners' Unions of Northumberland and Durham* (Cambridge, 1923), *passim*; A. J. Peacock, *Bradford Chartism 1838–1840* (Borthwick Institute Papers, No. 36; York, 1969), 19; A. R. Griffin, 'Methodism and Trade Unionism in the Nottinghamshire–Derbyshire Coalfield, 1844–1890', *WHS Proc.* 37 (1969), 2–9; P. R. Horn, 'Methodism and Agricultural Trade Unionism in Oxfordshire: The 1870s', *WHS Proc.* 37 (1969), 67–71.

[1] Asa Briggs (ed.), *Chartist Studies* (1967 reprint), 3–4, 129–40, 158, 220–5; E. R. Taylor, op. cit., 119; H. B. Kendall, op. cit., I. 336–41. See also H. U. Faulkner, *Chartism and the Churches* (New York, 1916), *passim*.

[2] W. J. Warner, op. cit., 264–6; A. W. Harrison *et al.*, *The Methodist Church*, 111 ff., 141.

[3] E. R. Taylor, op. cit., 85, 138–9. For an account of the Hanley revolt against the Conference and the formation of the New Connexion there, see 'Job Ridgway', in H. A. Wedgwood, *People of the Potteries* (Bath, 1970), 114–32. The Derby Faith was apparently known as 'Free Methodism': H. B. Snow, ' "Seth Bede and Dinah Morris" ', their Association with Wirksworth', *Wirksworth Urban District: Official Handbook* (n.d.), 21.

[4] E. P. Thompson, op. cit., Ch. 11. ii, 'The Chiliasm of Despair', and Postscript to Penguin edn. (1968), 919–23; E. J. Hobsbawm, *Labouring Men: Studies in the History of*

Swing riots (1830) 'riot and dissent' occurred simultaneously in some areas (Primitive Methodist strongholds like North Walsham, and places in Kent where Bible Christians were established) 'in too striking a manner to be wholly accidental'.[1]

Mixed expectations were created at such times by a rhetoric which equally conveyed social and religious implications, and could break out in a political or religious direction, often in both. For example, in the West Riding in 1802: '. . . there is a general expectation of they know not what. Like the second advent, the time is coming, the Day is at hand.'[2] The same conflating of possibilities is visible in the report from Berkshire about the activity of Primitive Methodists (autumn 1830): 'Riots by reading newspapers: burning by ranting. . . .'[3] More straightforwardly, religious language could be transferred directly to political situations: in the kind of union oath Disraeli seeks to frighten his readers with in *Sybil*, or in the Biblical language of vengeance with which Michael Hartley shoots down Moore the mill-owner in *Shirley*.[4] The language of radical and Dissenting grievance frequently coincided. 'Oh ye Church of England Parsins, who strain at a knat and swallor a cammell, woe woe woe be unto you, ye shall one day have you reward', ran one of the notices signed 'Swing' found in the possession of John Saville, a Luton straw-plait merchant, and probably a Ranter, when arrested (December 1830) in Suffolk.[5] Or take this fighting talk:

. . . we ever have, and ever shall oppose, denounce and assail the vile craft that would turn religion into a *state engine* or a trading speculation, and, that, like the Established Church of England, not only robs the people itself, but is a principal assistance in helping its robbery by others. Every man has a right to have what priest he chooses and to pay him what recompense he chooses, but no man or government has a right to force his God down my throat or his priestly hand into my pocket. . . .

That could almost be the voice of Miall, but it is in fact Ernest Jones in the *People's Paper* (9 July 1853).[6]

---

*Labour* (1964), Ch. 3, 'Methodism and the threat of Revolution in Britain'. For summary and discussion see S. Andrews, *Methodism and Society* (1970), 85–92.
[1] Hobsbawm and Rudé, *Captain Swing*, 186–7.
[2] E. P. Thompson, op. cit., 921, footnote 1.
[3] *Captain Swing*, 86.
[4] See E. P. Thompson, op. cit., 557–60 for examples; and cf. 431–3.
[5] *Captain Swing*, 161.
[6] Quoted by John Saville, *Ernest Jones: Chartist* (1952), 222.

This sort of language was not confined to the mid-century period. It was with a rhetoric of religion radically sympathetic to the slum-dweller and the 'criminal classes' that the Salvation Army went into battle against the comfortably affluent religion of the middle classes (including the Dissenters lampooned by Mrs. Booth: like Mr. Money-maker the Deacon, who is a sweater, an underpaying shopkeeper, or a trader in drink and opium [1]). Joseph Arch would exhort himself in 1872: 'You have got to trust in the Lord and in the power of His might, and speak out strong for Union.' [2] There was clearly a radical zone, frightening alike to Anglicans and the middle and ruling classes, where political and religious radicals spoke with, as it were, one voice, where radical issues—Dissent, Chartism, Teetotalism, Working-class educa-tion, and Unionism—overlapped, and where the personnel advocating the various causes was often the same group of people. [3] Nonconformity's part in the package was sometimes nicely illustrated. In 1872 for example, when Arch recruited for his Agricultural Labourers' Union on Tysoe village green, the chairman of the meeting was Josiah Smith, a Primitive Methodist local preacher; Arch stood on the Wesleyan Sunday School platform loaned by permission of the village smith who was a chapel trustee; and though the Vicar opposed Arch, and the local agent threatened redundancies, the band played 'Hold the Fort for I am coming' while the local men enrolled. [4]

One can see that overt political activity eventually outran chapel-inspired radical politics. Historians have pointed out how the denomi-nations lagged behind the developing labour movements towards the end of the century. In many cases, perhaps in most, late-nineteenth-century/early-twentieth-century Nonconformists supported socialist movements and policies in an attempt (which did not actually work, since socialist parsons and pastors did not necessarily attract large working-

[1] Mrs. Booth, *Popular Christianity* [1887], 131–43, 155–7.

[2] *Joseph Arch*, 72.

[3] Brian Harrison, ' "A World of Which We Had No Conception". Liberalism and the English Temperance Press: 1830–1872', *VS* 13 (1969–70), 125–58; 'The Temperance Question in England 1829–1869' (D.Phil. thesis, Oxford, 2 Vols., 1965), which is the basis of his *Drink and The Victorians: The Temperance Question in England 1815–1872* (1971); and B. Harrison and Barrie Trinder, *Drink and Sobriety in an Early Victorian County Town: Banbury 1830–1860* (*English Historical Review*, Supplement 4, 1969). The issue is however very complex: see Brian Harrison, 'Religion and Recreation in Nineteenth-Century England', *Past and Present*, No. 38 (1967), 98–125.

[4] M. K. Ashby, *Joseph Ashby of Tysoe 1859–1919: A Study of English Village Life* (Cam-bridge, 1961), 59–62. Howard Evans's short novel, *From Serfdom to Manhood: A Story of Agricultural Life* (Leamington, [1875]) equally nicely reveals these polarities.

class support) to keep the workers inside the chapels.[1] What emerges
from Stephen Mayor's study is that Nonconformists and the Nonconformist press were as likely as not to sympathize with the aims of
organized labour, but also that there was certainly no guaranteed across-
the-board support.[2] Socialist Nonconformists tended to be individual-
ists, not part of organized propaganda groups; indeed, Nonconformist
socialism tended to be vague and formless.[3] John Trevor's Labour
Church was a transitional phase for religious workers on the way to
overtly political activities and allegiances: it signalled a failure by Nonconformity to attract and keep workers, and was a protest over Dissent's
strongly maintained Liberal links.[4] Nevertheless, one should not ignore
the area covered by R. F. Wearmouth, the origins in Nonconformity
of Trade Union and Labour leaders and some of their claims: '. . . try
how one may, one cannot divorce Labour from religion' (George
Edwards); or, 'A man who did not revolt at what was enacted in this
country today was unworthy of the name of Nonconformist . . .'
(William Edwin Harvey).[5] And one should not forget what we have
called the 'implicit' radicalism of movements, chapels, mission halls,

[1] Peter d'A Jones, op. cit.: radical parsons attracted East-Enders, but R. J. Campbell
at the City Temple had massive congregations *before* embracing Socialism (63–4); all its
Christian Socialist clergy did not halt late-Victorian Anglican decline (305); the Congregation of John Clifford (Fabian Socialist) dropped from 2,479 (1886) to 2,213 (1903)
(64); and in East London the Nonconformists (usually accounted middle class in composition and tendency) were more successful than slum ritualists and High Churchmen
(cf. G. Best, *Mid-Victorian Britain 1851–75* (1971), 181, discussing his amazement that
Wesleyan Methodists, less overtly democratic than other Methodists, did surprisingly
better in most large towns). E. P. Thompson, 'Homage to Tom Maguire', *Essays in Labour
History: In Memory of G. D. H. Cole 25 September 1889–14 January 1959*, ed. Asa Briggs and
John Saville (revised edn., 1967), 276–316; John Kent, review of P. d'A. Jones, op. cit.,
and of Stephen Mayor, *The Churches and The Labour Movement* (1967), in *VS* 12 (1968–9),
375–7.

[2] Stephen Mayor, *The Churches and The Labour Movement* (1967).

[3] P. d'A. Jones, op. cit., 305–7; K. S. Inglis, 'English Nonconformity and Social
Reform, 1880–1900', *Past and Present*, No. 13 (1958), 73–88.

[4] E. J. Hobsbawm, *Primitive Rebels: Studies in Archaic Forms of Social Movement in the 19th
and 20th Centuries* (Manchester, 1959), 142–5; Henry Pelling, *The Origins of the Labour
Party* (2nd edn., Oxford, 1965), 125–44; K. S. Inglis, *Churches and the Working-Classes in
Victorian England* (1963), 215–49. Cf. George Haw's Introduction to *Christianity and the
Working Classes* (1906), ed. George Haw; and Beatrice Webb, *My Apprenticeship*, 162–4.

[5] R. F. Wearmouth, *Methodism and the Working-Class Movements of England, 1800–1850*
(1937); *Some Working-Class Movements of the 19th Century* (1948); *Methodism and the Struggle
of the Working-Class, 1850–1900* (Leicester, 1954); *The Social and Political Influence of
Methodism in the 20th Century* (1957); *Methodism and the Trade Unions* (1959). Hobsbawm's
discussion, *Primitive Rebels*, 134–42; George Edwards, op. cit., 43; Harvey (a Primitive
Methodist preacher, and a leader of the Derbyshire Miners' Association), in the *Derbyshire
Times*, 10 Dec. 1904: J. E. Williams, *The Derbyshire Miners* (1962), 217, 467.

which continued to take the Gospel to the poor: like the Salvation Army, early twentieth-century Pentecostalism, or the missions and tabernacles the *Daily News* census found flourishing alongside massive and empty chapels in Dissenting Gothic.[1]

The novelists acknowledge a connection of the poor and the working class with Nonconformity; some, like George Borrow, triumphantly declare it.[2] Dinah Morris preaches from the text John Wesley used in his first open-air sermon to the Kingswood colliers: Luke 4:18, 'The Spirit of the Lord is upon me, because he hath anointed me to preach the gospel to the poor.'[3] It is only natural that Silas Marner the weaver's religion should be Dissenting. The basis of Benson's congregation in *Ruth* is 'many poor': with a few farmers, shopkeepers and families of 'still higher worldly station', but only one Mr. Bradshaw (Ch. 14). Davenport and the Higginses are Methodists. Trollope's Primitive Methodist pastor, Puddleham, is intensely ignorant, but 'efficacious among the poor' (*The Vicar of Bullhampton*, Ch. 1). The Baptist chapel in *A Laodicean* is a Bethel for working people, 'worn and contorted by years of dreary toil'. Frank Capulett's people, unevangelical Anglicans, are not devoted to helping the poor like Jane Baxter's Baptist family and chapel.[4] In Silas Hocking's *Her Benny* Nell and Benny are welcomed at a poor man's chapel, and Benny becomes a Methodist Sunday School teacher among Liverpool's 'ragged and neglected children' (Chs. 7, 20, 24). A Mowbray collier in *Sybil* professes to have been 'a consistent methodist for many years'. Disraeli also puts in Wilkins, a Welsh Baptist teacher who brings news to the Committee for the National Strike that 'Glamorganshire is right to a man'; Dissenting chapels, where public thanksgivings are offered for Walter Gerard's bail; and Tummas and Sue 'of the Baptist school religion' who lead the Wodgate Hell-cats

---

[1] P. d'A. Jones, op. cit., 69.

[2] 'The crowd consisted entirely of the lower classes, labourers, and mechanics, and their wives and children—dusty people, unwashed people, people of no account whatever. . . .

'. . . There stood the preacher, one of those men—and, thank God, their number is not few—who, animated by the spirit of Christ, amidst much poverty, and, alas! much contempt, persist in carrying the light of the Gospel amidst the dark parishes of what, but for their instrumentality, would scarcely be Christian England.' George Borrow, *Lavengro*, Ch. 25.

[3] April 1739. Robert Southey, *The Life of Wesley And The Rise and Progress of Methodism*, ed. M. H. Fitzgerald (2 Vols., 1925), I. 174.

[4] [Edmund Gosse], 'The Unequal Yoke', *English Illustrated Magazine* (1886), Ch. 3.

in burning the Tommy-shop.[1] Kingsley made the same connections in *Yeast*: Lord Vieuxbois

. . . considered nothing more heterodox than the notion that the poor were to educate themselves. In his scheme, of course, the clergy and the gentry were to educate the poor, who were to take down thankfully as much as it was thought proper to give them; and beyond was 'self-will' and 'private judgement', the fathers of Dissent and Chartism, Trades'-union strikes and French Revolutions, *et si qua alia*.

But at this stage Kingsley's sympathies rather lay with Tregarva, the converted tin-miner, who sings Wesleyan hymns as he works, talks in 'the language of the Dissenting poor', exalts field-preaching as the method of reaching the labourers who will not come to church, and becomes a City-Missioner in London and later in Manchester.[2] Tregarva is an altogether muscular Christian.

Kingsley is not consistent: he has little time for 'the language of the Dissenting poor' when Alton Locke's mother or the Rev. Mr. Wigginton is doing the talking, and in *Two Years Ago* the Methodists are made anything but manly. Kingsley's Christian Socialism was strongly laced with conservatism, and the fact that the doted-on Tregarva is a gamekeeper indicates the narrowness of Kingsley's radical sympathies: that way lay his royalism, his hatred of Irishmen, his dismissal of them and blacks as 'human chimpanzees', his jingoism and support for Governor Eyre, and the evolution of muscular Christianity as an ideal for upper-middle-class Anglican graduates.[3]

Antipathy towards the association of Nonconformity with the discontented poor and with trade-unionism is perhaps only to be expected from anti-radical novelists. Disraeli believed in aristocracy not democracy, headed the Tory party, and upheld the Church of England as his party's 'great State-engine'.[4] Irreligion and Dissent in the manufacturing areas are to him much the same thing and equally horrifying: both testify to the absence of the Church of England, 'a main remedial agency in our present state'.[5] The alliance in *Sybil* of Dissenters and radicals proves

[1] *Sybil*, Bk. III, Ch. 1; Bk. V, Chs. 8 and 10; Bk. VI, Ch. 7.

[2] *Yeast: A Problem*, Chs. 3, 4, 11, 13, 15.

[3] R. B. Martin, *The Dust of Combat*, 213–15, 219, 221–2, 259–60. The face of Marie's black grandmother was withered, in death, 'as the wrinkled ape': *Two Years Ago*, Ch. 9. See G. M. Young, 'Sophist and Swashbuckler', *Daylight and Champaign* (1937), 102-11.

[4] Robert Blake, *Disraeli*, 397, 427–8, 476, 507.

[5] Disraeli's General Preface to the Collected edition of the Novels and Tales (1870–1), Vol. I (*Lothair*), xii. 'Under the plea of liberalism, all the institutions which were the bulwarks of the multitude had been sapped and weakened, and nothing had been substituted for them' (ibid., x).

his point: with friends like Sue and Tummas the Baptists hardly need opponents like Disraeli to expose their deficiencies, or so we are to read the novel.

Dislike and fear of Dissent make Disraeli do some odd things, and his manipulations actually show through the text of *Sybil*. This novel was presumably not what Engels had hoped for when he asked rhetorically if the middle classes had 'even done as much as to compile from those rotting blue-books a single readable book from which everybody might easily get some information on the condition of the great majority of "free-born Britons"?'[1] And if, as Edward Baines alleged, the 1842 Childrens' Employment Commission had sought out the most inflammatory evidence, and, being anti-Dissent in spirit, had exaggerated to excite the government to action in the industrial areas, then Disraeli compounded that exaggeration by selecting only what suited his particularly Anglican book. In Wodgate there is no church, and the grudging admission of Dissent ('. . . even the conventicle scarcely dares show its humbler front in some obscure corner') is quickly negatived ('. . . no churches, chapels . . .') (Bk. III, Ch. 4).

In Willenhall, the basis for Wodgate,[2] there was one Anglican Sunday School, one Wesleyan, one Baptist, one Primitive Methodist, and at Short Heath, two miles away, another Wesleyan. There was a Baptist day-school.[3] Sub-Commissioner Horne reported that in each Sunday School 'perhaps even a dozen boys, may be selected whose moral feelings and conduct are far above the average',[4] but Disraeli chooses only to conflate some of the more lurid statements into Suky's profession of faith ('. . . Moses, Goliath, and the rest of the Apostles'). Even some of Willenhall's worst cases were not entirely unenlightened: at the Wesleyan Sunday School, Walter Brindley, aged 17, 'has heard of the Apostles; does not know if St. Peter was one, nor if St. John was one, unless it was St. John Wesley'(!).[5]

---

[1] Engels's Address 'To the Working-Classes of Great Britain' (March, 1845), prefixed to *The Condition of the Working Class*, xxi. Disraeli was almost certainly not influenced by the Address: he finished *Sybil* at the end of April 1845, and had been hectically busy on it for the previous four months. *Lord Beaconsfield's Letters 1830–1852*, ed. by his brother (1887), 205.

[2] Sheila M. Smith, 'Willenhall and Wodgate: Disraeli's Use of Blue Book Evidence', *RES*, N.S. 13 (1962), 368–84.

[3] Reports by R. H. Horne Esq., *Children's Employment Commission. Appendix to the Second Report of the Commissioners [Trades and Manufactures] Part II. Reports and Evidence from Sub-Commissioners*, Parliamentary Papers, 1843 [432], XIV. 1, Q. 51, Sects. 547, 549.

[4] Ibid., Q. 49, Sect. 543.

[5] Ibid., Q. 34, No. 152.

' "Ah, me," thought Morley, "and could not they spare one Missionary from Tahiti for their fellow-countrymen at Wodgate!" ': an observation to be uttered most feelingly only after skipping Horne's tributes to the Sunday School teachers—locksmiths, key-makers, and miners (some barely literate themselves of course)—particularly the Nonconformists 'Richard Foster, key-stamper, and John Evans, miner'. Evans, a 'worthy and honest-minded *butty* of a coal-mine', superintendent of Short Heath Wesleyan Sunday School, protested to Horne that some 'Masters care but little' about their apprentices, and 'some method to compel masters to send them [to Sunday School] I think would be of much good':

I think the condition of the working class may be greatly improved by opening free trade whereby the working class may have sufficient labour to earn his bread for there are numbers of poor people would send their children to the Sunday School but have not clothing scarce to cover their Nakedness and shoes to wear, many Moral and Religious people are in this condition and I think that an alteration in the Corn Laws would bring about the better condition of the people and you may depend upon it Sir that I am Speaking the sentiments of 19 out of 20 in this parish.[1]

It is just this voice, radical, working-class, protesting, of the Non-conformist striving socially and morally to improve the Wodgates of the north, that Disraeli excludes and pretends does not exist. But it insists on being included: if there were 'no . . . chapels' then Suky could hardly have wanted her Baptist minister to marry her to Tummas, and if there were no schools she could not be 'of the Baptist school religion' (a memorable phrase from the Willenhall evidence that stuck).[2] Disraeli cannot at once imply the dangers of Baptist schools as generators of working-class rebels and yet deny their presence in Wodgate. 'It may be genteel to sneer at the Dissenters. It may be dignified to despise them.'[3] But it is a bit silly to deny their existence altogether.

Trollope is more relaxed than Disraeli and has less insistently political axes to grind, but he too finds the demoticism of Primitive Methodism not to his taste. A 'Conservative–Liberal', he believed that 'inequality is the work of God' and that the butcher's son was patently inferior to the parson's. And Puddlehamites were emphatically not 'gentlemen'.[4]

[1] Ibid., Q. 51, Sects. 551–7.
[2] Sheila M. Smith, art. cit., 383.
[3] Edward Baines, Letter to Lord Wharncliffe (25 Mar. 1843), Chairman of the Committee of the Council on Education. Appendix to *The Social, Educational, and Religious State of the Manufacturing Districts* (1969 impression), 72.
[4] Anthony Trollope, *An Autobiography* (2 Vols., 1883), I. 53–4; II. 129–30.

The Brontës were reared in anti-Radicalism: children of an Anglican parson who had been an anti-Luddite (and who had been happy to be supported by the notorious Rev. Hammond Roberson and Jabez Bunting).[1] He brought up his children to spot in the *Leeds Intelligencer* 'a most excellent Tory newspaper', and his creation of a youthful Tory in Charlotte is manifest in her letter to Branwell (17 May 1832) which mentions 'the extreme pleasure I felt at the news of the Reform Bill's being thrown out by the House of Lords, and of the expulsion, or resignation, of Earl Grey'.[2] It is to the discredit of the curates that Moses Barraclough, the 'preaching tailor', and Supplehough the Baptist are successful among the class of 'weaver girls'. And it is, of course, Michael Hartley, 'an Antinomian' and 'a violent Jacobin and leveller', who attempts to assassinate Robert Moore. Barraclough too is given to violence ('You were on the moor,—you wore a mask,—you knocked down one of my men with your own hand,—you! a preacher of the Gospel!'). But Helstone, who has the combined qualities of Patrick Brontë and Hammond Roberson, heroically opposes radicals and Dissenters: he boldly barges the Dissenting Sunday School leader into the ditch to the accompaniment of *Rule Britannia!*, which drowns the rivals' 'dolorous' canticle.[3] The anxieties of a class which fears the Non-conformist–radical alliance are as prominent in *Shirley* as they are in *Sybil*.

[1] Mrs. Gaskell, *The Life of Charlotte Brontë* (2 Vols., 1857), I. 52; J. Lock and Canon W. T. Dixon, *A Man of Sorrow: The Life, Letters and Times of the Rev. Patrick Brontë, 1777–1861* (1965), 100 ff.; E. P. Thompson, op. cit., 613–15; T. J. Wise and J. A. Symington, *The Brontës: their Lives, Friendships, and Correspondence* (4 Vols., Oxford, 1932), I. 99; T. P. Bunting, *The Life of Jabez Bunting D.D.*, completed by the Rev. G. Stringer Howe (2 Vols., 1859–87), II. 10–11.

[2] Mrs. Gaskell, *The Life of Charlotte Brontë*, I. 89, 110.

[3] *Shirley*, Chs. 1, 8, 17.

# IV.  THE PRESENCE OF DISSENT

THE 1851 Census revealed to alarmed Churchmen, and to jubilant Dissenters who had suspected as much, the extent of the Dissenting allegiance.[1] Granted all necessary cautions about Horace Mann's figures, the statistics gave a very real notion of the strength of Nonconformity: about half of the church attenders did not worship with the Established Church but with Dissent. Edward Miall 'said that as a dissenter he felt like the son of a peer, treated from birth as a menial, and suddenly finding himself in his ancestral home, recognised and receiving the attention due to his rank'.[2]

Dissent had increased massively between 1801 and 1851, and it increased commensurately in the second half of the century: more chapels were erected by the hundred, more sittings provided by the thousand.[3] In 1899 the Anglican communicant figure topped the Dissenting one (1,920,140 to 1,897,175) but the Free Churches claimed 875,000 more Sunday scholars and 175,000 more Sunday School teachers than the Church of England. The Church of England clergy numbered 21,164 and the Free Church only 8,802, but the Dissenters boasted 47,781 lay preachers. The Rev. Charles Herbert could assert: 'Without priest, without a pleasing ritual, with services often unattractive and prosy, in short without the strongest tendencies of a religion likely to be popular, they have not only continued to exist, but they have advanced.'[4]

What is more, Victorian Dissenting chapels tended to affect more people than their membership, not least through Sunday Schools.[5] The difference between Congregationalist members and attenders is spelled

---

[1] K. S. Inglis, 'Patterns of Religious Worship in 1851', *Journal of Ecclesiastical History*, 11 (1960), 74–86; W. S. F. Pickering, 'The 1851 religious census—a useless experiment?', *British Journal of Sociology*, 18 (1967), 382–407; D. M. Thompson, 'The 1851 Religious Census: Problems and Possibilities', *VS* 11 (1967–8), 87–97.

[2] Chadwick, *Victorian Church*, I. 367–8.

[3] G. K. Clark, op. cit., 171–3.

[4] 'Free Church Progress', *Puritan* (1899), 343–7.

[5] e.g., a survey (Sept. 1856) of the Aldercar, Langley, Loscoe, Codnor, and Eastwood parishes showed that of a population of 676 adults and 971 children (with C. of E. possessing 1 communicant, 17 regular attenders, and 26 occasional attenders), Dissenters, mainly Methodist, had 106 members, 45 regular attenders, 150 occasional attenders and 282 Sunday Scholars. A. R. Griffin, 'Methodism and Trade Unionism in the Nottinghamshire–Derbyshire Coalfield, 1844–90', *WHS Proc.* 37 (1969), 3.

out in the novels of William Hale White. The loss of the penumbra of
non-members was an early feature of the twentieth-century decline in
Nonconformist attendances. There was also clearly a fluid band of
church-goers between Church and Dissent: including the Anglicans who
would attend a near-by chapel on rainy days, or in the evening when
the Church was not open, and the Methodists who continued in Victorian
years the older habit of attending Church in the morning and chapel
later. Clergy complained in 1854 to the Bishop of Oxford that poor
parishioners were 'not decidedly dissenters nor church people'. In
1900 there were still West Riding Anglicans who thought it charitable
to 'give the chapel a turn'.[1] Charles Kingsley's West Country churchmen in *Two Years Ago* perplex the curate by occasionally attending the
Bryanite Chapel (Ch. 2), and Hardy adverts amusingly to the 'trimmers'
of Nether-Moynton:

. . . the mixed race which went to church in the morning and [Methodist]
chapel in the evening, or when there was a tea—as many as a hundred-and-ten
people . . . including the parish-clerk in the winter-time, when it was too dark
for the vicar to observe who passed up the street at seven o'clock. . . .
  It was owing to this overlapping of creeds that the celebrated population-puzzle
arose among the denser gentry of the district around Nether-Moynton: how
could it be that a parish containing fifteen score of strong full-grown Episco-
palians, and nearly thirteen score of well-matured Dissenters, numbered barely
two-and-twenty score adults in all?[2]

For Evangelical Anglicans, Dissent was more tolerable than Broad or
High Churches if access to an Evangelical Anglican Church was impossible. Evangelical Dissenters (the majority in this period) shared many
attitudes and theological assumptions with their Anglican counterparts,
and people like the Ruskins could fit theologically, if not socially, into
Dissenting pews—at a pinch.[3]
  Given the extent of nineteenth-century Nonconformity it is not
surprising that the novelists were variously in touch with, or related to,
Dissenters. The most obvious connection with Dissent is parental: this
is true of Edmund Gosse, son of Plymouth Brethren; Hale White, offspring of Congregationalists; Mrs. Oliphant, daughter of Free Churchmen of Scotland; Mrs. Gaskell, ensconced in the Unitarian cousinhood;
the Brontës, whose father and mother, as well as their aunt and servant

[1] D. M. Thompson, op. cit., 95–6; Henry Pelling, *Popular Politics and Society in Late
Victorian Britain* (1968), 23, 24.
[2] 'The Distracted Preacher', Ch. 1.
[3] John Ruskin, *Praeterita*, intro. Kenneth Clark (1949), 62–3; 121–2.

Tabitha, were followers of Wesley. Less obvious, but still more illustrative of Dissent's penetration into the marrow of the time, are relationships other than parental. Matthew Arnold's sister married a Quaker, W. E. Forster (who lost his membership for marrying out of the sect).[1] Dickens's sister became a convert to Congregationalism. Charles Kingsley married Fanny, the daughter of Pascoe Grenfell, whose sister Lydia was the girl whom Henry Martyn, so to say, left behind him when he went out as a missionary.[2] In 1844 Kingsley read 'with much emotion' the Life of the Cornish Church–Methodist who was Simeon's curate while Patrick Brontë was at St. John's, Cambridge, who got Brontë money from Wilberforce, and served as a basis for St. John Rivers in *Jane Eyre*.[3] Kingsley was himself proud of his descent from Cromwellian Independents, and the democratic and learned Congregationalists of the past are praised in *Alton Locke* at the expense of ignorant Baptists who, like the Fifth Monarchy Men, are Calvinists and allegedly therefore élitist.[4] Thackeray's mother was an Evangelical Anglican, and she and her circle were the basis for his satire of evangelicalism, but even the product of such a securely Anglican matrix became friendly at Cambridge with the son of a Dissenting solicitor, William Henry Brookfield; and his uncle, Mark Wood Carmichael Smyth, became a Plymouth Brother and wanted to give away all his possessions.[5]

Both George Eliot and Dickens attended Nonconformist schools, and it was the learned tradition of the Dissenting Academy that defined Disraeli's first contacts with Dissent. While still in the Jewish faith he boarded at a school in Blackheath whose headmaster was a Dissenter called Potticany; and in 1817 he went to the Rev. Eliezer Cogan's Unitarian Higham Hall, Epping Forest.[6] Robert Blake argues that *Contarini Fleming* suggests that Disraeli felt 'alienation and "apartness" from his schoolfellows' in these Dissenting Academies. Resentment against Dissent may thus have taken early root, reinforced by regrets for the Winchester he missed.[7]

[1] E. Isichei, *Victorian Quakers*, 202.
[2] J. H. Rigg, *Modern Anglican Theology* (3rd edn., 1880), 33–4.
[3] Ibid., 66; and J. Lock and Canon W. T. Dixon, *A Man of Sorrow*, 18–19.
[4] *Charles Kingsley: His Letters and Memories of His Life*, I. 183–4, II. 24; *Alton Locke*, Ch. 30.
[5] G. N. Ray, *The Buried Life: A Study of the Relation Between Thackeray's Fiction and His Personal History* (1952), 49 ff., 100; G. N. Ray (ed.), *The Letters and Private Papers of William Makepeace Thackeray* (4 Vols., 1945–6), I. xcv.
[6] 'Eli', according to Robert Blake, *Disraeli* (paperback edn., 1969), 12; but 'Eliezer' in H. McClachlan, *The Unitarian Movement in the Religious Life of England*, I (1934), 109. See entry for Eliezer Cogan (1762–1855), Boase, *Modern English Biography*.
[7] R. Blake, *Disraeli*, 12–13; and 'Disraeli: the Problems of a Biographer', *Cornhill Magazine*, 175 (1966), 301–2.

The general experience of Dissent was, of course, more mundane. Shopping on the High Street, with the grocer at least, if not with the butcher, meant contacting Dissenters: 'The names which figured highest in the benevolent lists of Salem Chapel, were known to society only as appearing, in gold letters, upon the backs of those mystic tradesmen's books which were deposited every Monday in little heaps at every house in Grange Lane.'[1] At Beresford Chapel, Walworth, the Ruskins rubbed shoulders with their plumber's wife. And even in the best families the servants were often Nonconformists. Beatrice Potter's family, lapsed Unitarians, had Martha Jackson, godly, faithful, Mrs. Potter's lifelong attendant, who married the Chadbandian Mills, railway guard turned butler, and a Baptist lay preacher.[2] Mrs. Thomas Hill, wife of a Primitive Methodist local preacher, helped out at entertainments at Dickens's home, Gadshill.[3] And even the virulently anti-evangelical Mrs. Trollope employed a Baptist nurse for her sons.[4] Esther Waters, so to say, was to be found in many a family, sometimes surprisingly.

Dissenters, like the poor (they often were the poor), were always with the parish priest, and were for Patrick Brontë's curates (lampooned in *Shirley*), or for Charles Kingsley, a problem. Brontë's High Church curates ('bigoted, intolerant') harangued Haworth Dissenters over Church Rates: if she had been a Nonconformist Charlotte would have horsewhipped them.[5] Kingsley was driven to consult F. D. Maurice about 'supra-lapsarian' Calvinists in his parish, and the mild reply contrasted sharply with Kingsley's views on the subject ('. . . the hungry sheep meanwhile looking up, foodless to the respective dunghills of particular and general baptist communions, whereon their respective hirelings sit muck enthroned . . .').[6]

Kingsley did get to know Dissenters: Philip Gosse in the 1850s; Thomas Cooper, on whom Alton Locke is calqued; J. H. Rigg, eminent Wesleyan, who got himself noticed by protesting against the caricatures in *Alton Locke* and inaccuracies in *Two Years Ago*.[7] Kingsley's aggression

[1] Mrs. Oliphant, *Salem Chapel*, Ch. 1; John Vincent, *Pollbooks*, 15–16.

[2] Beatrice Webb, *My Apprenticeship* (1926), 18 ff.

[3] H. Woodcock, 'The Religious Side of Charles Dickens and His Sister Fanny', *The Aldersgate Primitive Methodist Magazine*, N.S. 8 (1901), 109.

[4] T. H. S. Escott, *Anthony Trollope: His Work, Associates and Literary Originals* (1913), 224.

[5] Lock and Dixon, *Man of Sorrow*, 298.

[6] See Letters to Maurice (1844), to R. Cowley Powles (July 1844), and Maurice's reply (22 July 1844): *Charles Kingsley: Letters and Memories of His Life*, I. 127–33.

[7] R. B. Martin, *The Dust of Combat* (1959), 169 ff.; Edmund Gosse, *Father and Son*, 161–2; Louis Cazamian, *Kingsley et Thomas Cooper: Étude sur une source d'Alton Locke* (Paris, 1903); *LQR* 8 (1857), 1–49 and 276–8; *Charles Kingsley: Letters and Memories*, II. 22–3.

mellowed in time, but there is, nevertheless, some irony in his Chester botany group's being taken, while out on field-work, for a Dissenting congregation on the way to the opening of a new chapel in the country.[1] Trollope would have relished Kingsley's being regarded as leader of some Puddlehamite cohort! [2]

Like Kingsley, Thomas Hardy had Nonconformist forebears: his mother's family, Puddletown Symondses, contained Baptists in the eighteenth century.[3] Hardy rather insists that his mother 'had no non-conforming tendencies whatever', but she did send him to Dorchester's Nonconformist school because of the master's reputation for Latin.[4] One result of his architectural training is the detailed arguments about Baptism in the early part of *A Laodicean*. The architect Hicks's other pupil, Bastow, was a Baptist whose polemic on behalf of Adult Baptism, shared by the two Perkinses, sons of the Dorchester Baptist minister and graduates of Aberdeen, almost persuaded Hardy to accept a second baptism. There is a notably personal intensity about Hardy's account of Paula Power's baptismal dilemma, and the beginning of this famously bad novel is much the best part not least because Hardy convincingly enters the heart of her conflict:

What manner of man would it be who on an ordinary plodding and bustling evening of the nineteenth century could single himself out as different from the rest of the inhabitants, banish all shyness, and come forward to undergo such a trying ceremony? Who was he that had pondered, gone into solitudes, wrestled with himself, worked up his courage and said, I will do this, though few else will, for I believe it to be my duty?[5]

Hardy pays tribute to the courage and integrity of Woodwell, the Baptist pastor: unafraid to preach rebukingly to his landlady Paula, the richest member of the chapel, he shames Somerset into a sense of his insincerity in the Baptism argument, and exhausts himself in labours among the poor and ignorant. Of Dorchester's Baptist minister Perkins 'and his argumentative family' Hardy wrote:

They formed an austere and frugal household, and won his admiration by their thoroughness and strenuousness. He often visited them. . . . It was through

[1] R. B. Martin, *The Dust of Combat*, 274.
[2] See *The Vicar of Bullhampton*, Ch. 55 for Primitive Methodists processing to the opening of a chapel.
[3] Evelyn Hardy (ed.), *Thomas Hardy's Notebooks* (1955), 72.
[4] 'Florence Emily Hardy' [Hardy himself], *The Early Life of Thomas Hardy: 1840–1891* (1928), 22–3.
[5] *A Laodicean*, Ch. 2.

these Scotch people that Thomas Hardy first became impressed with the necessity for 'plain living and high thinking', which stood him in such good stead in later years. Among the few portraits of actual persons in Hardy's novels, that of the Baptist minister in *A Laodicean* is one—being a recognizable drawing of Perkins the father as he appeared to Hardy at this time, though the incidents are invented.[1]

Hardy was obviously faced, at least sometimes, with the outward and visible signs of evangelicalism and Nonconformity. Hermann Lea's *Thomas Hardy's Wessex* (1925) has a photograph of a fence painted, in the style of the evangelist Tess meets, with HOW SHALL WE ESCAPE IF WE NEGLECT SO GREAT SALVATION, and Lea informs us that the barn Alec D'Urberville preaches in 'was most probably drawn from the barn which stands near the centre of the village of Evershot and was originally used as a chapel'.[2] There is even a hint of Nonconformity about Tryphena Sparks, the cousin whose relationship with Hardy and influence on his work are now widely believed to have been of crucial importance. 'As like now,' says a relation of Hardy, referring to the Sparks family's Anglicanism, 'Church and Chapel overlap.' Tryphena is buried in Topsham cemetery, 'right at the far end': 'The gravedigger said to me, "Church that end chapel down there." '[3] Paula Power, Baptist waverer and gymnast, has some relation to Tryphena (Stockwell College had a gymnasium), and like her school at Athelhampton and the school in Plymouth where she became headmistress in 1871, Stockwell belonged to the British and Foreign Schools Society, officially interdenominational but in practice largely Nonconformist.[4]

Tryphena's relation to Nonconformity is speculative, but there is no doubt about the deep influence on Hardy of early contacts with local Dissenters. On his eighty-fourth birthday came a letter from one of the Perkins sons, and after a 60 years' gap Hardy was 'tempted to get in touch with him', but did not. And in the last months of his life Hardy recalled Bastow. Florence Hardy noted (17 November 1927):

Today T. H. was speaking, and evidently thinking a great deal, about a friend, a year or two older than himself, who was a fellow-pupil at Mr. Hicks's office. I felt, as he talked, that he would like to meet this man again more than anyone

---

[1] *The Early Life of Thomas Hardy*, 39–40.

[2] H. Lea, *Thomas Hardy's Wessex* (1925), 10, 24; Illustration 6, p. 30.

[3] John Antell, in a letter to me (18 Oct. 1970).

[4] See Lois Deacon and Terry Coleman, *Providence and Mr. Hardy* (1966), 33–4, 39–40, 78.

in the world. He is in Australia now, if alive, and must be nearly ninety. His name is Henry Robert Bastow; he was a Baptist and evidently a very religious youth, and T. H. was devoted to him. I suggested that we might find out something about him by sending an advertisement to Australian newspapers, but T. H. thought that would not be wise.[1]

If Dissent cut a wide swathe through the period, it also left a deep impression on those who had much to do with it, and especially in childhood. The instructive, because explicit, case is D. H. Lawrence. In 'Hymns in a Man's Life' he claims that though the poems of Wordsworth, Keats, Shakespeare, and Goethe may be 'woven deep into a man's consciousness', they 'are still not woven so deep in me as the rather banal Nonconformist hymns that penetrated through and through my childhood'. 'Galilee', 'Canaan's pleasant land', 'Sun of my soul, thou Saviour dear', 'the beauty of holiness': the tags of a Congregationalist childhood have gone deep, invested with 'wonder'. The hymns 'live and glisten in the depths of the man's consciousness in undimmed wonder, because they have not been subjected to any criticism or analysis'.[2]

The result of early contact with Dissent depends on its magnitude and nature, on the branch of Nonconformity involved, and even then need not be predictively straightforward. Lawrence, for example, dwells in 'Hymns in a Man's Life' on Congregationalism's 'beauty of holiness', its unsentimental vigour, its aloofness from the wildly emotional and energetically ranting Primitive Methodists who had 'revivals' and got 'saved'. But, of course, he belonged as a novelist, if anything, to the Primitive Methodists: as a writer he was a conversionist, an indulger in rant and 'personal emotionalism'. Birkin was recognized as being like a Sunday School teacher, and it was, as it were, at the Primitive Methodist Sunday School.

The novels of the Brontës and of Mrs. Gaskell will serve to show characteristic effects of upbringing and life at opposing ends of the Nonconformist axis.

---

[1] 'Florence Emily Hardy', *The Later Years of Thomas Hardy: 1892–1928* (1930), 237.

[2] Cf. George Orwell: 'The vestiges of an Anglican childhood clung to Orwell more tenaciously than he ever cared to admit, as was shown by . . . his extraordinary knowledge of hymns, which he remembered more exactly than any other agnostic I have ever met.' George Woodcock, *The Crystal Spirit: A Study of George Orwell* (Penguin edn., 1970), 81.

# V. THE BRONTËS

THE Brontë novels are effectively rooted in the eighteenth-century Evangelical Revival.[1] The myth of Patrick Brontë has it that he, 'an Irishman born Brunty, had worked his way up from a shanty in Roscommon to St. John's College, Cambridge, and preferment in the Church of England'.[2] In fact Patrick was early picked out as a candidate for the Evangelical ministry, sponsored to Cambridge, then promoted through a pipeline of 'awakened' parishes, eventually reaching the apotheosis of Church-Methodism—Grimshaw's old parish at Haworth.

Patrick Brontë was born 17 March 1777, at Drumballyroney-cum-Drumgooland, Co. Down.[3] He undoubtedly heard John Wesley preach on one of Wesley's biennial visits to the neighbourhood. Brontë's youngest brother was named after Thomas Walsh the Methodist preacher. Patrick became associated with local Presbyterians: he was befriended by David Barber, the Rathfriland Presbyterian minister (whom Wesley mentions in his Journals), and he taught in the Presbyterian school. Eventually, the Rev. Thomas Tighe, a friend of Wesley (like his brother who was host to Wesley and the preachers), engaged Patrick as a tutor for his children and coached him in theology.

It was as a protégé of Tighe that Patrick went up to St. John's, Cambridge, in 1802. There he was financially assisted, through the mediation of Henry Martyn, Simeon's curate, by Wilberforce, Henry Thornton, and the Church Missionary Society funds. The vicar at his first curacy in Wetherfield, Essex (1806) was Joseph Jowett, a friend of Simeon. The Evangelical Anglican, or Church-Methodist, old-boy network, by which Simeon secured for the Church of England an evangelical leaven which was yet untainted by Whitefield's or the Countess of Huntingdon's extreme Calvinism, was already visibly at work for Brontë.

Through a Cambridge friend, John Nunn, vicar at St. Chad's, Shrewsbury, Brontë got a curacy in Wellington, Shropshire (1808). His

---

[1] This chapter owes a good deal to Mrs. Grace Elsie Harrison, *Methodist Good Companions* (1935), *Haworth Parsonage: A Study of Wesley and the Brontës* (1937), and *The Clue to the Brontës* (1948). Writers on the Brontës have not given Mrs. Harrison due credit: she paved the way for serious consideration of Methodist influence on the Brontës.

[2] Geoffrey Moore, Foreword to Signet Classics edn. of *Wuthering Heights* (1959), v.

[3] Details of Patrick Brontë's life are from Lock and Dixon, *A Man of Sorrow*.

fellow-curate was William Morgan, a Welsh Church-Methodist with powerful friends: Crosse of Bradford, Mrs. Fletcher of Madeley, and John Fennell (John Fletcher's godson). Yorkshire had been for John Fletcher the 'Goshen of our land', and Brontë soon became one of Fletcher's widow's 'precious young men' whom she inevitably sponsored for Yorkshire parishes: Morgan became curate to Crosse at Bradford; Samuel Walter, the Madeley curate, got a parish near Huddersfield; and in December 1809 Brontë became curate at Dewsbury parish church.

In March 1811 Brontë moved on to the incumbency of Hartshead-cum-Clifton. And in January 1812 the Woodhouse Grove Wesleyan Academy opened, with the Rev. John Fennell from Madeley as first headmaster and his wife Jane (née Branwell) from Penzance as first matron. Brontë was appointed the first school examiner for 1812. At Woodhouse Grove he met Maria Branwell, Mrs. Fennell's niece. Maria's cousin Jane, Fennell's daughter, became engaged to William Morgan, and Patrick to Maria: Morgan and Brontë each married the other to Maria and Jane respectively, at a double ceremony in Guiseley Church.

The relation between Methodists and Anglicans was by this time becoming problematic, and the position of the Church-Methodists, with feet in both camps, uncomfortable. One trustee of Woodhouse Grove was the notorious Jabez Bunting (appointed superintendent of the Halifax Wesleyan Circuit, 1811), and when, about twelve months after the opening, the Woodhouse Grove trustees sacked Fennell because they wanted a straight Wesleyan as headmaster Bunting had his brother-in-law, Thomas Fletcher, appointed temporarily.[1] Bunting thus became anathema in the Brontë legend: congenial perhaps because of the antagonism to Luddites he shared with Brontë, he was nevertheless the man who had put uncle Fennell out of a job.[2]

In October 1815 Morgan became incumbent of Christ Church, Bradford, and Fennell succeeded him as Crosse's curate. Patrick had become incumbent at Thornton in May 1815, a place strong in Dissent with an ancient Puritan heritage, and here Charlotte (1816), Emily (1818), and Anne (1820) were born.[3] Then, in February 1820, after much delay because the Haworth trustees insisted on their ancient

---

[1] J. T. Slugg, *Woodhouse Grove School: Memorials and Reminiscences* (1885), 17, 34–5, 89–90.

[2] T. P. Bunting, *Life of Jabez Bunting D.D.* (2 Vols., 1859–87), completed by the Rev. G. Stringer Howe, II. 1–11.

[3] See William Scruton, *Thornton and the Brontës* (Bradford, 1898).

privilege of being consulted over their vicar, Patrick was finally able to reach out and take the plum he had been inching towards. Haworth had been William Grimshaw's parish from 1742 to 1763. John and Charles Wesley, George Whitefield, and John Newton had all preached there; Selina, Countess of Huntingdon, had been in the church when Whitefield preached and two men dropped dead and Grimshaw had urged Whitefield to 'cry aloud and spare not'. In 1761 John Wesley had exulted over the parish: 'What hath God wrought in the midst of these rough mountains!' [1] The legendary presence of the man Wesley designated as successor to himself and his brother was strong in the place. So Brontë 'had more than Abraham for his father when he married the niece of John Fletcher's god-son and drank out of Grimshaw's flagons at the Haworth Communion Service'. [2]

But Patrick also had, to say the least, bad luck in Haworth. His wife and all his children died there; Branwell became a drunkard and his father had to spend nights with him at bad times; many of the Church trustees were Dissenters and unready to grant funds for fabric repairs. Rivalry displaced the old Church/Methodism co-operation, and very ironically so, since Grimshaw was the father of Haworth Dissent. The Methodist chapel which Grimshaw had built bore, like the sounding-board in the Church, Grimshaw's favourite text ('For me to live is Christ . . .'); the first Baptist pastor at Haworth, like four other local Dissenting ministers and Dan Taylor, founder of the General Baptist New Connexion, was a Grimshaw convert; local Baptist and Congregationalist chapels had sprung up under Grimshaw's influence. [3] Nevertheless, Patrick stayed pro-Methodist: in old age he would go to West Lane Wesleyan Chapel for Sunday evening worship. And he remained, like all Methodists, mindful of John Wesley's youthful escape ('a brand plucked from the burning'): Haworth rectory must have no curtains, according to him, and inflammable clothes must be avoided. (When Heathcliff prays 'like a methodist', Joseph takes it as a sign 'that the Lord has touched his heart, and he is saved "so as by fire" '.) [4]

Patrick Brontë was not his children's only source of Methodist tales and impressions. His wife Maria—although she died in September 1821 when Charlotte was only 6 and Emily 3—was a Methodist, and Charlotte

---

[1] Frank Baker, *William Grimshaw 1708–1763* (1963), 187.

[2] G. E. Harrison, *The Clue to the Brontës* (1948), 46.

[3] 'An American Visitor at Haworth, 1861', *BST* 15 (1967), 134; Frank Baker, *William Grimshaw*, 270–1.

[4] Lock and Dixon, *A Man of Sorrow*, 282; *Wuthering Heights*, Ch. 17.

inherited her copy of Wesley's abridgement of the *Imitation of Christ*.[1] The sea-stained *Lady's Magazines* and, by implication of context, the 'mad *Methodist Magazines*' (Winifred Gérin gratuitously has them too 'stained with the salt-waves') which Caroline reads in Helstone's library (*Shirley*, Ch. 22) are probably related to the goods rescued from Maria Brontë's box smashed on its sea journey from Penzance to Yorkshire.[2] A more permanent source of Methodist influence, though, was Aunt Elizabeth Branwell, who brought to bear the full weight of Cornish Methodism. Her parents, Thomas and Anne Branwell, were long-standing Penzance Methodists; her own Aunt Elizabeth became Mrs. John Keam ('a fervent Methodist for 36 years' said Keam's *Methodist Magazine* obituary in 1876). Aunt Branwell's Aunt Jane was of course Mrs. Fennell; her sister Jane, another aunt to the Brontës, became Mrs. John Kingston, a Wesleyan missionary to the West Indies. Had she stayed in Penzance Aunt Branwell would undoubtedly have become a fully fledged Wesleyan like the rest of her family. Her teapot bearing Grimshaw's text is still extant.[3]

Another significant Methodist presence in Haworth rectory was Tabitha Aykroyd, faithful servant for thirty years (except for a 3 year break) from 1825 to 1855, when she died at the age of 85. She was a class leader at the Wesleyan Chapel, and not only remembered when fairies inhabited the area but had a fund of Grimshaw material (remembered 'his very words').[4]

The Brontës' work bears many signs of Patrick's stories, Tabbie's tales, Methodist hymnbooks, and the *Methodist Magazine*. Caroline Helstone reads 'some mad *Methodist Magazines*, full of miracles and apparitions, of preternatural warnings, ominous dreams, and frenzied fanaticism'. That Charlotte, at least, caught the tone and style of the *Methodist Magazine* is evident from her manuscript 'Julia' (dated 29 June 1837).[5] The narrator, Charlotte's favourite *persona*, Charles Townshend the rakish Methodist, describes, or at least begins to describe, the

---

[1] Clement Shorter, *Charlotte Brontë and Her Circle* (1896), 30–1.

[2] Mrs. Gaskell, *The Life of Charlotte Brontë* (2 Vols., 1857), I. 42; Wise and Symington *The Brontës: Their Lives*, etc., I. 21; Winifred Gérin, *Charlotte Brontë*, 35.

[3] For Miss Gérin's extravagantly horrified contemplation of Grimshaw's text, see *Anne Brontë* (1959), 36. There is a photograph of the teapot, ibid., facing p. 48.

[4] Lock and Dixon, *A Man of Sorrow*, 255; W. Gérin, *Charlotte Brontë*, 37–8; G. E. Harrison, *The Clue to the Brontës*, 52–3.

[5] MS. 'Julia' is now in the Miriam Lutcher Stark Library, Univ. of Texas. W. Gérin quotes extensively from it (*Charlotte Brontë*, 121–3), but since she silently emends the punctuation, constantly misreads, invents, and omits, my re-transcription is not redundant: see Appendix.

opening of a little chapel near Evesham, a monument to the labours of
Mr. Bromley, 'that great apostle of Methodism', who features elsewhere in the juvenilia.[1] 'My readers are,' Townshend says in 'Passing
Events', 'I have no doubt aware that on a Sunday evening I generally
make a point of attending the ministry of Mr. Bromley at the Wesleyan
Chapel, Slug Street. . . .' 'Julia' however digresses from the ministry
of Mr. Bromley to a long extract from the Journal of Mr. Barlow about
the persecutions resulting from the visit of a deputation of Methodists
to Mr. Rhodes, to rebuke his sin in trying to deprive them of a meeting-
place. The parody, which is exceedingly amusing, catches the tone of
the *Methodist Magazine*, if not its spirit, in describing this 'awful instance
of God's judgement upon the wicked', and nicely exaggerates the
Methodist style in illustrating, incidentally, the extreme gluttony of
the zealous servants of the Lord. The violence, which in the lives of the
early Methodist preachers was often all too actual, is done with a
Swiftian intensity, and reduced to absurdity to reflect the author's dis-
belief ('more than one pistol was discharged at my head'). God however
levels accounts: Barlow beholds Rhodes 'flung into that very horse-pond
where by his orders I had been nearly murdered'.

After this zestfully parodic excursion into Barlow's Journal, Townshend reverts to the chapel near Evesham: to be opened on the morrow
with four sermons and four collections. He must see to the 'penitential
benches' and the 'hamper of wine, spirits cold meat and bread and
cheese &c' for the Preachers.

Not only does 'Julia' indicate how much the *Methodist Magazine* has
been absorbed and exploit tellingly the ideolect of Methodism, the
Biblical phraseology, but it looks out to its contemporary, *Pickwick
Papers*, and anticipates Moses Barraclough, much as Barraclough anticipates Chadband. The extravagant jargon, the gluttony and drunkenness
of 'Julia' are all recognizably in the Dickensian zone.

Debris from Patrick's Methodist experience is widely strewn.[2]
Names from the Methodist mythology indicate his children's acquaint-
ance with early Methodist history. Selina Hastings, Countess of
Huntingdon, founder of the Calvinist Countess of Huntingdon's

[1] Townshend was originally Charles Wellesley: F. E. Ratchford, *The Brontës' 'Web of Childhood'* (New York, 1941), 122. See also Townshend's self-portrait, 'Passing Events: The History of Angria III' (Apr. 1836), *The Miscellaneous and Unpublished Writings of Charlotte and Patrick Branwell Brontë*, ed. T. J. Wise and J. A. Symington (2 Vols., Oxford, 1936–8), II. 167.
[2] Ellen Nussey tells of Patrick Brontë's story-telling to his children, Wise and Syming-ton, *Brontës: Lives*, etc., I. 114.

Connexion, and her first cousin, the notorious Lawrence Shirley, Earl of Ferrars, hanged unrepentant in 1760 for murdering his steward,[1] have generated a cluster of names: *Shirley*, Huntingdon (in *Tenant of Wildfell Hall*), Henry Hastings (the poet of *Angria*), Surena Ellrington (Charles Townshend's landlord, who occasionally acts the Methodist preacher).[2] Aristocratic sinners, Methodist pretenders, inhabit chapel galleries in the Juvenilia as they might have done at fashionable resorts. Charles Townshend, Surena Ellrington, Lord Macara Lofty, the Marchioness of Wellesley, and Alexander Percy—'Northangerland, the exclusive, the etherial' posing as 'our Dear Brother Ashworth'—attend Mr. Bromley at Slug Street, groaning, subduing their habitual smirks to 'canting gravity', whispering to the ladies.[3] But Charlotte always suggests authentic acquaintance with the jargon she exaggerates with such cheer-fully naïve zest:

Last night . . . coming home at twelve o'clock from Ebenezer Chapel and entering our back-parlour in a very sweet and heavenly frame of mind, I found Mr. Ellrington sitting by the fire with a foot of flesh in his mouth (All flesh is dust and dust bears an affinity to clay and pipes are made of that last commodity).

'We've had a blessed season,' said I as I took a seat opposite and clapped a corresponding cherry-stalk to my lips.

'Who exercised?' asked Surena, with that sparing frugality of language he always observes when smoking.

'Brother Chapman from the Chiselhurst District. Wrought the Lord with him signally, and also with Thomas Wouldsworth, who wrestled in prayer four mortal hours, and at last, as he said, prevailed to that extent that the very pulpit sides gave way before him. The carpenter was had up when he left it, to right matters a bit for Chapman.'

'Found many of the brethren liberty?'

'Several. Before the prayer was over we had eight women and three men dancing the heys in the body of the Chapel. By the time the sermon was con-cluded, the gallery was like Heaven, a play house heaven at least, where the gods dwell. I experienced a sense of special freedom. My windpipe is somewhat hoarse through crying for testimony to our labours. By the by, how is that d----d cold of yours Surena, which always comes on so on a Sunday night and prevents your attending the means of grace?'

'It's very bad still' answered Mr. Ellrington with a whine, at the same time

---

[1] *DNB*. Cf. *Wuthering Heights*, Ch. 17: '. . . I was as reckless as some malefactors show themselves at the foot of the gallows.'

[2] Wise and Symington, *Miscellaneous and Unpublished Writings*, II. 140, 232, 281–3; G. E. Harrison, *The Clue to the Brontës*, 13–14.

[3] 'Passing Events', Wise and Symington, *Miscellaneous and Unpublished Writings*, II. 140–3.

coughing once or twice and twitching the flannel wrapper about his throat: 'How so ever I trust that my time has not been unprofitably spent.'—And he looked towards a Bible which lay open before him.

I assented, glancing however, not at the sacred volume but at a thin meagre book ensconced underneath and peeping modestly from beneath the ample covers with the sober countenance of a Ledger.

'You have been questioning your heart Surena,' said I, 'and balancing accounts between yourself and Satan against the last day.'

'I trust I have,' he answered. 'Self-examination is the most laudable of Christian exercises.' [1]

And Surena's assertion is also the most laudable of Methodist sentiments.

When Patrick reached St. John Rivers in *Jane Eyre* he recalled Henry Martyn: Charlotte had probably worked as much from memory of what her father had told of his benefactor as from the published *Memoir* and *Journals and Letters*.[2] The fracas at Whitsuntide, 1810, when Patrick Brontë, leading his Dewsbury Sunday Schools procession, shouldered out of the way a drunken local bruiser, is transmuted into Helstone's conquest of impudent opposition from the amalgamated rival Dissenting Sunday Schools processing in Royd Lane. *Rule Britannia* drowns a 'most dolorous' canticle, and the 'hostile commander-in-chief', a spirit-merchant, fat and greasy, is shoved into the ditch to drink 'more water in that one afternoon than he had swallowed for a twelvemonth before'.[3] Jabes Branderham, whose sermon in Lockwood's dream is responsible for an unseemly babel in the Chapel of Gimmerden South, is related to Jabez Bunting:[4] he was leading the dedication service at the opening of Woodhouse Grove's New Chapel, 1833, when pandemonium broke out through visitors trying to rush the gallery. Mrs. Harrison suggests that making Heathcliff akin to the Rev. Jabes Branderham on his mother's side was part of Emily's revenge on restrictive Methodism.[5]

---

[1] 'The Return of Zamorna' (Dec. 1836/Jan. 1837), Wise and Symington, *Miscellaneous and Unpublished Writings*, II. 281–2. The narrator is again Charlotte's Townshend. For similar finding of 'liberty' and excited singing and shouting, cf. *Shirley*, Ch. 9.

[2] Cf. *Jane Eyre*, 624. The *Memoir* by John Sargent and the *Journals and Letters*, ed. by Wilberforce (2 Vols., 1837) were very famous. Kingsley read the *Memoir* (see Chapter IV, above) as did Janet Dempster ('Janet's Repentance', Ch. 23).

[3] *Shirley*, Ch. 17.

[4] *Wuthering Heights*, Ch. 3. *Jabez*, a good Northern name (the hero of Mrs. G. Linnaeus Bank's *Manchester Man* (1876) is Jabez Clegg) was sometimes written *Jabes* (e.g. *Lancaster Gazette* (8 Nov. 1845): nineteenth-century Cromwell material). Jabez/Jabes would be indistinguishable in pronunciation, and *Jabes* probably indicates that Emily had only heard of Bunting, never seen his name in print.

[5] Benjamin Gregory, *Side Lights on the Conflicts of Methodism During the Second Quarter of the Nineteenth Century 1827–1852* (1898), 539; G. E. Harrison, *Methodist Good Companions*, 110–13.

Joseph, in *Wuthering Heights*, has the kind of colloquial vigour for
which Grimshaw was famous. His rebuking Catherine and Heathcliff
for 'laiking' with 't'sahnd uh't gospel still i' yer lugs' recalls Grimshaw's reputed habit of praying outside the window if the dying would
not admit him: 'At least he will die with the word of God in his lugs.' [1]
And Joseph's vivid assimilation of the Authorized Version to everyday
speech is akin to Grimshaw's use of 'market language'. 'I' course, he
tells Dame Catherine hah hor fathur's goold runs intuh his pocket, and
her fathur's son gallops dahn t'Broad rood, while he flees afore tuh
oppen t'pikes?' [2]

Grimshaw's son John became a drunken reprobate, oddly a precedent
for Branwell and a model for Hindley Earnshaw. [3] Grimshaw's passion
for his wife, who died in 1739 after only four years of their marriage
(he was her third husband), his insistence on being buried 'in the same
grave with my deceased wife' at Luddenden, make him curiously like
Heathcliff. [4] If Mrs. Harrison is right and Heathcliff's arrival in the
Earnshaw family is related to Grimshaw's habit of fostering children,
Mrs. Leavis's suggestion of an incest theme in an early version of the
novel would become less plausible. [5] William Grimshaw's wife Sarah
was born Lockwood; his son John's widow married a Mr. Lockwood. [6]

Tabby's stories and Patrick's tales, reinforced perhaps by stories
Branwell brought home from Luddenden-foot railway station below
the Ewood house where John Grimshaw had lived, and near Luddenden
church where the Grimshaws were buried: we are close to the kind of
oral tradition Charlotte described:

My sister's disposition was not naturally gregarious; circumstances favoured and
fostered her tendency to seclusion; except to go to church or take a walk on the
hills, she rarely crossed the threshold of home. Though her feeling for the
people round was benevolent, intercourse with them she never sought; nor,
with very few exceptions, ever experienced. And yet she knew them: knew their
ways, their language, their family histories; she could hear of them with in-

[1] *Wuthering Heights*, Ch. 3; Lock and Dixon, *A Man of Sorrow*, 214.

[2] Frank Baker, *William Grimshaw*, 119–21; *Wuthering Heights*, Ch. 10.

[3] Lock and Dixon, *A Man of Sorrow*, 215.

[4] Frank Baker, op. cit., 39–40; Lock and Dixon, *A Man of Sorrow*, 215, 218; W. Gérin, *Charlotte Brontë*, 38–9.

[5] G. E. Harrison, *Clue to the Brontës*, 164–5; Grimshaw, Letter, dated 20 Aug. 1747, *Arminian Magazine* (1778), 475, about two foster children; 'A Fresh Approach to "Wuthering Heights"', F. R. and Q. D. Leavis, *Lectures in America* (paperback edn., 1969), 89–90.

[6] Frank Baker, op. cit., 34; G. E. Harrison, *Haworth Parsonage: A Study of Wesley and the Brontës*, 24.

terest, and talk of them with detail, minute, graphic, and accurate; but *with* them, she rarely exchanged a word.[1]

If being a Brontë in Haworth rectory meant knowing about Grimshaw it also meant contact with Haworth Dissent. Recalcitrant Church trustees financed a Strict Baptist chapel in Bridgehouse Lane in 1824, and like Barraclough in *Shirley* its first pastor was a Moses.[2] Patrick Brontë conducted a pamphlet war with him on Baptism.[3] Michael Hartley, weaver, a 'frantic Antinomian in religion, and a mad leveller in politics', a 'very Ezekiel or Daniel for visions', who tries to assassinate mill-owner Robert Moore while shouting Biblical slogans about the death of the wicked, is not too esoteric by Haworth standards: at 6 p.m. on 22 June 1830, when Patrick Brontë was in bed with inflammation of the lungs, an old man ('some fanatical enthusiast' Charlotte labelled him) called at the Parsonage. Tabby brought in the message: 'He desires me to say that the bridegroom is coming, and that we must prepare to meet him; that the cords are about to be loosed, and the golden bowl broken; the pitcher broken at the fountain.' Patrick Brontë lived.[4]

When Charlotte became a pupil in 1832 at Miss Wooler's academy, Roe Head, she widened her acquaintance with Methodism through her friends Ellen Nussey and Mary Taylor. The Nusseys were members of John Nelson's chapel at Birstall. The Taylors of the Red House, Gomersal, had built a Kilhamite Chapel opposite their home and attended the Parish Church in the morning and the chapel in the evening.[5] Joseph Taylor, Mary Taylor's grandfather, had been a friend of Wesley, but his son Joshua joined the New Connexion: he supported it with notes issued by his own bank.[6] Joshua Taylor's radical Methodism was new to Charlotte, as was, perhaps, the actual experience of Kilhamite enthusiasm in worship. The proximity in *Shirley* of Briar Chapel to the Yorkes' residence Briarmains derives from Charlotte's visits to Gomersal. Those visits however were not the only occasions

---

[1] Currer Bell, Preface, *Wuthering Heights and Agnes Grey*, by Ellis and Acton Bell (new and revised edn., 1850), xxi.

[2] Moses Saunders: Lock and Dixon, *A Man of Sorrow*, 266–7, 353.

[3] *A Brief Treatise on the Best Time and Mode of Baptism—Chiefly in Answer to a tract of Peter Pontifex, alias the Rev. M. S——, Baptist Minister* (1836); Lock and Dixon, *A Man of Sorrow*, 353 ff.

[4] Mrs. Gaskell, *Life*, I. 96–7; Lock and Dixon, *A Man of Sorrow*, 270–1; *Shirley*, Chs. 1, 30, 37.

[5] G. E. Harrison, *The Clue to the Brontës*, 81–2.

[6] *Journal of John Wesley*, Standard edn., ed. N. Curnock (8 Vols., 1909–16), VII. 521–2; W. B. Hoult, 'The Red House Gomersal', *Methodist Magazine*, 162 (1939), 158–62.

when she heard singing 'such as a very Quaker might feel himself moved
by the Spirit to dance to': she and Ellen Nussey, on holiday at Bridling-
ton in 1839, had lodgings opposite a Ranters' chapel, and Charlotte's
initial impulse was to go and see 'the violent excitement within its
walls'.[1] Nevertheless the Taylor ambiance is directly responsible for
much in *Shirley*. Its plot features Luddism in their region.[2] Canon
W. M. Heald recognized himself as Hall and 'the Yorke Family' as the
Taylors, and Mary Taylor found herself picturing clearly the Red House
as she read the novel.[3] But though Yorke has been claimed by Mrs.
Harrison as 'an excellent sketch of a Yorkshire Methodist', his exhortation in Chapter 30 to Robert Moore ('Confess, lad: smooth nought
down: be candid as a convicted, justified, sanctified methody at an
experience-meeting. Make yourself wicked as Beelzebub: it will ease
your mind') sounds as distant from an insider's comment, carries as
much outsider's irony, as the extravagant jargon of the *poseurs* of the
Juvenilia.[4] Mrs. Yorke's snowy-Sunday reading for the children (Ch. 34)
is 'John Wesley's Sermons: John Wesley, being a Reformer and an
Agitator, had a place both in her own and her husband's favour'—but
no place as founder of the sect to which, in fact, they do not belong.
Mr. Yorke is radically disposed, but he is no Barraclough.

There is significant variation in the way Emily and Charlotte present
Methodism. Charlotte has an eye for detail. Her use of hymns in *Shirley*
is entirely straightforward: she does not manipulate them like George
Eliot in *Adam Bede*. The congregation at Briar Chapel (Ch. 9) 'passed
jauntily from hymn to hymn and from tune to tune with an ease and
buoyancy all their own', but never inappropriately. Charlotte knows
her *Collection of Hymns, for the Use of the People Called Methodists*. The
first extract ('Oh! Who can explain') is from the hymn-book's section 'For
Believers Fighting'; then 'finding liberty' is celebrated by stanzas from
'Wesley's Birthday Hymn' ('What a mercy is this') and from 'Meet and
right it is to praise; /God the giver of all grace' ('Sleeping on the brink of
sin'), both from the section 'For Believers Rejoicing'.[5] The quotations
are on the whole accurate, but the stanzas of 'Oh, who can explain' are
written as 8 lines of 5 syllables each, whereas in the *Collection* they are

[1] Wise and Symington, *Brontës: Lives*, etc., I. 190.
[2] See Asa Briggs, 'Private and Social Themes in Shirley', *BST* 13 (1958), 203–19.
[3] Wise and Symington, op. cit., III. 64.
[4] G. E. Harrison, *Haworth Parsonage*, 20; cf. id., *The Clue to the Brontës*, 183.
[5] Respectively: stanzas 4 and 5 of Hymn No. 265; 6, 7, 8, 9 of No. 221; half of stanza
3 and all of stanza 4 (but quoted in two sections) of No. 228, in the 1780 *Collection*.

printed in 4 lines of 10 syllables each, and Charlotte begins halfway through an eight-line stanza in her quotation from 'Meet and right it is to praise', and quotes the stanza after 'Sleeping on the brink of sin' in two sections, clearly believing the hymn's stanzas to have four lines each. The implication is that she had the words by heart, but, easily done when working from memory, got wrong the stanza shapes.

On the other hand Emily is indifferent to detail, and the indifference corresponds to the fact that she had passed beyond the realm of evangelicalism while Charlotte was still thinking along lines laid down by it. *Jane Eyre* is as much a universalist tract, with Helen Burns as its exemplar of virtue, as Brocklehurst's *Child's Guide*, with its 'account of the awfully sudden death of Martha G———', is a Calvinist tract: they share the same basic shape and assumptions. In *Wuthering Heights* Emily stepped right outside that zone. And small details like distinguishing Church from Chapel and defining Joseph's religion are of no concern to her.

Haworth Church was a Chapel-of-Ease in Bradford Parish until August 1864, and that is perhaps an excuse for *Chapel* in *Wuthering Heights* to signify, like *Kirk*, the Church of England building.[1] In Chapter 3 Joseph and Lockwood go to the 'house': presumably the Methodist preaching-house, a word Wesley and the Methodists used to denote a building distinct from the Church.[2] But this 'house' is equated with the 'chapel', which 'now' has no 'Pastor' since the clergyman's stipend is too small and the manse is too dilapidated i.e. it is very like a Church of England. And the reference to the penny-pinching flock who will not increase the clergyman's stipend is a clear allusion to Patrick Brontë and St. Michael's, Haworth. In Chapter 30 Zillah tells Lockwood that 'Joseph and I generally go to chapel on Sundays' and Mrs. Dean explains that 'the kirk, you know, has no minister now . . . and they call the Methodists' or Baptists' place, I can't say which it is, at Gimmerton, a chapel'. That clarifies one problem: the 'chapel' with no minister does equal the Kirk i.e. the Church of England, so Branderham was preaching in the Church like the early Methodists at Haworth. But taken retrospectively Nellie's point is confusing, because *chapel* has often been used to denote *Church* through the novel, and now it suddenly means a Methodist or Baptist place of worship. And that refusal to specify which—Methodist or Baptist—is characteristic: Emily is obviously not bothered about the details of Joseph's religious allegiances. She even

[1] Lock and Dixon, *A Man of Sorrow*, 208 ff., 225, 531.
[2] e.g. 'Birstall house' and 'Dewsbury house', *Wesley's Journal*, ed. Curnock, VII. 522 (26 July, 1789), and 523 (1 Aug. 1789).

has him join with the Curate in reprimanding Earnshaw's carelessness over Heathcliff and Catherine's attending *church* (Ch. 6).

Certainly, however, it is difficult to construe predestinarian Joseph as a 'first-generation Methodist', as Kathleen Tillotson does.[1] 'Thank Hivin for all! All warks togither for gooid tuh them as is chozzen, and piked aht froo' th' rubbidge!' (Ch. 9) suggests something less mild than Arminianism. But Emily, to whom such subtleties are of slight concern, gives us little help: Nellie Dean's suggestion that Joseph might be a Baptist after all is the nearest we get to what might fit the theological statements he makes. And Emily's imprecision in this area is all the more marked because the genealogical structure, the multiple narrative and the time scheme are so precisely and minutely contrived.

But Emily could not entirely evade the effects of her upbringing. Methodism serves for her, as for Charlotte, two prominent functions. It is, firstly, a referent for passion. Extremes of feeling, behaviour, and religious enthusiasm can be defined by reference to Methodism. The grieving Heathcliff would lock himself in his room:

There he has continued, praying like a methodist—only the deity he implored is senseless dust and ashes; and God, when addressed, was curiously confounded with his own black father! After concluding these precious orisons—and they lasted generally till he grew hoarse, and his voice was strangled in his throat— he would be off again; always straight down to the Grange![2]

Lucy Snowe reacts tolerantly to a 'planted' Roman Catholic tract:

The little book amused, and did not painfully displease me. It was a canting, sentimental, shallow little book, yet something about it cheered my gloom and made me smile; I was amused with the gambols of this unlicked wolf-cub muffled in the fleece, and mimicking the bleat of a guileless lamb. Portions of it reminded me of certain Wesleyan Methodist tracts I had once read when a child; they were flavoured with about the same seasoning of excitation to fanaticism.[3]

Methodism also, one would suggest with Mrs. Harrison, provided for the Brontës a rhetoric of passion.[4] Declarations of love are made in the language of the Authorized Version, of hymns:

If all else perished, and *he* remained, I should still continue to be; and if all else remained, and he were annihilated, the universe would turn to a mighty stranger. I should not seem a part of it. My love for Linton is like the foliage in

[1] *Novels of the Eighteen-Forties*, 97.    [2] *Wuthering Heights*, Ch. 17.
[3] *Villette*, Ch. 36.                        [4] *The Clue to the Brontës*, 167 ff.

the woods. Time will change it, I'm well aware, as winter changes the trees. My love for Heathcliff resembles the eternal rocks beneath—a source of little visible delight, but necessary. Nelly, I *am* Heathcliff. . . .[1]

Catherine's language chimes in with Jane Eyre's:

I hold myself supremely blest—blest beyond what language can express; because I am my husband's life as he is mine. No woman was ever nearer to her mate than I am: ever more absolutely bone of his bone, and flesh of his flesh. . . .[2]

The language of Agnes Grey's secret love poems is similar:

> Oh, they have robbed me of the hope
> My spirit held so dear;
> They will not let me hear that voice
> My soul delights to hear.
>
> They will not let me see that face
> I so delight to see;
> And they have taken all thy smiles,
> And all thy love from me.
>
> Well, let them seize on all they can;—
> One treasure still is mine,—
> A heart that loves to think on thee,
> And feels the worth of thine.[3]

The world was taken aback by the frankness of the passion. Mrs. Gaskell took pains to excuse 'the existence of coarseness here and there' in Charlotte's works, 'otherwise so entirely noble'.[4] Evangelicals drew back their skirts from *Jane Eyre*. George Henry Lewes hailed Charlotte as a fellow-writer of 'naughty books'.[5] The Brontës' novels, though, are empty of real physicality; their dominant feeling is yearning for fulfilment, based on the authoresses' profound sexual innocence. But by appropriating the rhetoric of Methodism's love of God, exploiting the language of Divine love for earthly love, they deceived the

---

[1] *Wuthering Heights*, Ch. 9

[2] *Jane Eyre*, Vol. III, Ch. 12. A Methodist convert 'thus describes the manner in which he was "born of God. . . . Since that time the whole bent of my will hath been towards him day and night, even in my dreams. I know that I dwell in Christ and Christ in me; I am bone of his bone, and flesh of his flesh." This looks like Moravian language. . . .' R. Southey, *The Life of Wesley*, ed. M. H. Fitzgerald (2 Vols., 1925), I. 158–9. Given the Brontës' admiration for Southey and the correspondence with him, it is not unlikely that they were familiar with this and other similar passages in *The Life of Wesley*.

[3] *Agnes Grey*, Ch. 17.

[4] *Life*, II. 281.

[5] W. Gérin, *Charlotte Brontë*, 397, 430.

world. Harriet Martineau complained: 'I do not like the love, either
the kind or the degree of it. . . .'[1] The kind and the degree are, in
fact, borrowed from Methodism. 'Knowing nothing of earthly passion,
but being a connoisseur of the divine, she [Emily] must needs use the
thing she did know for the description of the love of which she was
ignorant.'[2] Shirley and Caroline in discussing love (again in Biblical
terms) provided the reply to a misunderstanding contemporary world:
'. . . in their dense ignorance they blaspheme living fire, seraph-
brought from a divine altar.' 'They confound it with sparks mounting
from Tophet!'[3]

A question like Edmund Gosse's of Hardy ('What has Providence
done to Mr. Hardy that he should rise up in the arable land of Wessex
and shake his fist at his Creator?')[4] is often asked of the Brontës. How
could three spinsters, brought up in an austere rectory in bleak
Haworth, produce work like this?[5] The Methodist matrix, while not
perhaps *the* clue, is certainly one clue.

---

[1] Quoted by Mrs. Leavis, Intro. to Penguin edn. of *Jane Eyre* (1966), 23.
[2] G. E. Harrison, *The Clue to the Brontës*, 168.
[3] *Shirley*, Ch. 17.
[4] Epigraph to Lois Deacon and Terry Coleman, *Providence and Mr. Hardy* (1966).
[5] Only Charlotte married, and that was on 29 June 1854, i.e. with the major works all
written and, except for *The Professor* (1857), published.

# VI. MRS. GASKELL

'Young ladies don't understand political economy, you know'.
Mr. Brooke, *Middlemarch*.

THE Brontës knew Methodism in its embryonic phase as a Dissenting movement; Mrs. Gaskell on the other hand was descended from old Presbyterian, now Unitarian, stock. Her family was securely ensconced in the complex web of relationships that made up the Unitarian cousinhood. Her mother, Mrs. Elizabeth Stevenson, née Holland, was connected with many important Unitarian families: Wedgwoods, Darwins, Turners.[1] Something of the, as it were, incestuous complexity of Unitarian relationships can be glimpsed in her double relatedness to William Turner (1761–1859), minister of Newcastle-upon-Tyne's Hanover Square Unitarian congregation.[2] Turner's first wife, Mary Holland, daughter of Thomas Holland of Manchester, was a cousin of Mrs. Stevenson; his second wife was the daughter of the Rev. William Willett of Newcastle-under-Lyme, a sister of Dr. Peter Holland's first wife Mary, and niece of Josiah Wedgwood, and this Mary Holland was Elizabeth Stevenson's aunt by marriage.[3]

William Stevenson (1772–1859), Elizabeth's father, was educated at Daventry and Northampton Academies and became minister of Dob Lane Unitarian chapel, Failsworth, near Manchester. He resigned, aged 25, in 1797, to become experimental farmer, editor of the *Scots Magazine*, *Edinburgh Review* contributor, private tutor, and finally keeper of the Treasury Records. Made motherless at 13 months, Elizabeth was cared for during the next twelve or thirteen years by her Unitarian aunt at Knutsford, Mrs. Hannah Lumb (née Holland). Brook Street Unitarian Chapel, Knutsford, built after the Toleration Act of 1689, where Matthew Henry had often preached, and Elizabeth Stevenson had taught in the Sunday School, and in whose graveyard William and Mrs. Gaskell are buried, gets into *Ruth* (Mrs. Gaskell's

---

[1] A. B. Hopkins, *Elizabeth Gaskell: Her Life and Work* (1952), 19.

[2] The inter-relatedness of Unitarians was very like that of Quakers: see E. Isichei, *Victorian Quakers*, 12, 66–7, 280–1.

[3] Mrs. Ellis H. Chadwick, *Mrs. Gaskell: Haunts, Homes and Stories* (New edn., 1913), 100–1.

'Newcastle story') as Thurstan Benson's chapel in the country-town of Eccleston: [1]

It stood on the outskirts of the town, almost in the fields. It was built about the same time of Matthew and Philip Henry, when the Dissenters were afraid of attracting attention or observation, and hid their places of worship in obscure and out-of-the-way parts of the towns in which they were built. Accordingly, it often happened, as in the present case, that the buildings immediately surrounding, as well as the chapels themselves, looked as if they carried you back to a period a hundred and fifty years ago. The chapel had a picturesque and old-world look, for luckily the congregation had been too poor to rebuild it, or new-face it, in George the Third's time. The staircases which led to the galleries were outside, at each end of the building, and the irregular roof and worn stone steps looked grey and stained by time and weather.

Mrs. Gaskell strikes the elegiac note characteristic of her accounts of the Dissent she approves of. She dwells on the wych-elm, lilac bushes, white rose-tree, and laburnums, 'all old and gnarled enough', in the chapel yard, on the ivy that covers the 'heavy-leaded, diamond-shaped panes' and makes the interior a 'green gloom, not without its solemnity', and on the birds, dwelling and singing in the ivy. Benson's chapel is in that austere tradition celebrated in Lawrence's 'Hymns in a Man's Life':

The interior of the building was plain and simple as plain and simple could be. When it was fitted up, oak-timber was much cheaper than it is now, so the woodwork was all of that description; but roughly hewed, for the early builders had not much wealth to spare. The walls were whitewashed, and were recipients of the shadows of the beauty without; on their 'white plains' the tracery of the ivy might be seen, now still, now stirred by the sudden flight of some little bird. [2]

Benson's name, Thurstan, was a Holland family name: Edward Thurstan Holland (1836–84), son of Mrs. Gaskell's cousin, Edward Holland, became Marianne Gaskell's husband. [3]

In the autumn after her father's death in March 1829, Mrs. Gaskell,

---

[1] A. B. Hopkins, op. cit., 15–29; Henry Green, *Knutsford, Its Traditions and History: With Reminiscences, Anecdotes, and Notices of the Neighbourhood* (1859), 62–4; C. S. Sargisson, 'Mrs. Gaskell's Early Surroundings and their Influence on her Writings', *Bookman*, 38 (Sept. 1910), 250; G. A. Payne, *An Ancient Chapel: Brook Street Chapel, Knutsford, with Allostock Chapel, Nr. Knutsford* (Banbury, 1934), 1, 33, 53; Alderman Thomas Beswick, 'Local Associations with Mrs. Gaskell', *Knutsford and Mrs. Gaskell* (Knutsford Gaskell Committee, 1960), 19.

[2] *Ruth*, Ch. 14.

[3] Mrs. Chadwick, op. cit., 115. Chapple and Pollard, *Letters of Mrs. Gaskell*, Biographical Index, 993; see Letter No. 553, pp. 736–7: Marianne's engagement to 'Thurstan'.

probably at the suggestion of her cousin Sir Henry Holland, went to stay with William Turner in Newcastle. Turner had been Holland's tutor, 1799–1803. His grandfather, John Turner, was minister at Knutsford, 1735–7. His father, William Turner, a friend of Joseph Priestley, had been first Unitarian minister at Allostock, near Knutsford, 1737–46, and in 1758 had married Mary Holland, sister of John Holland, supply-minister at Allostock, 1747–51. Turner acted as Elizabeth's guardian for two years.[1]

A daughter of Turner had married the Rev. John Gooch Robberds, minister of Cross Street Unitarian Chapel, Manchester, and on a visit to Mr. and Mrs. Robberds Elizabeth met the assistant minister, William Gaskell, whom she married at Knutsford, 30 August 1832.[2]

William Stevenson, William Turner, William Gaskell: they represent the cultured Dissent that helped define Unitarianism as the antithesis, on the whole, of nineteenth-century Methodism. Turner and Gaskell were both educated at Warrington Dissenting Academy and Glasgow University. Gaskell's father had also been at Warrington, and was taught by Priestley. Turner was a founder member of Newcastle's Literary and Philosophical Society (1793), Natural History Society (1824), Bible Society (1811), and sponsored its Mechanics' Society (1824). He campaigned against the Test and Corporation Acts, Capital Punishment, slavery; fought for prison reform; and was strenuous in good works and in education.[3] In 1838 two Bishops, Maltby of Durham and Stanley of Norwich, subscribed to a volume of his sermons.[4] Turner is supposed to have provided the basis for the kindly Thurstan Benson.[5]

William Gaskell was in Turner's learned mould: Professor of English History and Literature at Manchester's New College (1846–53),

---

[1] Mrs. Chadwick, op. cit., 99–100; G. A. Payne, *An Ancient Chapel*, 66–7.

[2] A. Cobden Smith, 'Mrs. Gaskell and Lower Mosley Street', *Sunday School Quarterly*, 2 (Jan. 1911), 157.

[3] *DNB*; George Harris, *The Christian Character, The Union of Knowledge and Benevolence, Piety and Virtue, As Illustrated in the Life and Labours of the late Rev. William Turner: A Discourse* . . . (Newcastle, 1859). *Declaration of the Objects of the Newcastle Upon Tyne Society for Promoting the Gradual Abolition of Slavery throughout the British Dominions* (Newcastle, 1823) lists Turner as a committee member. See also William Turner, 'Unitarianism in England', in J. R. Beard (ed.), *Unitarianism Exhibited in its Actual Condition*, (1846), 88–156.

[4] *DNB*, 'William Turner'; 'Edward Maltby (1770–1859)'. *Letters to the Right Reverend The Lord Bishop of Durham, Occasioned by the correspondence lately published in the newspapers and periodicals, relative to His Lordship's Subscription to a Volume of Sermons by the Rev. W. Turner, Newcastle-upon-Tyne* (1838).

[5] e.g., A. S. Whitfield, *Mrs. Gaskell: Her Life and Works* (1929), 10–11.

lecturer in English Literature at the Working Men's College (founded 1858) and later at Owens College, a constant speaker at Mechanics' Institutes, and a private tutor. He worked for sanitary improvements as well as popular education. His learned ministry attracted a large and influential congregation. His editorship of the *Unitarian Herald* lasted for its whole career (1861–75), he served on the Unitarian Home Missionary Board, wrote hymns, and translated sacred verse from German.[1]

The tone of this provincial and Dissenting culture could clearly bear comparison with the 'tone of the centre' Arnold was preoccupied with. Susanna and Catherine Winkworth were both William Gaskell's pupils, and Susanna wrote:

It may seem strange that among the names of those to whom we thus looked up for intellectual nourishment or guidance, none should occur of members of the Church of England. But the fact is, that although, as a Church of England family, the larger half of our acquaintance naturally were of the same persuasion, I cannot recall one distinctly intellectual person among them, either of the laity or clergy. Our Church friends were, many of them, excellent people, or perhaps on the average superior to the *average* of our orthodox Dissenting friends in education and refinement; but there was not one person of commanding intellect among them. And had there been one preacher of any remarkable power of thought in Manchester or its neighbourhood, I, at all events, should have gone any distance to hear him, but there was none. The Unitarians in Manchester were, as a body, far away superior to any other in intellect, culture, and refinement of manners, and certainly did not come behind any other in active philanthropy and earnest efforts for the social improvement of those around them. Most of the German merchants who were among our most intelligent and agreeable acquaintances, belonged either to Mr. Gaskell's or Mr. Tayler's congregation; not that they were all of them Unitarians in opinion, but because they found the preaching there better and more earnest, and the spirit more charitable than in other places of worship.[2]

---

[1] A. B. Hopkins, op. cit., 45–6; John Evans, *Lancashire Authors and Orators* (1850), 96–101; *Cross Street Chapel, Manchester: Commemoration of the Fifty Years' Ministry of the Rev. William Gaskell, M.A. Sermon preached by him August 4th; and Report of Proceedings at the Soirée Held in the Town Hall, October 15th, 1878; With the lists of subscribers to the Commemoration Fund* (Manchester, [1878]); Rev. S. Alfred Steinthal, *Funeral Sermon on the Late William Gaskell . . . June 15th, 1884* [Manchester, 1884]; 'The Late Rev. William Gaskell', *Manchester Guardian* (Thursday 12 June 1884). For Cross Street, see Benjamin Nightingale, *Lancashire Nonconformity* (6 Vols., Manchester, 1891–3), V. 81–107; and for both Turner's Newcastle Church and Cross Street, see George Eyre Evans, *Vestiges of Protestant Dissent* (Liverpool, 1897), 165–7, 182–3.

[2] *Memorials of Two Sisters: Susanna and Catherine Winkworth*, ed. by their niece Margaret J. Shaen (1908), 25–6; A. B. Hopkins, op. cit., 47–8.

Mrs. Gaskell shared that charity: assisted no doubt by her period at the Misses Byerly's school at Stratford. Although their Unitarian connections were impeccable (they were great-nieces of Sir Josiah Wedgwood and had taught the exiled Joseph Priestley's granddaughters) the Misses Byerly were nonetheless Anglicans, and five years' attendance at Holy Trinity, Stratford, reinforced Mrs. Gaskell's native Unitarian tolerance. She came to appreciate Gothic architecture, liturgies, and attended Anglican churches during Continental holidays when no Unitarian worship was available.[1]

But the chapel and its sanctions were dominant in Mrs. Gaskell's life. She was active in Cross Street's Sunday and Day Schools conducted in Lower Mosley Street, and even wrote articles for the *Sunday School Penny Magazine* edited by the Schools' director, Travers Madge.[2] And chapel opinion mattered: when two members burnt copies of *Ruth*, and a third forbade his wife to read it, Mrs. Gaskell, wife of the (still) assistant minister, felt 'improper' sitting beside them in chapel.[3] She told Anne Robson that her own children were not allowed to read *Ruth* on their own: and 'I can't tell you how much I need strength. . . . I had a terrible fit of crying all Saty night at the unkind things people were saying. . . .'[4]

Moral pressures like this might have come from any chapel. But Cross Street offered peculiar resistances to what Mrs. Gaskell was doing in her fiction. For Cross Street was where the bourgeoisie of Manchester worshipped God. Fifteen M.P.s and seven mayors had connections with the chapel, 'besides many borough and county magistrates'.[5] The German merchants and businessmen of the city, the Meyers, Schunks, and Schwabes, belonged to it.[6] The Trustees and members were the millocracy, the benefactors, the leaders, of Manchester society: corn millers, silk manufacturers, calico printers, patent-reed makers, engineers; bankers and barristers; founders of

[1] A. B. Hopkins, op. cit., 34–6; Elizabeth Haldane, *Mrs. Gaskell and Her Friends* (1930), 21–2.

[2] A. B. Hopkins, op. cit., 96–7, 302; Brooke Herford, *Travers Madge: A Memoir* (1867), e.g. 63–5; A. C. Smith, 'Mrs. Gaskell and Lower Mosley Street', *Sunday School Quarterly*, 2 (1911), 156–61; for Madge see also *Letters*, ed. Chapple and Pollard, No. 500, p. 677.

[3] *Letters*, No. 150, p. 223. Gaskell became senior minister in 1854 (A. B. Hopkins, op. cit., 45); *Ruth* was published 1853.

[4] *Letters*, No. 148, p. 221.

[5] Richard Wade, *The Rise of Non-conformity in Manchester, With a Brief Sketch of The History of Cross Street Chapel* (Manchester, 1880), 65.

[6] R. Wade, op. cit., 62; *Letters*, ed. Chapple and Pollard, No. 143, p. 215, and No. 94, pp. 149–51.

hospitals, libraries, educational institutes, charitable funds, missions to the poor.[1] The cousinhood extending outwards from the chapel was powerful indeed. The Potter family, for example, had long supplied Trustees for Cross Street. James Potter, son of John Potter, a Trustee, became one in turn (1782). His son Edmund became M.P. for Carlisle, and was Beatrix Potter's grandfather.[2] Edmund's younger brother Sidney, the calico printer, became a Trustee in 1840, and was a municipal councillor, 1844–50.[3] Thomas Potter, Manchester's first mayor, was a Trustee. His son, Sir John Potter, was three times the city's mayor; and his brother Thomas Bayley Potter—who remained a chapel member—became the M.P. for Rochdale. (Beatrice Webb's paternal grandfather, Richard Potter, brother of Thomas Potter, became M.P. for Wigan, 1832. Another of Richard's granddaughters, Mary Macaulay, daughter of Charles Zachary Macaulay, became Mrs. Charles Booth.)[4] And when Mrs. Gaskell wanted to present a copy of *Mary Barton* to the Manchester Free Library in 1852, she had to seek permission from Sir John Potter, its promoter. She feared Sir John's distaste: the distaste of the mill-owning class ('Of course I cannot be unaware of the opinions which you and your brother have so frequently & openly expressed with regard to *Mary Barton* . . .'). Neither did she want Sir John to think that she had callously exploited the murder of Thomas Ashton by unionists in 1831 as 'a mere subject for a story'. As it happened, the last person to speak to Thomas Ashton had been his sister Mary who, in 1847, married Thomas Bayley Potter. When she came to the murder in *Mary Barton* Mrs. Potter fainted away. The assistant minister's wife, the Potters suspected, had deliberately revived painful memories.[5]

And Mrs. Gaskell might well be wary: for Cross Street, she would know, did not take kindly to interfering criticisms of the free-market forces of political economy. Even apologists for Unitarian progressivism cannot mask the sect's illiberality in this respect: John Fielden, Unitarian and mill-owning advocate of the Factory Hours reforms, and

[1] R. Wade, op. cit., 60–6; R. V. Holt *The Unitarian Contribution to Social Progress in England* (1938), 21–2.

[2] Margaret Lane, *The Tale of Beatrix Potter* (revised edn., 1968), 14–34; *The Journal of Beatrix Potter: from 1881 to 1897*, transcribed by Leslie Linder (1966), 9, cf. 90–1.

[3] R. Wade, op. cit., 54–61; Sir Thomas Baker, *Memorials of a Dissenting Chapel* (1884), 105–6.

[4] Beatrice Webb, *My Apprenticeship* (1926), 2 and 217–18 (and footnotes); see also, Georgina Meinertzhagen, *From Ploughshare to Parliament: A Short Memoir of the Potters of Tadcaster* (1908).

[5] *Letters*, ed. Chapple and Pollard, No. 130, pp. 195–6; also footnote 1, p. 196.

Mrs. Gaskell were very isolated in their denomination. Many people in Cross Street Chapel and the Unitarian cousinhood of Cheshire and Lancashire agreed with the Macclesfield silk manufacturer who visited the Howitts (1854), 'whose workpeople are emphatically *hands*, and who thinks "Mary Barton" a dangerous, bad book'.[1] Manchester's Unitarian M.P.s, Mark Philips and John Potter, uncompromisingly opposed factory legislation in the Commons; the Unitarian *Inquirer* backed them up. Sir John Potter even thought legislation on behalf of chimney-sweeps undesirable. R. H. Greg (elected M.P. for Manchester against his will in 1838: he resigned 1841) wrote to the *Manchester Guardian* in opposition. He had already told the Children's Employment Commission that children were better able to study at evening classes than at day-school: they were less 'fatigued' after a day's work than after a holiday, and always wanted to go to bed earlier on Sundays, deprived of an energizing day in the mill.[2]

Robert Hyde Greg (1795–1875), older brother of Samuel (1804–76) and William Rathbone Greg (1809–81), was typical of the enlightened Unitarian employer who saw the need for 'model' conditions for his workers but who could still talk stupidly like that about child labour. The Gregs' father, Samuel, had been a mill-owner, and the sons made variously successful attempts at manufacturing. Their mother, Hannah Lightbody of Liverpool, was descended from Philip Henry (1631–96), father of Matthew Henry the Biblical commentator. W. R. Greg married Lucy Henry of Cross Street in 1835 (her grandfather and father were both buried at the chapel). Robert and Samuel both remained Unitarians.[3] Samuel Greg and his wife were close friends of Mrs. Gaskell, W. R. Greg was 'my old friend', and the Robert Gregs were people to have Sunday dinner with.[4] And it is important to note that some of Mrs. Gaskell's fiercest opposition came precisely from this bourgeois Dissenting quarter. The *British Quarterly Review* and W. R. Greg complained with one voice about the injustices and inaccuracies of *Mary Barton*: masters can be kind; the work is not arduous; workers are improvident and have families; they should rather be chaste, save money, and become capitalists in turn; salvation lies in self-help and

[1] Mary Howitt, *An Autobiography*, ed. Margaret Howitt (2 Vols., 1889), II. 106.

[2] R. V. Holt, op. cit., 186–95; Asa Briggs, *Victorian Cities*, 102–3; Shena D. Simon, *A Century of City Government: Manchester 1838–1938* (1938), 28–9.

[3] *DNB*, 'R. H. Greg'; 'S. Greg'; 'W. R. Greg'; 'William Henry (1774–1836)'; 'Thomas Henry (1734–1816)'.

[4] *Letters*, ed. Chapple and Pollard, Nos. 21, 42, 72a, 85, 104, 114, 136, 143, 167b, 186, 471.

*laissez-faire*—not in unions, charters, or enfranchisement.[1] It was the voice of Bounderby: these were the 'fictions' of Coketown, the manufacturers' standard rhetoric that Dickens and Morley rightly mauled in *Household Words* and *Hard Times*.[2]

Cazamian praised the tender female heart of Mrs. Gaskell for cracking open the hard 'Puritanisme' (as he has it) of the Northern Manufacturers.[3] And there is something in that opposition of female 'sentimentalité' and male hardness: it is strongly present in the regeneration of the hard, unpitying Dissenting businessman, Bradshaw, who will turn the blind eye to bribery so that his Liberal candidate may succeed in ousting the rival Tory, but who will not at first forgive Ruth her trespass. But in *Ruth*, as in *Mary Barton*, the protest is more than a woman's protest against a man's world: with exceptional courage Mrs. Gaskell is prepared to suggest that all is not well with the code of the Liberal-bourgeois-Dissenting millocracy. And the accused were not a distant and alien body of people: *Mary Barton* hurt friends.

W. R. Greg's review is filled with personal indignation. Masters suffer too:

It was only the more necessary to inform them [the workers] (as numerous stoppages of wealthy firms might indeed readily bring home to their conviction) that their masters *do* suffer, and suffer most painfully, from those reverses and stagnation of trade which they imagine to fall solely on themselves; to picture, however cursorily, the position of those employers who, on such occasions, have seen the accumulations of years of patient and honest industry suddenly swept away, and who, at an advanced period of life, have had to set to work to reconstruct the shattered fabric of their fortunes—and of those who, compromised more deeply still, find the prospects of their children blighted, their objects defeated, and their occupations gone.

And in a footnote he develops the point. Masters may not, in distress, be reduced to cellar-dwelling:

There is this approach, however, to a compensation in the case of the operative, that his trials, though more bitter and overwhelming for the time, are generally

---

[1] *BQR* 9 (1849), 117–36; [W. R. Greg], *Edinburgh Review*, 89 (1849), 402–35.

[2] *Hard Times*, Bk. II, Chs. 1, 2, 6, 8; 'Ground in the Mill', *HW* 9 (22 Apr. 1854), 224–7; 'Fencing with Humanity', *HW* 11 (14 Apr. 1855), 241–4; 'Death's Cyphering Book', *HW* 11 (12 May, 1855), 337–41. For views similar to Greg's, see B. Love, *The Handbook of Manchester* (Manchester, 1842), 99–102; and for a counter, Léon Faucher, *Manchester in 1844*, 109: 'We require from the work-people virtues which their masters themselves do not exhibit. We require that the lower classes should economise out of their necessities, at a time when the superior classes do not know how to economise out of their superfluity.'

[3] Louis Cazamian, *Le Roman social en Angleterre (1830–1850)* (Paris, 1903), 380–2.

shorter. The enterprising manufacturer, who loses in one desolating season the wealth accumulated by the patient and anxious labour of many preceding years, can seldom hope to regain either the fortune or the position he has lost; and he generally passes the remainder of his life a broken-spirited and unprosperous man—while as soon as employment returns, the operative is as well off, and too often as imprudent as ever; and though the thoughtful and sensitive among them may be occasionally depressed or irritated by anticipating the probable recurrence of such terrible visitations, it is certainly true that a far larger proportion of them soon recover their natural cheerfulness, than is the case with the unfortunate among their employers.[1]

It is a depressingly one-sided piece of special pleading from a man who has never had to go hungry (a possible state of affairs among the workers too easily brushed aside as 'bitter and overwhelming' but of short duration) and who has never wanted for anything, except perhaps the ability to keep his factories solvent. But the peculiar bitterness of the tone stems in no small measure from the bankruptcy in 1847, a matter of months before the appearance of *Mary Barton*, of his brother Samuel: the Sunday School, gymnasium, drawing and singing classes, baths, and libraries that he had instituted for his Bollington workers had been repaid with a strike over the introduction of technical innovations for stretching cloth, and Samuel Greg had been compelled to retire hurt from business. William Rathbone substantially assisted his brother, a broken man, after this distress.[2]

*Mary Barton*'s suggestions about uniquely suffering workers and careless bosses must have seemed a doubly barbed thrust. Mrs. Gaskell recognized as much and wrote a relieved letter to Mrs. Samuel Greg:

May I write in the first person to you, as I have many things I should like to say to the writer of the remarks on 'Mary Barton', which Miss Mitchell has sent me, and which I conjecture were written by your husband? Those remarks and the note which accompanied have given me great and real pleasure. I have heard much about the disapproval which Mr. Greg's family have felt with regard to 'M.B.', and have heard of it with so much regret that I am particularly glad that Mr. Sam Greg does not participate in it. I regretted the disapprobation, not one whit on account of the testimony of such disapproval which I heard was to arise out of it [a reference presumably to W.R. Greg's *Edinburgh Review* article], but because I knew that such a feeling would be conscientiously and thoughtfully entertained by men who are acquainted by long experience with the life, a portion of which I had endeavoured to represent; and whose actions during a

---

[1] *Edinburgh Review*, 89 (1849), 414–15, and footnote, 415–16.

[2] 'Samuel Greg', in H. A. Page [Alexander Japp], *Leaders of Men* (1880), 264–77; A. P. Stanley, Dean of Westminster, 'Brief Memoir', in *A Layman's Legacy in Prose and Verse: Selections from the Papers of Samuel Greg* (1877), 1–63.

long course of years have proved that the interests of their work-people are as dear to them as their own. Such disapproval, I was sure, would not be given if the writing which called it forth were merely a free expression of ideas; but it would be given if I had misrepresented, or so represented, a part as the whole, as that people at a distance should be misled and prejudiced against the masters, and that class be estranged from class.[1]

Given the pressures by which she was surrounded (and the tortuously roundabout prose of the letter gives some indication of how much on the defensive she was forced to be)—the Unitarian chapels full of Political Economists, 'model employers' among her friends, alongside the distressed employees she could see for herself—it is not surprising that Mrs. Gaskell disclaimed any knowledge of Political Economy, nor that she softened her case, fell back on 'comforting attitudes' in *Mary Barton*, and later wrote *North and South*.[2] The wonder is that she wrote *Mary Barton* at all.

Mrs. Chadwick suggested James Nasmyth, inventor of the steam-hammer, as the model for Thornton in *North and South*; David Shuster-man has countered with W. R. Greg.[3] A more likely candidate than either is Samuel Greg himself. In a letter to Lady Kay-Shuttleworth disclaiming her capacity for a novel about a good employer, which 'several people' have already suggested, Mrs. Gaskell indicates that it is Samuel Greg who comes readily to mind in that connection. It would be surprising in fact, after W. R. Greg's review, if any balancing of *Mary Barton*'s allegations in favour of the employers did not bear Samuel Greg very much in mind:

. . . whatever power there was in Mary Barton was caused by my feeling strongly on the side which I took; now as I don't feel as strongly (and as it is impossible I ever should,) on the other side, the forced effort of writing on that side would [be] \end in/ a weak failure. I know, and have always owned, that I have represented *but one* side of the question, and no one would welcome more than I should, a true and earnest representation of the other side. I believe what I have said in Mary Barton to be perfectly true, but by no means the whole truth; and I have always felt deeply annoyed at anyone, or any set of people who chose to consider that I had manifested the whole truth; I do not think it is possible to do this in any *one* work of fiction. You say 'I think there are good mill-

---

[1] *Letters*, ed. Chapple and Pollard, No. 42 [? early 1849], p. 73.

[2] Preface to *Mary Barton*. See John Lucas, 'Mrs. Gaskell and Brotherhood', in David Howard, John Lucas, John Goode, *Tradition and Tolerance in Nineteenth-Century Fiction* (1966), 162.

[3] Mrs. E. H. Chadwick, *Mrs. Gaskell: Haunts, Homes and Stories*, 147–8; David Shuster-man, 'William Rathbone Greg and Mrs. Gaskell', *PQ* 36 (1957), 268–72.

owners; I think the factory system might be made a great engine for good'; and in this no one can more earnestly and heartily agree with you than I do. I can not imagine a nobler scope for a thoughtful energetic man, desirous of doing good to his kind, than that presented to his powers as the master of a factory. But I believe that there is much to be discovered yet as to the right position and mutual duties of employer, and employed; and the utmost I hoped from Mary Barton has been that it would give a spur to inactive thought, and languid conscience in this direction. . . . I think the best and most benevolent employers would say how difficult they, with all their experience, found it to unite theory and practice. I am sure Mr. Sam Greg would. . . . It would require a wise man, practical and full of experience, \one/ able to calculate consequences, to choose out the best among the many systems which are being tried by the benevolent millowners. If I, in my ignorance, chose out one which appeared to me good, but which was known to business men to be a failure, I should be doing an injury instead of a service. For instance Mr. Sam Greg's plans have been accompanied with great want of success in a money point of view. This has been a stinging grief to him, as he was most anxious to show that his benevolent theories, which were so beautiful in their origin, might be carried into effect with good and *just* practical results of benefit to both master and man. He knew that he was watched in all his proceedings by no friendly eyes, who would be glad to set down failure in business to what they considered his Utopian schemes. I think, he, or such as he, might almost be made the hero of a fiction on the other side of the question [—] the trials of the conscientious rich man, in his dealings with the poor. And I should like some *man*, who had a man's correct knowledge, to write on this subject, and make the poor intelligent work-people understand the infinite anxiety as to right and wrong-doing which I believe that riches bring to many.[1]

Neither Dissent nor Unitarianism are specifically associated with Thornton in *North and South*. But Higgins's protest that Christian manufacturers prefer to 'din' their workers with Political Economy rather than with Christianity (Ch. 28) applies to the Dissenting millocrats. Like Samuel Greg, Thornton has to give up his business and he suffers the more from failure because the world knows of his new stand for religion and humanity (Ch. 50). And the set of Matthew Henry's commentaries, prominently, and apparently at first sight gratuitously, placed in the house of Thornton and his mother (Ch. 9), could be construed as a clue, by those who knew the family, to the link between Thornton and Greg, and to the, as it were, expiatory character of the novel: Greg's mother was, as we have seen, descended from Matthew Henry's father.

---

[1] *Letters*, ed. Chapple and Pollard, No. 72a (16 July [? 1851]), pp. 119–20.

Sally Leadbitter in *Mary Barton* plays a sort of Emily Brontë to Mary Barton's Mrs. Gaskell. Sally calls Alice Wilson a 'canting old maid' and a 'Methodee', but Mary, knowing better than to confuse things thus, insists, rightly, that Alice is Church of England. 'Well, well, Mary, you're very particular', is the reply (Ch. 8). And Mary's is Mrs. Gaskell's particularity: detail about religion is precise, when it is supplied (important proviso). The novels bear the stamp of an insider's information and sympathies. Mrs. Gaskell knew what it was to be on the receiving end of anti-Unitarian prejudice, the scorn of the orthodox for the theologically non-respectable. She feared that the High Church Nicholls would prevent Charlotte Brontë from continuing 'as intimate with us, heretics'; and when she wrote to Eliza Fox that 'We are going to the Ss. on Friday to go and call on the Bishop and Mrs Lee, who took the decided step of calling upon us, (Units) the other day', the parenthesis indicated the extent of her surprise that the Anglican Bishop of Manchester should seek out the acquaintance of a Unitarian, even a famous Unitarian novelist.[1] Not unnaturally then Mrs. Gaskell satirized Anglican attitudes towards Dissenters, notably in 'My Lady Ludlow'. Lady Ludlow's antipathy towards the Rev. Mr. Gray's Church-Methodism (reading and writing, which he intends to teach children of the parish, are the 'edge-tools' of Revolution) is laughed at, and so is her reaction to the Baptist baker from Birmingham: 'The mere idea of her agent being on the slightest possible terms of acquaintance with the Dissenter, the tradesman, the Birmingham democrat, who had come to settle in our good, orthodox, aristocratic, and agricultural Hanbury, made my lady very uneasy' (Ch. 14). But the baker turns out to be an irrefutably model farmer.

As another novelist might add an obtuse Dissenter to his novel, Mrs. Gaskell puts in obtuse Anglicans like Dixon (in *North and South*) and Sally (in *Ruth*). When Mr. Hale leaves the Church of England ministry, Dixon construes it (wrongly, I think) as a transfer to Dissent, and spots an analogy with her tailor–cousin who turned Methodist preacher at fifty: '. . . he had never been able to make a pair of trousers to fit, for as long as he had been in the trade, so it was no wonder; but for master!' (Ch. 5). And even after Thurstan Benson's moving tribute to Ruth— instead of a sermon at the funeral he reads from Revelation 7—Sally is apologetic: ' "He preaches sermons sometimes," said Sally, nudging Mr. Davis, as they rose from their knees. . . .' (Ch. 36).

Mrs. Gaskell's sympathies are with outsiders and minorities, victims

[1] Ibid., No. 191, p. 280; No. 55, p. 91.

of religious prejudice: with the girl wrongly hanged for witchcraft in her Salem story 'Lois the Witch'; with the Cagots in 'An Accursed Race'.[1] She sides with the man who dissents, conscientiously, from a religious orthodoxy: with Mr. Hale, or with Thurstan Benson who prolongs his deception about Ruth to shield her from the harsh censure of the righteous Cartwright, his leading member.

But Mrs. Gaskell's fictional dealings with Dissent have a particularly Unitarian, as well as a generally Nonconformist, flavour. Among Victorian novelists she is one of the most open towards Dissent as, for example, Davenport (the dying Methodist cellar-dweller in *Mary Barton*), *Ruth*, and *Cousin Phillis* witness. But—and here we are reminded of the strenuous intellectualism of Unitarianism—religious fanaticism always gets short shrift: 'Lois the Witch' bitingly exposes religious extremism. And it is fairly clear that the mildly satiric references to Methodist extremes imply that Mrs. Gaskell's view—though she is considerably less bitter to Methodism than most other novelists of the period—endorses some of the standard criticisms: Sally's tale about Jeremiah Dixon ('and them Methodees are terrible hands at unexpected prayers when one least looks for 'em'); Philip Hepburn's aunt Bell on Love Feasts ('Why, lad! what's been a-do? Thou'rt looking as peaked and pined as a Methody preacher after a love-feast, when he's talked hisself to Death's door'); the Gibsons' cook's puritanism ('. . . being a Methodist, she objected on religious grounds to trying any of Mrs. Gibson's new receipts for French dishes. It was not scriptural, she said . . . and now, if she was to be set to cook heathen dishes, after the fashion of the Papists, she'd sooner give it all up together'); or Jonas Barclay's asceticism (the Methodist minister, he 'told us as the pleasures o' this world were like apples o' Sodom: pleasant to look at, but ashes to taste')—these isolated cases endorse by contrast the insistence in *Ruth* on the cooler beauties of holiness.[2] The introspection of evangelicalism is absent from the Benson household:

. . . their lives were pure and good, not merely from a lovely and beautiful nature, but from some law, the obedience to which was, of itself, harmonious peace, and which governed them almost implicitly, and with as little questioning on their part, as the glorious stars which haste not, rest not, in their eternal obedience. (Ch. 40)

[1] 'Lois the Witch', *Right at Last and Other Tales* (1860). 'An Accursed Race', *Round the Sofa* (1859).

[2] *Ruth*, Ch. 16; *Sylvia's Lovers*, Chs. 11 and 13; *Wives and Daughters*, Ch. 15.

Unitarianism was, on the whole, much less puritanical than other Dissent: it lacked the evangelical's prohibitive attitudes to 'the world'. Unitarians were not Quakers: when Aunt Shaw sends Margaret Hale coral ornaments, but is 'afraid the Milton Dissenters won't appreciate them', the correction is given with, as it were, the authority of Mrs. Gaskell's Manchester Unitarian experience: 'She has got all her ideas of Dissenters from the Quakers, has not she?' (Ch. 18). Mrs. Gaskell's Unitarian openness to learning and culture emerges in *Cousin Phillis*. It is true that Ebenezer Holman's learning is at times almost crudely dwelt on: he will quote Virgil apropos of the landscape ('It's wonderful,' said he, 'how exactly Virgil has hit the enduring epithets, nearly two thousand years ago, and in Italy; and yet how it describes to a T what is now lying before us. . . .'). But Mrs. Gaskell does insist praiseworthily on the propriety of Phillis's reading Dante alongside Matthew Henry, and Holman withstands pressure from less liberal fellow-ministers like Brother Robinson (who 'told me that a poor little quotation I was making from the "Georgics" savoured of vain babbling and profane heathenism').[1]

For all the novel's adverse reception at Cross Street Benson's perception of redemptive hope in Ruth's illegitimate child must be attributed to the Unitarian liberalism of Mrs. Gaskell's theology. 'Teach her (and God will teach her, if a man does not come between) to reverence her child; and this reverence will shut out sin,—will be purification', urges Benson (Ch. 11), and the language of redemption is dilutedly unevangelical. Rather similar is Nicholas Higgins's transition to being able to encourage his son's reciting Methodist hymns or Thornton's reversion to piety at his mother's knee ('Speak to me again in the old way, mother. . . . If you would say the old good words, it would make me feel something of the pious simplicity of my childhood') : the experience is vague and the theology inexplicit. Mrs. Gaskell's liberality extends to Fred Hale's becoming a Roman Catholic, and creates sentimentally ecumenical scenarios ('Margaret the Church-woman, her father the Dissenter, Higgins the Infidel, knelt down together. It did them no harm').[2] And the logical end of this liberalism is the overlooking of sectarian distinctions altogether. Mrs. Gaskell is ultimately less interested in her Dissenters as Dissenters than as Christians. As Sally says, 'God forbid I should speak disrespectfully of Master

---

[1] *Cousin Phillis*, Pt. I, and Pt. IV.
[2] *North and South*, Chs. 28, 31, 41, 50.

Thurstan and Miss Faith . . . I never think on them as Church or Dissenters, but just as Christians.' [1]

And so sectarian distinctions are not insisted on. Piety in *Mary Barton* is not a sectarian property. Bessy Higgins's Methodism is not made an issue. Mr. Hale may dissent from the Church of England, but if he is supposed to be—as the reference in Chapter 4 to the Ejected of 1662 may be meant to imply—a kind of Dissenter, his new allegiances are unspecified. The 'body of Dissenters to which Mr. Benson belonged' is never (*pace* Laurence Lerner) identified.[2] And the religion Thornton returns to would probably be Dissenting and Unitarian if *North and South* is a tribute to Samuel Greg as well as a concession to the millocracy of Cross Street, but his sect is not particularized. All of which is, in fact, in keeping with James Martineau's version of Unitarianism, his attempts to propagate his liberal, open concept of Unitarian 'Church-life' rather than 'sect-life' (making precisely Troeltsch's distinctions), and to counter the aggressively sectarian Unitarianism of the British and Foreign Unitarian Association. John James Tayler, a minister at Brook Street Chapel, Manchester (1840–53), was one of Martineau's chief allies.[3]

Ironically, perhaps, this openness and liberality, which led to Mrs. Gaskell's eschewing the detection of the sectarian in the Christian, led finally to a merging of Dissent in the Church of England. The female characters of this wife and daughter of Unitarian ministers are often, like Margaret Hale and Miss Jenkyns of Cranford, daughters of Anglican ministers. The same tendency lay in Martineau's thought and work: he sought to promote a 'truly national church', a widening of the Anglican Church to include liberal Dissenters, and was accused of encouraging 'Unitarians to turn Anglican and Anglicans to refrain from becoming Unitarian'.[4]

In Manchester, of course, Unitarianism was as socially prestigious as Anglicanism, if not more so. Bishop Lee and his wife did, after all, call first. William Gaskell was, as R. N. Phillips, M.P., put it in his speech at the Golden Jubilee of Gaskell's ministry, himself a sort of Bishop:

[1] *Ruth*, Ch. 16.
[2] *Ruth*, Ch. 17. Laurence Lerner specifies: *Ruth*'s world is 'the world of Congregationalism'. Intro. to Penguin edn. of *Wives and Daughters*, ed. F. G. Smith (1969), 14.
[3] C. G. Bolam, J. Goring, H. L. Short, R. Thomas, *The English Presbyterians: From Elizabethan Puritanism to Modern Unitarianism* (1968), e.g. 256–7; 266–9; 274 ff.
[4] Ibid., 266, 275.

The Cross Street Chapel stands, I think—in the large and healthy influence which its members have exerted—second to none in this locality. Small in numbers, yet it has given to Manchester public men of high character and influential position; therefore its minister must have been, in the moral and spiritual concerns of life, the guide and friend of these influential citizens—(hear, hear). Few bishops of the Established Church, with all the aids and advantages of their high position, have been able to do in this respect a larger share of work than that which our friend, as a simple Nonconformist minister, has been privileged to accomplish.[1]

Not surprisingly, Mrs. Gaskell finds the worlds of *Cranford* and *Wives and Daughters* very congenial, and there is, of course, no Dissent in Cranford. The retreat to Cranford is an escape from the city, atheism, Dissent, the age of railways, the present. Symbolically the age of Dickens is made to submit to the age of Johnson and of Jane Austen: Captain Brown is run over by a train after reading a number of *Pickwick Papers*, a publication Miss Jenkyns disapproves of because it is unlike *Rasselas*.[2]

And where Dissent is most approved of it has about it the air of Cranford: the ivy-covered chapel of *Ruth*, the gently elegiac, rural Independency of Ebenezer Holman in *Cousin Phillis*. The psalm-singing scene is justly famous, but it is the contrast Holman makes with Holdsworth that is significant: 'I daresay you railway gentlemen don't wind up the day with singing a psalm together.' Mrs. Gaskell feels most at home, as it were, in Knutsford rather than in Cross Street or Lower Mosley Street, in a rural or small-town Dissent, whose relaxed and generous world approximates closely to the Anglicanism of Cranford. The convergence is total when the dying city-dweller Alice Wilson babbles of green fields: Anglican, she could be remembering Holman's world or Benson's chapel:

. . . old snatches of primitive versions of the Psalms (such as are sung in country churches half draperied over with ivy, and where the running brook, or the murmuring wind among the trees, makes fit accompaniment to the chorus of human voices uttering praise and thanksgiving to their God). . . .[3]

[1] *Commemoration of the Fifty Years' Ministry of the Rev. William Gaskell, MA*, 16.
[2] *Cranford*, Chs. 1 and 2.
[3] *Mary Barton*, Ch. 24.

# VII. GEORGE ELIOT

## 1. INTRODUCTORY

Shame on you, you Christians, noble and common, educated and uneducated Christians, *shame* on you, that an *antichrist* had to show you the essence of Christianity in its true, unveiled form! . . . And there is no other road for you to truth and *freedom* except that leading *through* the stream of fire [the *Feuer-bach*]. Feuerbach is the *purgatory* of the present times.

Marx, 1842

GEORGE ELIOT'S scientific, sociological interest in the poorer classes was declared before she wrote any fiction. She classified the sciences according to Comte, a pioneer sociologist (for *Felix Holt* she read again 'Comte's Social Science in Miss Martineau's edition').[1] She even fell in love with another pioneering sociologist, Herbert Spencer (whom she tried to get to read the *Politique Positive*: but he gave it up and instead got his knowledge of Comte from a popular summary in *The Leader* by George Henry Lewes). Spencer remained a life-long friend.[2] And it was the sociologist Riehl who taught her the value of the 'Natural History of social bodies' and the role she was to play as novelist:

If any man of sufficient moral and intellectual breadth, whose observations would not be vitiated by a foregone conclusion, or by a professional point of view, would devote himself to studying the natural history of our social classes, especially of the small shopkeepers, artisans, and peasantry,—the degree in which they are influenced by local conditions, their maxims and habits, the points of view from which they regard their religious teachers, and the degree in which they are influenced by religious doctrines, the interaction of the various classes on each other, and what are the tendencies in their position towards disintegration or towards development,—and if, after all this study, he would give us the result of his observations in a book well nourished with specific facts, his work would be a valuable aid to the social and political reformer.[3]

---

[1] F. C. Thompson, 'The Genesis of Felix Holt', *PMLA* 74 (1959), 577. Does she mean *The Positive Philosophy of Auguste Comte*, freely translated and condensed by Harriet Martineau (2 Vols., 1853)?

[2] J. D. Y. Peel, *Herbert Spencer: the Evolution of a Sociologist* (1971), 13–14, 27–8.

[3] 'The Natural History of German Life', *WR*, N.S. 10 (July 1856), 56, 72; Thomas Pinney (ed.), *Essays of George Eliot* (1963), 272–3, and 290, footnote 21. For Comte, see Raymond Aron, *Main Currents in Sociological Thought*, I. (Penguin edn., 1968), 63–109; and Basil Willey, *Nineteenth-Century Studies* (1949), ch. 7.

George Eliot, impatient with the genteel Evangelical themes of 'silly'
lady novelists ('Why can we not have pictures of religious life among the
industrial classes in England, as interesting as Mrs. Stowe's pictures of
religious life among the negroes?'), applied herself to fictional accounts
of religious life among the 'small shopkeepers, artisans and peasantry'.[1]
Her intent was serious, scientifically objective; no one, not even the
Dissenter, was to be declared common or unclean. The scientific
observer, the human-ecologist, did not make Mrs. Transome's mistake:
*she* 'hardly noticed Mr. Lyon, not from studied haughtiness, but from
sheer mental inability to consider him—as a person ignorant of natural
history is unable to consider a fresh-water polype otherwise than as a
sort of animated weed, certainly not fit for the table'.[2]

   The distinctive note here is the readiness to sympathize, in the novels,
with the religion of the 'middle and lower classes'. Outside the fiction
George Eliot could be as dismissive as anybody else about the 'miserable
etiquette' of sectarianism, as her reaction to Spurgeon reveals: '. . . the
most superficial, Grocer's-back-parlour view of Calvinistic Christianity
. . . seemed to look no farther than the retail Christian's tea and
muffins. . . .'[3] Her saturation in Evangelicalism under Miss Lewis
(principal governess of the Nuneaton School at which George Eliot
boarded, 1828–32), helped her to 'an especial interest in the weak
things of the earth, rather than in the mighty'.[4] Christianity, even when
abandoned, left its mark in her puritan seriousness, her moral insistence,
her presentation of the law of consequences and of determinism (clearly
related to the doctrines of the 'wages of sin' and predestination), and
notably (in the Feuerbachian phrase) the notion that 'Work is worship'.[5]
The Protestant sacramental awareness that saw worth in the commonest
person, in life's most menial activities (George Herbert's 'Nothing can
be so mean'), lingered on. What she admired in Cowper was legitimated

[1] 'Silly Novels by Lady Novelists', *WR*, N.S. 10 (Oct. 1856), 457; Pinney, op. cit.,
319.
[2] *Felix Holt*, Ch. 38. See C. T. Bissell, 'Social Analysis in the Novels of George Eliot',
*ELH* 18 (1951), 226, and A. J. Sambrook, 'The Natural Historian of our Social Classes',
*English*, 14 (1962–3), 131.
[3] *GE Letters*, I. 261, and V. 121–2.
[4] 'Silly Novels', *WR*, N.S. 10, 457; Pinney, op. cit., 318.
[5] R. H. Hutton, 'George Eliot's Heroines', *Spectator* (12 Feb. 1876): in L. Lerner and
J. Holmstrom, *George Eliot and Her Readers* (1966), 170; F. R. Leavis, *The Great Tradition*
(Penguin edn., 1962), 23; R. H. Hutton, *Essays on Some Modern Guides of English Thought in
Matters of Faith* (1887), 237 (cf. Samuel Butler, *The Way of All Flesh* (1903), Ch. 68);
George Levine, 'Determinism and Responsibility in the Works of George Eliot', *PMLA*
77 (1962), 268–79; Bernard J. Paris, *Experiments in Life* (1965), 102.

by Feuerbach: George Eliot's wide sympathies attached 'an uncommon significance' to 'common things', and 'to life, as such, a religious import'.[1] In *Adam Bede* work-worn hands are made to symbolize moral validity: 'old women scraping carrots with their work-worn hands' are declared to be legitimate artistic material; Adam looks at his hands, 'the hard palms and the broken finger-nails', when he thinks about Hetty's rejection of a 'common man' (Hetty, of course, bitterly regrets her work-coarsened hands); and before the tragedy of Hetty bursts upon them Adam and Mr. Poyser shake hands: 'the two honest men grasped each other's hard hands in mutual understanding'.[2] Dinah's authenticity is rooted in her being a working-girl. And though George Eliot may in the end insist on the contemporary redundancy of Dissent as of orthodox Christianity, and though her demonstration that Feuerbachian humanism is the essence of Dissent may in fact be more subversive than the frontal attacks of Dickens, she steadily eschews the easy dismissals, the cheap sneers, and genuinely sympathizes with what, ultimately, she rejects.

Admirers of her sympathetic fictional handling of Nonconformity thought George Eliot must have been brought up as a Dissenter; they had to be disabused.[3] But her experience of Dissent was extensive: 'My sketches both of churchmen and dissenters, with whom I am almost equally acquainted, are drawn from close observation of them in real life, and not at all from hearsay or from the descriptions of novelists', she wrote, apropos of 'Janet's Repentance'.[4] Her aunt and uncle, Mr. and Mrs. Samuel Evans, were Methodists: Wesleyans at first, they associated with the Primitive Methodists after the 1803 Wesleyan ban on women preachers, and later joined the Derby Faith Folk.[5] Marian and her father visited Wirksworth at least twice (the second time in June 1840), and

[1] Ludwig Feuerbach, *The Essence of Christianity*, trans. Marian Evans (1854), 274. For GE's enthusiasm about Cowper, see 'Worldliness and Other-Worldliness: The Poet Young', *WR*, N.S. 11 (1857), 39–42; Pinney, op. cit., 381–5.

[2] *Adam Bede*, Chs. 17, 30, 15, 38. Was George Eliot half-remembering Nicolas Maes's painting, *A Woman Scraping Parsnips* (1655, bequeathed to The National Gallery in 1838), when she connected Dutch painters with the viability of pictures of 'old women scraping carrots' in Ch. 17?

[3] See *GE Letters*, III. 429 (22 June 1861); VI. 68, 163.

[4] To John Blackwood, *GE Letters*, II. 347–8. Blackwood may have alluded to Scott's influence: Davie Deans is mentioned in GE's next sentence.

[5] J. Walford, *Memoirs of the Life and Labours of the late Venerable Hugh Bourne*, ed. Rev. W. Antliff (2 Vols., 1855–6), I. 216, 260. See the note by Rev. T. E. Brigden, *WHS Proc.* (1899), 124–5; and A. W. Harrison, 'The Arminian Methodists', ibid., 23 (1941–2), 25. Haight's note, *GE Letters*, I. 18, footnote 7, wrongly suggests that the Evanses 'founded the Arminian Methodist [i.e. Derby Faith] Methodist Chapel' at Wirksworth in or after 1814: the movement did not begin until 1831–2. Herbert Spencer's Uncle John was one of the leading Arminian Methodist seceders in Derby: J. D. Y. Peel, op. cit., 37.

Mrs. Evans stayed with them for a week in 1837—when Marian heard the Mary Voce story. Marian attended the school of the Misses Mary and Rebecca Franklin, daughters of the Rev. Francis Franklin, pastor of Cow Lane Particular Baptist Chapel, Coventry, and was deeply involved in the religious work, leading prayer-meetings among the girls and attending the chapel.[1] It was even rumoured, though wrongly, that she had 'submitted to the rite of adult baptism',[2] but she did, at least, enjoy breakfast with the Rev. John Howard Hinton the radical, 'of considerable note among Baptists'—Secretary of the Baptist Union (1841–66), and twice its president (1837 and 1863).[3]

George Eliot knew the family of John Sibree, pastor of Coventry's Vicar Lane Independent Chapel, but Sibree came to disapprove of her as a baneful influence on his children.[4] She corresponded with his son, who ditched his ambitions for the Congregational Ministry. Sibree did not abandon her to the German rationalists however: Francis Watts, a professor of theology at Spring Hill (Independent) College who had studied at Halle, was induced to visit and correspond, to help counter George Eliot's unbelief.[5] He had as little success as a Baptist minister introduced by Miss Rebecca Franklin for the same purpose ('That young lady must have had the devil at her elbow to suggest her doubts, for there was not a book that I recommended to her in support of Christian evidences that she had not read').[6]

Friendship with the Brays and Hennells was the entrée to a wide Unitarian/Rationalist circle.[7] At Rosehill she met George Dawson of Birmingham and W. J. Fox.[8] Unitarianism remained just tolerable: she appreciated its hymnody, was a bridesmaid when Fox married Rufa Brabant and Charles Hennell at his Finsbury Chapel, and bore with the

---

[1] J. W. Cross (ed.), *George Eliot's Life, As Related in Her Letters and Journals* (3 Vols., Edinburgh, 1885), I. 27.

[2] 'George Eliot as a Christian', *Contemporary Pulpit*, 2 (1884), 181.

[3] *GE Letters*, III. 328 (to S. S. Hennell).

[4] *GE Letters*, I. 306; cf. 309. For his earlier, more approving, phase, when Marian taught Mary Sibree German, see G. S. Haight, *George Eliot* (Oxford, 1968), 55.

[5] *GE Letters*, I. 135–6; 141–2; 143–4; 149–50; 154–5; 157–8.

[6] Cross's *Life* (Cabinet edn., 3 Vols.), I. 397–8 (Appendix by Mrs. John Cash, Sibree's daughter).

[7] For the ideas and allegiances these friendships led to, see Basil Willey, *Nineteenth-Century Studies* (1949), Ch. 8, 'George Eliot: Hennell, Strauss, and Feuerbach'; also U. C. Knoepflmacher, *Religious Humanism and the Victorian Novel* (Princeton, N.J., 1965), 44–59.

[8] Fox was the first contributor to Mill's *WR* (1824) and to Chapman's (1852); G. H. Lewes's *Biographical History of Philosophy* (1845–6) was based on lectures first given at Fox's Finsbury Chapel.

christening of Lewes's granddaughter by Dr. Thomas Sadler of Rosslyn
Hill Unitarian Chapel, which she and Lewes sometimes attended (Sadler
married Charles Lewes and Gertrude Hill, and conducted George Eliot's
funeral).[1] She heard James Martineau, whose wife was a cousin of Cara
Bray (*née* Hennell), preach at Coventry, and was later (1861) disap-
pointed that he was not after all the preacher when she attended Little
Portland Street Chapel to hear him. In 1844 George Eliot met Martineau
on a northern holiday with the Brays, when they introduced her to their
connections in the Manchester–Liverpool Unitarian cousinhood:
Hollands, Rathbones, Martineaus. And Edward Flower, the Unitarian
brewer from Stratford, whom George Eliot got to know through the
Brays, was induced to give financial support to the floundering *Westminster Review* (1852).[2]

## 2. ADAM BEDE

### (a) '*A Reflection of Facts*'

The welcome that Nonconformists afforded to *Adam Bede* is markedly
replete with the gratified surprise of readers long used to much less
friendly treatment of their fictional co-religionists. In Dinah Morris,
wrote the *Nonconformist*'s reviewer,

> . . . the author has done the ample justice to evangelical piety, which no novelist
> known to us (at least, no novelist of the same mark) has ever done before. The
> genuine spirituality and warm devotion of this simple, grave, loving young
> Methodist, are represented with a true appreciation and sympathy which are
> altogether beautiful and excellent; and the sermon preached by her on the com-
> mon, and the prayers she offered with the rude northern villagers, must com-
> mand the respect of the irreligious, and strongly move the hearts of the religious
> readers of the book. It is an unapproached picture. . . .[3]

Henry James had no reservations about the novel's accuracy:

> . . . Dinah Morris bears so many indications of being a reflection of facts well
> known to the author—and the phenomena of Methodism, from the frequency
> with which their existence is referred to in her pages, appear to be so familiar to
> her,—that I hesitate to do anything but thankfully accept her portrait.[4]

The novel is, for most of the time anyway, warmly open towards the
religious of all parties: to the Rev. Mr. Irwine, who will not (Ch. 5)

---

[1] *GE Letters*, I. 160, VI. 420; and Haight's *George Eliot*.

[2] *GE Letters*, III. 442, I. 178–80; and Haight's *George Eliot*.

[3] *Nonconformist*, 19 (6 Apr. 1859), 277.

[4] *Atlantic Monthly*, 18 (Oct. 1866), quoted by G. S. Haight, *A Century of George Eliot
Criticism* (paperback edn., 1966), 49–50.

incite Chad Cranage and other 'bull-headed fellows' to violence against
the Methodists, as well as to Dinah herself. Just as liberally, the data of
Methodism are borrowed from Southey's *Life of Wesley*. George Eliot
'made careful notes' from it

. . . on such matters as women's preaching, visions, the drawing of lots, divina-
tion of God's will by opening the Bible at hazard and reading the first text the
eye falls upon, belief in present miracles, visits to prisons and madhouses, and
Wesley's description of his preaching in the open air, standing 'in the calm
still evening, with the setting sun behind me' as Dinah Morris does in the second
chapter of *Adam Bede*.[1]

Some passages are densely packed with material from Southey. For
example, the end of Chapter 3:

And this blessed gift of venerating love has been given to too many humble
craftsmen since the world began, for us to feel any surprise that it should have
existed in the soul of a Methodist carpenter half a century ago, while there was
yet a lingering after-glow from the time when Wesley and his fellow-labourer fed
on the hips and haws of the Cornwall hedges, after exhausting limbs and lungs
in carrying a divine message to the poor.[2]

That after-glow has long faded away; and the picture we are apt to make of
Methodism in our imagination is not an amphitheatre of green hills,[3] or the deep
shade of broad-leaved sycamores,[4] where a crowd of rough men and weary-
hearted women drank in a faith which was a rudimentary culture, which linked
their thoughts with the past, lifted their imagination above the sordid details of
their own narrow lives, and suffused their souls with the sense of a pitying,
loving, infinite Presence, sweet as summer to the homeless needy. . . .
. . . I cannot pretend that Seth and Dinah were anything else than Methodists—
not indeed of that modern type which reads quarterly reviews and attends in
chapels with pillared porticoes; but of a very old-fashioned kind. They believed
in present miracles, in instantaneous conversions, in revelations by dreams and
visions; they drew lots, and sought for Divine guidance by opening the Bible

G. S. Haight, *George Eliot*, 249–50. 'At Gwennap . . .', Wesley says, 'I stood on the
wall, in the calm still evening, with the setting sun behind me, and almost an innumerable
multitude before, behind, and on either hand.' [11 Apr. 1744]. R. Southey, *The Life of
Wesley*, I. 347.
[2] John Wesley and John Nelson in Cornwall, R. Southey, op. cit., I. 341.
[3] Heptonstall Bank: '. . . an oval spot of ground, surrounded with spreading trees,
scooped out, as it were, in the side of a hill, which rose round like a theatre'. Ibid., I.
349.
[4] 'Sometimes, in a hot and cloudless summer day, he and his congregation were under
cover of the sycamores, which afford so deep a shade to some of the old farm-houses in
Westmoreland and Cumberland.' Ibid., I. 347.

at hazard; having a literal way of interpreting the Scriptures which is not at all sanctioned by approved commentators. . . .[1]

Southey supplied data, reinforced what she knew already and what she had learned from her Methodist aunt. Reading the *Life of Wesley* may even have given George Eliot the name Hetty: Southey discusses at some length the unhappy love life of Wesley's sister Hetty (Mehetabel).[2] And her account corresponds in its emphases to Southey's. Methodists are a hymn-singing people.[3] Arminians, they repudiate Calvinism. When Arthur receives in a book-parcel from London 'pamphlets about Antinomianism', Irwine is interested: 'they let one see what is going on'. George Eliot probably had in mind John Fletcher's *Checks to Antinomianism*.[4] Arthur's unconcern about the theological debate is ironic: his antinomianism had all too obviously evil results; he lacked, and fatally, Dinah's 'inward holiness'. George Eliot insists, with Southey, on the Quaker-like dress and asceticism of the Methodists.[5] Friends and relations recognized Aunt Samuel in Dinah not least in the Quaker-like costume: Mrs. Evans, like other Methodist ladies, wore a black dress and 'coal-scuttle bonnet' in protest against 'the vanities of the time'.[6] Even on her wedding day Dinah wears a grey dress. Hetty and Bess Cranage are presented as shallowly fond of trinkets and finery: George Eliot approves of the seriousness that eschews such frivolity. The 'Methodist cap' suits Dinah as the cup contains the acorn (Ch. 20); Hetty's dressing up in sober garb only emphasizes her moral distance from her cousin. In Hetty's bedroom, and on the village green, Dinah's

[1] Leavis quotes this passage as an example of GE's precision as 'sociologist and social historian', *Anna Karenina and Other Essays* (paperback edn., 1967), 56–7. For 'present miracles': Southey, op. cit., I. 321–2; II. 179 ff.; 'instantaneous conversions': ibid., II. 64–5, and note VI, 'Instantaneous Conversion', 381; 'dreams and visions': ibid., I. 182–5; II. 19–20, footnote 1; 38–39; drawing lots: ibid., I. 95, 96, 132, 268–70 (cf. R. A. Knox, *Enthusiasm* (Oxford, 1962 reprint), Ch. 17, and p. 452); 'opening the Bible at hazard': Southey has many examples of what he calls Bibliomancy or *Sortes Biblicae*: I. 121, 154, 170, 183, 193, 246; II. 21. See also Wesley, *Works* (3rd edn., 13 Vols.; 1829–31), VIII. 449–51; R. Green, 'Scripture Playing cards', *WHS Proc.* I (1897), 15–25; C. D. Hardcastle, 'Scripture or Draw Cards', *WHS Proc.* 4 (1903), 6–8; H. J. Foster, ibid., 40–3.
[2] Southey, op. cit., I. 314–16.
[3] Ibid., II. 97.
[4] Ibid., I. 260 ff.; and Ch. 25, *passim* (particularly II. 198–217); *Adam Bede*, Ch. 5.
[5] Southey, op. cit., II. 287–91.
[6] William Mottram, *The True Story of George Eliot: In Relation to 'Adam Bede', giving the real life history of the more prominent characters* (1905), 185. (Partly published in *Leisure Hour*, 52 (1902–3). Mottram was great-grandson of George Evans, brother to Robert and Samuel Evans.)

chastely decorous style confronts the triviality of Hetty and Bessy Cranage. Hetty's road to hell was paved with ornamental presents; Bessy tears off her trinkets with tears of repentance (as Mrs. Evans cut off her curls, and abandoned her lace).[1]

Dinah's abstemiousness—in Mrs. Poyser's agricultural terms, as part of the symbolic antithesis between Stonyshire and Loamshire, Dinah and Methodism are the 'bare-ribbed runts' on the common rather than 'a fine dairy o' cows' in a pasture—is in line with Wesley's instructions to his preachers ('Do you eat no flesh suppers? no late suppers? . . .'; 'Breakfast on nettle or orange-peel tea').[2] Commentators have stressed the worldly benefits of this Methodist discipline, of what Weber called 'intramundane asceticism'; it is the 'work-discipline' that paid.[3] Will Maskery, once a work-shy drunkard, is now 'thrifty and decent' (Ch. 5). But any material advantage was incidental; holiness was an end in itself. The unworldly ideal (Dinah's gravity and self-sacrifice, Seth's repugnance for Wiry Ben's 'wicked songs', his refusal to join the dancing at Arthur's coming-of-age celebration) was less the manifestation of gloom than the results of optimistically striving for perfection.[4] But, optimistically pursued or not, the path to perfection, as Southey sufficiently indicated, was thorny.[5] Seth discussed the matter with John Barnes, who had 'lately professed himself in a state of perfection, and I'd a question to ask him about his experience. It's one o' them subjects that lead you further than y'expect—they don't lie along the straight road' (Ch. 30).[6]

Southey's account of Wesley's distaste for farmers stands behind Dinah's admission that rural areas are less susceptible to Methodism than the towns (Ch. 5), and Mr. Poyser's dismissing Methodism as a matter for 'tradesfolks', not farmers (Ch. 18).[7] The villagers' notion that Methodists 'goes stark starin' mad wi' their religion', that 'folks allays

[1] Guy Roslyn, *George Eliot in Derbyshire* (1876), 36.

[2] Southey, op. cit., II. 87; *Minutes of Conference* (1778), Q. 24.

[3] R. N. Flew, *The Idea of Perfection in Christian Theology* (Oxford, 1934), 338; W. J. Warner, *The Wesleyan Movement in the Industrial Revolution* (New York, 1967), 141–3.

[4] John Walsh, in *A History of the Methodist Church in Great Britain*, ed. R. Davies and G. Rupp (1965), 314.

[5] Southey, op. cit., II. 70 ff.

[6] Cf. R. N. Flew, op. cit., 323; A. C. Outler (ed.), *John Wesley* (New York, 1964), 251–305; W. E. Sangster, *The Path to Perfection: An Examination and Restatement of John Wesley's Doctrine of Christian Perfection* (1943).

[7] Op. cit., I. 350–2. Southey quoted Burnet's *History of His Own Times*, on the proneness to religion of townsmen: 'As for the men of trade and business, they are generally speaking, the best body in the nation. . . .' Op. cit., I. 351–2, footnote 1.

groon when they're hearkenin' to th' Methodys . . .', and Sandy Jim's and Bessy Cranage's responses, are paralleled in Southey's extensive descriptions of revival phenomena.[1] Like many of Wesley's converts, Bessy Cranage falls away.[2]

Dinah's sermon is characteristic in form and content, as well as in effect. Her text (Luke 4:18), 'The spirit of the Lord is upon me, because he hath anointed me to preach the Gospel to the poor', was Wesley's when he 'submitted to be more vile' in his first sermon in the fields, and, with a sure sense of occasion, took the statement with which Christ initiated His public ministry.[3] Dinah claims to follow 'That man of God . . . Mr. Wesley, who spent his life in doing what our blessed Lord did—preaching the Gospel to the poor. . . . (Ch. 2).[4] Particularization ('Here Dinah turned to Bessy Cranage . . .') was the regular tactic of Wesley that brought the sermon home to John Nelson ('I thought his whole discourse was aimed at me'). Wesley and Whitefield would dramatically invoke Christ: 'Thus look unto Jesus! There is the Lamb of God, who taketh away thy sins! . . .', 'Look yonder! . . . what is it that I see? It is my agonizing Lord! Hark, hark! do you not hear? . . .'[5] Just so:

. . . Dinah had that belief in visible manifestations of Jesus, which is common among the Methodists, and she communicated it irresistibly to her hearers; she made them feel that he was among them bodily, and might at any moment show himself to them in some way that would strike anguish and penitence into their hearts.

'See!' she exclaimed, turning to the left, with her eyes fixed on a point above the heads of the people—'see where our blessed Lord stands and weeps, and stretches out his arms towards you. Hear what he says. . . .'[6]

According to Wesley, 'the Scriptural way, the Methodist way, the true way' of preaching was:

[1] e.g. op. cit., I. 168 ff.; 174 ff.; 199 ff.; II. 166–79. Cf. *Minutes of Conference* (1749), Q.3, Tuesday 13 May 1746; John Cennick, 'Account of the Most Remarkable Occurrences in the Awakening at Bristol and Kingswood . . .', Written April 1750, *WHS Proc.* 6 (1908), 101–10, 133–41; L. Tyerman, *The Life and Times of the Rev. John Wesley, M.A.* (3 Vols., 1870–1), I. 255–68; R. A. Knox, op. cit., 520–35.

[2] Southey, op. cit., I. 352–4; *Adam Bede*, Ch. 25.

[3] Southey, op. cit., I. 174.

[4] Cf. Southey, op. cit., I. 350: 'If I might choose, I should still, as I have done hitherto, *preach the gospel to the poor.*'

[5] Southey, op. cit., I. 295; II. 108.

[6] Cf. Discussion of this technique in review of a volume of sermons, *Methodist Magazine*, ser. iii, Vol. 2 (1823), p. 32. The Puritans came near the same technique: J. A. Newton, *Methodism and the Puritans* (1964), 6.

At our first beginning to preach at any place, after a general declaration of the love of God to sinners, and his willingness that they should be saved, to preach the law, in the strongest, the closest, the most searching manner possible; only intermixing the gospel here and there, and shewing it, as it were, afar off.

After more and more persons are convinced of sin, we may mix more and more of the gospel, in order to 'beget faith', to raise into spiritual life those whom the law hath slain; but this is not to be done too hastily neither. Therefore, it is not expedient wholly to omit the law; not only because we may well suppose that many of our hearers are still unconvinced; but because otherwise there is danger, that many who are convinced will heal their own wounds slightly. . . .[1]

Dinah follows this 'Methodist way'. She begins with a 'Gospel' declaration of Christ's love for the poor. Then her announcement of Christ's coming to call sinners to repentance, and the dramatic 'The *lost!* . . . Sinners! . . .', mark the transition to the 'Law':

. . . a new current of feeling . . . as she tried to bring home to the people their guilt, their wilful darkness, their state of disobedience to God—as she dwelt on the hatefulness of sin, the Divine holiness, and ['intermixing the gospel here and there'] the sufferings of the Saviour, by which a way had been opened for their salvation.

With, as it were, 'more and more' becoming 'convinced of sin', she 'mixes more and more of the gospel', drawing attention to Christ's presence among them, full of pity and love. After effecting Bessy's 'conversion', Dinah outlines the love, joy, and peace of the believer, and calls them all to 'take this blessedness'.[2] The pattern was Wesley's: small wonder that people thought George Eliot had copied one of her aunt's actual sermons.[3]

---

[1] John Wesley, *Letter on Preaching Christ*, *Works*, XI. 480–1, 486. (For 'The Terrors of the Lord' see W. L. Doughty, *John Wesley: Preacher* (1955), 106.) For a discussion of this passage see William Sargant, *Battle for the Mind: A Physiology of Conversion and Brain-Washing* (paperback edn., 1966), 85–6. (Sargant's case has been attacked by Ian Ramage, *Battle for the Free Mind* (1967).) Cf. discussion of the importance of the *Law* in preaching, in review cited in note 6, p. 151: *Methodist Magazine*, ser iii, Vol. 2 (1823), p. 30.

[2] Chad's Bess is initially hostile (amused at the Methodists' making faces, i.e. looking with melancholy compassion at the villagers). Interestingly Sargant suggests that negative emotional involvement is as likely to lead to conversion as positive attraction: op. cit., 86–7.

[3] S. Parkinson, *Scenes from the 'George Eliot' Country* (Leeds, 1888), 114. G. S. Haight, 'George Eliot's Originals', *From Jane Austen to Joseph Conrad: Essays collected in Memory of James T. Hillhouse*, ed. R. C. Rathburn and M. Steinmann (Minneapolis, 1958), 183. Miss L. Bulkley, 'Dinah Morris and Mrs. Elizabeth Evans', *Century Magazine*, N.S. 2 (1882), 552.

## (b) '*My Aunt's Story*'

G. S. Haight has stressed the importance of Southey's assistance at the expense of the influence of Mrs. Samuel Evans ('the supposed original').[1] But George Eliot's aunt had been a living and known example of early Methodism. Her conversion (1797) was as spectacular as any Southey had to describe:

. . . while I was looking to Christ, the mighty power of God fell upon me in an instant. I fell to the ground like one dead, I believe I lost my senses for a season, but when I recovered, the dear friends were praying with me, and I was trembling and weeping most bitterly. It pleased the Lord in about two hours to speak peace to my soul; I arose from my knees, and praised God for that opportunity.[2]

With access to such a source it is not surprising that Dinah and Methodism appear to be more than simply reifications of a close reading of Southey.

The equation between Dinah Morris and Mrs. Evans became a firm folk-belief, written into the Primitive Methodist record, and testified to by a tablet in the Methodist Chapel at Wirksworth ('Erected by Numerous Friends / to the Memory of / Elizabeth Evans / Known to the World as "Dinah Bede" . . .').[3] The myth inflated George Eliot's contact with her aunt: Miss Bulkley, native of Wirksworth and daughter of a Methodist associate of Samuel Evans, added to the visits recorded by George Eliot a week's stay in 1842 with the younger Samuel Evans.[4] She alleged daily meetings, notes in George Eliot's 'little book', and the aunt's lament that her niece took away 'the notes of the first sermon I preached on Ellaston Green'.[5] William Mottram, a distant relation of George Eliot, made over £1,400 by lecturing on *Adam Bede* and Elizabeth Evans.[6]

Privately, the connection was acknowledged. George Eliot's Journal contains an account (30 November 1858) of the *History of 'Adam Bede'*:

---

[1] *George Eliot*, 250.

[2] Z. Taft, 'Mrs. Elizabeth Evans', *Biographical Sketches of the Lives and Public Ministry of Various Holy Women* (2 Vols., 1825–8), I. 148.

[3] H. B. Kendall, *The Origin and History of the Primitive Methodist Church*, I. 142–4; Joseph Ritson, *The Romance of Primitive Methodism* (1909), 134; S. Parkinson, *Scenes From the 'George Eliot' Country*, 109–11; C. S. Olcott, *George Eliot: Scenes and People in her Novels* (1911), 44–5.

[4] Letter to Sophia Hennell (7 Oct. 1859), *Letters*, III. 174 ff.

[5] S. Parkinson, op. cit., 112–14 (where Miss Bulkley becomes Miss 'Buckley'). H. B. Kendall identifies Hayslope as Ellaston Green, op. cit., I. 142.

[6] Information about Mottram, and his kinship with GE, is in a letter to me from G. S. Haight.

The germ of 'Adam Bede' was an anecdote told me by my Methodist Aunt Samuel (the wife of my Father's younger brother): an anecdote from her own experience. We were sitting together one afternoon during her visit to me at Griffe, probably in 1839 or 40, when it occurred to her to tell me how she had visited a condemned criminal, a very ignorant girl who had murdered her child and refused to confess—how she had stayed with her praying, through the night and how the poor creature at last broke out into tears, and confessed her crime. My Aunt afterwards went with her in the cart to the place of execution, and she described to me the great respect with which this ministry of hers was regarded by the official people about the gaol. The story, told by my aunt with great feeling, affected me deeply, and I never lost the impression of that afternoon and our talk together. . . .[1]

This, George Eliot's most circumstantial account of her aunt's involvement (as Elizabeth Tomlinson) with Mary Voce, hanged in Nottingham (Tuesday 16 Mar. 1802) for murdering her illegitimate child, indicates the source of details in the novel: the refusal to confess, the typically Methodist procedure of accompanying the criminal to the gallows after a night in the condemned cell, and the subsequent public approval ('All Stoniton had heard of Dinah Morris, the young Methodist woman who had brought the obstinate criminal to confess . . .' (Ch. 47)).[2] Lewes suggested that the prison scene, which became 'the climax towards which I worked', might go well in a *Scene of Clerical Life*, and she 'began to think of blending this and some other recollections of my aunt in one story with some points in my father's early life and character'. When proposed publication as a *Scene of Clerical Life* fell through she 'determined on making what we always called in our conversations "My Aunt's Story", the subject of a long novel'. Dinah is not, of course, exactly like Mrs. Evans, she does not have black eyes, and her gentle preaching manner resembles more the old age than the exuberant youth of Mrs. Evans. But there is a sizeable enough debt for knowledge of the aunt to throw valuable light on the presentation of Dinah. And the context ('The character of Dinah grew out of recollections of my aunt') certainly qualifies George Eliot's assertion that 'Adam is not my father any more than Dinah is my aunt, indeed there is not a single *portrait* in *Adam Bede* . . .'.[3] (This anxious insistence related to

---

[1] *GE Letters*, II. 502 (GE, 'Autograph Journal 1854–61'; MS. in Beinecke Library, Yale).

[2] Details about Mary Voce are in the broadsheet tract the Methodists issued: Henry Taft, *An Account of the Experience and Happy Death of Mary Voce, Who was Executed on Nottingham Gallows, on Tuesday, March 16, 1802, for the Murder of Her Own Child.* (Mrs. Gaskell thought the murderess was called Mary Don, *Letters*, ed. Chapple and Pollard, No. 444, p. 579.)

[3] *GE Letters*, II. 502–3.

charges that *Scenes of Clerical Life* represented real people, charges resented because close to the truth.)[1] The letter to Sophia Hennell (7 October 1859) makes the same claim, but adds details that serve only to reveal *Adam Bede*'s further indebtedness to Mrs. Evans: her Arminian 'optimism' about God's tolerance, which shocked the Calvinist niece; her joining the 'New Wesleyans' (i.e. Primitive Methodists) *'when women were no longer allowed to preach'*; and 'one or two accounts of supposed miracles in which she believed—among the rest, *the face with the crown of thorns seen in the glass'* (which Dinah invokes to rebuke Bessy Cranage's vanity about lace).[2] So, although she insists that Dinah is not a portrait, George Eliot's most private accounts do not minimize her aunt's role in planting many a fruitful seed.

Disconcerting public events led however to anxiously excessive public disclaiming. The Liggins affair, Bracebridge's scouting for originals and finding a witness to George Eliot's copying Dinah's sermon from Mrs. Evans's manuscript, the word about 'originals' becoming fairly common knowledge, were all felt to impugn her integrity as a person and a novelist.[3] The Journal entries show the mounting sense of strain. Blackwood brings letters denying Liggins's authorship, that he has written to 'several people' (27 May, 1859). Letters to the *Times* have to be 'concocted' (5 June). 'Letter from the troublesome Mr. Quirk of Attleborough, still wanting satisfaction about Liggins' (20 July). Less pleasant than the journey (October 1859) to Lincolnshire is 'a correspondence with a *crétin* named Bracebridge . . . who undertakes to declare the process by which I wrote my books . . .' (7 Oct.). So distressed was she by November that she came near to ending her relationship with the Blackwoods because they did not act promptly enough for her over Newby's advertising *Adam Bede, Junior. A Sequel* ('not being strongly moved, apparently by what is likely to injure me more than

---

[1] 'Mr. Tryan is not a portrait of any clergyman, living or dead. He is an ideal character . . .', GE to John Blackwood [18 Aug. 1857], *GE Letters*, II. 375. Cf. '. . . I mentioned to G. that I had thought of the plan of writing a series of stories containing sketches *drawn from my own observations of the Clergy*, and calling them "Scenes from Clerical Life . . ."' [my italics], "How I came to write Fiction" (6 Dec. 1857), "Autograph Journal, 1854–1861" (Beinecke MS.); and GE's talking of "the real Dempster" and "the real Janet" ' (11 June 1857), *Letters*, II. 347.

[2] *GE Letters*, III. 174–7.

[3] R. N. Currey, 'Joseph Liggins: A slight case of literary identity', *TLS* 57 (26 Dec. 1958), 753; G. S. Haight, in *From Jane Austen to Joseph Conrad*, 182–3; G. S. Haight, *George Eliot*, 231, 244–5, 267, 280–7, 289–91, 308, 312. See also, *The Letters of Mrs. Gaskell*, ed. Chapple and Pollard, 566–7, 583–6, 592, 594, 903–5, 908–9.

them').[1] Being driven to identify herself was less galling for her (she who yearned always for acclaim and reassurance about her talent) than it was to hear of Liggins stealing her thunder (for example, a deputation of Dissenting ministers, including W. T. Rosevear, minister at Coventry's Bailey Lane Baptist Chapel, visited Liggins to urge him to contribute to the *Eclectic Review*), or to be accused of merely copying her characters and their words from the life.[2] 'How curious it seems to me that people should think Dinah's sermon, prayers, and speeches were *copied*—when they were written with hot tears, as they surged up in my own mind!'[3] When *Seth Bede 'The Methody': His Life and Labours. Chiefly Written by Himself* appeared (1859), purporting to be the life of Samuel Evans (alias Seth Evans and Seth Bede), George Eliot claimed to have reconciled herself to the 'silly falsehoods and empty opinions afloat in some petty circles' as 'the shadow to the bright fact of selling 16,000 in one year'.[4] But in indignation and self-defence she conceded less to Charles Bray than she would to Sophia Hennell ('I knew my aunt and uncle and they were Methodists—my aunt a preacher; and I loved them: so far only they resembled Seth and Dinah'), and played down the aunt's seminal role.[5] She professed 'some surprize—incredulity, rather' to hear of a journal; she did not believe her aunt '*could* write'.[6] But while she may not have seen any 'journal' (though a written account of Mrs. Evans's religious experience is drawn on by 'Guy Rosyln', and Zachariah Taft's quotations indicate a written account—'what I have written is intended to his glory . . .', 'since I have written this scrawl . . .'), George Eliot knew very well that Mrs. Evans could write. In 1839 she herself had written to her aunt: 'You know how it will delight me to see your handwriting whenever you feel able to bestow a little time on me.'[7] But the skeletons were being rushed back into the cupboard. Bracebridge, she wrote (22 September 1859), '. . . is informing his acquaintances that Dinah and Seth are portraits of my aunt and uncle—two aged people,

---

[1] 'Autograph Journal, 1854–1861' (Beinecke MS.); G. S. Haight, *George Eliot*, 314.

[2] *GE Letters*, III. 44; G. S. Haight, *George Eliot*, 281.

[3] *GE Letters*, III. 176. 'It is happy for me that I never expected any gratification of a personal kind from my authorship. The worst of all this is that it nauseates me—chills me and discourages me in my work', ibid., III. 157.

[4] (5 Dec. 1859), *GE Letters*, III. 226.

[5] [19 Sept. 1859], ibid., III. 155.

[6] Ibid., III. 157, 185.

[7] GE to Mrs. Samuel Evans (5 Mar. 1839), ibid., I. 20; Guy Roslyn, *George Eliot in Derbyshire* (1876), 31 ff.; Z. Taft, *Biographical Sketches of the Lives and Public Ministry of Various Holy Women*, I. 157–8. George Eliot was sceptical about the existence of Taft and his book, which Bracebridge claimed to have seen: *GE Letters*, III. 171, and footnote 8.

dead these twelve years with no other resemblance to my characters than that they were pious Wesleyans.'[1] In fact, of course, Mrs. Evans died in 1849, and Samuel Evans not until December 1858: he was still alive when *Adam Bede* was finished![2]

This public stance was kept up. Lewes wrote to Bracebridge that Seth and Dinah only resembled Mr. and Mrs. Evans 'as good and pious people of the same sect resemble each other'.[3] He informed 'Guy Rodgers' (alias Guy Roslyn) that George Eliot

. . . begs you to understand that *Dinah Morris was never intended to be a representation of Mrs. Elizabeth Evans*; and that any identification of the two (or of any other characters in Adam Bede with real persons) would be protested against as not only false in fact and tending to perpetuate false notions about art, but also as a gross breach of social decorum.[4]

But the strained circumstances of the insistence should alert us to the greater value of the cooler admissions of the Journal and the letter to Sophia Hennell. Dinah is of course not a *portrait*, but acquaintance with the aunt does throw light on *Adam Bede*. To take a minor example, Dinah's curious working habits, her ability to leave the Snowfield mill for preaching virtually at will, are really explicable only by reference to Mrs. Evans. Elizabeth Tomlinson was so valuable a hand to her employer at the Nottingham lace factory that he wanted to keep her services, whatever outrageous terms her career as a preacher dictated.[5]

(c) *Female Preacher*

Dinah replies to Irwine's query as to whether the Wesleyan Society sanctions women preachers (Ch. 8):

It doesn't forbid them, sir, when they've a clear call to the work, and when their ministry is owned by the conversion of sinners, and the strengthening of God's people. Mrs. Fletcher, as you may have heard about, was the first woman to preach in the Society, I believe, before she was married, when she was Miss Bosanquet; and Mr. Wesley approved of her undertaking the work. She had a great gift, and there are many others now living who are precious fellow-helpers in the work of the ministry. I understand there's been voices raised against it in the Society of late, but I cannot but think their counsel will come to nought. It isn't for men to make channels for God's Spirit, as they make channels for the water-courses, and say, 'Flow here, but flow not there'.

[1] GE to John Blackwood (22 Sept. 1859), ibid., III. 162.
[2] Adam Bede was completed 16 Nov. 1858: ibid., II. 497–8.
[3] (19 Sept. 1859), ibid., III. 159.
[4] (8 Dec. 1872), ibid., V. 339.     [5] Z. Taft, op. cit., I. 155.

The reply accurately reflects Wesley's acquiescence in the extraordinary call of women when 'God owns them in the conversion of sinners.'[1] Dinah's drawing on the analogous experience of a fellow-Methodist is also characteristic of Methodism. And George Eliot's use of the analogy (Adam reminds Seth in Chapter 51 that Mrs. Fletcher married, and therefore so might Dinah) reflects her reading of Henry Moore's *Life of Mrs. Mary Fletcher*.[2] She borrowed it in March 1839 from her aunt ('You were very kind to remember my wish to see Mrs. Fletcher's life') and returned it probably about August 1840.[3] Dinah's 'channel' image perhaps relates to Mrs. Fletcher's seeing herself as a 'pipe' through which God's blessing flows.[4]

There were indeed many 'precious fellow-helpers', and Mary Bosanquet was not the first to progress (like Dinah) from work with women, children, and the sick, to class-testifying, class-leadership and, thence preaching. Sarah Crosby and Grace Walton had been advised by Wesley about their exhorting before he sanctioned Mary Bosanquet (1771).[5] And of all the female preachers of early Methodism Sarah Crosby has particular relevance to *Adam Bede*. She was a friend of Miss Bosanquet and Sarah Ryan, and converted the future Mrs. Dobinson to Methodism at the Foundry (1759). In 1761 she moved with Mr. and Mrs. Dobinson to Derby where they pioneered Methodism. Wesley was forced to allow Sarah Crosby's right to preach, and she was probably 'the first authorised woman preacher in Methodism'.[6]

Mr. and Mrs. Dobinson's home became the centre of Derby Methodism, and Mrs. Dobinson encouraged Mrs. Elizabeth Evans to become a

[1] Leslie F. Church, *More About the Early Methodist People* (1949), 137. Cf. H. Moore (ed.), *The Life of Mrs. Mary Fletcher, Consort and Relict of the Rev. John Fletcher, Vicar of Madeley, Salop. Compiled from her Journal and other authentic documents* (Birmingham, 1817), 397–8.

[2] Henry Moore, op. cit. Southey only mentions Mrs. Fletcher in connection with her husband, who 'married Miss Bosanquet': *Life of Wesley*, II. 325.

[3] *GE Letters*, I. 18, 61.

[4] H. Moore, op. cit., 93.

[5] L. F. Church, op. cit., 139.

[6] A. W. Harrison, 'An Early Woman Preacher—Sarah Crosby', *WHS Proc.* 14 (1924), 104–9; Frank Baker, 'John Wesley and Sarah Crosby', ibid., 27 (1949–60), 76–82. For the unfortunate Sarah Ryan and Wesley, see Southey, op. cit., II. 154–5, footnote 1. And for other Methodist woman preachers, see L. F. Church, op. cit., Ch. IV, pp. 136–75; W. Parlby, 'Diana Thomas of Kington. Lay Preacher in the Hereford Circuit 1759–1821', *WHS Proc.* 14 (1924), 110–11; W. F. Swift, 'The Women Itinerant Preachers of Early Methodism', *WHS Proc.* 28 (1951–2), 89–94, and ibid., 29 (1953), 76–83; O. A. Beckerlegge, 'Women Itinerant Preachers', ibid., 30 (1956), 182–4; Z. Taft, op. cit., (2 Vols., 1825–8); Annie E. Keeling, *Eminent Methodist Women* (1889); Abel Stevens, *The Women of Methodism* (1873).

Derby Class-Leader.[1] Mrs. Evans may thus have heard of Sarah Crosby, and of her subsequent labours with the Misses Ryan and Bosanquet in Leeds. And it is probable, as A. W. Harrison suggests, that she generated Sarah Williamson, the 'holy' and 'blessed woman' whom Dinah visits in Leeds, 'a preaching woman as the Methodists think a deal on'.[2]

The 'voices raised', 'of late', against women preachers did not come to naught: the Wesleyan Conference forbade them 'in general' in 1803.[3] By the 'Epilogue' of *Adam Bede* (set in 1807) Dinah has abandoned preaching, unlike Mrs. Evans, who, in Seth's words, 'left the Wesleyans and joined a body that 'ud put no bonds on Christian liberty'. The Conference had become less liberal than Wesley and the breakaway Methodists; Bunting, editor of the *Methodist Magazine* after 1821, reportedly even suppressed details about preaching from women's obituaries.[4]

In his questioning of Dinah Irwine is also curious about possible embarrassments to the young woman preacher: 'And you never feel any embarrassment from the sense of your youth—that you are a lovely young woman on whom men's eyes are fixed?' Dinah disclaims the notion: even the 'hard and wild' men, 'rough ignorant people' around Snowfield, are not uncivil, because they see the woman less than God's presence felt through her. Nevertheless the matter is raised, and Wiry Ben's jeer in Chapter 1 ('What come ye out for to see? A prophetess? Yea, I say unto you, and more than a prophetess, an uncommon pretty woman') endorses Irwine's concern, a concern elaborated in Mrs. Fletcher's autobiography. She acknowledged that, preaching in the ball-room of a Harrogate inn, she might appear 'a bad woman, or a stage player' and be treated 'rudely'. However conscious she was of the power of God Mrs. Fletcher knew she looked 'ridiculous' preaching on a horse-block in the street at Huddersfield. But, like Whitefield and Wesley in beginning field-preaching, she gladly submitted to be 'more vile'.[5]

It might at first appear strange that George Eliot should thus imply

---

[1] Z. Taft, op. cit., I. 151.

[2] A. W. Harrison, art. cit., 108; *Adam Bede*, Chs. 8, 38, 40.

[3] *Minutes of Conference* (1803); S. Warren, *Chronicles of Wesleyan Methodism*, I (1827) 290–1.

[4] W. F. Swift, *WHS Proc.* 28 (1951–2), 90–2; cf. W. Parlby, *WHS Proc.* 14 (1924), 111, footnote by M. Riggall; L. F. Church, op. cit., 156. See also J. E. Alcock, *Notes on the Progress of Wesleyan Methodism in the Mansfield Circuit* (Mansfield, 1900), 10: quotation from Local Preachers' Minute Book (25 Sept. 1831), 'A female has very improperly been employed by one of the brethren to preach for him at Annesley Woodhouse.'

[5] H. Moore, op. cit., 89, 109; Southey, op. cit., I. 174; *The Journal of the Rev. John Wesley, A.M.*, ed. N. Curnock, II. 172, and footnote 1.

that Dinah might feel the social indignity of field-preaching, and as it were share John Wesley's and Mrs. Fletcher's sense of impropriety. Wesley had been a Fellow of Lincoln and was an Anglican clergyman; Mary Bosanquet became an Anglican minister's wife; while Dinah was, as R. H. Hutton twice, slightingly, insists, only a 'Wesleyan factory-girl'.[1] But George Eliot, rightly, sees Methodism as a sort of 'rudimentary culture'. Wesley wrote of the Nottingham Methodists: 'Most of our society are the lower-class, chiefly employed in the stocking manufacture, yet there is generally an uncommon gentleness and sweetness in their temper, and some elegance in their behaviour.'[2] Wesley and the Methodist system worked to heighten the tone, to make decorous the style, of the societies. The success of the effort may be gauged by the fact that Seth (who is, after all, only a rural carpenter) reads 'a newly-bought book—Wesley's abridgement of Madam Guyon's life' (Ch. 50).[3] (Henry Moore refers to it in his Preface to Mrs. Fletcher's *Life*.) Adam reads standard works of English, Protestant, spirituality, like *Pilgrim's Progress* and Taylor's *Holy Living and Holy Dying* (Ch. 19), but Seth is reading, in 1801, about a French Roman Catholic mystic: Wesley's cheap reprints, his encouraging Methodists to read widely, have cracked English insularity and anti-French prejudice.[4]

Wesley's literary values were characteristic of the eighteenth century: 'Perspicuity and purity, propriety, strength and easiness joined together. Where any of these is wanting, it is not a good style.'[5] Clarity and simplicity in preaching, he quickly learned, were essential: 'brown-bread', or plain style, for 'plain people'.[6] Dr. Johnson himself approved the Methodists' 'plain and familiar manner, which is the only way to do good to the common people . . .'[7] He would have extended the approval to Dinah. Her decorously plain style in speech and dress is rooted in Wesley's eighteenth-century sensibility. She

[1] R. H. Hutton, *Essays on Some of the Modern Guides of English Thought in Matters of Faith* (1887), 178.

[2] Quoted by G. H. H., *The History of Wesleyan Methodism in Nottingham and its Vicinity* (Nottingham, 1859): W. J. Warner, op. cit., 176.

[3] John Wesley, *An Extract of the Life of Madam Guion* (1776): entry No. 314 in Richard Green's *Bibliography* of Wesley's works (1896), 186.

[4] See A. C. Outler (ed.), *John Wesley* (New York, 1964), 252. For Wesley's literature programme, see F. K. Baskette, 'Early Methodists and their literature', *Emory University Quarterly*, 3 (1947), 207–16; and Southey, op. cit., I. 358; II. 86–7.

[5] Quoted by T. B. Shepherd, *Methodism and the Literature of the Eighteenth Century* (1940), 253–4; cf. F. W. Bateson, *English Poetry and the English Language* (Oxford, 1934), 50 ff.

[6] Southey, op. cit., I. 360.

[7] Boswell's *Life* (Everyman edn., 1962), I. 283–4.

sacrifices the family shame that Mrs. Poyser talks about to her vocation, but that is not to say she is not conscious of it. Bartle Massey is surprised at her lack of forwardness: 'These preaching women are not so back'ard commonly . . .' (Ch. 46). But if he, like George Eliot, had read Mrs. Fletcher's *Life* he would have seen that not all female preachers were 'forward'.[1] He too might have spotted in Wesley's friend the kind of ideal character Wesley sought to produce, and of which Dinah is no mean example.

In Mrs. Fletcher's *Life*, besides the sort of material that interested her later in Southey—sortilege, the dreams and visions, the Bibliomancy—George Eliot also learned of the wearing life of itinerant preachers. (In the novel, Brother Marlowe's exhaustion from years of combining secular work and 'watching and praying, and walking so many miles to speak the Word' took its toll (Ch. 8): Mrs. Poyser's concern about Dinah's asceticism is clearly no joke.) The novelist could even find in Mrs. Fletcher a precedent for Dinah's delay in marrying: Mr. and Mrs. Fletcher weighed the prospect of marriage for twenty-five years.[2]

And there are linguistic parallels between Dinah and Mrs. Fletcher. To be sure, a phrase like their 'drawn out in prayer' may be from stock and, like 'borne in upon my mind' (which was allegedly 'frequently used' by Mrs. Samuel Evans), readily available to friend or foe who wanted to represent an evangelical.[3] Likewise the style glutted with allusions to, and phrases and metaphors from, the Authorized Version. But it is important to see that this Biblical language is characteristic of Methodists like Mrs. Fletcher: if Dinah spoke differently she would be less truly Methodist. Those who complain about her Methodist idiom ('once she opens her mouth she fails' (W. J. Harvey); 'a self-conscious and irritating mode of speech' symptomatic of 'self-righteousness' (Joan Bennett)) have taken an unwise cue from the 'canting jargon' tradition, neither apprehending the necessity of this ideolect if Dinah is truly to represent Methodism, nor perceiving its wholly serious nature, the real communication by means of it, and its indication of the life lived in, as it were, the light of Scripture.[4]

[1] e.g. H. Moore, op. cit., 104: 'August 30. Yesterday it was given out for me to be at
——. For a whole month it lay on my mind. None, O my God, but thyself knows what I go through for every public meeting! I am often quite ill with the prospect.'
[2] H. Moore, op. cit., 129.
[3] L. Bulkley, *Century Magazine*, N.S. 2 (1882), 550. Cf. Mrs. Trollope's *Vicar of Wrexhill*, II, Ch. 7.
[4] W. J. Harvey, 'George Eliot and the Omniscient Author Convention', NCF 13 (1958–9), 96; J. Bennett, *George Eliot: Her Mind and Her Art* (Cambridge, 1954), 108–9. See G. A. Starr, *Defoe and Spiritual Autobiography* (Princeton, 1965), 21 ff.; 'On the

## (d) '*By the word of their Testimony*'

The Methodist Revival propagated 'experimental' religion: the Methodist was a man who had had, and was supposed to enjoy still, a religious experience.[1] Experience was to be checked by Scripture, and Henry Moore, bearing in mind Wesley's objection that Madame Guyon subordinated Scripture to experience, stressed that Mrs. Fletcher always tested her experience by the Bible.[2] So Dinah, like a good Wesleyan, ensures that her leadings are endorsed by direction from the Bible, albeit randomly opened (Ch. 3). Nevertheless, as outsiders scornfully insisted, the stress on experience meant that pre-eminence did tend to get granted to the feelings. Dinah feels led back to Stonyshire; she talks of 'assurances' and 'direction'. Mrs. Poyser is sceptical: 'You feel! yes. . . . That's allays the reason I'm to sit down wi', when you've a mind to do anything contrairy' (Ch. 49). 'When there's a bigger maggot than usual in your head you call it "direction" . . .' (Ch. 6). The scepticism was George Eliot's:

No one can have talked to the more enthusiastic Methodists and listened to their stories of miracles without perceiving that they require no other passport to a statement than that it accords with their wishes and their general conception of God's dealings; nay, they regard as a symptom of sinful scepticism an inquiry into the evidence for a story which they think unquestionably tends to the glory of God, and in retailing such stories, new particulars, further tending to his glory, are 'borne in' upon their minds.[3]

She was probably recalling here her conversations with her aunt, her exposure to the characteristic Methodist compulsion to bear witness. Sanctioning Sarah Crosby's ministry, Wesley urged her to tell 'nakedly' what was 'in [her] heart'.[4] Dinah is as ready to declare the intimacies of her soul to Irwine and Lisbeth Bede as Mrs. Evans was to her niece. In class and band meetings, in love feasts and 'experience meetings', the

---

ludicrous use of the language of the Holy Scriptures, in matters of common life', *Methodist Magazine*, ser. iii, Vol. I (1822), p. 173; 'On the Peculiarities of Religious Phraseology', ibid., ser. iii, Vol. II (1832), pp. 172–80; Ian Robinson, 'Religious English', *Cambridge Quarterly*, 2 (Autumn, 1967), 303–38.

[1] R. E. Davies, *Methodism* (Penguin, 1963), 72; R. A. Knox, *Enthusiasm* (1962 edn.), 513–48 (Ch. XXI, 'Wesley and the Religion of Experience').

[2] J. Wesley, *An Extract of the Life of Madam Guion* (1776), Preface, v–vii; H. Moore, op. cit., Preface, xx–xxi (cf. xxiii, for mention of 'Madam Guion').

[3] 'Evangelical Teaching: Dr. Cumming', *WR*, N.S. 8 (1855), 442; T. Pinney (ed.) *Essays of George Eliot*, 166–7.

[4] A. W. Harrison, *WHS Proc.* 14 (1924), 106.

Methodists eagerly testified of their religious experiences.[1] Mutual confession was the principle of fellowship, and the basis of the discipline
Dinah described to Irwine: 'There's a very strict order kept among us,
and the brethren and sisters watch for each other's souls as they that
must give account' (Ch. 8).[2]

The confessions were written in journals and autobiographies as well
as uttered in public. In this Methodists consciously imitated the Puritans.
Wesley was, of course, descended from Nonconformists. His paternal
grandfather and namesake was a protégé of John Owen, ejected in 1662
and imprisoned four times. Samuel Annesley, his maternal grandfather,
was Defoe's schoolmaster. Samuel Wesley, John's father, was educated
at Dissenting Academies, and once heard Bunyan preach.[3] And though
his parents had become High Church, Wesley absorbed Puritan influences with, as it were, his mother's milk.[4] His mother read Puritan
divines (Richard Baxter was her favourite), led an ordered life, medi-
tated regularly, and kept a spiritual day-book. And Methodism's debt
to Puritanism is symbolized not only in the number of Puritan authors
in Wesley's *Christian Library*, but in his encouragement of diary-keeping
and autobiography.[5]

The first Conference (1744) decided that the 'Assistant' preachers
should keep journals for 'our satisfaction' and 'the profit of their own
souls'. After 1793 every preacher had to 'draw out a sketch of his life
and experience'.[6] Wesley got his preachers to write accounts of their
lives for the *Arminian Magazine*; in the later years of his life the Conference Minutes began to carry biographies of the preachers who died.
Verbal and written testimonies made a focus for self-examination;
they also provided models for others' experience, and sources of comfort, encouragement, example. *The Form of Discipline* (1797) suggested,
as a stimulus for revival: 'Let every Preacher read carefully over the
Life and Journals of the late Mr. Wesley, the Life of Mr. Fletcher, the

[1] *Rules of the Band Societies* (1738); *Rules of the Society of the People Called Methodists* (1743):
in Samuel Warren, *Chronicles of Wesleyan Methodism*, I (1827), 262, 284–6; Davies and
Rupp, op. cit., 272, 311; *Samuel Sellars: Memoirs and Remains* (1875), 29.
[2] See John Lawson, 'The People called Methodists. 2 Our Discipline', Davies and
Rupp, op. cit., 188–91.
[3] A. Skevington Wood, 'John Wesley's Reversion to Type: The Influence of his Nonconformist Ancestry', WHS Proc. 35 (Dec. 1965), 88, 89; R. E. Davies, *Methodism*, 44,
footnote.
[4] J. A. Newton, *Methodism and the Puritans* (1964), 7.
[5] For Puritan works on self-examination in Wesley's Christian Library, see R. C. Monk,
*John Wesley: His Puritan Heritage* (1966), 171–3.
[6] *Minutes of Conference* (1744), Q.4; *Minutes of Conference* (1793), Q.25.

Life of David Brainerd; and let us be followers of them as they were of
Christ. . . .'[1] Published *Lives*, like verbal testimonies, constituted
*exempla*; the individual Methodist drew strength from his sense of
partnership with the person he heard testifying or whose *Life* he had
read. Mrs. Fletcher used memoirs as texts for her sermons.[2] Diarists
recorded their reading: Mrs. Fletcher noted in her diary her impressions
of 'the Life of Mr. David Brainard', of the *Magazine* accounts of Prudence Williams and 'a little diary of dear Mrs. Yate', and recorded
gobbets of the experience of people she knew.[3] Each *Memoir* thus became
a kind of sum of previous accounts and written records of spiritual
experience: just as the individual Methodist was the product of an
accretion, a coalition of testimony—the sum of all his fellows and predecessors.

In this context it is possible to see *Adam Bede*'s affinities with the
characteristic Methodist memoir. The typical memoir alludes to the
antecedent analogous lives that have been influential; and the 'memoir'
of Dinah Morris draws on and declares parallels with John Wesley's,
Mrs. Fletcher's, Sarah Williamson's experiences. And, in a curious
way, the novel and Dinah can be said to have been generated and formed,
like the typical Methodist, by a coalition of testimony and biography:
Mrs. Evans's verbal testimony, Mrs. Fletcher's *Life*, Southey's *Life of
Wesley*. It was indeed, as George Eliot put it, 'a combination from widely
sundered elements of experience'.[4] As Defoe's novels grew out of
Puritan autobiography, so *Adam Bede* has affinities with, is generated
by, Methodist testimony.[5] *Adam Bede* is, in this sense, the first truly
Methodist novel. It is easy to see why that posse of Dissenting parsons
called on Liggins.

Methodist hymns were prime expressions of phases of the Methodist
experience, what it was to *know, feel,* and *prove* Christ.[6] The *Collection of*

[1] *Minutes of the Methodist Conferences from the first, held in London, by the late Rev. John
Wesley, A.M., in the year 1744*, Vol. I (1862), p. 683.

[2] L. F. Church, op. cit., 146.

[3] H. Moore, op. cit., 271–2, 287, 291, 209.

[4] GE to Chas. Bray [19 Sept. 1859], *GE Letters*, III. 155.

[5] For the novel's debt to Puritan autobiography, see G. A. Starr, op. cit.; Ian Watt,
'Defoe as Novelist', in *From Dryden to Johnson*, Pelican Guide to English Literature, ed.
B. Ford (1957), Vol. 4, pp. 203–16. Also, on affinities between Methodist autobiography
and fiction: T. B. Shepherd, *Methodism and the Literature of the Eighteenth Century* (1940),
148–62.

[6] 'Are we reading, we may ask, so many studies in autobiography?' W. F. Lofthouse,
'Charles Wesley', Davies and Rupp, op. cit., 135; G. H. Findlay, 'Two Verbs: Feel and
Prove', *Christ's Standard Bearer: A Study in the hymns of Charles Wesley* . . . (1956), Ch. 5,
pp. 39–46.

*Hymns, For the Use of the People called Methodists* was arranged to represent stages of Christian experience, it was 'a little body of experimental and practical divinity'.[1] In fact John Wesley arranged it 'as a spiritual biography of the sort of person whom he called in the Preface a real Christian'.[2] Singing a Methodist hymn was an expression of personal experience like a testimony or autobiography, and a declaration of affiliation with the Wesleys' experiences, with this characteristic Methodist life of faith epitomized in John Wesley's arrangement of his brother's hymns. The hymns expressed and demonstrated the Methodist experience; and they provided a code-language equally as important as the words of the Authorized Version, if not more so.

Naturally the Methodists in *Adam Bede* use hymns (and in fact, not only the Methodists: Adam's hymn is Anglican—Bishop Ken's morning hymn). Dinah reinforces her sermon's optimistic proclamation of the Arminian gospel with a verse from Charles Wesley ('Enough for all, enough for each').[3] But, unlike Charlotte Brontë, George Eliot rarely quotes straightforwardly from the Hymn Book; she *uses* the verses she quotes. Seth ('very fond of hymns') naturally repeats two stanzas of a favourite hymn, 'Dark and Cheerless is the morn' (Ch. 38). They refer ironically, of course, to Hetty's plight, the darkness of her friendless, alienated journey, and anticipate her spiritual illumination in the prison ('Fill me, Radiancy Divine'). Noteworthily, though, George Eliot has selected stanzas containing no specifically Christian terminology, preparing the way for the humanist ending of the novel. The hymn's last couplet, for example ('Haste, my Lord, no more delay!/Come, my Saviour, come away!'), is excluded.[4] Similarly Dinah sings to herself only stanzas 1, 2, and 5 of 'Eternal Beam of Light Divine' (Ch. 50), thus making that hymn a plea for resolution of conflict, with more than a hint of her struggle about the prospect of marriage ('Speak to my warring passions, "Peace!" '). Intact, the hymn reads quite differently:

---

[1] John Wesley, *A Collection of Hymns* . . . (1780), Preface, iv.

[2] B. L. Manning, *The Hymns of Wesley and Watts* (1942), 11.

[3] Stanza 4 of No. 241, in *A Collection of Hymns* (2nd edn., 1781), from the section 'For Believers Rejoicing'.

[4] It is difficult to say exactly which verses George Eliot omits. Before 1780 the last stanza of this hymn was 'Christ, whose Glory fills the Skies,/Christ the true and only light', but as No. 150 in the 1780 *Collection*, it had become 'O disclose the lovely face': Frank Baker, *Representative Verse of Charles Wesley* (1962), 19. Omission of 'Christ, whose Glory . . .' would be damning; but Seth's 'Till *thou* inward light impart', incorporates the *thou* (for previous *they* and *thy*) which only got into the hymn in the 2nd (1781) edn. George Eliot was, then, almost certainly using at least a post-1781 Hymn Book. Cf. below, note 3, p. 166.

it is a prayer of acquiescence in God's will, an acceptance of suffering, even death; it anticipates pain and death, and is taken from the section 'Discipline and Resignation: For Believers Suffering'. Dinah may be suffering now, but the novel hardly equates her marriage to Adam with suffering and dying. So the inconvenient stanzas are silently omitted.[1]

Alteration of hymns has never been malpractice, and is a testimony to the way hymns are made personal property.[2] But George Eliot lets Seth bear the blame for her most blatant and daring alteration. He apologizes, as well he might, for improving on Watts's 'My God, the spring of all my joys':

Perhaps I feel more for you than I ought to feel for any creature, for I often can't help saying of you what the hymn says—

> In darkest shades if she appear,
> My dawning is begun;
> She is my soul's bright morning-star,
> And she my rising sun.

That may be wrong, and I am to be taught better. . . . (Ch. 3)[3]

The change of pronouns is like the blasphemous inscription (*Illumina Tenebr[as] Nostras Domina*) on the portrait of Donne.[4] The implication is clear, even without George Eliot's humanist point: 'Love of this sort is hardly distinguishable from religious feeling. What deep and worthy love is so?' Clearly the hymns have a face value in the novel, they are to signal the Methodist mentality; but they are also tailored to serve the novel, especially its humanism.

### (e) *The Ending: Conversion and Marriage*

With its story of imprisonment for child-murder and release from prison *Adam Bede* obviously owes something to *The Heart of Midlothian*; but, in making the prison scene climactic, and equating release from physical prison with spiritual emancipation, George Eliot related her novel even more closely to *Moll Flanders*.[5] And to turn Biblical metaphor

[1] No. 328, in the 1781 *Collection*. GE has 'holy fear' in stanza 2; all the Hymn Book versions I have seen have 'lowly fear'.

[2] See Martha Winburn England and John Sparrow, *Hymns Unbidden* (New York, 1966), 39.

[3] The hymn was inserted into the *Collection* ('New Edition', 1797), p. 90, between 87 and 88, as 87*. George Eliot's edition of the *Collection* was thus probably a post-1797 edn. Cf. above, note 4, p. 165.

[4] J. B. Leishman, *The Monarch of Wit* (1951; 6th edn., 1962), Frontispiece.

[5] There is no actual statement that she read *Moll Flanders*, but it is extremely likely given her acquaintance with Defoe's *Robinson Crusoe* ('Balzac and His Writings', *WR*, N.S.

into plot, as Defoe had done in *Moll Flanders*, was extremely apposite in a novel treating of Methodism.

'Methodists are great folk for going into prisons', Adam says to Irwine. The early Methodists, from Holy Club days at Oxford onwards, made it a central and characteristic function.[1] Their literature and hymns reflected this orientation and their awareness that conversions effected in prison were an appropriate acting out of New Testament metaphor: salvation was a release from the bondage and captivity of sin.[2] Charles Wesley's hymn, 'And can it be, that I should gain', made the imagery particularly memorable:

> Long my imprisoned spirit lay
> Fast bound in sin and nature's night:
> Thine eye diffused a quickening ray;
> I woke; the dungeon flamed with light;
> My chains fell off, my heart was free,
> I rose, went forth, and followed thee.[3]

In many of its details Hetty's case follows a well-established routine: a Methodist stays overnight in the condemned cell, elicits confession and repentance, and accompanies the malefactor to the gallows, ministering comfort. Mary Voce had gone to the gallows accompanied by 'above one hundred voices singing penitentiary hymns on the way to and at the gallows, and three or four persons attending voluntarily in the cart, administering comfort and consolation'.[4] The Methodists encouraged confession of crime as an indication of repentance towards God. Silas Told exhorted Mrs. Brownrigg, condemned for murder:

I am afraid you do not sufficiently permit the Spirit of God to convince you of the enormity of the crime for which you are condemned. Are you condemned in your own conscience? Do you judge yourself, that you may not be judged of

4 (July 1853), 212; *GE Letters*, I. 21) and *History of the Devil* (Cross's *Life*, (1st edn.), I. 23; P-G. Maheu, *La Pensée religieuse et morale de George Eliot* (Paris, 1958)).

[1] Charles Wesley's *Journal*, ed. Thomas Jackson (2 Vols., 1849), I. 117 ff. (July 1738); L. F. Church, op. cit., 196 ff.; *An Account of the Life and Dealings of God with Silas Told*, written by Himself (1786), particularly 104 ff.; Southey, op. cit., II. 312–13; W. J. Warner, op. cit., 237 ff.

[2] John Wesley, *A Word to the Condemned Malefactor*, *Works*, XI. 179–82; Charles Wesley, *Prayers for Condemned Malefactors*, G. Osborn (ed.), *The Poetical Works of John and Charles Wesley* (11 Vols., 1868–71), VIII. 339–53.

[3] No. 193, *Collection* (1780); Frank Baker, *Representative Verse of Charles Wesley* (1962), 9–10.

[4] *The Nottingham Date Book 1750–1879* (Nottingham, 1880), 237.

God? Condemn yourself, that you may not be condemned in the day of judgement, when the secrets of all hearts will be open to God. . . .[1]

The Nottingham Methodists, including Elizabeth Tomlinson, persuaded Mary Voce to confess her guilt only after weeks of effort. Confession was the necessary step towards conversion. Of a recent murder trial the *Methodist Magazine* (1824) said:

. . . we see in this case nothing to indicate genuine religious feeling;—no mark, no proof of that true, and, if true in his case especially, that deep and heart-rending repentance, and *full and honest confession*, which was called for by God and by society. . . . He was not frankly dealt with by his spiritual adviser, if he did not urge him to confess his crimes, as the only means of reparation to injured society; as fulfilling the injunctions of the Gospel. . . . But whether reminded of this or not, a true penitence would have opened the heart and the lips. . . .[2]

The exhortations to confession in the novel are, then, customary, but the results in Hetty's case hardly conform to the pattern. Mary Voce was typical: the euphoria on the way to the gallows ('This is the best day I ever saw, I am quite happy, I had rather die than live'), the joy at the moment of death ('Glory! Glory to Jesus! . . . I shall soon be in Glory,—Glory is indeed already begun in my soul, and the angels of God are about me!'), exhortations to the crowd ('She desired the people at the gallows to take warning by her'), occur repeatedly in the accounts of Charles Wesley and Silas Told. That was what always happened on the way to execution. And the executed became focuses of propaganda: on the evening of Mary Voce's execution Mr. Kane preached in the crowded Halifax Lane Chapel, Nottingham, on 'Is not this a Brand plucked from the fire?'; a broadsheet account of her death was issued;[3] and one of the Methodist women who accompanied Mary Voce wrote a ballad about her.[4]

Even discounting the reprieve, there is little in Hetty's repentance that would have given substance to a Methodist sermon. There is no joy or repose in the sense of God's pardon; we cannot imagine her addressing the crowd. The tone of the account is quite different from

[1] Silas Told, op. cit., 162–3.

[2] 'Christian Retrospect . . . XVI . . . Thurtell's alleged penitence . . .', *Methodist Magazine*, ser. iii, Vol. 3 (1824), pp. 123–4.

[3] *An Account of the Experience and Happy Death of Mary Voce.*

[4] Mottram, op. cit., 200–1, quotes the ballad. A Letter in the Nottingham *Guardian* (12 Aug. 1911) names Sarah Cummins (or Cummens) as the author of what is probably the same poem.

the jubilation of the Methodist broadsheet about Mary Voce. And the difference is rooted in the fact that, although Hetty confesses and becomes a 'penitent', hers is no turning to a supernatural fountain of forgiveness and strength. She leans on Dinah as a human being, rather than on a Divine source of comfort: 'She was clinging close to Dinah; her cheek was against Dinah's. It seemed as if her last faint strength and hope lay in that contact; and the pitying love that shone out from Dinah's face looked like a visible pledge of the Invisible Mercy' (Ch. 46). In the characteristic Methodist account, the convict leans, with manifest assurance, on his new-found Saviour; Hetty clings to Dinah, the only saviour she knows: 'the only visible sign of love and pity' (Ch. 47). Dinah's words (in her prayers and counsel she is perhaps at her most authentically Methodist) thus fall curiously flat: they could generate the Mary Voce result, instead they merely affirm a humanist, Feuerbachian point. Hetty's 'regeneration' is as non-Divine as Adam's.[1] George Eliot as it were demythologizes the traditional formulas of repentance and conversion as Feuerbach had reinterpreted, humanistically, the Christian symbols and theology. Hetty repents superficially to God, but most movingly to Adam: the human connection is the most prominent.

And the result is less a concession wrung from the reader that, after all, Dinah's words about, and faith in, God are a mistaken and now untenable gloss on what is essentially human sympathy, than the feeling that all that has gone before is wasted. A great deal of research, of labour, went into creating the authentic feel and tone of Dinah's Methodism. George Eliot was perhaps even too sympathetic, too involved: the 'hot tears' as she wrote Dinah's prayers and sermons deflected the critical, objective eye that bears on, say, Dorothea Brooke. She recognized early in her life where her sympathies tended: 'I hardly know,' she once wrote to Mrs. Pears, 'whether I am ranting after the fashion of one of the Primitive Methodist prophetesses with a cart for her rostrum, I am writing so fast.'[2] And much of that sympathy and that 'deep feeling' as she listened to her aunt's account of the prison scenes ('I only remember her tone and manner, and the deep

---

[1] Cf. U. C. Knoepflmacher, *Religious Humanism and the Victorian Novel*, 55–9, and *George Eliot's Early Novels: The Limits of Realism* (Berkeley, Calif., 1968), 111–12.

[2] GE to Mrs. Abijah Hill Pears [28 Jan. 1842], *GE Letters*, I. 126. Cf. George Eliot's note on the manuscript of *Adam Bede* presented to Lewes (23 Mar. 1859): 'A large portion of it was written twice . . . but other parts only once, and among these the descriptions of Dinah and a good deal of her sermon . . .' (BM MSS.).

feeling I had under the recital')[1] gets into *Adam Bede*. Dinah carries a great deal of authorial weight. The ending must, then, be construed as George Eliot's wrenching away from the novel her emotional support, her sympathy with Dinah, and the imposition, in intellectual allegiance to Feuerbach, of the humanizing reinterpretation. The novel, having schooled the reader to accept the, if anything, over-sympathetic handling of Dinah, then throws him off balance by, so to speak, sharply tugging away the rug.

Having done that much damage George Eliot then let her novel go: let it run aground firmly on the sunken rocks of melodrama and convention. Hetty is reprieved, and must be transported. There is nothing else the novel can do with her, for Adam, on George Henry Lewes's regrettable suggestion, is to be married to Dinah.[2] Bulwer Lytton objected to the marriage (perversely, perhaps, in view of his own hand in *Great Expectations*), as did, and most forcibly, Henry James:

> If the story had ended, as I should have infinitely preferred to see it end, with Hetty's execution, or even with her reprieve, and if Adam had been left to his grief, and Dinah Morris to the enjoyment of that distinguished celibacy for which she was so well suited, then I think Adam might have shared the honors of pre-eminence with his hapless sweetheart. . . .
>
> I doubt very much whether the author herself had a clear vision, for instance, of the marriage of Dinah Morris to Adam, or of the rescue of Hetty from the scaffold at the eleventh hour . . . an evidence of artistic weakness; they are a very good example of the view in which a story must have marriages and rescues in the nick of time. . . .[3]

Debris from another ending lies about at the end and Seth is left oddly stranded, a supernumerary actor in Dinah's marriage, talking of the possibility of their leaving the Wesleyans and joining a more liberal body. His possessive tone towards Dinah hints that before Lewes made his suggestion Seth might have been intended for her, and the rightness of that tone supports the Methodist literature that points out that 'Seth Evans' had in fact in the life married his 'Dinah Morris'.[4] However, in the blur of the ending, having given Dinah Feuerbach in exchange for

---

[1] GE to Sophia Hennell (7 Oct. 1859), *GE Letters*, III. 176.

[2] 'Autograph Journal, 1854–1861' (30 Nov. 1858); *GE Letters*, II. 503.

[3] *GE Letters*, III. 264 (23 Feb. 1860); Henry James, *Atlantic Monthly*, 18 (Oct. 1866), in G. S. Haight, *A Century of GE Criticism*, 47, and *Atlantic Monthly*, 55 (May, 1885), quoted by F. R. Leavis, *The Great Tradition* (Penguin, 1962), 50.

[4] e.g. '. . . the author has taken warrantable liberty, and represented Dinah as the wife of Adam Bede. This . . . was not the case, Dinah preferring to cast her lot with "the Methody".' *Seth Bede 'The Methody'*, Introduction, [4].

her Christ, George Eliot obviously felt little compunction in stripping
her of her vocation and marrying her to the agnostic, or at best nominally
Anglican, Adam. The abandonment of preaching (where Mrs. Evans
continued after the Conference ban) and the marriage to Adam (where,
as the reading of Southey, to say the least, would show, Methodists
strenuously opposed mixed marriage) indicate some change of heart, a
change of character. But the switch is abruptly contrived and left un-
explained. There is no credible transition to humanism; Feuerbach is
simply imposed on Dinah, on a Methodism whose very real life, convincingly portrayed, is not at all extinguished. The marriage and the
abandonment of preaching are, one supposes, to indicate Dinah's silent
concession to Feuerbach, to George Eliot. But this is sleight of hand,
not argument or demonstration: a victory is conceded, but we know the
contest has been rigged. The early chapters, the Dinah of Hayslope
Green, can't convincingly be put down just like that.[1]

### 3. FELIX HOLT

The pious ones, from the Pope to the yogis of California, are great on the
'change of heart', much more reassuring from their point of view than a change
in the economic system.

George Orwell, 'Looking Back on the Spanish War'.

*Felix Holt* was written less compulsively than *Adam Bede*.[2] The Methodist
style had come almost too readily: George Eliot realized in that novel,
as we have seen, her propensity for 'ranting' after the fashion of a
Primitive Methodist prophetess. But what *Felix Holt* lost in spontaneity
(it had to be made up for as in *Romola* by research and hard reading) was
compensated for by objectivity. Dissent could not be treated with irony
as well as with sympathy and tolerance; the debilitating emotional
involvement with Dinah, that prevented the kind of focus and control
that are manifest in the clear-eyed handling of Dorothea, was of the
past: George Eliot had journeyed that much further from her early
evangelicalism. She set the pace, manifested the authority and objectivity
she sought in this account of Dissent, in the magisterial social–historical
survey of the 'Author's Introduction'.

[1] 'The superlative effect reached by George Eliot in her delineation of Dinah preaching
on the village green and in the bed-chamber or the condemned cell of Hetty . . . renders
it inexpressibly disappointing that Dinah Morris should be metamorphosed in so commonplace, not to say undignified a manner, into the beer-chronicling, fool-suckling Mrs.
Adam Bede.' 'George Eliot', *BQR* 45 (Jan. 1867), 166.
[2] For its shaky start, see F. C. Thompson, 'The Genesis of Felix Holt', *PMLA* 74 (1959),
576–84.

Nevertheless, the going was hard. She wrote in her diary (23 July
1865), almost four months after she had begun the new novel, that she
was 'going doggedly to work . . . seeing what determination can do in
the face of despair. Reading Neale's [*sic*] History of the Puritans.'[1]
(Readers of Neal will appreciate that 'determination'.) Research was her
defence against the threat of silence, and the resultant patchwork of
memories of Nuneaton and Coventry, invention, reading, and legal
problems (obligingly sorted out by Frederic Harrison) is often un-
wieldy. The footnotes tend to show glaringly through: Rufus Lyon is
(Ch. 6) 'a bishop—i.e. the overseer of an Independent church and
congregation'.

The most apparent assistance from Neal was the suggestion for Lyon's
challenging to public debate the representative of the Church, when the
Independent pastor's reputation as logician and preacher ('a talking
machine') frightens off the opposition. This abortive encounter helps
along the plot (Christian finds out that Esther is not a Jermyn), illustrates
the antagonism between Church and Dissent, and places Rufus Lyon as
an old-fashioned puritan, conscious of his Nonconformist heritage,
eager for debate, following established precedents in the puritan manner
('He evidently feels himself in company with Luther and Zwingle and
Calvin and considers our letters part of the history of Protestantism'
(Ch. 23)):

How had that man of God and exemplary Independent minister, Mr. Ainsworth,
of persecuted sanctity, conducted himself when a similar occasion had befallen
him at Amsterdam? He had thought of nothing but the glory of the highest
cause and had converted the offer of recompense into a public debate
with a Jew on the chief mysteries of the faith. Here was a model: the case was
nothing short of a heavenly indication, and he, Rufus Lyon, would seize the
occasion to demand a public debate with the Rector on the Constitution of the
true Church. (Ch. 15)[2]

Rufus is modelling himself on not only a learned puritan divine ('the
learned Mr. *Ainsworth*, the *Rabbi* of his age'), but a Brownist, a pioneer
Congregationalist.[3] The reader familiar with Neal might have anticipated

---

[1] *GE Letters*, IV. 97.

[2] Ainsworth was reputedly an ancestor of W. Harrison Ainsworth, the novelist and man
of letters. 'Memoir of W. Harrison Ainsworth, Esq.', *Mirror of Literature, Amusement and
Instruction*, N.S. 1 (1842), v–xvi. (Disputed by John Evans, 'The Early Life of W. Harrison
Ainsworth', *Manchester Quarterly*, 1 (1882), 136–55.) For Ainsworth see above, note 3,
pp. 57–58.

[3] Daniel Neal, *History of the Puritans* (2nd corrected edn., 2 Vols., 1754), I. 363. (The
original edn. (1732–8) was published in 4 Vols.) GE knew about Ainsworth: in the

Lyon's failure; but at this stage in the novel (Ch. 15) George Eliot has
Lyon keep Ainsworth's failure to himself.[1] Her notebook, however,
told the whole story in a note drawn from Neal:

> Mr. Ainsworth's death (a Brownist minister) was sudden, and not without sus-
> picion of violence; for it is reported, that having found a diamond of very great
> value in the streets of Amsterdam, he advertised it in print, and when the
> owner who was a Jew, came to demand it, he offered him any acknowledgement he
> would desire; but Ainsworth though poor, would accept nothing but a confer-
> ence with some of the rabbies upon the prophecies of the Old Testament relating
> to the Messias, which the other promised but not having interest enough to obtain
> it, and Ainsworth being resolute, it is thought he was poisoned.[2]

Other notes in the notebook went straight into the novel, e.g. ' "The
bottomless perjury of an *et caetera*" Lord Digby at opening of th [*sic*]
long Parliament', and 'Root and Branch Petition, 1640'. Rufus is sure
Felix 'will not deny that you glory in the name of Radical, or Root-and-
branch man, as they said in the great times when Nonconformity was in
its giant youth' (Ch. 27). '*Root and Branch*, or the total extirpating of
episcopacy', was Neal's sharp definition.[3] Again, knowledge of Nonconformist history, or a reading of Neal, helps to illuminate the
squirearchy's unease over the *carte blanche* given to Rufus: ' "You are
afraid of my committing myself to the 'bottomless perjury of an et
cetera'," said Philip, smiling . . .', and quoting Lord Digby, as well
he might (Ch. 14).[4] Neal had explained the objection of the Commons:

> It was argued likewise against the *oath itself*, that in some parts it was very
> ambiguous and doubtful. . . .
> . . . And the ambiguity is further increased by that remarkable *et caetera*,
> inserted in the body of the oath; for whereas oaths ought to be explicit, and the

---

'Quarry' ('Felix Holt the Radical: autograph manuscript notebook of memoranda,
statistics, historical notes and quotations collected preparatory to writing *Felix Holt the
Radical*, No place [1861]', MS. Vault Eliot 10, Yale Univ. Library) she noted that the
Puritan founders of New Plymouth were 'Brownists under the pastoral care of W.
Robinson at Leyden', and (Neal, I. 380), 'Mr. Robinson pastor of the church at Leyden,
first struck out the congregational or independent form of church government.'

[1] The two points (Lyon's seeking ancient analogues for his behaviour, and the failure of
the debate already implicit in Neal) are missed by Arnold Kettle, '*Felix Holt the Radical*',
*Critical Essays on George Eliot*, ed. Barbara Hardy (1970), 108–9. And by W. J. Harvey, who
suggests several reasons why the debate does not occur, but misses the most obvious one,
*The Art of George Eliot* (1961), 134.

[2] Neal, op. cit., I. 436–7 (George Eliot's note, 'Neale II. 42', indicates that she had
access to the 1st, 4 Vol. edn.).

[3] Op. cit., I. 675 ff., 680.

[4] Neal, op. cit., I. 647.

sense of the words as clear and determined as possible, we are here to swear to we know not what, to something that is not expressed; by which means we are left to the arbitrary interpretation of the judge, and may be involved in the guilt of perjury before we are aware.[1]

With George Eliot making full use of her reading of Neal the novel is, if anything, over-informative about Congregational polity and theory. The *Nonconformist* reviewer thought Rufus Lyon untypical, but, 'such illusions as are occasioned by the introduction of his character are generous in tone and display knowledge more or less intimate of what the author puts into her picture . . . .'[2] Lyon's declarations of the primitive validity of Congregationalism have the air of gobbets from Neal. Too often his presentation signals to the reader that authorial research has gone on *here*. It is, for example, bluntly put to us that Rufus 'was susceptible concerning the true office of deacons in the primitive Church' (Ch. 4).[3]

But George Eliot can do better than this. She invests Rufus with a very real sort of life: the 'odd-looking rusty old man', jeered at by schoolboys as 'Revelations', with his little legs and large head, and 'large, brown, short-sighted eyes' (exactly like Silas Marner), is sympathetically observed. And she shows, does not simply state, the outworkings of the Congregationalist polity. She presents the leading members, the deacons Nuttwood and Muscat, asserting their critical rights. Division threatens over the choir; individual jealousies and vanities emerge. The minister under the Voluntary system is subject to his congregation's constant scrutiny, they can dismiss him for theology too 'high' or for theology not 'high' enough. Rufus resigned his Skipper's Lane pastorate when regard for Annette modified his doctrine of Reprobation and the congregation detected this 'laxity'. Malthouse Yard was a less auspicious post, but here, too, his orthodoxy is suspect: Mrs. Holt's late husband ('he'd have been as good a judge of your gifts as Mr. Nuttwood or Mr. Muscat') would have had to ponder whether Lyon's doctrine was 'high enough' (Ch. 4). (Malthouse Yard chose a successor with higher doctrine.) And the minister was regarded as a servant, albeit the servant of a democracy:

[1] Neal, op. cit., I. 651–2.

[2] *Nonconformist*, 26 (15 July 1866), 606.

[3] Cf. F. R. Leavis, Introduction to Everyman (1966) edn., ix: Lyon is 'another of the book's liabilities, produced by her attempt to endow with a lovable personality the precipitation from her reading up, for the purpose of the novel, of Neale's [*sic*] *History of the Puritans*'.

. . . at that time the preacher who was paid under the Voluntary system was regarded by his flock with feelings not less mixed than the spiritual person who still took his tithe-pig or his *modus*. His gifts were admired, and tears were shed under best bonnets at his sermons; but the weaker tea was thought good enough for him; and even when he went to preach a charity sermon in a strange town, he was treated with home-made wine and the smaller bedroom . . . the good Dissenter sometimes mixed his approval of ministerial gifts with considerable criticism and cheapening of the human vessel which contained those treasures. Mrs. Muscat and Mrs. Nuttwood applied the principle of Christian equality by remarking that Mr. Lyon had his oddities, and that he ought not to allow his daughter to indulge in such unbecoming expenditure on her gloves, shoes, and hosiery, even if she did pay for them out of her earnings. (Ch. 6)

This aspect of Voluntaryism was commonly dwelt on, familiarized to the reading public by Mrs. Oliphant's and Mark Rutherford's novels and by anti-sectarian literature like the *Physiology of the Sects* and William Pitt Scargill's *Autobiography of a Dissenting Minister* (1834). But, for all the 'narrowness or asperity' of Dissent that George Eliot insists on, sincere men of integrity like Rufus are not to be sneered at:

. . . his person altogether seemed so irrelevant to a fashionable view of things, that well-dressed ladies and gentlemen usually laughed at him, as they probably did at Mr. John Milton after the Restoration and ribbons had come in, and still more at that apostle, of weak bodily presence, who preached in the back streets of Ephesus and elsewhere, a view of a new religion that hardly anyone believed in. (Ch. 6)

Only occasionally does George Eliot overdo the account. Calvinist despondency was a fact, but the constant weeping of Lyddy, Lyon's servant, over Alleyne's *Alarm to Unconverted Sinners* is exaggerated almost to the point of caricature.

Nevertheless, despite the accuracy, the sympathy, and the minimal caricature, Rufus Lyon is unsatisfactory. He is being pressed into two irreconcilable roles: George Eliot's attempt to put into one person features which belong to two distinct and quite separate directions of the novel generates the kind of unease that is widely felt about his character and about the novel. On the one hand he is made to appear, to the eye of 1866, as a relic of days gone by: like Seth and Dinah, he belongs to the past, an example of the disappearance of his sort of Non-conformity and Christianity from contemporary relevance. His relevance and worth in the past are not minimized, but his essential qualities are to survive in Felix Holt, rather than in any Congregationalist after the thirties. On the other hand, Rufus has a role for the sixties;

he belongs as well to that part of the novel that is demonstrating that mob rule does not pay, that Felix's kind of moral insistence in the quest for political change, for the Second Reform Bill, is the only valid political attitude. And in this zone of the novel Rufus is a 'political dissenter', of a sort that became prominent only after 1832. The two aspects are not really compatible, Rufus Lyon cannot stand the contrary strains of the imposed significances.

The novel is set in 1832, just after the First Reform Bill. Congregationalists whose 'ecclesiastical and doctrinal' stance Rufus shared were at that time considered 'conservative'.[1] George Eliot insists that we see him as a 'rusty old Puritan', a 'seedy old ranter'. He carries into the nineteenth century the last surviving remnants of a seventeenth-century tone and spirit. He is the now archaic 'learned minister'; like the Puritans, he is logical, rational, systematic in discourse as in theology: 'Already he was beginning to sketch the course his argument might most judiciously take in the coming debate; his thoughts were running into sentences, and marking off careful exceptions in parentheses . . .' (Ch. 15).

Seventeenth-century Puritans declared that individuals and congregations must not be allowed to 'put a fallacy upon their own souls',[2] a principle Rufus applied to politics: the reasons against the ballot 'need not be urged lengthily; they only require complete enumeration to prevent any seeming hiatus, where an opposing fallacy might thrust itself in' (Ch. 16). There was an intimate historical connection between the systematic theology inspired by Ramus and Congregationalism: Ramus's Congregationalism was denounced (at Nismes, 1572) as 'pernicieuse' because 'démocratique'. In New England,

. . . the congregational theory developed hand-in-hand with the application of Ramus' dialectic to the Bible . . . there was a deep-seated affinity between the logic and polity. . . . [T]he New England divines freely acknowledged him as a discoverer of 'the *Congregational way* of Church Government', and in their expositions used his logic to establish it.[3]

George Eliot wants to expose the disparity between logic-chopping Puritanism and the mid-nineteenth century: to set up the same sort of conflict as C. M. Davies noted at Goodman's Fields, where 'the only

---

[1] John Stoughton, *Reminiscences of Congregationalism Fifty Years Ago* (1881), 17.

[2] Perry Miller, *The New England Mind* (New York, 1939), 68.

[3] Perry Miller, op. cit., 120. See also W. J. Ong, *Ramus: Method, and the Decay of Dialogue* (Cambridge, Mass., 1958), and K. L. Sprunger, 'Technometria: A Prologue to Puritan Theology', *Journal of the History of Ideas*, 29 (1968), 115–22.

symptom of the nineteenth century visible', the Blackwall Railway arches, clashed oddly with the learned ministry and systematic exposition of Scripture of W.H. Black the Seventh-Day Baptist.[1]

Rufus's old-fashioned character is buttressed by literary references. In keeping with the generation of this part of the novel out of Neal, its bookish nature, both Church and Dissent have their opposing sets of authors. Sherlock, the Church's advocate, who sees himself momentarily as another Philpotts, Bishop of Exeter and doughty right-wing Anglican champion, is told to read 'Jewel, Hall, Hooker, Whitgift, and the rest: you'll find them all here. My library wants nothing in English divinity. Sketch the lower ground taken by Usher and those men, but bring all your force to bear marking out the true High-Church doctrine' (Ch. 23). (Ussher is always spelt Usher in Neal.) Likewise, the Dissenters are referred to literary sources (Ch. 14):

'How did Dissenters, and Methodists, and Quakers, and people of that sort first come up uncle?' said Miss Selina, a radiant girl of twenty, who had given much time to the harp.

'Dear me, Selina,' said her elder sister Harriet, whose forte was general knowledge, 'don't you remember *Woodstock*? They were in Cromwell's time.'

This limited general knowledge of the girl who has, in the manner of Mr. Brooke, 'gone into' *Woodstock* is satirized, but the indices of George Eliot's own account of Rufus are names culled from Neal: Alleyne, John Howe, Matthew Henry, Richard Baxter. Rufus 'hastened to disencumber a chair of Matthew Henry's Commentary' for a visitor (Ch. 14), and absent-mindedly offers people 'reflections that were occupying his mind . . . about a peculiar incident narrated in the life of the eminent Mr. Richard Baxter' (Ch. 6). 'Why don't you always go to chapel, Mr. Holt,' demands Esther, 'and read Howe's "Living Temple" . . .?' (Ch. 10).[2]

The reference is always to historical analogues for Rufus: the 'good little father, whose thoughts and motives seemed to her [Esther] like the "Life of Dr. Doddridge", which she was content to leave unread. . . .'[3] The 1866 reader is invited to see Rufus in a lengthening

[1] C. M. Davies, *Unorthodox London* (1873), 228.
[2] Howe's *Living Temple* was the 'most famous book' by Cromwell's domestic chaplain (A. Peel, *A Hundred Eminent Congregationalists* (1927), 57–9). See Neal, op. cit., II. 792; 808–9.
[3] Ch. 10. Philip Doddridge (1702–51), who ran a well-known Academy in Northamptonshire, was author of *The Rise and Progress of Religion in the Soul* (1745) and *The Family Expositor* (Andrew Kippis, 'Life of Philip Doddridge', prefixed to *The Family Expositor* [1792], Vol. I).

historical perspective, as a relic of the Puritan past who has survived only
freakishly into 1832. In this sense Rufus is intended to be wooden, the
kind of Dissenter you can, in 1866, only read about in books like
Neal's. And the novel's critics have, almost too liberally, taken the
point ('. . . the quaint but tediously mannered polemics of the Rev.
Lyon'; '. . . the Congregationalist minister, heroically quaint reminder
of the heroic age of Puritanism . . . is incredible and a bore').[1]

But Rufus Lyon has a function relevant to the novel's facing the political issues of the 1860s. George Eliot is using the problems of 1832 to
highlight solutions for the 1860s.[2] Felix Holt's attack on those who
merely seek political change without the morally regenerative strength
of his humanism is directed at the turbulent masses who shaped the
fears of Matthew Arnold and Thomas Carlyle. George Eliot's 'Address
to Working Men, by Felix Holt', written at the behest of Blackwood
(who suspected he was a 'radical of the Felix Holt breed'), spells out the
conservative political message of the novel.[3] Instead of advising democratic support for increased suffrage, Felix '. . . talks boyish Carlyl-
ism about the worthlessness of votes, and practically proceeds upon the
hypothesis that the people must be lectured into models of virtue before their voting this way or that can be of any importance.'[4] *Felix Holt*
and 'The Address to Working Men' share the anxieties of *Culture and
Anarchy* and Carlyle's 'Shooting Niagara'.[5] The *Nonconformist* saw that
the 'Address' coincided in spirit with Arnold's 'Anarchy and Authority'
(*Cornhill Magazine*, January 1868): both reflected conservative responses
to 'the advancing tide of democratic feeling'.[6] Apocalyptic feelings were
in the air: George Eliot's old foe, Dr. Cumming, had predicted 1867 as
the year of the Second Advent.[7] The measure of George Eliot's conservative response can be taken by comparing *Felix Holt* and the 'Address'
with R. W. Dale's *The Politics of the Future: A Lecture to the New Electors*

[1] Ian Milner, '*Felix Holt, The Radical* and Realism in George Eliot', *Casopis pro Moderní
Filologii*, 37 (Prague, 1955), 169; F. R. Leavis, *The Great Tradition*, 65.

[2] Arnold Kettle, op. cit., 99–100. For the period, see Maurice Cowling, *1867:
Disraeli, Gladstone and Revolution, The Passing of the Second Reform Bill* (Cambridge, 1967),
and Michael Wolff, 'The Uses of Context: Aspects of the 1860s', *VS*, Supplement to
Vol. 9 (Sept. 1965), 47–63.

[3] 'Address to Working Men, by Felix Holt', *Blackwood's*, 103 (1868), 1–11; *GE Letters*,
IV. 246. See Ian Milner, 'The Genesis of George Eliot's Address to Working Men and its
relation to Felix Holt, the Radical', *Acta Universitatis Carolinae* (1963), *Philologica*, 2
(*Prague Studies in English*, 10), 49–53.

[4] *BQR* 45 (January, 1867), 175–6.

[5] 'Shooting Niagara: and After?', *Macmillan's Magazine*, 16 (1867), 319–36.

[6] *Nonconformist*, 28 (11 Jan. 1868), 42.

[7] John Francis Witty, *What Have We, and What Has Dr. Cumming to do with 1867?* (1862).

given in Birmingham Town Hall, 19 November 1867. Dale was not of those who 'a year ago, were prophesying that a moderate extension of the suffrage would involve us all in portentous misery and ruin'. He is aware that the people need educating; democratic might, he insists, but without Carlyle's lurid and violent imagery, is not *per se* right; 'moral laws' are 'mightier than even the united force of a great people'. Nevertheless, unlike George Eliot, or Arnold and Carlyle, he does not see the people as a potential mob: 'Whatever may be the political action of the new electors, their enfranchisement must greatly increase the stability and security of the State.'[1]

George Eliot read Matthew Arnold. In the notebook she used for *Felix Holt* material one finds: ' "One of the causes which please noble spirits but not destiny, which have Cato's adherence, but not Heaven's". Matt: Arnold.' She does not name the source, but she is quoting from *On the Study of Celtic Literature*, Part I, which appeared in the *Cornhill Magazine*, 13 (March 1866): she was manifestly keeping up with Arnold's latest work whilst writing her novel.[2] In November 1867 she thanked Frederic Harrison for his article, 'Culture: a Dialogue', which had *inter alia* questioned Arnold's definition of 'culture': 'Only in one point I am unable to see as you do. I don't know how far my impressions have been warped by reading German, but I have regarded the word 'culture' as a verbal equivalent for the highest mental result of past and present influences.'[3] And Felix Holt's conservatism in the 'Address' is rooted in a view of the cultural heritage:

Do anything which will throw the classes who hold the treasures of knowledge— nay, I may say, the treasure of refined needs—into the background . . . and. . . . You injure your own inheritance and the inheritance of your children. You may truly say that this which I call the common estate of society has been anything but common to you. . . . Nevertheless, that these blessings exist makes life worthier to us, and urges us the more to energetic, likely means of getting our share in them; and I say, let us watch carefully, lest we do anything to lessen this treasure which is held in the minds of men, while we exert ourselves . . . that we and our children may share in all its benefits. Yes; exert ourselves to the utmost, to break the yoke of ignorance. . . .[4]

---

[1] R. W. Dale, *The Politics of the Future* (1867), 2, 4, 7 ff., 18–20.

[2] Arnold actually has 'those causes'.

[3] *GE Letters*, IV. 395 (7 Nov. 1867). Frederic Harrison, 'Culture: A Dialogue', *Fortnightly Review*, N.S. 2 (Nov. 1867), 603–14, replying to Arnold's 'Culture and its Enemies', *Cornhill Magazine*, 16 (July 1867), 36–63. See U. C. Knoepflmacher, *Religious Humanism and the Victorian Novel*, 60 ff.: 'George Eliot, Matthew Arnold, and Tradition'.

[4] *Blackwood's*, 103 (1868), 8; T. Pinney, op. cit., 426.

The antithesis between political radicalism and cultural conservation is not, of course, a necessary one; but in declaring it George Eliot lines up with Arnold and Carlyle (whose 'unclassed Aristocracy by nature' includes the talented, the intellectuals, threatened by the 'unanimous torrent of brutish hoofs and hobnails').[1] And the social groupings of *Felix Holt* are oddly akin to Arnold's. That we find Populace, Barbarians, Philistines, and the Cultured class-alien in the novel, much as they appear, in their most developed form, in *Culture and Anarchy*, shows how very much the novel is of the *Zeitgeist* of the sixties, in which Arnold developed this analysis.[2]

The Barbarians are represented by Mrs. Transome's aristocratic emptyheadedness. Esther's illusions shatter on that dullness, that absence of any high demand: '. . . a life of middling delights, overhung with the languorous haziness of motiveless ease, where poetry was only literature, and fine ideas had to be taken down from the shelves of the library when her husband's back was turned' (Ch. 44). The Philistines are the Dissenters, seen in two categories, the mercantile and the narrow. Felix Holt stands out against the 'pence-counting, parcel-tying generation such as mostly fill your chapels' (Ch. 5); like Will Ladislaw who rebukes Bulstrode's shady business ethics, Felix opposes the dishonest trading of his father's quack medicine business, and offends the chapel's business sense:

He had set himself up for something extraordinary, and had spoken ill of re-spectable tradespeople. He had put a stop to the making of saleable drugs, contrary to the nature of buying and selling, and to a due reliance on what Providence might effect in the human inside through the instrumentality of remedies unsuitable to the stomach, looked at in a merely secular light. . . . (Ch. 37)

The chapel's response is being caricatured; George Eliot is perhaps rather less seriously engaged with this moral problem here than she is in *Middlemarch*, and the point does not rise much above the common-place. But in depicting the narrowness of Rufus Lyon himself she transcends the more conventional suggestions about his congregation ('Dorcas

---

[1] 'Shooting Niagara', *Macmillan's Magazine*, 16 (1867), 329.

[2] See Raymond Williams, *Culture and Society 1780–1950* (Penguin, 1966), 112–19, and Arnold Kettle, op. cit., 113–14. Arnold misunderstood Carlyle's distinction between Aristocrats 'by title, by fortune, and position' and Aristocrats 'by nature', 'supreme in faculty, in wisdom, human talent', *Culture and Anarchy*, ed. J. Dover Wilson, 83–5. For the growth of Arnold's ideas in the sixties, culminating in *Culture and Anarchy*, see J. Dover Wilson, ed. cit., xviii ff. See also S. M. B. Coulling, 'The Evolution of *Culture and Anarchy*', *SP* 60 (Oct. 1963), 637–68.

meetings, biographies of devout women, and that amount of ornamental knitting which was not inconsistent with Nonconforming seriousness', 'sleek well-clipped gravity' (Ch. 5)). Lyon eschews Byron and Shakespeare ('. . . the fantasies therein were so little to be reconciled with a steady contemplation of that divine economy which is hidden from sense and revealed to faith, that I forbore the reading, as likely to perturb my ministrations' (Ch. 28)), but his is no stereotyped narrowness. George Eliot takes us close to his restricted channels for effort, his rising in importance as a denominational speaker: there are only constricted forms that ambition can take 'in the mind of a man who has chosen the career of an Independent preacher' (Ch. 6). George Eliot seeks in fact to reinvest with interest the notion of 'narrowness', as it were to reinstate it, as she does in the case of Bulstrode:

Again he heard himself called for as Brother Bulstrode in prayer meetings, speaking on religious platforms, preaching in private houses. . . . That was the happiest time of his life: that was the spot he would have chosen now to awake in and find the rest a dream. The people among whom Brother Bulstrode was distinguished were very few, but they were very near to him, and stirred his satisfaction the more. . . . (Ch. 61)

The sting is taken out of 'narrowness', as Lawrence takes the sneer out of 'provincial' with the triumphant provincialism of *Sons and Lovers* ('They looked down the darkness of the railway. There was London!' Ch. 4). This perceptiveness helps George Eliot comprehend the bitterness of a man like Lyon faced with a feeble but privileged Establishment:

What was more exasperating to a zealous preacher, with whom copious speech was not a difficulty but a relief—who never lacked argument, but only combatants and listeners—than to reflect that there were thousands on thousands of pulpits in this kingdom, supplied with handsome sounding-boards, or occupying an advantageous position in buildings far larger than the chapel in Malthouse Yard—buildings sure to be places of resort, even as the markets were, if only from habit and interest; and that these pulpits were filled, or rather made vacuous, by men whose privileged education in the ancient centres of instruction issued in twenty minutes' formal reading of tepid exhortation or probably infirm deductions from premises based on rotten scaffolding? (Ch. 15)

As the *BQR* reviewer recognized, George Eliot could get 'into the heart' of men like Felix, understand 'their life motives', appreciate 'the nobleness of their aims and aspirations'.[1]

The Populace is an election mob, dangerous to law and order, but embroiling Felix Holt, the cultured class-alien, and so highlighting,

[1] *BQR* 45 (Jan. 1867), 145.

actually and symbolically, the Arnoldian antithesis. Trained as a doctor, Felix disdains the bourgeoisie, the professional occupation, and chooses to be a journeyman watchmaker: he inhabits an uneasy zone between the working and middle classes. And his culture is insisted on, at least towards the end of the novel: Esther perceives that he is 'a highly cultivated man', has a 'cultured nature' (Ch. 43). He is of that order of class-aliens 'who are mainly led, not by their class spirit but by a general *humane* spirit, by the love of human perfection', who propagate reason apart from the 'machinery' of party politics or dogmatic religion.[1] And culture triumphs: Esther is saved from Transome Court, and converted not to Dissent and Calvinism but to Felix's humanism that supersedes them.

   In these concerns, *Felix Holt* is clearly a sixties' novel. And the kind of political Dissenter we are invited to see Rufus Lyon as representing is indeed hardly appropriate to 1832. Some effort is made to capture the atmosphere of the earlier period by reference to the Catholic Emancipation Act of 1829, and by having Rufus speak of Brougham and Wellington. But the political atmosphere is more substantively that of the period after 1832. There is the emphasis on the Liberal–Dissent alliance, and on Rufus's hold over Liberal voters ('conscious of his political importance as an organ of persuasion') so that he has to be wooed by Harold Transome (Ch. 16). There is the rhetoric of 'voluntaryism' against the 'State Church' (Ch. 41), and mid-century issues like Church Rates and Church-Rates contests are not unprominent: if Felix, we are informed, had 'fought about Church-rates, or had been worsted in some struggle in which he was distinctly the champion of Dissent and Liberalism, his case would have been one for gold, silver, and copper subscriptions, in order to procure the best defence' (Ch. 37). The *Patriot*, the radical organ to which Lyon is urged by Brother Kemp to send an account of the disputation fiasco, was not founded until February 1832: it was a harbinger of the developed political activity of Dissenters.[2] Of course it is just possible that George Eliot might have intended a clever topical allusion to a recent publication; but the tone of Rufus Lyon's political activities belongs firmly to the era of Miall's *Nonconformist* (started April 1841) and the British Anti-State-Church Association (founded in 1844: it became the Society for the Liberation of Religion from State Control —the Liberation Society—in 1853), or to 1862, and the Bicentenary Celebrations of the Great Ejection, which, it has been suggested, helped

[1] *Culture and Anarchy*, ed. J. Dover Wilson, 109.
[2] John Stoughton, *Reminiscences*, 77.

worsen Arnold's jaundiced view of Dissent.[1] When she talks of Rufus Lyon's political Dissent George Eliot brings to bear slogans, a tone, reflecting precisely the period which she has just lived through, between 1832 and 1865 to 1866.[2]

The Janus-like character of Rufus Lyon—old-fashioned Puritan, new political Dissenter—is clarified when we look at the matrix that is supposed to have generated him, in particular at the Rev. Francis Franklin, minister at Cow Lane Baptist Chapel, Coventry (1798–1852).[3] The links between Treby Magna and Coventry are close. In 1832 election rioting at Coventry was severe.[4] The industries of Treby Magna, tape-weaving and watchmaking, were Coventry trades. Felix's occupation as a journeyman watchmaker allows him to work at home and therefore (good humanist) teach boys as he works. The trade was not subject to periodic fluctuation: it confers on Felix working-class status, but it is also a stable job for supporting his mother. Since he has served no apprenticeship, and has not enough property, he has no vote: the seven years' apprenticeship was the only qualification for the franchise before 1832, and the Freeman vote distinguished Coventry before and after 1832.[5] Like Rufus Lyon (Ch. 5), Francis Franklin possessed a bust of Whitefield.[6]

Whitefield symbolizes the reconciliation of Calvinism with evangelism, which Rufus Lyon's ministry among the Sproxton miners exemplifies.[7] Franklin's village-evangelism was a sign of the moderate Calvin-

[1] For Miall, see Arthur Miall, *Life of Edward Miall* (1884), and James Ewing Ritchie, 'Edward Miall, Esq., M.P.', *The London Pulpit* (1854), 120–31. For the Liberation Society, see R. G. Cowherd *The Politics of English Dissent* (New York, 1956; 1959), 153 ff.; O. Chadwick, op. cit., I. 151. For the 1862 Bicentenary, see Jean A. Smallbone, 'Matthew Arnold and the Bicentenary of 1862', *BQ*, N.S. 14 (1951–2), 222–6.

[2] Cf. Richard Masheder's breakdown in *Dissent and Democracy* (1864), 1–2. 1832–44: Dissent was identified with, but not allied to Radicalism or Whiggism; 1844–59: 'Dissent was both identified with, and allied to, democracy, or Radicalism'; after 1859: 'Dissent became both identified with, and allied to, Liberalism. . . . Liberalism accordingly is playing the part of accomplice to the Liberation Society.'

[3] Irene Morris, *Three Hundred Years of Baptist Life in Coventry* (1926), 44, 56.

[4] F. W. Humberstone, 'Coventry in Relation to George Eliot's Fiction', *Coventry Herald* (14 Nov. 1919), in *George Eliot, 1819–1919, A Record of the Centenary Celebrations held at Coventry November 1919* (Coventry, 1920), Collected, Mounted and Arranged by Joseph Sidwell: in Coventry and Warwickshire Collection, Coventry City Reference Library; Peter Searby, *Coventry Politics in the Age of the Chartists 1836–1848* (Coventry, 1964), 9; T. W. Whitley, *The Parliamentary Representation of the People of Coventry* (Coventry, 1894), 296–8.

[5] See John Prest, *The Industrial Revolution in Coventry* (Oxford, 1960).

[6] There is a photograph of it in the Coventry Library's *Record of the Centenary Celebrations*.

[7] O. C. Robison, 'Particular Baptists in England 1760–1820' (D.Phil. thesis, Oxford, 1963), 152–3.

ism that became widespread among Particular Baptists in the early nineteenth century. (Franklin and the moderate Calvinists were not, however, as Arminian as the General Baptists, a mistake G. S. Haight makes.[1]
Mrs. Holt's faith in works rather than grace (Ch. 4) is related to the
Arminianism of the General Baptist connection—parodied thus by
George Eliot—in which she was born, and which excludes her from
church membership at Lyon's chapel.) Franklin, converted in Oxford
under James Hinton, pastor of Oxford's New Road Baptist church, and
baptized at Abingdon in April 1793, was trained by Hinton to evange-
lize the villages about Oxford. He took the practice to Coventry.[2]
While a student at Bristol Baptist Academy under John Ryland the
elder, he accompanied Steadman on an evangelistic tour of Cornwall
(1797). The first-ever organized Baptist Home Missions tour had been
made only the year before, by Saffrey and Steadman under the auspices
of the Baptist Missionary Society.[3] And the B.M.S., at home or over-
seas, was very much a product of moderating Calvinism.

Felix Holt discovers Lyon (Ch. 5) skimming through a missionary
report. And Franklin was closely associated with missionary work. He
married (November 1799) Rebekah Dyer, sister of John Dyer, first
full-time secretary (1817–41) of the B.M.S. Andrew Fuller, prominent
moderate Calvinist and first secretary of the B.M.S., was succeeded
jointly in that office in 1815 by John Ryland, Franklin's old principal,
and James Hinton, his old pastor. Franklin's fourth daughter, Eliza,
died (aged 21) of cholera in India, where she was assisting her Baptist
missionary husband. Her brother James died in 1827 (aged 20) while
studying at the Bristol academy preparatory to working for the B.M.S.[4]
Rufus Lyon's reservations about the report he is reading ('emitting occasionally a slight "Hm-m" that appeared to be expressive of criticism
rather than of approbation') indicate the reluctance with which even
men like Andrew Fuller reconciled missionary activity with the theology
of grace.[5]

The association of Lyon with Franklin has become as much a part of

---

[1] *George Eliot*, 19.

[2] Irene Morris, op. cit., 42; [anon.], 'Three Hundred Years of Baptist Life in Coventry',
*BQ*, N.S. 3 (1926–7), 142.

[3] Irene Morris, op. cit., 43; O. C. Robison, thesis cit., 95–7.

[4] Irene Morris, op. cit., 44, 47; E. A. Payne, 'The Diaries of John Dyer', *BQ* 13 (1949–
50), 253. In 1927 a Franklin descendant was a Baptist missionary in China: A. S. Langley,
'Some Notable Names in Midland Baptist History', *BQ*, N.S. 3 (1926–7), 283.

[5] S. Pearce Carey, *William Carey* (8th, enlarged, edn., 1934), 54 ff., 80 ff.; E. D. Potts,
*British Baptist Missionaries in India 1793–1837* (Cambridge, 1967), 8, footnote 1.

the record as Dinah Morris's with Mrs. Evans.[1] The accuracy of some of the claims is difficult to authenticate; their existence, however, testifies to the strength of the connection. It is claimed that in Franklin's study over the archway at Cow Lane the books were arranged like Rufus Lyon's in rows on the floor, and that he walked up and down these passages composing sermons; and that Lyon's 'little legs' are like Franklin's.[2] Franklin's portrait does give some impression of a 'large head' and small body; and the eyes are prominent.[3] His shortage of small talk sounds very like Lyon's greater preoccupation with Baxter than with mundane affairs:

He seldom made any remark upon ordinary topics, such as the state of the weather, but perhaps quoted some passage of Scripture, on which he made some useful comment, or cited some wise maxim or proverb, or some quotation from Bunyan's 'Pilgrim', or Watts' Psalms and Hymns, of both which books he was passionately fond; or it may be he gave the outlines of a sermon he had been preaching on the previous Sunday.[4]

Clearly, not a few details of Lyon's portrait originate in Franklin, and the sympathy of George Eliot's account is connected with the gratitude she expressed to Cross ('. . . my wife impressed on my mind the debt she felt that she owed to the Miss Franklins for their excellent instruction, and she had also the very highest respect for their moral qualities').[5] Among her frequent guests were Dr. Joseph Frank Payne and his brother John Burnell Payne, grandsons of John Dyer, and first cousins once removed of Mary and Rebecca Franklin; and Dr. James Hinton, son of the John Howard Hinton with whom she once breakfasted and grandson of Franklin's old pastor, became a visitor at the Priory, and treated Lewes's ears.[6]

But while Franklin is just the kind of Dissenter who might generate 'an old-fashioned Puritan' like Lyon, he was emphatically not a 'political

---

[1] Cross's *Life* (1st edn.), I. 24–5. *Records of An Old Association, Being a Memorial Volume of the 250th Anniversary of the Midland, Now the West Midland, Baptist Association, formed in Warwick, May 3rd, 1655*, ed. R. Gray, J. Ford, J. M. Gwynne-Owen (1905), 155; A. S. Langley, art. cit., 283.

[2] Irene Morris, op. cit., 49; *Our Times* (1881), quoted by Cross (1st edn.), I. 25.

[3] Portrait in Irene Morris, op. cit., facing p. 42; cf. description of Lyon (*Felix Holt*, Ch. 4): '. . . little legs . . . large head . . . short-sighted. . . .'

[4] John Sibree, *The Funeral Oration* [1852], 17. A copy of this pamphlet is in an interleaved and annotated copy of John Sibree and M. Caston, *Independency in Warwickshire* (Coventry, 1855), in the Coventry and Warwickshire Collection, Coventry City Library.

[5] Cross's *Life* (1st edn.), I. 26.

[6] E. A. Payne, 'Gleanings from the Correspondence of George Eliot', *BQ*, N.S. 17 (1957–8), 181; *GE Letters*, III. 328–9, 438; V. 436; VI. 142, footnote 5.

Dissenter'. Although he survived until 1852 and thus witnessed the Victorian recrudescence of political Dissent, he remained quietist: the Coventry newspapers record almost no participation by him in the local meetings on politics, education, the State Church, public health, that drew activist Dissenting support. John Watts, however, who came to Cow Lane to assist Franklin in 1841, publicly declared himself a Chartist in 1842.[1]

John Sibree makes a marked contrast with Franklin. He came to Vicar Lane chapel in 1819, 21 years after Franklin had come to Cow Lane: the gap was a generation gap; Sibree was the political 'new man'. He published sermons and tracts 'in support of nonconformist principles': on education, in favour of Voluntaryism, advocating refusal to pay Church Rate and repeal of the Corn Laws.[2] His property was distrained for non-payment of Church Rate. Sibree chaired a meeting (February 1842) at St. Mary's Hall between Chartists and Anti-Corn-Law Leaguers; Vicar Lane schoolroom was used for political meetings (e.g. of the Complete Suffrage Movement in 1843). Under Sibree, Vicar Lane was far more political than Cow Lane under Franklin: the Congregationalists in 1847 returned on principle £200 granted them by the government for school-building in 1835; William Taunton, one of Sibree's Sunday School teachers, was a physical-force Chartist, an Owenite Socialist, manager of Coventry's first Co-operative store, and a member of Coventry's Anti-Corn-Law Committee.

Franklin belonged to that older generation of Dissenters which may have supported in principle democratic and liberal movements, but eschewed open and active political action. He came to Cow Lane in 1798—a significant date, for reaction against radicals, sparked by events in France, caused many Dissenters to become politically circumspect. James Hinton had been attacked as a 'Jacobin' at Woodstock in 1794; and though he defended Oxford Dissenters against the Rector of Lincoln College, strenuously opposed Lord Sidmouth's Bill (1811) curtailing the activities of Nonconformist preachers, and was a friend of American

---

[1] J. Sibree and M. Caston, *Independency in Warwickshire* (1855), 114–16; Peter Searby, op. cit., 18. Searby, p. 15, records a rare political act by Franklin: chairing lectures (1839) on *The Errors of Socialism*.

[2] B. Poole, *Coventry: Its History and Antiquities* (1870), 234. Sibree's pamphlets include: *A Plea for the Liberty of Education* (1843); *Why Not? or Seven Objections to the Educational Clauses of the Factories Regulation Bill* (1843); *The Case of the Manchester Educationalists* (1852–4); *A Few Plain Words on the two Educational Bills now before the Country* (1852); *The Test of Experience, or the Voluntary Principle in the United States* (1851); *The Law of Church Rate Explained, and the Duty of Dissenters Recommended* (1836); *The Corn-monopoly condemned by the Scriptures* (1841). Peter Searby, op. cit., supplies details of Sibree's political acitivities.

colonial emancipation, he never 'meddled' with politics, and declared that he neither had, nor did he 'wish to have, the least political influence' over his congregation.[1] His son, John Howard Hinton (1791–1873), on the other hand, agitated against slavery and was connected with the Voluntary Church Society and the Liberation Society. His *Church Property—whose is it?* was published (1848) by the British Anti-State-Church Association. The Liberation Society published his *Civil Establishments of Religion Impeach the Intrinsic Power of the Gospel*. An anonymous and hostile pamphleteer quoted a speech of his at an Anti-Church-Rate Conference (1861): 'I have been a soldier in this battle from my youth, and I am in better hope today than I have ever been, of seeing victory won (Loud cheers). And I say this, that whether Parliament chooses to give us this sort of justice or not, we will have it without them. (Loud cheers.)'[2]

The same generation gap may be observed in Leicester and Birmingham. Robert Hall of Leicester's Harvey Lane Baptist Chapel was a 'decided Radical'; he helped framework knitters evade the Combination Laws (1819), but he 'preferred on the whole to remain aloof from political meetings and speechmaking'. But his successor at Harvey Lane in 1826, J. P. Mursell, was a friend of Edward Miall at the nearby Bond Street Independent Chapel, and together they actively campaigned against the Church Rates and for Disestablishment. It was Mursell who suggested that Miall himself should edit their new magazine, the *Nonconformist*.[3]

R. W. Dale became assistant to John Angell James at Carr's Lane, Birmingham, in 1853, and his successor in October 1859. There was no more political a Dissenter.[4] John Angell James, however, though liberal

---

[1] James Hinton, *A Vindication of the Dissenters in Oxford, addressed to the Inhabitants; in reply to Dr. Tatham's sermon, lately published, after having been preached in Oxford many Sundays successively* (1792); J. H. Hinton, *A Biographical Portraiture of the Late Rev. James Hinton, M.A.* (Oxford, 1824), 355–7, 358, 367; 'A Narrative of the Riotous Proceedings at Woodstock, Oxfordshire, on May 18, 1794, when the Rev. Mr. Hinton, Minister at Oxford, opened a Lecture at that Place', *Protestant Dissenters Magazine*, 2 (1795), 252–6; W. H. Summers, *History of the Congregational Churches in the Berkshire, South Oxon, and South Bucks Association* (Newbury, 1905), 246–50.

[2] G. F. C., *A Warning to Churchmen: Extracts Exposing the bitter Hostility of Dissenters Towards the Church, and their ultimate aims* (3rd edn., 1862), 17.

[3] A. Temple Patterson, *Radical Leicester* (1954); F. Boase, *Modern English Biography* (2nd impr., 1965), II, Col. 1057.

[4] See A. W. W. Dale, *Life of R. W. Dale of Birmingham* (1899); R. W. Dale: *Churchmen and Dissenters: their mutual relations as affected by the proposed celebration of the Bi-Centenary of St. Bartholomew's Day 1662* (1862); *Nonconformity in 1662 and in 1862* (1862); *The Politics of Non-conformity* (Manchester, 1871); 'The Religiousness of Political Dissent', *Congregationalist*, 2 (1873), 112–23.

in outlook and opposed to the Church of England, never spoke in 'the last twenty years of his life' about politics except in his own pulpit. The style and tone of the new men distressed him: '. . . during that period he stood distinctly aloof from organized hostility to the Established Church. . . . He doubted the wisdom of the leaders of the Anti-State-Church movement.'[1] James, like Rufus Lyon, looked for his models in previous ages: 'holy Baxter', 'that great and serene spirit, John Howe', George Whitefield.[2] In reference to the claim that 'the life of modern Independency is one of contest—a contest that embraces politics as well as religion', the Physiologist of the Sects rightly claimed that 'John Angell James . . . may be taken as the type of old Independency, and Mr. R. W. Dale, the present minister of the same chapel, if not the same congregation, as the type of the new.'[3]

I would suggest that Rufus Lyon is a sort of Mr. Facing-Both-Ways, a disjunctive combination of two different kinds of Dissenting pastor, the old and the new. To serve the various uses to which the novel is put, Lyon is made a kind of schizophrenic amalgam; Sibree has been disconcertingly grafted on to Franklin. It is as though George Eliot had combined the learned and retiring William Henry Black of the Seventh Day Baptists in Goodman's Fields with a man like W. T. Henderson, pastor of Banbury's Bridge Street Baptist Chapel, who led the 1852 campaign which ended the town's Church Rate, was a Chartist sympathizer, supported Edward Miall's radical candidacy in 1859, and confessed it was his custom 'to preach without reserve on public events'.[4] Men like William Black preferred to view the mid-nineteenth century as a reflection of Biblical prophecy, rather than as an arena for their personal political involvement. Black published interpretations of Daniel.[5] And Esther finds Lyon (Ch. 41), not inappropriately for a 'rusty old puritan', but much less suitably for a political Dissenter:

. . . absorbed in mastering all those painstaking interpretations of the Book of Daniel, which are by this time well gone to the limbo of mistaken criticism; and Esther, as she opened the door softly, heard him rehearsing aloud a passage in

---

[1] R. W. Dale, *The Life and Letters of John Angell James* (new edn., 1862), 120. See J. A. James, *Dissent and the Church of England* (3rd edn., 1831).

[2] J. A. James, *An Earnest Ministry: The Want of the Times* (4th edn., 1848).

[3] *The Physiology of the Sects*, 82–3.

[4] B. S. Trinder, 'The Radical Baptists', *Cake and Cockhorse*, 2 (Jan. 1965), 179–92.

[5] W. H. Black, *Gabriel's Prophetic Numbers, in Daniel ix. 24–26 (commonly translated and explained as 'weeks' of years) now shown to relate to the duration of the Persian Empire only* (Mill Yard Lecture, 14 Aug. 1869); *Explanations of the Chronology and Prophetic Numbers, in the Book of Daniel. As Summed up in the Eighth Lecture thereon* (Mill Yard lecture, 28 Aug. 1869).

which he declared, with some parenthetic provisoes, that he conceived not how a perverse ingenuity could blunt the edge of prophetic explicitness, or how an open mind could fail to see in the chronology of 'the little horn' the resplendent lamp of an inspired symbol searching out the germinal growth of an antichristian power.

No great English novelist has got closer than George Eliot to the heart of the Dissenting matter. And one's necessary criticisms of her manipulation of Dinah and Rufus Lyon, and one's exposing of her designs on history, should never for a moment cause one to detract from her necessary stature as the novelist with a very unique compassion for and insight into the Nonconformist spirit, the enthusiastic character, the Puritan temper, and with an authentic grasp of some aspects of Nonconformist history and historical process. And though her novels became progressively more distanced from the early tearful sympathy of her treatment of Dinah, until finally her Dissenter had become an out-and-out hypocrite in Bulstrode, George Eliot never lost her compassion and insight, her openness. They are qualities that her imitators, Mrs. Oliphant and William Hale White, manifest more rarely in their dealings with Nonconformity than one might have hoped. And they are certainly opposite to the way the Dickens tradition contemplates Nonconformists.

# VIII. CHARLES DICKENS

## I. WHAT DICKENS KNEW

ABOVE all, George Eliot treated Dissent, like so much else in her writing, with high seriousness. It would perhaps be asking too much to require Dickens to begin to match that seriousness. Indeed, everything tended to become a joke in his fiction. Even institutions he actually approved of, like the Ragged Schools, got satirical treatment in the novels.[1] He did recognize that laughter, other people's laughter anyway, was sometimes inappropriate: Lord Seymour should not have cut jokes ('which were received with laughter') about a raging typhoid epidemic.[2] The recognition did not, however, extend, as we shall see, to prayer at Joseph Hone's funeral, or prayer at Bunsby's marriage. Nor, indeed, to Christ's own words: Mr. Weller is allowed his jeer at the New Birth as a Methodistical 'inwention'. Dissenters would clearly be over-optimistic to anticipate a respect even Christ was not afforded. Dickens's unthinking contempt for Christian theology and Christianity's Dissenting practitioners is ironically revealed in a description of Chadband's getting up steam. One person's groan, the outward expression of the 'inward working', 'being echoed by some elderly lady in the next pew, and so communicated, like a game of forfeits, through a circle of the more fermentable sinners present, serves the purpose of parliamentary cheering'.[3] Had he remembered his *Measure for Measure* ('Why, all the souls that were, were forfeit once . . .'), Dickens might well have paused before reducing preaching to a 'game of forfeits'.

The immaturity, the failure of seriousness, are commensurate with Dickens's always seeking the child's point of view. Doubtless, in an age of the industrial exploitation and the domestic oppression of children, Dickens's viewpoint generated, to say the very least, valid and necessary sympathies. But there is such an unflagging insistence on the child's view of religious behaviour and language that one wonders whether Dickens was capable of sustaining any other. It may be bad for a child to

---

[1] Philip Collins, *Dickens and Education* (1963), 90 ff.

[2] 'To Working-Men', *HW* 10 (7 Oct. 1854), 170; Edgar Johnson, *Charles Dickens: His Tragedy and Triumph* (2 Vols., 1953), II. 826.

[3] *Bleak House*, Ch. 25.

be exposed for two hours to Boanerges Boiler's outstretched coat-sleeve ('as if it were a telescope with the stopper on'), but other reasons must be offered for adults to eschew his ministrations. Children may not be able to understand phrases like 'the Lamb of God', or words like 'Sepulchre', but Dickens shows few signs of conceding that adults might.[1] One should never minimize the virtue of his appeal on behalf of the child in its exposure to Christian teachers: he shares the protest of, say, *Jane Eyre* and *Father and Son*. But what is gained is purchased at the expense of any real concession in the fiction that Jo, or Kit Nubbles, might not be the best or the only judges of the religious worth of a Dissenting minister.[2]

But why this clamant unseriousness about Nonconformity? It cannot be said that Dickens knew nothing at all of Dissent as it really was. His beloved sister Fanny, whose little boy was the 'original' of Paul Dombey, was, with her husband Henry Burnett, converted evangelically under the ministry of James Griffin, minister of Rusholme Road Congregationalist Chapel, Manchester.[3] The couple gave up their secular musical career to take charge of the chapel music. Burnett's grandmother had been a Dissenter, thought he had been brought up in the Establishment.[4] But there is a curious joint evasiveness about all this in Forster's *Life*. Dickens's letter of 5 July 1848 simply told Forster that Fanny had been buried in unconsecrated ground, and Forster merely adds for explanation that 'Mr. Burnett's family were dissenters'.[5] There is no mention by either man of Fanny's conversion to Congregationalism, nor that the funeral was conducted at her request by Griffin. Dickens's reaction must be interpreted from that silence: there is no actual evidence, however, of increased resentment against Dissent for capturing his sister.[6] Rather, the use of Fanny's 'little deformed child' Harry, who 'loved his Bible and evidently loved Jesus',[7] for Paul Dombey, endorses the deep contradictions of Dickens's relations with Dissenters in life

---

[1] Philip Collins, op. cit., 55–6, 90–1; *Our Mutual Friend*, Bk. II, Ch. 1.

[2] For more examples of the constant reference to the child's point of view in religious instruction, see: 'A December Vision', *HW* 2 (14 Dec. 1850), 265–7, and K. J. Fielding (ed.), *The Speeches of Charles Dickens* (1960), 129, 242, 284–5, 293.

[3] James Griffin, *Memories of the Past: Records of Ministerial Life* (1883), 165 ff. For Rusholme Road (opened 31 Aug. 1826) and Griffin, its first minister, see Benjamin Nightingale, *Lancashire Nonconformity* (6 Vols., Manchester, 1891–3), V. 166–7.

[4] Griffin, op. cit., 167, 177.

[5] John Forster, *The Life of Dickens*, ed. and intro. J. W. T. Ley (1928), 521–2.

[6] *Pace* A. H. Adrian, 'Dickens and the Brick-and-Mortar Sects', *NCF* 10 (1955), 200, and footnote 20.

[7] James Griffin, op. cit., 209.

and in fiction. Fanny's Congregationalism must at least have given pause
to the author of Stiggins.

Dickens's acquaintance with Dissent began early. He went to the
school in Chatham run by the younger Rev. William Giles, son of the
William Giles who was pastor of Zion Baptist Chapel and possibly of
the neighbouring Providence Chapel as well.[1] The schoolmaster
Giles had apparently attended courses at Oxford, was scholarly, and
earned Dickens's everlasting gratitude by praising him. It was Giles who
gave his pupil the nickname 'The Inimitable'. Dickens started sending
Giles copies of his books, beginning with *Pickwick* ('To the Reverend
William Giles from his old and affectionate pupil, Charles Dickens'),
after Giles had sent a silver snuff-box to 'the inimitable Boz'. Giles continued after leaving Chatham to combine the Baptist ministry and keeping schools, and he continued being involved with aspects of Dickens's
life and work. One of his referees for a school he opened in 1831 was
Daniel Grant, one of the originals for the Cheeryble Brothers.[2] Dickens
himself allowed his name to be used as referee in 1845, after he had
met Giles again. In October 1843 Dickens had presided at a soirée at
Manchester's Free Trade Hall in aid of Manchester Athenaeum, and
stayed with the Burnetts. Nearby lived Giles's young brother, Samuel,
known (presumably a Dissenting connection) to the Burnetts, and a
meeting between Dickens and his old master was arranged at Samuel
Giles's house. In 1849 Dickens was a member of the committee for a
testimonial fund raised by Giles's old pupils.[3]

Dickens's attitude towards the Chatham Baptists of his childhood was
obviously more ambivalent than critical orthodoxy about Boanerges
Boiler would suggest. Everybody seems to agree that Dickens's account
in 'City of London Churches' (Ch. 9 of *The Uncommercial Traveller*) is
based on experience of William Giles, senior, at Chatham.[4] The
'traveller' claims to have had enough of 'powerful preachers'. As a child
he was

. . . caught in the palm of a female hand by the crown . . . violently scrubbed
from the neck to the roots of the hair as a purification for the Temple . . .

[1] Details in Philip Collins, *Dickens and Education*, 10–11, and Arthur Humphreys,
*Charles Dickens and His First Schoolmaster* (Manchester, 1926).

[2] Cf. Rev. W. Hume Elliot, *The Country and Church of the Cheeryble Brothers* (Selkirk,
1893).

[3] Not, as Collins suggests (op. cit., 11) as its president; Dickens was invited to preside
at the presentation but declined: Humphreys, op. cit., 17–18.

[4] Edgar Johnson, op. cit., I. 19–20; Jack Lindsay, *Charles Dickens* (1950), 37; A. H.
Adrian, art. cit., 198; T. Blount, 'The Chadbands and Dickens' View of Dissenters',
*MLQ* 25 (1964), 296.

carried off highly charged with saponaceous electricity, to be steamed like a potato in the unventilated breath of the powerful Boanerges Boiler and his congregation, until what small mind I had, was quite steamed out of me. . . .

He was catechized about Boiler's 'fifthly, his sixthly, and his seventhly' and (it is one of Dickens's best child's-eye-view descriptions)

. . . sat under Boanerges when he specifically addressed himself to us—us, the infants—and at this present writing I hear his lumbering jocularity (which never amused us, though we basely pretended that it did), and I behold his big round face, and I look up the inside of his outstretched coat-sleeve as if it were a telescope with the stopper on, and I hate him with an unwholesome hatred for two hours.[1]

The account is, as usual, compelling, but two points mitigate against the over-simple orthodox equations. Dickens is casting himself in this passage as the child of evangelical parents, familiar to Victorian literature, exposed to endless 'powerful' preaching. But Dickens was no such child, no matter how many visits he may have made to Providence Chapel. Mr. and Mrs. John Dickens were so far from being evangelical that they were unused even to the family prayers that Fanny and her husband held, and 'interested in the new character and new associations of their daughter'.[2] So all the evangelical, repressed childhoods of the fiction must be seen as an imaginative *tour de force*, a sympathetic entering into an experience Dickens himself had not shared, but which was, perhaps, the definitive middle-class childhood experience of his time. And, one might add, if Boiler is indeed generated only by experience of Giles senior, why is it found sweetly reasonable that Dickens's view of Dissent should, so to speak, ignore Giles junior? (Edgar Johnson: 'These experiences laid the foundations for his lifelong hatred of Nonconformity and his revulsion from any formal religious affiliation.')[3]

At one stage, of course, Dickens did not eschew 'formal religious affiliation', even with Dissent. Much has been made of his taking a family pew at Edward Tagart's Little Portland Street Chapel, after attending a memorial service for Channing, on 12 November 1842. The Unitarian network was quickly alerted: Mrs. Tagart wrote about it to Mrs. Robberds, wife of William Gaskell's colleague at Cross Street, Manchester ('He says Mr. Tagart has opened up a new field of thought and

[1] *The Uncommercial Traveller*, in *NOID, The Uncommercial Traveller and Reprinted Pieces*, etc.
[2] James Griffin, op. cit., 198.
[3] Edgar Johnson, op. cit., I. 20.

inquiry to him'). Dickens composed the inscription on a salver presented to Tagart by the congregation (July 1844):

. . . not as a quittance of the debt they owe him for his labours in the cause of that religion which has sympathy with men of every creed and ventures to pass judgement on none, but merely as an assurance that his learning, eloquence, and lessons of divine truth have sunk into their hearts and shall not be forgotten in their practice.

Dickens and Tagart remained friendly until the minister's death in 1858.[1]

Dickens was attracted to Channing, and thus to Unitarianism, by his reputation for learning and philanthropy, particularly his stand against slavery. He had found New England Unitarians admirable for their approval of 'innocent and rational amusements'.[2] And at home, cultured and tolerant Unitarians were on every hand: Forster, of course—introduced to Dickens by Harrison Ainsworth, probably himself a Unitarian; W. J. Fox; and, later, Mrs. Gaskell.[3] Dickens's declaration to C. C. Felton of his new allegiance is unequivocal: 'Disgusted with our Established Church, and its Puseyisms, and daily outrage on common sense and humanity, I have carried into effect an old idea of mine and joined the Unitarians, who *would* do something for human improvement, if they could; and who practise Charity and Toleration.'[4] And the theological coolness of Unitarianism chimed in with Dickens's own liberal views to such an extent that his *Life of Our Lord* has been taken as a Unitarian document.[5] Robertson Nicoll even claimed that there was 'sufficient documentary evidence to show that Dickens was to the end a Unitarian', that is even after he gave up regular attendance at Little Portland Street in the late 1840s.[6] And Robert Browning went so far as to regard Dickens as a hypocrite in that he was 'an enlightened Unitarian' who nevertheless had his children baptized into the Church of England.[7] Be that as it may, Dickens's relation with Unitarianism certainly serves usefully to indicate the great gulf fixed between the revivalist/fundamentalist and the decorous/learned/liberal

---

[1] F. S. Johnson, 'Dickens and the Tagarts', *Dickensian*, 21 (July 1925), 157–8; J. M. Connell, 'The Religion of Charles Dickens', *Hibbert Journal*, 36 (1937–8), 229–34; Adrian, NCF 10 (1955), 197.

[2] *American Notes*, Ch. 3.

[3] Edgar Johnson, op. cit., I. 186, 464.

[4] Published for the first time in The Pilgrim Edition of *The Letters of Charles Dickens*, III, ed. House, Storey, and Tillotson (Oxford, 1974), 455.

[5] Philip Collins, *Dickens and Education*, 54–5.

[6] Quoted by J. M. Connell, art. cit., 225.

[7] Edgar Johnson, op. cit., I. 573–4.

wing of Dissent, and importantly spotlights the difference between Dickens's almost uniformly antagonistic fictional accounts of Dissent and his actual everyday attitudes.

It is, of course, most interesting that Dickens should be well enough disposed to Dissent in the shape of aristocratic Unitarianism. For although he is commonly acclaimed as a radical and a sympathizer with the poor, and doubtless saw himself as that, he seems oddly antagonistic to just those sorts of Dissent that in fact constituted the religious sphere of the poor. He might inform his children that Christianity was on the side of the poor: 'And when people speak ill of the Poor and Miserable, think how Jesus Christ went among them and taught them, and thought them worthy of his care. And always pity them yourselves, and think as well of them as you can.'[1] But the actual religious practices of the poor get mercilessly lampooned. It does not seem to occur to Dickens that the signs of the poverty and misery with which Christ sympathized might well be an ill-conditioned and ill-sited chapel (the poor neighbourhood of the Dissenting chapels in Chapter 15 of *The Old Curiosity Shop* seems oddly to be held against them). Or an ill-educated lay preacher ('ignorant enthusiasm',[2] and 'Volunteer Apostles' are everywhere attacked). Or precisely the 'poor and ignorant' who are so subject to revivalism, 'the labouring classes' among which Goosetrap Witness has such deplorable success.[3] And any attempt by these 'Poor and Miserable' Christians to appropriate for themselves Christ's words or the New Testament's (say, about the New Birth) becomes apparently good reason for distaste or scorn. The author of 'Volunteer Apostles' seems not to have heard of the Disciples, or of St. Paul's theology of grace: 'Brother Witness did not parade much human learning or education. It was all miracle and grace, and very bad grammar. . . .' And as the *Eclectic Review* said of *Pickwick*: these 'doctrines and expressions . . . do not originate with the extravagancies of enthusiasts, but are part and parcel of the sacred Scripture'.[4]

Dickens's curious blindness to the role Dissent played among the poorer classes has not gone unnoticed: 'Dickens had *his* place in the sun. It was no hardship for one who was daily basking in the warmth of public approbation to sink into the obscurity of a pew on Sunday. . . .' 'Had Dickens, like his admirer, George Gissing, been well-nigh extinguished

[1] *The Life of Our Lord* (1934), 28.
[2] *Sunday Under Three Heads*, 8.
[3] 'Hysteria and Devotion', *AYR* 2 (5 Nov. 1859), 32; 'Volunteer Apostles', *HW* 5 (5 June 1852), 263.
[4] *Eclectic Review*, N.S. 1 (1837), 355.

by economic struggle, he might have looked eagerly for some opportunity of rearing his diminished head in self-expression once a week, and
found it, like many a Labour leader today, in Little Bethel.'[1] Mrs.
Oliphant vented the same sort of complaint in *Blackwood's* (1855):
Dickens libels the preachers of the poor:

We have another quarrel with Mr Dickens—one of long standing, dating back
to the period of his first work: the 'shepherd' of Mr Weller's widow, the little
Bethel of Mrs Nubbles, have effloresced in *Bleak House* into a detestable Mr
Chadband, an oft-repeated libel upon the preachers of the poor. This is a very
vulgar and common piece of slander, quite unworthy of a true artist. Are we
ready to believe, then, that only those who are moderately religious are true
in their profession?—that it is good to be in earnest in every occupation but one,
the most important of all, as it happens? What a miserable assumption is this!
Mr Dickens' tender charity does not disdain to embrace a good many equivocal
people—why then so persevering an aim at a class which offends few and
harms no man? Not very long since, we ourselves, who are no great admirers of
English dissent, happened to go into a very humble little meeting-house—
perhaps a Bethel—where the preacher, at the beginning, we are ashamed to say,
tempted our unaccustomed faculties almost to laughter. Here was quite an opportunity for finding a Chadband, for the little man was round and ruddy, and
had a shining face—his grammar was not perfect, moreover, and having occasion
to mention a certain Scripture town, he called it Canar of Galilee; but when we
had listened for half an hour, we had no longer the slightest inclination to laugh
at the humble preacher. This unpretending man reached to the heart of his
subject in less time than we have taken to tell of it; gave a bright, clear, individual view of the doctrine he was considering, and urged it on his hearers with
homely arguments which were as little ridiculous as can be supposed. Will
Mr Dickens permit us to advise him, when he would next draw a 'shepherd',
to study his figure from the life? Let him choose the least chapel on his way, and
take a chance for a successful sitting: we grant him he may find a Chadband,
but we promise him he has at least an equal chance of finding an apostle instead.[2]

What Edmund Gosse wrote of his father's congregation, we may
apply generally to the anti-Dissenting novelists; but the reproach is
particularly directable at Dickens, the strongest claimant perhaps among
the novelists as a sympathizer with the poor:

. . . in those earliest years the 'brethren' and 'sisters' were all of them ordinary
peasants. They were jobbing gardeners and journeyman carpenters, masons and
tailors, washerwomen and domestic servants. I wish that I could paint, in colours
so vivid that my readers could perceive what their little society consisted

---

[1] W. Kent, *Dickens and Religion* (1930), 94–5.
[2] [Mrs. Oliphant], 'Charles Dickens', *Blackwood's*, 77 (Apr. 1855), 463–4.

of, this quaint collection of humble, conscientious, ignorant and gentle persons. In chronicle or fiction, I have never been fortunate enough to meet with anything which resembled them. The caricatures of enmity and worldly scorn are as crude, to my memory, as the unction of religious conventionality is featureless.[1]

This failure in sympathy and understanding towards Dissent may be partly put down to Dickens's southern-ness. He was, as Orwell put it, 'a south of England man, and a cockney at that, and therefore out of touch with the bulk of the real oppressed masses, the industrial and agricultural labourers'. And in consequence he has little idea of the kinds, the strengths, and the rootedness of Dissent in some northern communities. The antipathy between North and South revealed in this connection in Dickens is as crucial and as marked as the division in V. S. Pritchett's family:

On my mother's side they were all pagans, and she a rootless London pagan, a fog-worshipper, brought up on the folk-lore of the North London streets; on my father's side they were harsh, lonely, God-ridden sea or country people who had been settled along the Yorkshire coasts or among its moors and fells for hundreds of years. There is enough in the differences between North and South to explain the battles and uncertainties of a lifetime.[2]

Most of Dickens's observation of chapel-going is in a southern context. There are the Baptist chapel at Chatham, and Tagart's Unitarian chapel. 'The Devil's walk', verses which Dickens added to Maria Beadnell's book (1831), mentions Irving's London church:

> Then to Irving's chapel he gaily hied
> To hear the new 'unknown tongue'
> And he welcomed with great pleasure and pride
> The Maniacs he'd got among:
> For it always fills the Devil with glee
> To hear Religion mocked,
> And it pleases him very much to see
> Sights at which others are shocked.[3]

Little Bethel in *The Old Curiosity Shop* was reputedly based on a Baptist Chapel in Goodman's Fields, Whitechapel.[4] *Household Words* attacked, as we have seen, the Peculiar People of Essex. In *The Uncommercial*

[1] Edmund Gosse, *Father and Son*, 125.
[2] V. S. Pritchett, *A Cab at the Door*, 1.
[3] Walter Dexter, *The Love Romance of Charles Dickens* (1936), 46.
[4] Lily Watson, 'Charles Dickens and Dissenters', *N & Q*, ser. **xi**, Vol. 5 (29 July 1912), 511–12.

*Traveller* Dickens spots a 'fierce-eyed spare old woman' in a 'slate-coloured gown' going to 'some chapel'—up Aldersgate Street.

Dickens had, of course, been to the North. But according to *Hard Times* nobody went to the chapels of Coketown's 'eighteen religious persuasions': the 'perplexing mystery of the place was, Who belonged to the eighteen denominations? Because, whoever did, the labouring people did not.' There is a rudimentary hint that local radicalism may be linked with Dissent in the masters' minds (Bounderby: 'I am acquainted with these chaps. . . . What warning did I give that fellow, the first time he set foot in the house, when the express object of his visit was to know how he could knock Religion over, and floor the Established Church'), but Dickens makes nothing more of it. And oddly so, given Chadband's symbolic presentation as a miniature northern town in the novel that preceded *Hard Times*. In fact the nearest Dickens gets to associating the likes of Chadband with Coketown is in Slackbridge's talk. His rhetoric and manner are very akin to Chadband's. They both have hot foreheads to wipe, both address their 'friends', both build verbal houses of cards ('Devoid of parents, devoid of relations, devoid of flocks and herds, devoid of gold and silver, and of precious stones': 'this degrading and disgusting document, this blighting bill, this pernicious placard, this abominable advertisement'), and both expose their victims in vividly destructive detail and at length ('a Gentile and a Heathen, a dweller in the tents of Tom-all-Alone's and a mover-on upon the surface of the earth': 'What do you say, *now*, of Stephen Blackpool, with a slight stoop in his shoulders, and about five foot seven in height . . . how he sneaked, and slunk, and sidled, and splitted of straws'). But further than this likeness Dickens eschews going. And of course he fails to make any vital connection, or to perceive that in the Coketowns of the North there might possibly be a connection, between some of the eighteen denominations and a worker's acquaintance with the star of Bethlehem. As Leavis concedes, *Silas Marner*, in making the connection, has greater perception than *Hard Times*:

The kind of self-respecting steadiness and conscientious restraint that he [Dickens] represents in Stephen did certainly exist on a large scale among the working-classes, and this is an important historical fact. But there would have been no such fact if those chapels described by Dickens had had no more relation to the life of Coketown than he shows them to have.[1]

And Dickens's own record bears witness against him. There is almost

[1] F. R. Leavis, *The Great Tradition*, 60, footnote 1; 271.

as notable a difference between what his article 'On Strike' reveals about Nonconformity in Preston and what *Hard Times* says about it, as there is between Slackbridge and the real orator described in the article under the name of Gruffshaw. Where Gruffshaw, the 'professional speaker' Dickens saw in action at Preston, was given little rein by the serious and worthy unionists, Slackbridge is made eloquently dominant. And Dickens is as little disposed to be fair in his novel to Dissenters as to the unionists. So *Hard Times* refuses to take note of the signs of northern chapel life and mentality the novelist could not help evincing in the article. Like the Preston lockout's anonymous financial supporters who identify themselves by Scriptural titles: 'Bear ye one another's burdens' (who 'sent one Pound fifteen'), and 'We'll stand to our text, see that ye love one another' (who 'sent nineteen shillings'). Or the hymn with which a union meeting opens:

> Assembled beneath thy broad blue sky
> To thee, O God, thy children cry.
> Thy needy creatures on thee call
> For thou art great and good to all.
>
> Thy bounty smiles on every side
> And no good thing hast thou denied;
> But men of wealth and men of power
> Like locusts, all our gifts devour.
>
> Awake, ye sons of toil! nor sleep
> While millions starve, while millions weep;
> Demand your rights; let tyrants see
> You are resolved that you'll be free.[1]

## 2. STEREOTYPES

What first made me sceptical was Charlwood, the Dissenting grocer. He was too much of a caricature and too stagey. Mr. Neale belonged to the High Church party, and it was natural to him, as Charlwood was a Dissenter, to describe him as a cheat, a drunkard, and given on provocation to the use of profane language.

William Hale White,
on the Rev. J. M. Neale's account of the 'Gill's Lap' murder:
'The Growth of a Legend', *Athenaeum*, No. 3517 (23 March 1895), 378–9.

Dickens is the most notorious of the novelists who are content with stereotypes of Dissenters. Stereotypes constitute a semiotic available to

[1] 'On Strike', *HW* 8 (11 Feb. 1854), 553–9.

the writers for signalling, without too much effort and originality, the presence of a Dissenter as it were on stage.[1] The stereotypes are sufficiently in touch with reality, sometimes more and sometimes less, to convince the unknowing reader that he has truly met a Dissenter. But novelists who only employ this signal system, and never go beyond its limited resources in their fictional treatment of Dissent, are really evading extensive contact with, or new thought about, Nonconformity.

Stereotypes, always indicative of the absence of openness, are also labour-saving devices: they can be a valuable kind of shorthand for satirists or commentators, especially if they have their audiences entirely with them. In time, the code having been established, one need only allude to one aspect of the type, agitate the signal-flag ever so slightly, to induce recognition in the pre-conditioned audience, and get a result—anger, laughter, acknowledgement—which the novelist refusing to deal in stereotypes would have to work a deal harder for. Matthew Arnold and Dickens are adepts in a period of experts. But the emptiness and the flatness of the character are exposed as soon as the signal is made to a reader who does not share the code, who, like nineteenth-century Dissenters, knows that the novelists are sometimes *only* talking code-language, and that all preachers do not squint or use bear's grease on their hair. Too many readers and critics have not recognized even yet that the novelists are often merely dealing with a conventional set of types, in a zone where 'Everyone knows'—and therefore most people only vaguely know—what is the case.

Rich men finance Dissenting affairs. Usually they are *nouveaux riches*, free-trading philistines, who have acquired their money through industry. Hardy's John Power and Mrs. Oliphant's Copperhead fulfill the type. Arnold's Bottles Esquire is the type rampant:

. . . a Radical of the purest water; quite one of the Manchester School. He was one of the earliest free-traders; he has always gone as straight as an arrow about Reform; he is an ardent voluntary in every possible line, opposed the Ten Hours' Bill, was one of the leaders of the Dissenting opposition out of Parliament which smashed up the education clauses of Sir James Graham's Factory Act; and he paid the whole expenses of a most important church-rate contest out of his own pocket. And, finally, he looks forward to marrying his deceased wife's sister.[2]

[1] For 'semiotic', see Edwin Ardener, 'Introductory Essay: Social Anthropology and Language', in *Social Anthropology and Language*, A.S.A. Monographs, 10, ed. E. Ardener (1971), particularly xli ff., and footnote 16, lxxxvi.

[2] *Friendship's Garland*, Letter VI; R. H. Super (ed.), *Culture and Anarchy* (Ann Arbor, 1965), 69.

Interestingly, Power and Copperhead, both railway-builders, seem to have been based on the same Baptist, Sir Samuel Morton Peto (1809–89), who built the Crimean railway (1854–5). He was a Liberal M.P., and built Baptist chapels and the Dorset portion of the London and South-Western railway (1846): which would indicate him as the model for John Power—Baptist, Radical M.P., Wessex-railway and chapel builder. Among his many Baptist benefactions, Peto had the Regent's Park Diorama reconditioned as a Baptist chapel: and Copperhead the (Congregationalist) railway-builder is a member of the Crescent Chapel, 'near Regent's Park', 'evidently meant to be Regent's Park Baptist Chapel', according to Robertson Nicoll.[1]

Some Nonconformists were proverbially rich, like Peto and the Gurneys (as W. S. Gilbert's Judge in *Trial by Jury* has it: 'At length I became as rich as the Gurneys'). And such men were commonly expected to develop away from Dissent, seeking social prestige in the Church of England to match their financial status: '. . . your friend Bottles, who is now a millionaire and a Churchman, was then a Particular Baptist.' 'No carriage drives to chapel after the third generation':[2] there was lots of evidence for that in the Quaker Pease and Whitwell families, the originally Baptist Marshalls of Leeds, Henry Bolckow the Middlesbrough Wesleyan, the Milnes family, and so on and on.[3] It seemed the natural transition for Galsworthy's Forsytes: 'Originally, perhaps, members of some primitive sect, they were now in the natural course of things members of the Church of England. . . .'[4] There were plenty like Obadiah Newbroom:

. . . of the well-known manufacturing firm of Newbroom, Stag and Payforall. A staunch Dissenter himself, he saw with a slight pang his son Thomas turn Churchman, as soon as the young man had worked his way up to be the real head of the firm. But this was the only sorrow which Thomas Newbroom, now Lord Minchampstead, had ever given his father. 'I stood behind a loom myself, my boy, when I began life; and you must do with great means what I did with little ones. I have made a gentleman of you, you must make a nobleman of yourself.'

---

[1] 'Mrs. Oliphant', *BW* 22 (1 July 1897), 177. For Peto see A. C. Underwood, *A History of the English Baptists* (1947), 239–40; *DNB*; Nicolas Bentley (ed.), *Russell's Despatches from the Crimea, 1854–1856* (Panther edn., 1970), 159, 173, 175; Harold Perkin, *The Age of the Railway* (Panther edn., 1970), 117.

[2] Henry Allon (1881), quoted by J. C. G. Binfield, thesis cit., 316.

[3] E. Isichei, op. cit., 142; W. G. Rimmer, *Marshalls of Leeds Flax Spinners 1788–1886* (Cambridge, 1960), 11, 102–3; Asa Briggs, *Victorian Cities*, 257; J. Pope-Hennessy, *Monckton Milnes* (1949), 7 ff.

[4] John Galsworthy, *The Man of Property* (1906), Ch. 1.

Those were almost the last words of the stern, thrifty, old Puritan craftsman, and his son never forgot them. From a mill-owner he grew to coal-owner, ship-owner, banker, railway director, money-lender to kings and princes; and last of all, as the summit of his own and his compeer's ambition, to land-owner.[1]

And there were plenty of smaller fry, like Alton Locke's Cousin George, who left Dissent to become an Anglican clergyman as a stratagem for rising in the world, or William Hale White's Mrs. Furze (in *Catharine Furze*), who sought gentility and respectability in the transfer. On the other hand, however, Hardy and Mrs. Oliphant recognized that the more interesting case is the person like John Power or Mr. Copperhead: who doggedly sticks to his Dissent when to leave it would be socially advantageous. Morton Peto is a good example of the rich man who, as it were, chose rather to suffer social affliction with the people of God, even after his bankruptcy lost him his eminence among the Baptists. Quakers provide further examples, and, at the end of the century, Charles Booth noticed among Primitive Methodists that 'an advance in worldly position may come without bringing with it any desire to leave the community'.[2]

If he stayed in Dissent, a rich man was likely to be the Leading Member, a force to be reckoned with in chapel and denomination. 'No squire', it was said, 'ever entered the family pew of the parish church with a more conscious feeling that he was exercising his hereditary right' than Albert Spicer 'entered any Congregational church which he chose to attend'.[3] And locally the Leading Member's word could be law to the minister and his family. In the minister's conflicts with his deacons the Leading Member must above all be appeased, for he was a considerable contributor to the funds. The loss of the coal-merchant's money was as serious to Basil Martin as loss of Bradshaw's pew-rent to Thurstan Benson in *Ruth*. Leading Members patronized their pastors, scrutinized their theology and behaviour: Tozer in *Salem Chapel* was not an isolated nuisance. George Macdonald was harried out of his pastorate by his deacons.[4] The story was an old one: Benjamin Patchett, an elder

[1] *Yeast*, Ch. 6. (The 1851 edition has Payforall, as does the original, *Fraser's Magazine*, 38 (Sept. 1848), 287. The De Luxe edition, p. 78, misprints 'Playforall'.)

[2] Charles Booth, op. cit., ser. iii, Vol. 7, pp. 140–1.

[3] *Albert Spicer 1847–1934: A Man of His Time*, by One of His Family (1938), 15, 20, quoted by Binfield, thesis cit., 341.

[4] Greville Macdonald, *George Macdonald and His Wife* (1924), 177–83; cf. *The Physiology of the Sects*, 66: 'In such contests the laymen are always victors, for they hold the purse strings. . . .'

at a Halifax Independent chapel, would call out to his minister in the pulpit when things displeased him, and in 1759 he published *A Short Inquiry into the proper qualification of Gospel Ministers: with some Directions how we, who are hearers, may know whether the Doctrines our Ministers deliver from the pulpit are according to God's mind and will, or not.*[1] Benson's subterfuge to protect himself and Ruth from Bradshaw testifies to the power of the Leading Member; Benson's eventual victory is like a sublimation of all a minister and his wife might crave.

So far the stereotypes have run fairly true to life: it was more difficult for the type to break free from the objective data when the number of wealthy Dissenters was so comparatively small. But the stereotypes relating to larger groups, to the ministers and the ordinary members, drift away much more from mere fact, are far more simply distorted and, indeed, abusive. The larger the group, of course, the easier it is to generalize about its characteristic member, and to get away with insult —to retreat, for that matter, as Dickens does in the 1847 Preface to *Pickwick*, into the defensive claim that, after all, one does not mean that all Dissenters are as bad as the stereotype which one will, however, persist in putting forward as characteristic.

Everybody knew that Dissent was shopkeepers' religion. 'It's on'y tradesfolks as turn Methodists', as Mr. Poyser put it. Nonconformity was for Brown, Jones, and Robinson, who were in trade. Hawkyard and Gimblett are dry-salters; the wife of the whip- and harness-maker who keeps a Post Office is a member of the Doubly Seceding Little Emmanuel persuasion.[2] Mrs. Gaskell offers a Baptist Baker (*My Lady Ludlow*) and Quaker brothers who keep a grocery, drapery, and mercery shop (*Sylvia's Lovers*). The core of Mrs. Oliphant's Salem Chapel is 'Greengrocers, dealers in cheese and bacon, milkmen . . .': the leading ladies are Mrs. Tozer, the grocer's wife, Mrs. Pigeon the poulterer's wife, and Mrs. Brown of the Devonshire Dairy. In *Vanity Fair*, Briggs's Dissenting relations are a 'hatter and grocer', and a 'shoemaker's lady'. George Macdonald's Mr. Appleditch, the grocer, attends his Salem Chapel 'in sleek black clothes, with white neck-cloth, and Sunday face composed of an absurd mixture of stupidity and sanctity'.[3]

And Dissent is commonly presented in terms of trade: the chapel is a 'schism-shop', an 'opposition shop', its inhabitants talk, like the text-

[1] R. W. Dale, *History of English Congregationalism*, 599, footnote 31.
[2] Dickens, 'The Haunted House', Ch. 1, (*Christmas Stories*, 232).
[3] George Macdonald, *David Elginbrod* (3 Vols., 1863), III, Bk. 3, Ch. 6.

painter to Tess, in a 'trade voice'.[1] The often-drawn corollary is that in
Dissent, as a branch of trade, run by tradespeople, there is money to
be made. Coketown's churches and chapels are 'pious warehouses'.
Chadband would like to do a little business ('Air we in possession of a
sinful secret, and doe we require corn, and wine, and oil—or, what
is much the same thing, money—for the keeping thereof?'). Jonas
Mudge, a member of the Brick Lane Temperance Association, is a
'chandler's shopkeeper, an enthusiastic and disinterested vessel, who
sold tea to the members'.[2] Raffles pinpoints the connection in Bulstrode's case: 'I thought you were trading and praying away in London
still . . .' (Ch. 53).

Bulstrode is perhaps the best example in nineteenth-century fiction
of the common enough charge that Nonconformity and a corrupt commercial ethic go together. George Eliot's earlier treatment of the theme
in *Felix Holt* must have been considerably reinforced by Arnold's dealing
with 'the growth of commercial immorality in our serious middle
class' in *Culture and Anarchy*:

. . . may we not be disposed to say, that this confusion [of thought and practice]
shows that his new motive-power of grace and imputed righteousness has become
to the Puritan as mechanical, and with as ineffective a hold upon his practice, as
the motive-power of the law was to the Jew? and that the remedy is the same as
that which St Paul employed,—an importation of what we have called Hellenism
into his Hebraism, a making his consciousness flow freely round his petrified rule
of life and renew it?

And the comparatively innocent business of Holt's Elixir is developed
into the larger scale villainy of the Dissenting pawnbroker whose corrupt spirit, so to say, inspires Bulstrode.[3]

The implications for Dissent of this charge cannot simply be dismissed out of hand as conventionally stereotyped and unsupported.
Indeed, Edward Miall's chapter on 'The Trade Spirit' in *The British
Churches in Relation to the British People* (1849) provides ammunition for
the accusers: 'Saintship, using the term not in a sarcastic, but a sober
sense, does not pass nowadays as a trustworthy security for commercial
uprightness.'[4] However, and here the reason for including this case

---

[1] Charlotte Brontë, 'Passing Events', Wise and Symington, *Miscellaneous and Unpublished
Writings*, II. 143; *Shirley*, Ch. 1; *Tess*, Ch. 12.

[2] *Bleak House*, Ch. 54; *Pickwick Papers*, Ch. 33.

[3] 'Porro Unum est Necessarium', *Culture and Anarchy*, Ch. 5. U. C. Knoepflmacher has
seen other parallels between *Culture and Anarchy* and *Middlemarch: Religious Humanism and
the Victorian Novel*, 69–70.

[4] P. 305. The whole of Miall's Ch. VI, 291–341, on the relationship between Christianity and Business, is very important.

among the stereotypes becomes clear, Miall's book was written to all Christians, including those in the Establishment. *His* case applied across the religious spectrum, for, obviously, there was no reason why Dissenters should have a premium on commercial dishonesty.

Equally, there were plenty of Anglicans in trade; and just as all shopkeepers were not Dissenters, not all Dissenters were shopkeepers. It was not good enough, as George Eliot knew, to dismiss Dissent as a mere shopocracy ('It is too possible that to some of my readers Methodism may mean nothing more than low-pitched gables up dingy streets, sleek grocers, sponging preachers, and hypocritical jargon—elements which are regarded as an exhaustive analysis of Methodism in many fashionable quarters').[1] Shopkeepers there were in Dissent, with stock doubtless supplied by the Quakers who were strongly entrenched in tea (Hornimans), blue (Reckitts), biscuits (Huntley and Palmer), matches (Bryant and May), soap (Crosfields), and chocolate (Cadburys, Frys, Rowntrees).[2] Shopkeepers were, after all, 'the class of the age; they represent its order, its decency, its industry'—according to Disraeli's Vavasour.[3] But they were not all of one type: 'shopocracy' as a designation is deceptively unifying. *Vanity Fair*'s radical 'hatter and grocer', and *Ruth*'s shopkeepers, 'thoughtful and reasoning, who were Dissenters from conviction', would seem short on sleekness. Some shopkeepers, particularly grocers, were as notoriously radical as cobblers. There were recognizable lines of differentiation on the High Street: butchers, saddlers, wine-merchants, and others who sought custom among the better-off, could not afford to alienate Churchman and Tory; but 'Mr. Tiliot, the Church spirit-merchant, knew now that Mr. Nuttwood, the obliging grocer, was one of those Dissenters, Deists, Socinians, Papists, and Radicals, who were in league to destroy the Constitution.'[4]

Sometimes Nonconformists did act out the type of commercialized religionism. Pugin professed disgust at what he called 'the horrible impiety of trading in religious edifices':

With respect to the style of that class of chapels built on speculation, it is below criticism. They are erected by men who ponder between a mortgage, a railroad,

[1] *Adam Bede*, Ch. 3.

[2] E. Isichei, op. cit., 182 ff.

[3] *Tancred; or the New Crusade*, Bk. II, Ch. 14.

[4] *Felix Holt*, Ch. 3; Vincent, *Pollbooks*, 14–16. Cf. *Mark Rutherford's Deliverance* for a contrast between the Tory wine-merchant who goes to church and the ironmonger who is a Dissenting deacon.

or a chapel, as the best investment of their money, and who, when they have resolved on relying on the persuasive eloquence of a cushion-thumping, popular preacher, erect four walls, with apertures for windows, cram the same full of seats, which they readily let; and so greedy after pelf are these chapel-raisers, that they form dry and spacious vaults underneath, which are soon occupied, at a good rent, by some wine and brandy merchant.[1]

Pugin had in mind episodes like the Wesleyan Centenary Hall scandal, exposed by teetotal Wesleyans in an effort to rouse the conscience of the Connexion.[2] But Thackeray at least did not suppose that this sort of cashing-in was confined to Dissent: his (Anglican) Rev. C. Honeyman lets out the vaults of his chapel to a wine-merchant, and we would be wrong to make Pugin's extension to all chapel-builders, most Nonconformists.[3] Edmund Gosse's Capuletts make the mistake ('I know these Dissenters perfectly well') of assuming that the Baxters will want to maximize the loss of their daughter's affluent fiancé by a breach-of-promise action ('Religious feeling never comes in when there is money in the case'). But the Baxters' unworldly innocence of any commercial intent is a sufficient rebuke to that kind of generalization.[4]

The generalization was underpinned by common prejudice against trade, and was widespread because so easily available to social snobs as a way of dismissing Dissent as a whole as merely vulgar. Only if one believed there to be an inherent discrepancy between the smell of cheese and bacon, and religious or poetic aspirations, was it possible to endorse Thomas Hughes's sneer at 'John Smith, the great grocer' and financier of Dissenting affairs, or Kingsley's dismissal of Browning ('He was born and bred a Dissenter of the trois état, and . . . nothing will take the smell of tallow and brown sugar out of him. He cannot help being coarse and vulgar . . . if he had been born either a gentleman (of course I mean a churchman, for *all gentlemen owe that name to Church influence over themselves or their parents*) or a hard-working man, in contact with

---

[1] *Contrasts* (1836), 28.

[2] B. Harrison, thesis cit., II. 902; James Buckle, *The Wesleyan Centenary Hall Spirit Vaults Exposed, and the Temperance Principles of John Wesley Defended Against the Practical Opposition of the Methodist Conference and Missionary Committee* (n.d.). In fairness, the Methodists did not actually 'form dry . . . vaults', but found themselves in possession of the vaults in the building purchased (1839) for the Wesleyan Centenary Hall. They did not, however, eschew the 'One Hundred to Two Hundred Pounds annual rent' to be gained from the vaults (Buckle, 25). In his *Drink and the Victorians* (1971), 310, Harrison dates the episode 1846.

[3] *The Newcomes*, Ch. 11.

[4] *The Unequal Yoke*, Ch. 12 (*English Illustrated Magazine* (1886), 612–15).

iron fact, he might have been a fine poet').¹ Of course a soul (does one still need to say it?) could be a merchant.²

The congregations of tallow and brown-sugar vendors took to themselves appropriate teachers: their pastors were as often as not self-selected illiterates, good for little else than posing as preachers of the Gospel. The assumption came easily to those who could talk, as Arnold did, of Wesley's 'third order' mind.³ Moses Barraclough is a 'preaching tailor', like Dixon's cousin in *North and South* who became a Methodist preacher at the age of 50 ('. . . but then he had never been able to make a pair of trousers to fit, for as long as he had been in the trade, so it was no wonder . . .').⁴ Goosetrap Witness is a cobbler, '. . . and it is a singular circumstance that no craft has furnished so many field-preachers and religious enthusiasts as that of St. Crispin. George Fox was a Shoemaker. . . .' So was the pastor of Little Bethel ('. . . by trade a Shoemaker, and by calling a Divine'), and Thackeray's 'Reverend Giles Jowls, the illuminated cobbler, who dubbed himself reverend as Napoleon crowned himself emperor. . . .' Kingsley's Tom Thurnall would not attend the Methodist Chapel—where 'some inspired tinker' was likely to send his hearers to hell ten times an hour.⁵

The connection between ignorance and the working-class preacher is often made explicit. Puddleham's work is done 'in spite of the intensity of his ignorance'; the note purporting to have been written by Allan, the Wesleyan minister, about a proposed marriage of John Caldigate to Euphemia in Australia is couched in the language of an uneducated man, and that seems to be accepted by Trollope as only fitting; and Dickens venomously underlines the point:

Mr. Stiggins did not desire his hearers to be upon their guard against those false prophets and wretched mockers of religion, who, without sense to expound its

---

¹ Hughes was taking up John Clifford's attack on the State Church, in a debate (1872) on one of Miall's disestablishment motions: M. R. Watts, thesis cit., 34. M. F. Thorp, *Charles Kingsley, 1819–1875* (Princeton, 1937), 95. Ironically, of course, Kingsley was similarly judged by Hopkins: he alleged that Browning's way of talking 'with the air and spirit of a man bouncing up from table with his mouth full of bread and cheese and saying that he meant to stand no blasted nonsense' came in with Kingsley and the Broad Church men. Hopkins to R. W. Dixon (12–17 Oct. 1881), *The Correspondence of Gerard Manley Hopkins and Richard Watson Dixon*, ed. C. C. Abbott (1935), 74.

² *Pace* Walter Bagehot, quoted by John Gross, *The Rise and Fall of the Man of Letters* (1969), 78.

³ *Civilisation in the United States* (Boston, 1888), quoted by A. C. Whitby, thesis cit., 29.

⁴ *Shirley*, Ch. 1; *North and South*, Ch. 5.

⁵ *HW* 5 (5 June 1852), 263; *Old Curiosity Shop*, Ch. 41; *Vanity Fair*, Ch. 33; *Two Years Ago*, Ch. 4.

first doctrines, or hearts to feel its first principles, are more dangerous members of society than the common criminal; imposing, as they necessarily do, upon the weakest and worst informed, casting scorn and contempt on what should be held most sacred, and bringing into partial disrepute large bodies of virtuous and well-conducted persons of many excellent sects and persuasions. But as he leant over the back of the chair for a considerable time, and closing one eye, winked a good deal with the other, it is presumed that he thought all this but kept it to himself.[1]

Of those 'well-conducted persons of many excellent sects and persuasions' Dickens had little or nothing to say; the usual implication, here and elsewhere, is that Stiggins is characteristic of the freelance Nonconformist preacher, and that Anglican ministers, educated as they are at ancient universities, are obviously better equipped to be spiritual guides. Beatrice Webb discerned otherwise when she met the new Bacup Dissenting minister,

. . . one of the 'new college men', with measured phrases and long words; a poor exchange for the old-fashioned minister 'called of God from among the people', no more educated than his fellows but rising to leadership by force of character. . . . He has a certain influence over the people, through his gift of the gab; but even they half unconsciously feel that the 'real thing' is passing away, and grieve that there [are] 'na more plain men as *feel* the word of Christ'. He is a snob into the bargain . . . but then he is not of 'Lanky' breed. . . .[2]

Silas Hocking shared the same feeling about the passing of the old individualist (even if ignorant) preachers.[3]

And ignorance and illiteracy were not universal among Nonconformist preachers, though their qualifications are often sneeringly minimized. For example: Spurgeon 'was not illiterate, like some of the Dissenting ministers, but he had had only an ordinary school education, and had left school when he was fifteen. He had read little except the ordinary Nonconformist literature.' To Arnold's claim that a man had read nothing who had read only his Bible, Amy Cruse thus added the Puritan classics as not really counting. Perpetrators of this kind of slur can never have glanced at the scores of authors Spurgeon preoccupied himself with, nor really pondered just whom they are dismissing so readily: as a boy Spurgeon had read Milton for light relief from Doddridge, Baxter, and the rest![4]

[1] *The Vicar of Bullhampton*, Ch. 1; *John Caldigate* (3 Vols., 1879), II, Chs. 3 and 9; *Pickwick Papers*, Ch. 45.

[2] Beatrice Webb, op. cit., 169.       [3] Silas K. Hocking. *My Book of Memory*, 61–4.

[4] Amy Cruse, *The Victorians and their Books* (1935), 77; E. W. Beacon, *Spurgeon: Heir of the Puritans* (1967), 15.

The word of novelists on Nonconformist ignorance is even more suspect. The 'old Baptist Conventicle, situated at the north-west corner of Goodman's Fields, Whitechapel', confidently identified by Lily Watson as the basis for Dickens's Little Bethel, is presumably the Seventh-Day Baptist chapel in Mill Yard, Goodman's Fields, visited by C. M. Davies ('. . . it reminded me forcibly of scenes in Dickens's "Old Curiosity Shop" ').[1] There may have been, as Lily Watson claims, 'an occasional preacher there who was also a shoemaker', but the minister, William Henry Black (1808–72), was a noted scholar and antiquary, Assistant Keeper of the Public Record Office, cataloguer—to name just one of his scholarly enterprises—of the Ashmolean MSS., member of the Camden Society and author and editor of numerous scholarly publications.

> I noticed that Mr. Black bore with him, for use in the pulpit, a Greek Harmony of the Gospels with a Latin running commentary. I certainly had not been prepared for this. I expected to find some illiterate minister, with a hobby ridden to death, when lo! I found myself in the presence of a profound scholar and most courteous gentlemen, who informed me that he thought in Latin, said his prayers in Hebrew, and read his New Testament lessons from the original Greek!

Kit Nubbles's reaction to *that* is open to conjecture.[2]

The fictionally stereotypical preacher is not only illiterate but dirty and ugly. Chadband is bear-like and oily: bear's grease, a hair-dressing advertised in the monthly parts of *Bleak House*, was suspected of fostering dirt, certainly at the Crimea.[3] His 'dirty thumb-nail' and 'oily smile' go together. The Dissenter Boultby in *Shirley* (Ch. 17) is, likewise, a 'large greasy man with black hair combed flat on his forehead'. Dissenters have poor complexions (Chadband is 'yellow', Hawkyard 'yellow-faced'); their faces, hair, and physique are 'lank'. Perspiration at prayer and when preaching signify inspiration to them, and vulgarity to the reader: Gimblet felt the Lord 'at it, while I was perspiring'.[4] Noncon-

---

[1] *N & Q*, ser. xi, Vol. 5 (29 June 1912), 511–12; C. M. Davies, *Unorthodox London*, 227–37.

[2] C. M. Davies, op. cit., 229. Black had been ministering there since at least 1838; his Friday Evening Bible Readings at Mill Yard began October 1840 (*Old Curiosity Shop* was published 25 Apr. 1840–6 Feb. 1841): *Praelectiones Theologicae Miliarenses* (1868), 2 and 3. See also *DNB*; British Museum and Bodleian Catalogues; and W. T. Whitley, 'Seventh Day Baptists in England', *BQ*, N.S. 12 (1946–8), 252–8.

[3] Trevor Blount, 'The Chadbands and Dickens's View of Dissenters', *MLQ* 25 (1964), 300; Nicolas Bentley (ed.), *Russell's Despatches from the Crimea, 1854–1856*, 33.

[4] 'George Silverman's Explanation', Ch. 6.

formists share their physical deformities with other evangelicals: where Trollope's Low Churchman Maguire (in *Miss Mackenzie*) is a 'horrid, greasy, evil-eyed parson', suffering from a 'most terrible squint in his right eye', Barraclough has a wooden leg and Stiggins squints ('a semi-rattlesnake sort of eye').[1] In precisely the same syndrome are the members of Browning's Zion Chapel Meeting.

The irrelevance of ugliness and deformity to any case against an ideology is obvious to some of the novelists. Thurstan Benson is deformed, but his Sunday dignity makes 'his bodily deformity be forgotten in his calm, grave composure of spirit'.[2] Hardy's Baptist minister's 'steaming face' indicates whole-heartedness in his denunciation of Paula the Laodicean (his 'heart was full and bitter; no book or note was wanted by him; never was spontaneity more absolute than here . . .').[3] And Dickens even indicts himself in *The Life of Our Lord*: 'The most miserable, the most ugly, deformed, wretched creatures that live, will be bright Angels in Heaven if they are good here on earth.'[4]

But what Dickens assures us is good enough for heaven somehow rarely contrives to please Charles Dickens. For he ensures that these ugly Dissenters will never claim his acceptance, nor Christ's if we believe his word on the qualifications for heaven, by making it quite clear that they are not 'good here on earth'. Like other novelists he makes 'a canting vulgar hypocrite of every Dissenter'.[5] The Pharisees, asserted Kingsley preaching on 'Hypocrisy', 'crept into widows' houses, and for a pretence made long prayers. Does no one do so now?' Of course, reply the novels, that is just what the Baptist Wigginton in *Alton Locke* and the Bryanite preachers in *Two Years Ago* do.[6] Every claim to morality or holiness is exposed as a cover under which these evangelical rogues (and Low Churchmen are usually included in the charge with Dissenters) can indulge their massive appetites for food, drink, sex, and other people's money. Charlotte Brontë's Timothy Steighton is representative: 'Tim was a "religious man" himself; indeed, he was "a joined Methodist", which did not (be it understood) prevent him from being at the same time an ingrained rascal. . . .'[7]

---

[1] *Miss Mackenzie* (2 Vols., 1865), I, Ch. 4; II, Ch. 6; *Pickwick Papers*, Ch. 27.

[2] *Ruth*, Ch. 14.

[3] *A Laodicean*, Bk. I, Ch. 2.

[4] *The Life of Our Lord* (1934), 27–8.

[5] Review of *Two Years Ago*, BQR 25 (1857), 415.

[6] 'Hypocrisy', Sermon 37, *Town and Country Sermons* (1861), 350; *Alton Locke*, Ch. 3; *Two Years Ago*, Ch. 4.

[7] *The Professor*, Ch. 3.

The outward and visible signs of the Dissenting hypocrite are bawling in the pulpit like Barraclough (Thackeray's Mr. Bawler is a Darbyite), 'snuffling' (Barraclough), 'snivelling' (the pastor of Little Bethel), and peculiarities of pronunciation: Barraclough's *Looard*, Chadband's *untoe* and *Terewth*.[1] Almost invariably these impious hypocrites roll their eyes, raising them and their hands to heaven. According to Hurrell Froude, the Dissenter was a man 'who turned up the whites of his eyes and said Lawd'.[2] Enthusiasts, asserts Dickens, 'turn their eyes, and not their thoughts to Heaven . . .'[3]

Dickens tended to reduce all his Nonconformists and his Evangelical Anglicans to this one level. The names they are given are revealing: Melchisedech Howler; Goosetrap Witness; the Rev. Jared Jocks, Montgolfian (Montgolfier invented the hot-air balloon), a member of whose church is the father of Cinderalla, who belongs to the Juvenile Band of Hope; the Rev. Jabez Fireworks and Mr. Glib, members of a Teetotal Committee; the Hon. Member for Whitened Sepulchres, and his constituents, whose 'lank hair' stands on end, pointing 'straight up to the skylights of Exeter Hall', at the thought of Sunday jaunts.[4] And evidence has survived giving us a glimpse of Dickens actually moulding a Dissenting minister into the stereotype.

In November 1842 Dickens and Cruikshank attended the funeral of William Hone the publisher and bookseller, an old friend of Cruikshank, who had been converted to Nonconformity and had become a member of Thomas Binney's King's Weigh House Chapel—where he sometimes used to preach—and a sub-editor of the *Patriot*. Dickens described his hilarious journey to the funeral with Cruikshank, and the funeral itself, to C. C. Felton, an American acquaintance, but the letter (dated 2 March 1843) was not made public until 1871, when J. T. Fields published a version of it in *Atlantic Monthly* in July of that year and in his *Yesterdays with Authors* of the same year. 'Was there ever,' whooped Fields, 'such a genial, jovial creature as this master of humor!', forgetting just for a moment perhaps that Dickens was describing a funeral. The original letter to Felton had run thus vividly and jovially:

[1] Bawler the Darbyite is in *Vanity Fair*, Ch. 64. Cf. V. S. Pritchett, op. cit., 34: 'Nonconformists often affected small changes of consonant, "p", becoming "b" and an "s" becoming a "z". . . .'

[2] Much quoted, e.g. A. L. Drummond, *The Churches in English Fiction* (Leicester, 1950), 244.

[3] *Sunday Under Three Heads*, 34.

[4] 'Frauds on Fairies', *HW* 8 (1 Oct. 1853), 97–100: a pastiche Teetotal version of the story of Cinderella; 'Whole Hogs', *HW* 3 (23 Aug. 1851), 505–7; 'The Sunday Screw', *HW* 1 (22 June 1850), 289–92.

There was an Independent clergyman present, with his bands on and a bible under his arm who as soon as we were seated, addressed George thus, in a loud emphatic voice: 'Mr. Cruikshank. Have you seen a paragraph respecting our departed friend, which has gone the round of the morning papers?'—'Yes Sir,' says George, 'I have'—looking very hard at me the while, for he had told me with some pride, coming down, that it was his composition. 'Oh!' said the clergyman. 'Then you will agree with me, Mr. Cruikshank that it is not only an insult to me who am the servant of the Almighty, but an insult to the Almighty whose servant I am'—'How's that Sir?' says George. 'It is stated, Mr. Cruikshank, in that paragraph,' says the Minister, 'that when Mr. Hone failed in business as a bookseller, he was persuaded by *me* to try the Pulpit, which is false, incorrect, unchristian, in a manner blasphemous, and in all respects contemptible. Let us pray.' With which, my dear Felton—and in the same breath I give you my word—he knelt down, as we all did, and began a very miserable [jumble] of an extemporary prayer. I was really penetrated with sorrow for the family, but when George (upon his knees, and sobbing for the loss of an old friend) whispered me 'that if that wasn't a clergyman, and it wasn't a funeral, he'd have punched his head,' I felt as if nothing but convulsions could possibly relieve me.

The clergyman's pomposity is, of course, Chadband's, and so is that bathetic drop ('Let us pray'): 'My friends, may I so employ this instrument as to use it toe your advantage, toe your profit, toe your gain, toe your welfare, toe your enrichment! My young friend, sit upon this stool.' [1] And the ludicrous exchanges between Dickens and Cruikshank while the clergyman is praying are strongly reminiscent of Captain Cuttle's conversation with Bunsby while Howler offers up 'some extemporary orisons'. [2] George Orwell at least had the decency to feel ashamed ('it stuck in our throats a little') about laughing and joking during the prayers of the lady who gave tea to the tramps. [3]

Forster published extracts from the letter in his *Life*, and Dickens's distortions were thus publicized in Britain. Thomas Binney recognized himself as the 'independent clergyman' and published a corrected version of the event. He wore, he claimed, no professional garb at the funeral, indeed he 'never wore bands'; a Bible was placed on the table for his use, so he had no need of one 'under his arm'; the 'loud, emphatic voice' was exaggeration, and the words put into his mouth invention.

---

[1] *Bleak House*, Ch. 25. George Macdonald attempted the same device less well with his Dissenting minister in *David Elginbrod*: ' "Brethren, we have this treasure in earthen vessels, and so long as *this* vessel lasts"—here he struck his chest so that it resounded—"it shall be faithfully and liberally dispensed. Let us pray".' (III, Bk. 3, Ch. 6.)

[2] *Dombey and Son*, Ch. 60.

[3] *Down and Out in Paris and London* (1933), Ch. 26.

The conversation with Cruikshank, in which he admitted writing the article about Hone, but not the offensive paragraph (which implied a connection between Hone's failure as a coffee-house keeper and his preaching at Binney's chapel), had occurred before the domestic service. The bathetic transition ('Let us pray') was impossible, because 'according to Nonconformist custom', as on this occasion, that service 'is always begun by reading an appropriate passage of Scripture, and generally with a few words of consolation and sympathy rising out of it: *then* follows the prayer.' And as 'Mr. Dickens's *testimony* to what he sees is inaccurate, his opinion as to what he probably did not understand [the "miserable jumble of an extemporary prayer"] may pass without remark.' Cruikshank had denied the conversation with Dickens (*Daily Telegraph*, 23 November 1872), as well he might; and in fact Dickens and Cruikshank had not sat, or knelt, together. Binney's purpose was to '. . . expose and protest against those worse than mere literary immoralities in which our writers of fiction indulge, not only in their novels, where they may be allowed a licence, but even when they "give us their word" for the truthfulness of their description of facts.'[1]

The *BQR* agreed that Binney had been distorted: 'The truth is, that out of a few elements of fact Dickens has drawn an exaggerated and worthless caricature. . . .'[2] He saw what he wanted to find; and so did Forster (who noted Binney's challenge in Vol. III among 'corrections made in the thirteenth thousand of the second volume', but in 1876 expunged the whole affair, and thus covered up valuable evidence of Dickens the caricaturist of Nonconformity at work). Forster's marginal note to the original passage in Vol. II reads 'Shop and pulpit'.[3]

To claim always to see only stock figures of fun and hypocrisy everywhere was not an adequate response to the evangelical claims of Nonconformity.

---

[1] See Thomas Binney, 'Charles Dickens, As an Observer and Reporter of Facts', *Evangelical Magazine and Missionary Chronicle*, N.S. 5 (1873), 3–9; J. T. Fields, *Atlantic Monthly* 28 (July 1871), 110–11, and *Yesterdays With Authors* (Boston, [1871]; 1900), 146–8; W. Robertson Nicoll, *Dickens's Own Story: Sidelights on His Life and Personality* (1923), 147–70; E. Paxton Hood, *Thomas Binney: His Mind, Life and Opinions* (1874), 229–32; E. Wagenknecht, *The Man Charles Dickens: A Victorian Portrait* (new edn., Norman, Oklahoma, 1966), 203–6. The full and accurately transcribed text of the letter to Felton has become for the first time available in The Pilgrim Edition of *The Letters of Charles Dickens*, III, ed. House, Storey, and Tillotson (Oxford, 1974), 451–6. A. H. Adrian, 'Dickens and the Brick-and-Mortar Sects', *NCF* 10 (1955), 198–9, accepts the episode as Dickens gives it.

[2] Review of Forster's *Life*, *BQR* 57 (1873), 230.

[3] John Forster, *The Life of Charles Dickens*, II (1873), 12; III (1874), 520–1.

Thackeray and Dickens, on the whole, did not face the problem. For they assumed, generally at least, that their evangelical characters were hypocrites. As long as this is so, all is well. Feigned asceticism need be no challenge to the most worldly. But it is doubtful whether this escape from the difficulty satisfied even those who devised it. They are always contrasting the religion of their evangelical characters with some vague undefined ideal of 'true' or 'real' Christianity. But what this may be we are never told. By implication we are allowed to guess that it lays great stress on one or two of the moral precepts of the gospels, such as the duty of forgiveness and of generosity, to the exclusion of others. It concentrates, in fact, on those moral qualities which the ordinary good-natured man of the world usually imagines himself to possess.[1]

A passage, to which we have already referred, in a letter from James Denney to Robertson Nicoll is worth quoting as a coda to Mr. Cockshut's observations:

Like you, I have sometimes wondered at Dickens's representation of nonconformity in people like Stiggins. . . . All the novelists like Dickens, Thackeray, and Fielding represent the *natural man* and his goodness—that is, goodness in *instinctive* forms; but all sorts of nonconformity stand for goodness in *reflective* forms—that is, in forms which have a tendency to be self-conscious, and, if they are not watched, Pharisaic. Now self-consciousness and Pharisaism are very odious to the natural man, whose goodness must be impulsive and instinctive or null, and hence he pitches into them whenever he gets the chance, with or without provocation.

I was struck once by a remark of Birrell in his life of F. Lockwood, to this effect: that Lockwood had not a particle of nonconformist about him; he was born in the Church of England and on the edge of Doncaster Racecourse, and saw no reason why a man should not be equally at home in both. That is the sort of man Dickens understands, but a man who takes away these congenial environments and gives nothing as good in their place, he delights to represent as an odious humbug. I think I sympathise with this quite enough to understand it, and even to see a certain justification for it; but the novelists should have had good nonconformists as well as bad. I believe they would have had but for the feeling that goodness must be spontaneous and not a matter of 'principle' at all. A character that implies dissent implies comparison, and comparison is odious.[2]

[1] A. O. J. Cockshut, *Anthony Trollope* (1955), 71.

[2] (23 Dec. 1911), *Letters of Principal James Denney to W. Robertson Nicoll 1893–1917* (1920), 191–2.

## 3. DICKENS AND THE ANTI-DISSENTING TRADITION

Horace Smith has lent me his manuscript called 'Nehemiah Muggs, an exposure of the Methodists' perhaps I may send you a few extracts.
> Keats, letter to George and Thomas Keats (14 Feb. 1818).

. . . a perfect Jakes of Uncleanness.
> Bishop Lavington, on George Whitefield's *Account of God's Dealings*.

Dickens's consistently grotesque image of the Dissenting preacher is clearly a traditional thing. His preachers are interestingly close, for example, to the Brontës' Methodists, who are usually mad, ugly, violent in word and deed, most inspired when most drunk, and hypocritical. Moses Barraclough is an Ur-Chadband: their pronunciations are similar; and, perhaps revealingly, there is an Hortense in both *Shirley* and *Bleak House*. Moreover, the Brontës' published work has clear connections with their juvenilia. There—and it is most developed in Branwell—the hypocrisy of the Methodist *poseurs* is broached with a curious intensity. Branwell in particular seems so disturbingly committed to the violence of his gothic protagonists' language and their self-deceits, and his own guilt, self-hatred, and revulsion from the flesh appear so strongly, that the reader can only feel that he is present at some perturbingly sick revelation:

O Lord God Creator of heaven and Earth who hast in thine Infinite Justice so long chastised man for sin and who hast declared that untill he repent thou wilt punish him eternally. look in thy infininite mercy upon these thy creatures kneeling here before thee Thou knowest O Lord their act of kneeling is but filthy and self righteous hypocrisy that their groans and sighs and ejaculations now are either the besotted drivillings of spirits lying to themselves or impious efforts of spirits lying unto thee. . . . Through thy Holy Spirit give unto these wretched sinners a knowledge of their state—a horrible blasting and consuming vision of their sin—hurl them into the dust that they may cast ashes upon their heads and in howling and gnashing of teeth behold the frightful life they have dragged on Grant that they may so hate and abhorr themselves as the instruments of Satan as to wish that they had never never been born. and so heartily and truly repent of their transgressions as to shout aloud for VENGEANCE VENGEANCE against their blaspheming and accursed heads Give them that sense of their own hatefulness which shall cast them headlong hopeless of mercy for such Hellish Sin and praying aloud for eternal punishment And howling We are unworthy to see thee Oh shut out Heaven from our eyes!—Yes O Lord Hear me I entreat thee hear me. Crush this roof above our guilty heads and cast us at once into the Lake that burneth with brimstone and the worm wich gnaweth for ever—Why wilt thou delay thy vengeance will not I say the very Elements rebel will not the Heavens sin when they see sin spreading thus unpunished over the world Come down O Lord Come down annihilate our Bodies—And cast O cast our souls for ever into ——

The preacher concluded in exu[lt]ation he stood his head bowed and trembling with the exertion. Throughout this SERMON His Voice and gesture had been awfully emphatic at length fearfully terrific For his hollow hoarsened voice then rung in cracks of thunder on our ears his brow shone and his eyes flashed while his wasted hand[s] quivered as they were raised in his Blasphemous Impiety. No one but Northangerland COULD throw himself into that madness of passion none other could so work upon his own or his hearers feelings. For the Direty Rascals—I could not for my heart give them another name—seated in the pit and front of the Gall[ery] Groaned ejaculated and Amen'ed at every climax of the discourse—unmindful of the preachers constan[t] Sallies of bitterness at them they only Groaned the deeper the more he lashed them many were acting the arrant hypocrite more were doing it for the sport and rascality of the thing but numbers of weak heads were drawn away by Ashworths divine fury till they did know wether they stood on their heads of their heals. 'Oo Loard' 'Come down Loard' 'Slay us' 'Do take vengeance' was reverberated through the assembly. . . .[1]

Branwell was only 19 when he wrote that (the fragment is dated 4 May 1836), but it is easy to see—and this is the point—that Barraclough and Chadband are never too far away. So perhaps they too were ministering to neurosis. And, as Iris Murdoch argues, 'The great novels are victims neither of convention nor of neurosis. The social scene is a life-giving framework and not a set of dead conventions or stereotyped settings inhabited by stock characters. And the individuals portrayed in the novels are free, independent of their author, and not merely puppets in the exteriorisation of some closely locked psychological conflict of his own.'[2]

Charlotte Brontë's juvenilia never have anybody as extravagantly violent as Branwell's Methodists: at least, she never concedes so much to the violence of her Methodist parodies as Branwell, and never leaves us in much doubt that they are merely parodic. Her Bromley prays:

O shed thy grace upon us like a water-spout; wash us, scour us with sand and soap, heave us neck and heels into Nebuchadnezzar's furnace, bound in our coats and hosen, our garments, our shoes and our hat, our bed and our bedding, our sheets, blankets, bolster-drawers and pillow slips. In with our fish-kettle and warming-pan, our gridiron and our porridge pot, our tureen and our soup-ladle; let nothing escape. . . .[3]

[1] Wise and Symington (eds.), *Miscellaneous and Unpublished Writings*, II. 171.

[2] 'The Sublime and the Beautiful Revisited', *Yale Review*, 49 (1959–60), 257.

[3] Wise and Symington, op. cit., II, 141.

Bromley is extravagant in his way, but the passage is so much more *healthy* than Branwell's: the bolster-drawers and the porridge pot are located too securely in domestic reality (and rather endear Bromley to us in the way Joseph's rooted, earthy language does) for us to worry about Charlotte's sanity in the way we do about Branwell's. And, of course, Dickens's preachers' ideolect is rather in Charlotte's than in Branwell's manner. Chadband enquires (Ch. 25) if Jo's parents

. . . after casting him forth to the wolves and the vultures, and the wild dogs and the young gazelles, and the serpents, went back to their dwellings and had their pipes, and their pots, and their flutings and their dancings, and their malt liquors, and their butcher's meat and poultry, would *that* be Terewth?

But we can say, at least, that the sustained grotesquerie of Chadband, Barraclough, and the Methodists of Charlotte's juvenilia reflect juvenile fantasy, and that they are almost entirely an immature vision. And further, worryingly, there is the threateningly adjacent and diseased fantasy world of Branwell which this sort of grotesquerie, indulged in too long, built and sustained. Adult writers playing children's games might become a danger to themselves.

And immaturity characterizes a whole body of literature opposing religious or quasi-religious out-groups. Fantasy played a large part in nineteenth-century anti-Catholic literature, which, like anti-Mormon and anti-Freemason propaganda, dwelt 'persistently on themes of brutal sadism and sexual immorality'. Opponents imposed their own sexual fantasies on these closely-knit or secret groups: '. . . they obviously took pleasure in imagining the variety of sexual experience supposedly available to their enemies. . . .'[1] And what Stephen Marcus says of anti-Catholic literature applies also to some nineteenth-century anti-Nonconformist material:

. . . Roman Catholicism is a pornographer's paradise, and there is, as they say, evidence to back up every charge. All priests are lechers, satyrs, pimps, all nuns are concubines or lesbians or both. The confessional is the locus of meeting of lubricity and piety. This perfect balance of outrage and envy is matched by a similar ambivalence of idea; the Church of Rome, like everyone's parents, is at

[1] G. F. A. Best, 'Popular Protestantism in Victorian Britain', in *Ideas and Institutions of Victorian Britain: Essays in Honour of George Kitson Clark*, ed. Robert Robson (1967), 115–42; see also, David Brion Davis, 'Some Themes of Counter-Subversion: An Analysis of Anti-Masonic, Anti-Catholic, and Anti-Mormon Literature', *Mississippi Valley Historical Review*, 47 (1960), 205–24.

once ascetically denying us the gratification of our impulses and hypocritically wallowing in a highly sexualised existence, making love over the nasty stye.[1]

In *Sunday Under Three Heads* Dickens comments on a Puritan account of a woman who murdered an illegitimate child conceived after dancing instigated by the *Book of Sports*: 'Such "sports" have taken place in Dissenting Chapels before now. . . .'[2] The iniquities of Shepherds are sexual ones: the 'kiss of peace' is by no means innocent. 'The worst o' these here shepherds is, my boy, that they reg'larly turns the heads of all the young ladies, about here.' Brother Humm discourses on the attractions of the temperance brothers for the ladies ('He was always first oars with the fine city ladies'). The sisters rush to fling their arms around their favourite brothers, to protect them from Stiggins's violence: Brother Humm, very popular, is almost suffocated by caresses. The lights are extinguished, and the reader is left to imagine that more is going on than just Weller punching Stiggins on the head.[3] Similarly, sinister implications are attached to Chadband's relationship with his female coterie: Mrs. Snagsby, it is lubriciously remarked, is his 'handmaid'.

The eighteenth-century novel was kinder than this to Nonconformity.[4] Humphry Clinker, a 'complete fellow', is no hypocrite, and represents the democratic following of Methodism: if he converts all the poor to abandon swearing 'there will be little or nothing left to distinguish their conversation from that of their betters', says Bramble.[5] Richardson, in *Sir Charles Grandison*, at least acknowledged the democratic intent of the early Methodists: 'I am sorry that our own clergy are not as zealously in earnest as they. They have really, my dear, if we may believe Aunt Eleanor, given a face of religion to subterranean colliers, tinners, and the most profligate of men, who hardly ever heard either of the word, or thing.'[6] Grave's *Spiritual Quixote*, only mildly satirical, insists on Wildgoose's eating and drinking, and on Whitfield's large appetite; but

---

[1] S. Marcus, *The Other Victorians: A Study of Sexuality and Pornography in Nineteenth Century England* (Corgi edn., 1969), 63.

[2] *Sunday Under Three Heads*, 37–9.

[3] *Pickwick Papers*, Chs. 27, 33.

[4] Chs. 9 and 10 of T. B. Shepherd, *Methodism and the Literature of the Eighteenth Century* (1940), marshall much valuable evidence; A. M. Lyles, *Methodism Mocked: The Satiric Reaction to Methodism in the Eighteenth Century* (1960), covers a lot of literary ground.

[5] Tobias Smollett, *The Expedition of Humphrey Clinker* [1771], ed. L. M. Knapp (Oxford, 1966), 84, 100.

[6] *The History of Sir Charles Grandison in a Series of Letters* (7 Vols., 1754), VI, Letter 9 (Lady G. to Miss Byron), 32.

if the Rev. Dr. Greville is opposed to Methodism as potentially schismatic, and warns that Wesley will be succeeded by less zealous men who
'after prejudicing the people against their proper Pastors . . . will leave
them a prey to the ignorance, and perhaps much greater immorality,
of illiterate Plebeians', he does acknowledge 'the seriousness' of the
Methodists' lives and the 'vehemence and earnestness of their harangues'
which have 'really awakened many indolent and careless Christians to
a sober and devout life', and especially among the 'middling and lower
ranks of mankind'.[1] Graves was, of course, a clergyman seriously
interested in the spiritual health of the Church of England, and his novel
has little connection with the stereotypes of the drama which are, one
feels, as much insulting to religion itself as to Methodism. Fielding, on
the other hand, shares the tone of the stage attacks. He opposes himself
to 'the pernicious principles of Methodism'; the Spirit has failed to
move Whitefield's sister-in-law (*Tom Jones*, Bk. 8, Ch. 8), and, most
damningly, Blifil becomes, in the novel's last chapter, a Methodist
'in hopes of marrying a very rich' Methodist widow in the North. In
*Amelia* (Bk. I, Ch. 4) a canting Methodist antinomian robs Booth in
prison.

But Fielding is not typical of the eighteenth-century novelists in this
matter, and it is a novel, Richard Cumberland's *Henry*, that counters
the scurrilous anti-Puritan, anti-Methodist canard of the dramatists,
poets, and pamphleteers. Ezekiel Daw, Arminian Methodist, opposes
the tendency towards antinomianism among Calvinist Methodists like
Jemima Cawdle. She deals 'the kiss of peace with a fervency most edi-
fying', is most inspired by brandy, and advocates faith and grace: 'How
often have I preached to you upon the vanity of works!' Where she
contends for Calvinism 'with the argument of the brandy-bottle launched
at his head; Ezekiel preached regeneration, repentance, and a new life,
which he illustrated with the inference of the wash-hand bason.' And
Daw effectively applies the cold water to Dickens and Mrs. Trollope as
well as to the eighteenth-century traders in sexual fantasy. At Henry's
trial Daw takes up the 'kiss of peace' charge:

. . . scoff not at me John Jenkins, nor put thy sensual fancies to my account, as
if I had given warrant to familiarities between young people of different sexes:
though the kiss of peace, of friendship, nay of love itself, may be innocent and
void of offence, yet mark me, neighbours, I recommend it not, especially to the
adult; I say unto you, as the wise man saith, 'Give not your lips unto women, for

[1] Richard Graves, *The Spiritual Quixote, or the Summer's Ramble of Mr. Geoffrey Wildgoose:
A Comic Romance* [1773], ed. C. Tracy (Oxford, 1967), Bk. VII, Ch. 1; Bk. XII, Chs. 5, 13.

in the lips there is as it were a burning fire; for ye know that a whore is a deep ditch, and a strange woman is a narrow pit'.

Daw was thin, yellow-haired, irascible, bilious, 'in short he was a creature compounded of most benevolent and excellent qualities, with a strong tincture of enthusiasm all over'. The title of the chapter where he is so described is *When the Heart is right, the Man will be respectable, though his Humours are ridiculous*.[1]

'[N]or put thy sensual fancies to my account': do not impose your own sexual fantasies on me. Mrs. Trollope in her accounts of Evangelical Anglicans, and Dickens in his presentation of Dissenters, looked rather to the closed tradition than to Cumberland's open account. They pass on the old charges of hypocrisy made in Burns's 'Holy Willie's Prayer', his 'Address to the unco' Guid, or the Rigidly Righteous', or 'The Kirk's Alarm'; of gluttony (represented in *Bartholomew Fair*'s Zeal-of-the-Land Busy); of the mechanic inspiration of the spirit and spirits bottle; of the sexual hypocrisy that fascinates Anstey in *The New Bath Guide*. They trade all over again in that hoary apparatus of pious-sounding hypocrites whose language may come from the Authorized Version but whose sensuality is merely mortal, of Shepherds, Flocks, Chosen Vessels, Holy Kisses, twanging voices, squinting preachers, and Methodist processes that was spelled out in Bickerstaffe's *Hypocrite* (out of Molière's *Tartuffe*, by Cibber's *Non-Juror*), and in Samuel Foote's *The Minor* and the *canaille* it spawned. *The Minor* looked forward to Dickens and Anthony Trollope (Squintum, i.e. Whitefield, obviously answered the taste that found Stiggins and Maguire appropriate), and back to Joseph Reed's *The Register Office* (1761), apparently written before it (Reed's Advertisement claimed that Foote had copied Mrs. Cole, the bawd and follower of Squintum, from Mrs. Snareswell, devotee of Mr. Watchlight, Tallow-Chandler and minister of the Tabernacle: another Whitefield figure).[2]

The twin themes of (deplorable) demotic sectarianism and sexual

---

[1] *Henry* (4 Vols., 1795), I, Bk. 1, Ch. 6; II, Bk. 4, Ch. 2; I, Bk. 3, ch. 5; I, Bk. 2, Ch. 10; I, Bk. 2, Ch. 11.

[2] Isaac Bickerstaffe, *The Hypocrite: A Comedy* (1769); Samuel Foote, *The Minor, A Comedy* (1760); *The Methodist: A Comedy; Being a Continuation and Completion of the Plan of the Minor*. . . . (n.d.). There was a pamphlet 'in dramatic shape' called *The Spiritual Minor*: [John Genest], *The English Stage* (10 Vols., Bath, 1832), X. 180. See also, Samuel Foote, *Apology for the Minor, In a Letter to the Rev. Mr. Bain* (Edinburgh, 1771), and *A Letter from Mr. Foote, to the Reverend Author of the Remarks, Critical and Christian, on the Minor* (1760). Amid the outraged attacks, Foote was supported by 'A Genius', *Observations, Good or Bad, Stupid or Clever, Serious or Jocular, On Squire Foote's Dramatic Entertainment Intitled the Minor* (1761). Joseph Reed, *The Register Office* (1761), 47.

hypocrisy had already appeared in *The Connoisseur* in 1755.[1] Earlier still, Steele had connected Cant with Andrew Cant ('a Presbyterian minister in some illiterate part of Scotland') and Addison had blamed Restoration impiety on over-reaction against 'Those Swarms of Sectaries that over-ran the Nation in the time of the great Rebellion' who 'carried their Hypocrisie so high, that they had converted our whole language into a Jargon of Enthusiasm. . . .'[2] Christopher Anstey could claim the respectable company of Bishop Lavington: '. . . if the reader will please to look into the Bishop of *Exeter*'s book, entitled *The Enthusiasm of Methodists and Papists Compared*, He will find many instances (particularly of young People) who have been elected' to Methodism in the manner of Miss Prudence B-R-D (and hers was 'election' by rape).[3] Goldsmith's Tony Lumpkin chimed in with the general chorus:

> When Methodist preachers come down,
> A preaching that drinking is sinful,
> I'll wager the rascals a crown,
> They always preach best with a skinful.[4]

Dickens, of course, knew his eighteenth-century novelists, and it **is** interesting that he looked to Fielding rather than to Smollett in connection with Nonconformity. He was probably also familiar with the dramatic tradition. *The Minor* and *The Register Office* were both performed in the early nineteenth century. Maw-worm, Bickerstaffe's illiterate shopkeeper ('We deals in grocery, tea, small-beer, charcoal, butter, brick-dust, and the like'), disciple of Cantwell, victim of his own malapropisms, ambitious to preach ('I have made several sermons already, I does them extrumpery'), was familiar to nineteenth-century playgoers.[5] *The Hypocrite* went through many editions.[6] Lamb praised Dowton's acting of Dr. Cantwell: he had the very tone of hypocritical Methodism ('The spirit of WHITFIELD seems hovering in the air, to suck the blessed

---

[1] *The Connoisseur*, by Mr. Town, Critic and Censor-General, No. 61 (Thursday 27 Mar. 1755), 361–6.

[2] *Spectator*, No. 147 (18 Aug. 1711); No. 458 (15 Aug. 1712), *The Spectator*, ed. Donald Bond (5 Vols., Oxford, 1965), II. 78–81; IV. 115–18.

[3] Anstey, *The New Bath Guide: Or, Memoirs of the B-R-D Family* (1766), 99.

[4] *She Stoops to Conquer*, Act I, *Collected Works of Oliver Goldsmith*, ed. A. Friedman, (5 Vols., Oxford, 1966), V. 117.

[5] [John Genest], *The English Stage* (1832), I. lxxxiii, cii.

[6] 3rd edn., 1769; another edn. 1792; *Sharpe's British Theatre* (Vol. 6, 1804); *New English Drama* (Vol. I, 1818); Cumberland's British Theatre (Vol. 3, 1829); and other collections and series like *Lacy's Acting Edition of Plays* (Vol. 76, 1867?) and *Dick's Standard Plays* (No. 51, 1884).

tones, so much like his own upon earth').[1] Thackeray apparently refers to a performance of the same period:

Do you remember, dear M—, O friend of my youth, how one blissful night five-and-twenty years since, *The Hypocrite* being acted, Elliston being manager, Dowton and Liston performers, two boys had leave from their loyal masters to go out from Slaughter House School where they were educated, and appear on Drury Lane stage, amongst a crowd which assembled there to greet the King?[2]

Dickens knew *The Register Office* from Chatham days, if indeed he read 'over and over' Mrs. Inchbald's *Collection of Farces*, though he would have missed Mrs. Snareswell and Mr. Watchlight if he did not actually see a performance or read it elsewhere than in Mrs. Inchbald's expurgated *Collection*.[3] He knew *The Spectator*; and modelled *Household Words* on it.[4] He acted in Jonson's *Every Man In His Humour*; read Goldsmith; and, as if completely to give away the game, quoted Swift in the 1847 Preface to *Pickwick*:

. . . it is never out of season to protest against that coarse familiarity with sacred things which is busy on the lip, and idle in the heart; or against the confounding of Christianity with any class of persons who, in the words of SWIFT, have just enough religion to make them hate, and not enough to make them love, one another.[5]

Reviewers familiar with the tradition needed little prompting. The *Eclectic* recognized that *Pickwick*'s generalizing to a whole body from individual cases was 'the course adopted by the infamous Foote' in *The Minor*. Thomas Hood recalled Zeal-of-the-Land Busy in his review of *Barnaby Rudge*. The *Athenaeum* reviewer called Chadband 'a greasy, preaching *Mawworm*'; *Putnam's Magazine* thought he had become the definitive specimen: '. . . how superior he is to the Maworms of the stage, and all other attempts to delineate his species. He will for ever

---

[1] *Examiner* (1 and 2 Aug. 1819), *The Works of Charles and Mary Lamb*, ed. E. V. Lucas (7 Vols., 1903–5), I. 188. Lamb was writing about a performance at the English Opera House (27 July 1819): Lucas, I. 461.

[2] *Vanity Fair*, Ch. 48.

[3] *Register Office*: Mrs. Inchbald, *A Collection of Farces and other After-pieces, which are acted at the Theatres Royal, Drury Lane, Covent-Garden, and Hay-Market* (7 Vols., 1809), VII. 137–69. Forster's *Life*, 8.

[4] Forster's *Life*, 8, and 443, footnote: 'I strongly incline to the notion of a kind of *Spectator* (Addison's)—very cheap, and pretty frequent.'

[5] Preface to First Cheap Edn. (1847), x; *NOID*, *Pickwick Papers*, xiii. Dickens certainly read Goldsmith's *Citizen of the World* (Forster's *Life*, 8), and *The Bee* (P. Collins, *Dickens and Education*, 10).

stand as the type of that numerous band of evangelists whom he so vividly calls to mind.' [1] And Mrs. Trollope well knew the nature of her own work: *The Vicar of Wrexhill* was entitled *The Unco' Guid* in draft, and Cartwright is labelled in the novel as 'that odious hypocritical Tartuffe'. [2]

Dickens and Mrs. Trollope, then, take up the eighteenth-century case, particularly the stage case, against the Methodists, and as it were make it again available for the Victorian period. 'Dickens gibbeted cant in the person of Dissenters,' said Trollope, 'of whom I never knew anything. I have done so in Mr. Slope, an Anglican, but the unbeneficed descendant of my mother's Vicar of Wrexhill.' 'I think,' he unsurprisingly opines, 'I may have inherited some of my good mother's antipathies towards a certain clerical school.' [3] Dickens and Mrs. Trollope influenced each other: he read her *Domestic Manners of the Americans* before he visited America, and kept his copy; she read and liked his *American Notes*. [4] *The Vicar of Wrexhill* is almost certainly a cashing-in on *Pickwick*'s success, a try at doing for Evangelical Anglicanism what Dickens had done for Methodism.

Dickens's case is reinforced by what he has learned from the essayists. From Leigh Hunt perhaps, who supported the charges that Methodist 'love-feasts, watchnights, and revivalist fervour became occasions for promiscuous sexual intercourse', in his *An Attempt to Shew the Folly and Danger of Methodism* (1809). [5] Dickens sent him *Pickwick* hoping he would find some 'vibration of the old chord you have touched so often and sounded so well. . . .' [6] Dickens received presentation copies of Hunt's *Poetical Works* (1844) and his *Religion of the Heart* (1853). [7] And Dickens was not the only one familiar with Hunt's work: Branwell Brontë chose him, in December 1827, as a chief man on his imaginary island. [8]

William Hazlitt, many of whose works, including *The Round Table*, were in Dickens's library, also charged Methodism with hypocrisy, with

[1] *Eclectic Review*, N.S. 1 (1837), 354–5; *Athenaeum*, No. 743 (Jan. 1842), 79; *Athenaeum* (17 Sept. 1853), and *Putnam's Magazine* (Nov. 1853), quoted in A. E. Dyson (ed.), *Dickens, Bleak House: A Casebook* (1969), 51, 80.

[2] Chadwick, op. cit., I. 447; *Vicar of Wrexhill*, II, Ch. 10.

[3] T. H. S. Escott, *Anthony Trollope: His Work, Associates and Literary Originals* (1913), 111–12.

[4] Edgar Johnson, op. cit., I. 357, 360, 422–3; J. H. Stonehouse (ed.), *Reprints of the Catalogues of the Libraries of Charles Dickens and W. M. Thackeray* (1935), 114.

[5] E. P. Thompson, op. cit., 410, footnote 1.

[6] Edgar Johnson, op. cit., I. 220.

[7] J. H. Stonehouse, op. cit., 63.

[8] Mrs. Gaskell, *Life of Charlotte Brontë*, I. 87.

being the resort of 'religious invalids', who like Mawworm suppressed
their 'animal spirits' ('Melancholy tailors, consumptive hair-dressers,
squinting coblers'), to sit under 'sleek and corpulent' pastors who had
married 'thriving' widows. A religion for the vulgar and the foolish,
conveyed in unintelligible jargon, ' "Vital Christianity" is no other
than an attempt to lower all religion to the level of the capacities of the
lowest of the people.'[1] The coincidence of opinion with Dickens is
clear; and even clearer is Dickens's admiration for Sydney Smith, the
*Edinburgh Review*'s scourge of the evangelicals. Smith's *Works* (4 Vols.,
1839–40) were on Dickens's shelves.[2] Before they met in 1839 Dickens
wanted most to meet Smith 'of all the men I ever heard of and never
saw'.[3] Dickens admired Smith's 'noble wit'; Smith loved Dickens's
'humor most'.[4] Dickens referred to him after his death as the 'wisest
and wittiest of the friends I have lost'.[5]

It is not true that 'Theologically speaking, it might be said of him as
Shaftesbury said of Palmerston, that he did not "know the difference
between Sydney Smith and Moses".'[6] He almost certainly knew Smith
as the author of satirical attacks on 'Methodism', by which he understands evangelicalism in all its forms. Smith opposed the notion of
special providences, of a religion of feeling; he charged Methodists with
anti-worldly gloominess, with hypocrisy (they stress grace not works),
with a 'shocking familiarity with words and images, which every real
friend to religion would wish to keep sacred'. Methodism leads to madness; gives 'ploughmen and artisans' too elevated opinions; gains popularity by vulgar antics in the 'Tabernacle'. '[T]o the learning, the moderation, and the rational piety of the Establishment, we most earnestly wish
a decided victory over the nonsense, the melancholy, and the madness
of the tabernacle.'[7] Baptist missionaries are 'little detachments of
maniacs', merely devout tinkers.[8] In 1809 Smith reviewed a book re-

---

[1] 'On the Causes of Methodism', *The Round Table*, No. 15 (22 Oct. 1815), *The Collected
Works of William Hazlitt*, ed. A. R. Waller and Arnold Glover (13 Vols., 1902), I. 57–61.

[2] J. H. Stonehouse, op. cit., 103.

[3] *The Letters of Charles Dickens*, ed. M. House and G. Storey (Pilgrim edn.), I (Oxford,
1965), 546; cf. 641 (Wednesday 19 June 1839: 'Sydney Smith's . . .').

[4] *Letters* (Pilgrim edn.), II (Oxford, 1969), 261, footnote 3, and *Letters of Charles Dickens*,
ed. W. Dexter (Nonesuch edn.), II. 395.

[5] K. J. Fielding (ed.), *The Speeches of Charles Dickens* (Oxford, 1960), 405. See also
Forster's *Life*, 161, 291, 327, 371–2; K. J. Fielding, op. cit., 144; *Letters* (Pilgrim edn.),
I. 686; *Letters* (Nonesuch edn.), I. 593.

[6] K. J. Fielding, *Charles Dickens: A Critical Introduction* (1958; 1961 impression), 138.

[7] Review of *Causes of the Increase of Methodism and Dissension*, by R. A. Ingram, *Edinburgh
Review*, 12 (1808): *Works* of the Rev. Sydney Smith (4 Vols., 1839–40), I. 95–129.

[8] On Indian Missions, *Edinburgh Review*, 12 (1808); *Works*, I. 172–3.

plying to his two previous articles, and, using even more violent and insulting language, he repeated his charges. The Methodist and Baptist claims on Providence are disgustingly impious; Scriptural language is debased by this 'illiterate and ungrammatical prelacy'; Methodism is 'not Christianity . . . but . . . debased mummery and nonsense'. A 'nest of consecrated cobblers'; 'such a perilous heap of trash'; 'the nasty and numerous vermin of Methodism'; 'didactic artisans'; 'delirious mechanic'; 'drunken denunciations of Methodism'; 'thousands of canting hypocrites and raving enthusiasts—men despicable by their ignorance, and formidable from their madness'; 'self-ordained ministers' —the charges are familiar, the imagery unusually intense. '[C]urse us with any evil but the evil of a canting, deluded, and Methodistical populace. Wherever Methodism extends its baneful influence, the character of the English people is constantly changed by it. Boldness and rough honesty are broken down into meanness, prevarication, and fraud.'[1] '[I]t is very possible,' he wrote in a review of Hannah More's *Coelebs in Search of a Wife* (1809), 'to be a good Christian, without degrading the human understanding to the trash and folly of Methodism.'[2]

Dickens named his fifth son, born on 18 April 1847, Sydney Smith Haldimand Dickens.

#### 4. THE DICKENS TRADITION

Here is a portrait of the founder and first editor of the 'Daily News', Charles Dickens, who needs no introduction to any English audience.

> *The Religious Life of London: A Lantern Lecture*,
> by the Superintendent of the 'Daily News' Church Census
> [R. Mudie–Smith], [1903].

We have talked of Dickens and Mrs. Trollope in the same category as retailers to Victorian fiction of the earlier anti-evangelical tradition, the one setting the tone for anti-Dissenting novels, the other for anti-Evangelical-Anglican novels. Dickens was, of course, much more influential, because he made himself more acceptable, than Mrs. Trollope. Sydney Smith approved, as one might expect, of *The Vicar of Wrexhill*, and Trollope himself was influenced by it, as we have seen.[3] But

---

[1] Review of *Strictures on Two Critiques in the Edinburgh Review, on the Subject of Methodism and Missions*, by John Styles (1809), *Edinburgh Review*, 13 (1809); *Works*, I. 185–201.

[2] *Edinburgh Review*, 13 (1809); *Works*, I. 210. Of these articles, Mrs. Oliphant wrote: 'These extraordinary productions are already altogether out of date, as indeed they must have been behind the time in which they were written, and of right belonged to a less enlightened generation . . .', 'Sydney Smith', *Blackwood's*, 79 (Mar. 1856), 359.

[3] T. H. S. Escott, op. cit., 30, 31, 111–12.

Tractarians rebuked it for immorality, and Thackeray, who agreed that there was 'much cant and hypocrisy . . . among those who desecrate the awful name of God, by mixing it with their mean private interests and petty projects', thought it 'unscrupulously filthy' and 'coming from a woman's pen . . . most odiously and disgustingly indecent'. In suggesting that Evangelicals were interested above all in gaining sexual advantage under the cloak of religion, the novel was 'a shameful and wicked slander'.[1] The reception of *Domestic Manners of the Americans*, an account obsessed with the sexual opportunities of revivals and of camp meetings and the sensual proclivities of itinerant Methodist preachers, likewise included charges of 'gross' exaggeration by an 'unblushing vixen': Mrs. Trollope was altogether too much of the eighteenth century, and unrepentantly so, to be entirely congenial to the Victorians.[2] But Mr. Popular Sentiment, as Trollope labelled him in *The Warden* (Ch. 14), had charms which soothed even outraged Nonconformist breasts. He blended the scurrility of the eighteenth-century stage and the sneers of the essayists with enough credentials like social indignation, religious sentiment, pathos, and humour, to pacify many otherwise indignant Dissenters: he was too good, too much *there*, to be ignored on a simply party basis.[3]

But he did nevertheless, release into Victorian fiction treating Dissent an older virulence, the more widespread because of his enormous and wide-ranging readership. This animus was conveyed not only in the persons of Stiggins and Chadband, but in the numerous imitations triggered by *Pickwick* and *Bleak House*.[4] The imitative prose narratives and

[1] O. Chadwick, op. cit., I. 447; [W. M. Thackeray], 'Our Batch of Novels for Christmas, 1837', *Fraser's Magazine*, 17 (Jan. 1838), 79–85.

[2] *American Criticisms on Mrs. Trollope's 'Domestic Manners of the Americans'* (1833), 42, 67. Cf. [James Grant], *The Great Metropolis* (2nd ser., 2 Vols., 1837), I. 132–3.

[3] Dickens was favourite reading for A. L. Rowse's Bible Christian aunt and uncle (*A Cornish Childhood*, 58–9); a Salvation Army Officer's report could describe a down-and-out as a 'Kind of Mark Tapley' (William Booth, *In Darkest England* (6th edn., 1970), 29); Lily Watson's family knew their Dickens 'intimately' ('Charles Dickens and Dissenters', *N & Q*, ser. xi, Vol. 5 (29 June 1912), pp. 511–12); J. C. Francis's Baptist father 'read Dickens with delight, month by month as fast as the parts were published' ('Charles Dickens', *N & Q*, ser. xi, Vol. 5 (15 June 1912), pp. 461–3); a Nonconformist preacher in the 1840s classified 'the London City Mission; the novels of Mr. Dickens; the cholera' as the 'three great social agencies' (G. M. Young, *Early Victorian England*, quoted by G. H. Ford, *Dickens and His Readers: Aspects of Novel-Criticism Since 1836* (paperback edn., 1965), 81, footnote): he could just, one supposes, be construed as having approved as little of Dickens as of the cholera, rather than as having approved of him as much (presumably) as of the London City Mission.

[4] For accounts and lists, see F. G. Kitton, *Dickensiana* (1886), 362–405, and *The Minor Writings of Charles Dickens* (1900), 234–44; W. Miller, *The Dickens Student and Collector*

stage performances made Stiggins and Chadband still more familiar to the period, and there is even some evidence of their being conflated into a single stereotype of the Nonconformist preacher. In George Lander's *Bleak House: or, Poor 'Jo'*, first performed at the Pavilion Theatre, Monday 27 March 1876, Chadband's costume includes a 'large black cotton umbrella'. The umbrella is however the stock property of Stiggins (because gloomy evangelicals always expect rain?).[1]

Stiggins's reputation was thoroughly advertised, not only in the pastiche *Penny Pickwick*, and the plays like W. T. Moncrieff's *Samuel Weller, or The Pickwickians* [1884], or W. L. Rede's *Pickwick*, first performed at the Adelphi, 3 April 1837, but in the pictorial tradition. Stiggins and his umbrella, rolling-eyes, red-nose, brandy-and-water, and the violence done to him, were favourite subjects for the numerous illustrators of *Pickwick*.[2]

And in the imitations one tends to find an intensification of the violence, a stepping-up of the scurrility, as though the imitators had fewer qualms about re-creating a fuller-blooded eighteenth-century case, once Dickens had made available the material, given them as it were his sanction. The audience for *The Penny Pickwick* and the theatre versions had obviously less sense of the proprieties than some of Dickens's own readers.[3] Smirkins of *The Penny Pickwick* is Stiggins raised to a new power: he not only rolls his eyes, but his 'ghastly eyes were constantly rivetted on the ceiling'; he and his flock eat and drink more, the 'stream of grace' flows more freely; and Smirkins not only bestows the 'kiss of redemption', but fathers a child on one of his 'pious lambs'. And the Swiftian violence done to Stiggins in *Pickwick Papers* is intensified: Smirkins is degraded, pelted, bloodied, muddied, be-sooted and be-greased, horse-whipped, his eyes blackened, his nose dislocated.

Compared with that, *Pickwick Papers* seems almost moderate, and certainly its sexual innuendo seems mild, even if it is no less sinister,

---

(1946), 241–56; Louis James, *Fiction for the Working Man 1830–1850* (1963), 45–71; W. Miller, 'Imitations of Pickwick', *Dickensian*, 32 (Winter, 1935–6), 4–5.

[1] George Lander, *Bleak House: or Poor 'Jo': A Drama in Four Acts* (?1884).

[2] See Joseph Grego (ed.), *Pictorial Pickwickiana* (2 Vols., 1899).

[3] *The Penny Pickwick: Post-Humorous Notes of the Pickwickian Club*, ed. by 'Bos' (2 Vols.). Kitton dates it 1842 or *c*. 1842; John Medcraft, *A Bibliography of the Penny Bloods of Edward Lloyd* (Dundee, 1945), gives [1838–42]. Lloyd moved from Wych-Street, Strand, to 62 Broad Street between Nos. 17 and 18 of *The Penny Pickwick*, a move that took place between 1836–7 and 1838–9: Philip A. H. Brown, *London Publishers and Printers: A Tentative List—c. 1800–1870* (British Museum, 1961), 59. The Penny Pickwick has 112 numbers, so [1838–42] looks right.

beside the pornographic *Rosa Fielding, Or, A Victim of Lust* (1876). But again, Dickens is not blameless: he can be said to have generated Mr. Bonham, a 'sanctimonious elder of the chapel which he patronized', who lives at Rutsden Lodge, and who fails, because of incontinence, to seduce 16-year-old Rosa whom he wants for his wife, and after a night with two girls at a brothel voices regret over the innocent pleasures he has for a lifetime ignorantly debarred himself from. A story is put about by military friends of Bonham's daughter libelling the Reverend Brother Stiggins of Little Bethel: it is alleged that a major had seduced a maiden lady in Little Bethel beneath the eyes of Stiggins while he was preaching and that Stiggins tried to blackmail the major, who was however able to kick out the saintly divine because he had evidence that he had been found in a pig-pen, rogering a young sow. Enraged at the rumour, Stiggins comes up to the barracks, is got dead-drunk, is tarred and feathered, wheeled on a wheelbarrow into town, and dumped on the steps of Miss Larcher's Temperance Coffee-House. Miss Larcher, the lady supposed to have been seduced in the chapel, is outraged ('Oh, my, what a state for a babe of grace, a minister of the word'), but is easily seduced by a dragoon-officer in her Coffee-House. Bonham himself is anxious that the missionaries to the Fukkumite Islanders, whom he supports, should be supplied with special pants for the female natives: so that their 'bare bottoms' should not be displayed 'to the unhallowed gaze of the unregenerate sailors of whale ships', but reserved for the private pleasure of our 'self-sacrificing brethren, the missionaries'.[1]

Dickens provided, as *Rosa Fielding*'s development of motifs from *Pickwick*, *The Old Curiosity Shop*, and *Bleak House* indicates, Dissenting themes and characters which had clearly become well-known reference points in any discussion of Nonconformity. And they were evidently regarded in many quarters as a complete description rather than an abusive shorthand. It was a kind of apotheosis of the stereotype: Dickens's semiotic, so to say, bid fair to replace the vernacular—as though semaphore or morse-code should displace human speech. Everybody read Dickens, according to M. K. Ashby, and all 'tyrants and fools could be transmogrified into Dickens characters. . . .'[2] The *Ragged School Union Magazine* complained in 1864 that Borrioboola-Gha was still 'the worldling's nickname for foreign missions'.[3] Thackeray, making fun of a

---

[1] Described and discussed by Stephen Marcus, *The Other Victorians*, 220–38.

[2] M. K. Ashby, *Joseph Ashby of Tysoe* (Cambridge, 1961), 94.

[3] Quoted by Philip Collins, 'Dickens and the Ragged Schools', *Dickensian*, 55 (1959), 106, footnote 5. See Miss E. J. Whateley, 'Charles Dickens', *Leisure Hour* (1870), 730, for the same point.

sabbatarian letter to the *Times*, signed 'ONE OF THE PEOPLE CALLED CHRISTIANS', claimed to have spotted the author: Mr. Punch 'was awake all night after it had appeared, tossing about in his bed in a fury, and exclaiming "STIGGINS—it's STIGGINS—I know it is—the rascal! . . ." '[1] A Black Country song, 'Bright Crowns laid up', attributes 'pie in the sky' notions to a Methodist called Twiggins (which I take to be a variant of *Stiggins*):

> I heard the voice of Twiggins say
> Come let us work no more,
> Lay down thy ommer and thy tongs
> And beg from door to door
>
> Bright crowns laid up,
> Laid up for you and me,
> Bright crowns, bright crowns
> There's a crown of victory.[2]

Dickens's stereotypes are still in circulation: Ezra Pound's article 'Mr. Housman at Little Bethel' (1934), and Rabbi Warshaw in *Portnoy's Complaint* ('. . . a character out of Dickens is what he is': 'And doesn't he speak in those fucking syllables', i.e. like Chadband), indicate the deep roots that Dickens's images have put down in the western literary tradition.[3] Not surprisingly one finds in the nineteenth century that accounts of religious events and people will use Dickens's stereotypes as a kind of touchstone. A Salvation Army congregation at prayer reportedly 'flopped' themselves down: 'flopping' is Cruncher's word for the act of kneeling in *A Tale of Two Cities*.[4] C. M. Davies approved the absence of a 'Stiggins element' at a Kensal New Town Free Church tea-and-experience meeting; the Walworth Jumpers greeted each other with a 'good whacking' 'kiss of peace'; their new meeting-place was 'a certain Little Bethel down a back slum in Chelsea'; the

---

[1] 'Mr. Punch on the Fine Arts', *Punch*, 8 (1845), 224. See also 'Stiggins in New Zealand', *Punch*, 9 (1845), 3. M. H. Spielmann, *The Hitherto Unidentified Contributions of W. M. Thackeray to 'Punch'* (1899), 121–2, 131–2, 288.

[2] Michael and Jon Raven, *Folk Out of Focus* (Wolverhampton, 1965), 65. The song alludes to the Wednesbury anti-Methodist riots (1742–3), but is of later provenance: e.g. *rifle* = 'fire-arm' (to shoot down pigeons for pie in the sky)—1st date in *OED* is 1775. Twiggins is too close to Stiggins to be accidental.

[3] *Criterion* (Jan. 1934), in *Literary Essays of Ezra Pound*, ed. T. S. Eliot (paperback edn., 1963), 66–73; Philip Roth, *Portnoy's Complaint* (1969), 73–4.

[4] 'A Press Skirmisher', *The Service of the Salvation Army with their Mad March-Outs, Knee Drill, Song Drill, Groan Drill and Cash Drill* (n.d.), 4. (Bodleian Library, John Johnson collection.)

locale of the Seventh-Day Baptists was like something out of *The Old Curiosity Shop*.[1]

In time, Dickens's stereotypes having become so exactly synonymous in everybody's mind with the actuality (all pastors becoming 'shepherds' and all chapels 'Little Bethels'), Nonconformists clearly felt they should try and inject some approbative content into what had become merely antagonistic (so to say, wresting the best tunes from the devil). In his speech at the Baptist Union Assembly (1906) when Lloyd George presented him with a portrait, John Clifford praised the 'godly and heroic folk in a little Bethel near Nottingham' where he was brought up; Joe Wrag, in Hocking's *Her Benny*, found a place of worship in 'a little Bethel near his home'.[2] Nonconformists had to try and remind the readers of Dickens that they had after all been calling their chapels Bethel long before *The Old Curiosity Shop*. A similar process can be seen with 'Salem Chapel'. Mrs. Oliphant's rather disparaging account of the chapel whose name she probably drew from 'Janet's Repentance' was instantly confirmed by other novelists (Mr. Appleditch, the grocer in *David Elginbrod* (1863) worships at Salem Chapel, Dervish Town; Puddleham's chapel (1869–70) is 'Salem' or 'New Salem'), but already in 1877 the sting was being drawn by Clifford ('It is a trifle that "Society" in its superior enlightenment treats "Salem Chapel" as a vulgar impertinence. . . . But it is intolerable that landowner and squire, justice of the peace and priest of the Church, should form a confederacy to close the chapel down, and stamp out the hated pestilence of Dissent . . .').[3]

Dickens taught his period to see Dissent through his spectacles. His models were only too available to succeeding novelists. 'We are grieved,' wrote the *British Quarterly* reviewer of *Two Years Ago*, 'to think that Mr. Kingsley should stoop to imitate the scurrilous caricatures which Mr. Dickens has drawn. . . .'[4] Mrs. Oliphant was another who did not hesitate in stooping to imitate Dickens's popular material.

---

[1] *Mystic London* (1875), 83; *Unorthodox London* (1873), 91, 101.

[2] M. R. Watts, thesis cit., 392; Silas Hocking, *Her Benny*, Ch. 16.

[3] *Baptist Handbook* (1877), 109, 318–19. Mrs. Oliphant claimed that she made suggestions for improving the marketability of *David Elginbrod* and persuaded Blackett to publish it, *Autobiography and Letters of Mrs. M. O. W. Oliphant*, ed. Mrs. Harry Coghill (2nd edn., 1899), 190.

[4] *BQR* 25 (1857), 416–17.

# IX. MRS. OLIPHANT AND THE TRADITION

Are you, then, so eager to return to Scott, who never seems to have suffered
from writer's cramp?

George Moore to Edmund Gosse, in George Moore, *Avowals*.

NEW GRUB STREET was a world away from George Eliot, but Mrs.
Oliphant was often confused with her major rival.[1] Joseph Langford
suspected Mrs. Oliphant of having written 'Amos Barton'.[2] George
Eliot resented the imputation that *Salem Chapel* was a novel of hers: 'I
am NOT the author of the Chronicles of Carlingford. They are written
by Mrs. Oliphant. . . .' She had not read the instalments in *Blackwood's*,
'but from what Mr. Lewes tells me, they must represent the Dissenters
in a very different spirit from anything that has appeared in my books'.[3]
The *Spectator* thought *Salem Chapel* 'could take its place besides George
Eliot's "Scenes from Clerical Life", without being hurt by the
comparison'.[4] And George Eliot suspected poaching: 'Of course every
writer who produces an effect on the public suggests to others a choice
of subjects or of manner which is more or less conscious imitation and
in some cases the inevitable result of a certain affinity.'[5]

It seems perhaps hardly coincidental that *Salem Chapel* (1862–3)
follows *Adam Bede* (1859), and that *Phoebe, Junior* (1876) follows *Felix
Holt* (1866).[6] But if the general similarity of subject-matter recruited
George Eliot's readers for *Salem Chapel*, in the end Mrs. Oliphant could
only lose by any comparison.

To Henry James Mrs. Oliphant's fecundity was 'extraordinary': 'no
woman had ever, for half a century, had her personal "say" so publicly

---

[1] Mrs. Kathleen Watson thinks there is much more to this muddled assimilation than I
think viable. See 'George Eliot and Mrs. Oliphant: A Comparison in Social Attitudes',
*E in C* 19 (1969), 410–19. For discussion of contrasts see, Review of M.O.W.O's
*Autobiography and Letters*, *Quarterly Review*, 190 (July 1899), 256.

[2] *GE Letters*, II. 435, footnote 5.

[3] GE to S. S. Hennell (23 Apr. [1862]), *GE Letters*, IV. 25.

[4] *Spectator*, 36 (14 Feb. 1863), 1639.

[5] GE to S. S. Hennell (1 May [1862]), *GE Letters*, IV. 28.

[6] Cf. M.O.W.O. to Blackwood (1862): '. . . the faintest idea of imitating or attempt-
ing to rival the author of "Adam Bede", never entered my mind.' *Autobiography and
Letters*, 185–6.

and irresponsibly.'[1] In her hey-day (the 1860s–80s) she continually rivalled the exemplary day's toil Gissing's Jasper Milvain puts in (*New Grub Street*, Ch. 14): 'there is so much of me!' she justifiably exclaimed.[2] James dubbed her 'a great *improvisatrice*, a night-working spinner of long, loose, vivid yarns, numberless, pauseless' (Trollope was 'the great *improvisatore* . . .'). He admired reluctantly, but was puzzled by

. . . a love of letters that could be so great without ever, on a single occasion even, being greater. It was of course not a matter of mere love; it was a part of her volume and abundance that she understood life itself in a fine freehanded manner, and, I imagine, seldom refused to risk a push at a subject, however it might have given pause, that would help to turn her wide wheel.[3]

Mrs. Oliphant marshalls her thin resources to the best advantage, works over the same ground a second and third time, tackles a subject in *Blackwood's*, in a biography, in a novel. Novels are followed by sequels, sequels become a sequence; no possibility of restating a theme is lightly waived. An article on Irving (1858) becomes a fully fledged biography (1862); and with this material, plus an interest in revivalism stimulated by work on Wesley,[4] she produces a novel about charismatic revivalism, *The Minister's Wife* (1869). Admiration for Wilkie Collins, which provided material for an article (May 1862),[5] and her notion of how inferior deacons and elders could blunt the genius of a preacher (theme of the Irving article and *Life*), helped to shape the sensationalist plot and the religious matter of *Salem Chapel* (February 1862 to January 1863). Tozer of *Salem Chapel* was too profitable a seam to leave unworked, so he reappears, with his granddaughter, in *Phoebe, Junior: A Last Chronicle of Carlingford* (1876): the parting note of the title not unconnected with Trollope's *Last Chronicle of Barset* (1867).

At least some of Mrs. Oliphant's badness, the resort to popular sentiments about mothers and religion, conventionally plotted intrigue, and sensationalism, can be put down to financial calculation. There is a distinct gap between her cheaply melodramatic novels and the critical voice which deplores Bulwer's 'sham and cheap melodrama' and Charles Reade's theatricality and melodrama, which withstands the shallowness

---

[1] 'London Notes', *Harper's Weekly* (Aug. 1897): *Notes on Novelists with some Other Notes* (1914), 358.

[2] *Autobiography and Letters*, 258 (20 Apr. 1876).

[3] *Notes on Novelists*, 358–9; 'Anthony Trollope', *Century Magazine* (July 1883), reprinted in *Partial Portraits: The House of Fiction*, ed. Leon Edel (paperback edn., 1962), 90.

[4] 'Historical Sketches of the Reign of George II. No. VII.—The Reformer', *Blackwood's*, 104 (Oct. 1868), 428–56.

[5] 'Sensation Novels', *Blackwood's*, 91 (May 1862), 564–84.

with which female novelists 'discussed and settled' the 'vexed questions
of social morality, the grand problems of human experience', and which
rejects the 'froth of flirtation and folly which has lately invaded like a
destroying flood the realms of fiction', the books 'by millions, which . . .
depreciate instead of elevating the intellectual taste of the multitude'.[1]
As anonymous critic Mrs. Oliphant scorns precisely those strategies
she deploys as novelist:

Out of the mild female undergrowth, variety demands the frequent production
of a sensational monster to stimulate the languid life. . . . Murder, conspiracy,
robbery, fraud, are the strong colours upon the national palette. Even when we
try to be Arcadian, it is Arcadia '*plus* a street-constable', as Carlyle says; and
over that ideal world Mr. Justice Somebody looms supreme upon the bench,
and the jurymen are always within call. . . .[2]

To attempt a popular success she crosses to the side of popular taste,
and her fiction quite knowingly exploits the vices of Charles Reade and
Mrs. Henry Wood that she attacks in Maga.[3] And this resort to the
*kitsch* factors of sensationalism, conventional plotting, and so on, as
guarantors of popular esteem, comes with curious readiness. Given the
leisure she occasionally regretted not having, Mrs. Oliphant might have
ironed out minor inaccuracies (Beecher of *Salem Chapel* becomes
Beecham in *Phoebe Junior*; a few pages of *The Minister's Wife* after Horace
Stapylton had 'begun to glide out of the habits of a lover' he is described
as 'still so lover-like'; at the beginning of *Phoebe*, Vol. II, Horace
Northcote's white tie is said to be always 'of the stiffest' as a sort of
clerical uniform: at the end of Vol. I he had, however, appeared with
white cravat 'carelessly tied').[4] But more worrying, though the lapses
of memory about what she has written are symptomatic of the serious
fault, is the consistent evasion of close imaginative engagement, what

[1] '*Autobiography and Letters*', 434 (30 Apr. 1897); 'Charles Reade's Novels', *Blackwood's*,
106 (Oct. 1869), 510; 'Modern Novelists—Great and Small', *Blackwood's*, 77 (May 1855),
555; M. O. and F. R. Oliphant, *The Victorian Age of English Literature* (1892), II. 200;
M.O.W.O., ' 'Tis Sixty Years Since', *Blackwood's*, 161 (May 1897), 619.
[2] 'Novels', *Blackwood's*, 94 (Aug. 1863), 168–9.
[3] See R. D. Altick, *The English Common Reader* (Chicago, 1957), Appendix B. Charles
Reade's *It is Never Too Late to Mend* (1856) sold 65,000 in seven years, and was attacked for
melodrama, which Mrs. Oliphant's novels are not exactly free of (*Blackwood's*, 106
(Oct. 1869), 510). Mrs. Henry Wood's *East Lynne* (1861) sold 430,000 up to 1898; it was
charged with glorifying vice as a purifier (*Blackwood's*, 91 (May 1862), 567) but imitated in
*Salem Chapel* (see Vineta and Robert A. Colby, *The Equivocal Virtue: Mrs. Oliphant and the
Victorian Literary Market Place* (Hamden, Conn., 1966), 51–2).
[4] *The Minister's Wife* (3 Vols., 1869), III. 257 and 269; *Phoebe, Junior* (3 Vols., 1876),
I. 280, II. 3. Cf. M.O.W.O.: 'I don't remember much one year what I wrote the year
before . . .', *Autobiography and Letters*, 241.

James called a 'full, pleasant, reckless rustle over depths and difficulties'.

Revealingly, she was 'astonished beyond measure' at the 'established
intimacy' with his characters that Trollope claimed, and advocated, in
his *Autobiography*: 'I am totally incapable of talking about anything I
have ever done in that way.' [1] This self-confessed failure is not insignificant: it underlies the hand-me-down air of parts of her account of
Dissent, the reworking of novels on other novels. Honest toil at the
anvil of fiction ('. . . this does not mean that I was indifferent to the
work as work, or did not beat it out with interest and pleasure . . .')
would be no substitute for originality and imaginative engagement.

Mrs. Oliphant's novels about Scottish Nonconformity—*Margaret
Maitland*, *Magdalen Hepburn*, *Lilliesleaf*, *The Minister's Wife*—are notice-
ably different in spirit and tone from her novels about English Dissent,
*Salem Chapel* and *Phoebe, Junior*.[2] Scottish Nonconformity is more congenial to her than English; she knows more about it. The Scottish
novels were all written early (except for *The Minister's Wife*, which
however stems from the early interest in Irving), generated in the
period when Mrs. Oliphant's sympathies for the Scottish Free Church
cause were at their strongest.

Henry James discerningly spotted where her strength lay:

She showed in no literary relation more acuteness than in the relation—so profitable a one as it has always been—to the inexhaustible little country which has
given so much, yet has ever so much more to give, and all the romance and reality
of which she had at the end of her pen. Her Scotch folk have a wealth of life, and
I think no Scotch talk in fiction less of a strain to the patience of the profane.[3]

*Margaret Maitland* is little more than a ramblingly pious tale of love and
intrigue. And the treatment it incidentally affords the 1843 Disruption
of the Church of Scotland, out of which emerged the (technically Nonconformist) Free Church of Scotland in which Mrs. Oliphant grew up,
consists of scarcely more than sympathetic noises and a sketchy map
of the dispute. But even that little does bring to the novel a bit of

---

[1] *Autobiography and Letters*, 4; Trollope, *An Autobiography*, II. 49–51.

[2] *Passages in the Life of Mrs. Margaret Maitland*, by Herself (Henry Colburn, 3 Vols.,
1849); *Magdalen Hepburn: A Story of the Scottish Reformation* (Hurst and Blackett, 3 Vols.,
1854); *Lilliesleaf . . .*, written by Herself (Hurst and Blackett, 3 Vols., 1855); *The
Minister's Wife* (Hurst and Blackett, 3 Vols., 1869); *Salem Chapel* (Blackwood, 2 Vols.,
1863); *Phoebe, Junior* (Hurst and Blackett, 3 Vols., 1876).

[3] *Notes on Novelists* (1914), 350 (London Notes, Aug. 1897).

sociological muscle, some saving realism. It is a recruited strength that helps specify the dimensions of a world of religious experience that Mrs. Oliphant had herself inhabited, and could move freely about in, and through it the novel impinges, however slightly, on a world of real moral conflict and decision that considerably stiffens its backbone.

This reinforcement is found again in *The Minister's Wife* (1869): its engagement with the charismatic revivalism associated with Edward Irving redeems a little its trivialities of plot, its tired story-lines, and weakness of invention. But this novel, based on 'the religious movement in the West of Scotland about the year 1830',[1] one of Mrs. Oliphant's best fictions, a serious attempt to enter the revivalist mind, to penetrate the heart of a revival, comes characteristically near to shipwreck because of the banality and conventionalism with which it is associated. Once again Mrs. Oliphant had failed to perceive where her best interests might lie; the melodrama, the mysteriousness where (as in *Salem Chapel*) there is really no mystery, are allowed to undermine the religious theme. In Book III she is not content with a sometimes very moving account of the prophetess who feels left derelict by God: she must draw out the flagging Stapylton case to its bitter end, with Isabel's struggles over the baby he wants her to leave behind in Scotland when they emigrate to America, tedious maternal delight over baby's perambulatory efforts, a secret drawer's contents exposing Stapylton as murderer, murder threats, a loaded pistol, grinding and gnashing of teeth. The unimaginative ordinariness of this lifeless third volume almost completely obscures Ailie Macfarlane's reconciliation to her God.

Mrs. Oliphant professed her incapacity for assessing her material's worth ('Sometimes I find it totally impossible to form any opinion of what I have done, and send it off in hopeless perplexity, not knowing whether it is good or bad . . .'),[2] but one suspects the financial calculation all the time, a recipe for fiction that would inevitably try granting a novel as many various appeals as possible. And in striving to manage several jobs at once *The Minister's Wife* fails to do itself justice: it ends up satisfying neither as a tale of mystery and horror, nor as a religious novel.

Doubtless, one of the better-done things in the novel is the prophet John's blackmailing the prophetess Ailie into marrying him by means of religious shibboleths ('. . . hear the Word of the Lord! and see that ye sin not against the Holy Ghost'). But, characteristically, the strength of the account undoubtedly derives from St. John Rivers's

---

[1] Preface to *The Minister's Wife*.       [2] *Autobiography and Letters*, 178.

pressures on Jane Eyre—pressures that are also professedly religious
but are really purely sexual—to become a missionary. And any insight
into the ambivalent mixture of nature and grace in these cases is
weakened in the conventionalized passion—usual with Mrs. Oliphant—
of Black John ('his great, heavy, passionate eyes').

Mrs. Oliphant's accounts of English Dissent lack first-hand experience. Of *Salem Chapel* she wrote:

As a matter of fact I knew nothing about chapels, but took the sentiment and a
few details from our old church in Liverpool, which was Free Church of Scotland, and where there were a few grocers and other such good folk whose ways
with the minister were wonderful to behold. The saving grace of their Scotch-
ness being withdrawn, they became still more wonderful as Dissenting deacons,
and the truth of the picture was applauded to the Echoes.[1]

Her love for the English Establishment had grown, and acquaintance
with the French monastic revival and with the Montalambert family
helped shape her into a High Churchwoman.[2] The drift away from
Free Church sympathies paralleled her social and political progress. The
girl who collected signatures in Liverpool against the Corn Laws, worshipped at the Presbyterian church with 'the engineers and their families
who worked in the great foundries', never went to dances, theatres, or
art galleries, and who was therefore at one, culturally, socially, and
politically, with the mass of Dissenters in her novels, grew up to abhor
second-class rail travel and cheap clothes ('not fit for any gentlewoman
to wear'), sent her sons to Eton and Balliol, and 'could say more easily
than most people the things that stab and blister' about persons whose
cultural position she had once shared.[3] Her strenuous scorn for provincial vulgarity is a repudiation of the Liverpool childhood (and in fact
Copperhead's view of his Turner as an investment, his equation of
aesthetic and monetary value, is uncomfortably close to Mrs. Oliphant's
treatment of her own art as commodity). The *British Weekly* writer
(presumably Nicoll) had 'often been surprised that her hard experience
never seemed to school her into charity and restraint'. Her sons lacked

[1] Ibid., 84.

[2] *Blackwood's*, 92 (Aug. 1862), 215. W. W. Tulloch, 'Mrs. Oliphant', *Bookman*, 12
(Aug. 1897), 115. She translated Count Charles Forbes René de Montalembert's *The
Monks of the West from St. Benedict to St. Bernard* (7 Vols., 1861–79) and wrote *Memoirs of the
Count de Montalembert: A Chapter of Recent French History* (2 Vols., 1872). Both were
published by Blackwood.

[3] *Academy* (3 July 1897), 15–16, quoted by V. and R. A. Colby, op. cit., 237; 'Mrs.
Oliphant', *BW* 22 (1 July 1897), 177; *Autobiography and Letters, passim*.

charity too, in their priggish Toryism. Frank (Cecco), namesake of his uncle Frank who had been, like Mrs. Oliphant's mother, 'tremendously political and Radical', could class demonstrations of 'young roughs, *soi-disant* the unemployed' among the London amusements of 1887: 'Many people think that the unemployed are not bad fellows on the whole, as long as you don't ask them to work, but they are certainly an abominable nuisance.'[1]

The Free Church of Scotland had a comparatively short history of protest against the Established Church, and though its membership was to some extent socially inferior, the difference was less marked than in England: research has merely shown that the eldership of the 'Frees' (in Aberdeen) tended to be drawn from the lower middle class and that of the Establishment from the upper middle class.[2] In England, of course, Dissent's social inferiority was marked and long-entrenched, and by her shift towards Anglicanism Mrs. Oliphant was precluding very much chance of learning the English situation. In general terms she understands, and presents, the caste difference between Anglicans and Dissenters, but she is quite capable of effectively negating the barriers she points to by putting a Dissenter on the kind of socially equal footing with the Establishment he might easily have enjoyed in Scotland. Only one chapter of *Salem Chapel* after Vincent's firm impression that 'society' in Carlingford is closed to 'a poor Dissenting minister' (Ch. 5) he gets his wished-for entrée to that 'society' through meeting Lady Western in Masters's bookshop. The improbability here was protested against by George Eliot: 'And certainly no dissenting life I ever came in contact with in the provinces, could furnish an example of a dissenting minister being invited to visit her by a lady of title on a first interview in a shop.'[3]

Vincent's love for Lady Western was, according to the *Nonconformist*, 'infatuation, not to say madness'.[4] There is more of this sort of madness in *Phoebe, Junior*, where Mrs. Oliphant is less interested in analysing seriously the social problems of Dissent than in developing the ironies of the fictional situation she has designed. Her ironic interest in caste

---

[1] *Autobiography and Letters*, 10, 348.

[2] See A. A. Maclaren, 'Presbyterianism and the working class in a mid-nineteenth century city', *Scottish Historical Review*, 46 (1967), 115–39, and Geoffrey Best, *Mid-Victorian Britain 1851–1875* (1971), 185. The secession had included all classes, 'even nobles and gentry and eminent professional men'; and it set out absolutely to replicate the Establishment, on the basis of the claim to be the 'true' Church of Scotland. J. H. S. Burleigh, *A Church History of Scotland* (1960), 352, 354.

[3] (23 Apr. [1862]), *GE Letters*, IV. 25–6.

[4] 'Salem Chapel', *Nonconformist*, 23 (25 Feb. 1863), 158.

concentrates on the margins where genteel poor (the May family, whose father is a Carlingford clergyman) and rising middle class (the ex-shopocracy as presented by Phoebe) overlap, and Dissenting railway magnates brush against third-rate peers. Phoebe feels inferior as a Dissenter to Ursula May; Ursula for her part feels inferior to Phoebe because she has shone in 'grand society'—the Copperheads' ball, grand only to Ursula. The Rev. Mr. May forges a bill drawn on Tozer, a socially despised, but nevertheless prosperous Dissenting grocer. Northcote, sometime missionary of the Liberation Society, and Anti-State-Church lecturer, is introduced into the May family, where Clarence Copperhead, son of the Dissenting millionaire, is being coached for Oxford examinations, and where Reginald May has just accepted a sinecure chaplaincy to an almshouse (shades of Trollope!). Northcote had attacked May at an Anti-State-Church meeting attended by Carlingford's enthusiastic Dissenters (Vol. II, Chs. 1 and 2). May's dismissiveness towards the Liberation Society ('A parcel of trumpery agitators, speechifiers, little petty demagogues, whom nobody ever heard of before'; 'Shopkeepers', Vol. II, Ch. 5) confronts Northcote's virulent political Dissent, but the party allegiances of both are softened over tea at Tozer's, where the butterman and leading elder is moved (unrealistically, objected the *Nonconformist*) to declare that there is no need to perpetuate public stances in private.[1] The two young men recognize mutual problems of faith and doubt in the nineteenth century, and of irksome authority (the congregation and elders in one case, and May's Dissent-abhorring, duty-shirking Rector in the other). The 'old faith' represented by the fifteenth-century Chapel of the Charity Foundation is a rebuke to Northcote's unlovely 'new agitations', and May perceives how immoral the Rector must look to Dissenting eyes. The two young, hopeful ministers turn out to be only factitiously opponents (both are 'foolish, wrong and right'), and realize their true *rapport* in the Mays' drawing-room where Northcote woos Ursula and May yearns after Phoebe. Copperhead plays his fiddle while Churchman and Dissenter burn with passion for girls of the opposite parties.[2]

[1] *Phoebe Junior*, Vol. II, Ch. 10. 'Dissent in Fiction', *Nonconformist*, 37 (5 July 1876), 675.

[2] *Phoebe*, Vol. II, Chs. 12 and 15. Cf. Mrs. Oliphant's account of Church–Dissent relations in [Frederick William Robinson's] *Church and Chapel* (1863): 'The object of the book, as it lies on the surface, is to show how entirely external are the disagreements between the good Churchman and the good Dissenter; and how the two require only to be brought together and see each other's hearts, to secure their entire brotherhood and co-operation in all good works'. 'Novels', *Blackwood's*, 94 (1863), 179.

   The ludicrous inadequacy of this as a solution to the differences between Church and Dissent is abundantly clear, and equally clearly this simplistic but confident resolution is based on ignorance of the problem and the issues. The ease with which Dissenters are made to abandon their opposition to the Church reflects Mrs. Oliphant's simplified view of the quarrel: for her, Dissenting antagonism is simply a matter of inverted snobbery, Arnold's 'jealousy of the Establishment'. Snubbed, as he thinks, by Lady Western, Vincent delivers his sensational 'course' on Establishment evils: his passion, Mrs. Oliphant says, simply an underdog's reaction against the privileged class (*Salem Chapel*, Ch. 8). Acceptance by Lady Western dampens Vincent's ardour against the Church; friendship with Reginald May makes Northcote embarrassed by his own early antagonism; 'social elevation' modifies Phoebe's 'sectarian zeal' as it had toned down her parents' sense of social inferiority and of spiritual superiority to the Establishment (*Phoebe*, I, Ch. 2). Mrs. Oliphant hardly touches on the details of Dissenters' social and political deprivation and displays her usual lack of interest in the detailed theological differences between the parties. Northcote's speech against the Establishment is, she claims, no routine agitation, but she evades telling us what he said, coyly adding that it would be dangerous to do so.[1] Mrs. Oliphant's mentions of the Liberation Society, the 'Dis-Establishment Society', the *Nonconformist* and the *Patriot*, convey a superficial impression of knowledge. But these details were widely available, especially in and about 1862, Bicentenary of the Great Ejection (when *Salem Chapel* began to be published). The *Nonconformist* pointed out that Congregational Dissenters did not, as they do in *Salem Chapel* and *Phoebe*, talk of the 'connexion': that was Methodist jargon. Nor were the students at Homerton College, as the first chapter of *Salem Chapel* asserts, 'brought up upon the *Nonconformist* and *Eclectic Review*': 'this journal [sic] had the distinction of being tabooed by the quasi-Conservative alumni of that venerable institution'. The author of *Salem Chapel* was obviously 'not personally familiar with the life that he has undertaken to depict'; 'absence of that special and minute knowledge which intimate acquaintance confers' was noticeable: *Phoebe, Junior* 'could only have been written by one who knows little really of Dissent'.[2]

---

   [1] *Phoebe*, II, Ch. 2. Cf. a similar evasion in her novel *A Son of the Soil* (1866), in reference to Colin's first Scottish *Tracts for the Times*: 'It would be doing Colin injustice to reproduce here this revolutionary document . . .' (Vol. II, Ch. 21).
   [2] 'Salem Chapel', *Nonconformist*, 23 (25 Feb. 1863), 157; 'Dissent in Fiction', *Nonconformist*, 37 (5 July 1876), 675.

According to the Colbys, *Salem Chapel* has the

... ring of truth and of originality—an inside view of an independent congregation presented with candor and humor and with just enough snobbish condescen-
sion to appeal to a predominantly Church of England reading public for whom
the popular image of the Dissenter was still a vulgar, hymn-singing tradesman.[1]

But *Salem Chapel* is clearly deficient in truth, not entirely satisfactory
as an inside view, less original than compounded of popular notions, and
calqued on fictional accounts.

The sensation of 'horror', lightly dismissed by Mrs. Oliphant in
*Blackwood's* in May 1855 as a mere stimulant to the jaded palates of
novel-readers, was embraced as a profitable gambit in *Salem Chapel*.[2]
The novel's melodramatic 'machinery'—the mysterious Mrs. 'Hilyard';
Susan Vincent's abduction; the abductor Colonel Mildmay's being shot;
Susan accused of the crime; an atmosphere of murkily rainy evenings;
fleeting glimpses of the avenging Mrs. Mildmay's hauntingly white face
(shades of *The Woman in White*); overheard conversation; appropriately
inflated rhetoric—fulfils Mrs. Oliphant's prediction that 'What Mr.
Wilkie Collins has done with delicate care and laborious reticence, his
followers will attempt without any such discretion. . . .'[3] The only
discretion Mrs. Oliphant allowed herself, remembering her fear that
Collins's imitators would glorify vice, and her rebuking *East Lynne* for
representing 'the flames of vice as a purifying, fiery ordeal, through
which the penitent is to come elevated and sublime', was to guarantee
that the abducted Susan Vincent passed through no real 'flames of vice',
had no need of penitence. She remains unscorched, if rather flushed.
Mrs. Oliphant did not, however, eschew borrowing from *East Lynne*:
Mildmay changes his name, calling himself Fordham, as Levison took
the alias Captain Thorn; Tozer, like Mr. Joe Jiffin, owns a shop in 'the
cheese and ham and butter line', with a comfortable parlour behind,
and a well-furnished drawing-room upstairs.[4]

The 'sensation' element, aimed to appeal to the large audience of *The
Woman in White* and *East Lynne*, constantly diverts attention from the
chapel. From the vestry (Ch. 10) Vincent overhears an argument
between Mrs. 'Hilyard' and Colonel Mildmay (' "She-wolf!" cried the
man, grinding his teeth'). Vincent has just made a tea-meeting speech

[1] V. and R. A. Colby, op. cit., 46.

[2] 'Modern Novelists—Great and Small', *Blackwood's*, 77 (May 1855), 566.

[3] 'Sensation Novels', *Blackwood's* 91 (May 1862), 567, 568. 'Machinery' was Mrs.
Oliphant's word, *Autobiography and Letters*, 187; *Victorian Age of English Literature*, II. 186.

[4] See V. and R. A. Colby, op. cit., 51–2.

which invoked melodramatic circumstance ('the dark streets which thrilled round' his congregation). We are invited to agree that the banal events of the Hilyard–Mildmay melodrama are weightier than the interests of a Dissenting community or the preoccupations of a Dissenting pastor.

What, then, were the poor dialectics of Church and State controversy, or the fluctuations of an uncertain young mind feeling itself superior to its work, to such a spectacle of passionate life, full of evil and of noble qualities—of guilt and suffering more intense than philosophy dreams of? (Ch. 11)

Reviewers recognized that this rejection was ill-judged: '. . . almost any novelist could do as well or better' than the 'Mildmay melodrama'; and the *Spectator* wished '. . . that in some new edition the Mildmay film might be skilfully removed from the book, by some neat surgical operation, and the simple squabbles of the Salem Independents left in all their purity and majesty.' [1] But while the plot advanced, the Dissenting life was treated mostly as backcloth and kept static, limited to a few basic propositions about narrowness and the congregation's power over its minister. Once stated, these are simply repeated; and they are almost all Mrs. Oliphant has further to add in *Phoebe, Junior*.

Not surprisingly, given *Salem Chapel*'s abundant literary indebtedness and Mrs. Oliphant's ignorance, Dickens's influence is strong. Mrs. Oliphant, using her familiar smokescreen device, was publicly cool about Dickens. [2] As we have seen, she rebuked his contempt for the 'preachers of the poor'. Andrew White, a character in *The Minister's Wife*, is said to look, in funeral garb, '. . . like the conventional type (often very far from the reality), which the public accepts as that of a Dissenting pastor. It was not Chadband, benign and oily, but a more melancholy and meagre specimen' (Vol. III, Ch. 1). This double-edged rebuttal—conventional public images are often untrue, and Chadband does not represent the conventional type (a rebuke to Dickens for selecting badly)—hardly prepares the reader for Mrs. Oliphant's trading in stereotypes, and Dickensian ones at that.

---

[1] *Spectator*, 36 (14 Feb. 1863), 1639. Sensation 'marred the effect' of *Salem* and *The Perpetual Curate* ('The Brownlows', *The Literary World: A Monthly Supplement to the Christian World*, 1 (14 Mar. 1878), 18); it was 'quite out of place' in *Salem* (*Nonconformist*, 23 (25 Feb. 1863), 157), and happily was absent from 'The Rector' and 'The Doctor's Family' (*Nonconformist*, 23 (17 June 1863), 494). 'The plot may be dismissed as not only bad but unnecessary' (*National Review* (1863), quoted by V. and R. A. Colby, op. cit., 49).

[2] 'Sensation Novels', *Blackwood's* (May 1862), 564–84, compares him adversely with Wilkie Collins.

Old Mr. Tufton's 'large soft flabby ministerial hand' (*Salem*, Ch. 3), and Tozer's unction, blending with grease from the bacon and butter, are by no means distant from Chadband. In *Phoebe*, Tozer has become more completely the greasy shopkeeper, the unctuous Dissenter: by the time he turns stagily on Mr. May demanding his pound of flesh ('I'll have him rot in prison for it') his sturdy support of his sect and class has been swamped by the author's satiric intent. His final speech rejecting 'clever young men' and advocating 'strong opinions' and 'no Charity' towards other denominations, was, observed the *Nonconformist*, 'not so much humorous as funny, after the manner of many of the extravagant dramatic attitudinisings of Charles Dickens'.[1]

The Salem womenfolk are cruelly pilloried: their complacent ignorance of social and cultural barrenness, their love of tea-parties ('the urns . . . well filled, the cake abundant'), their meagre ambitions and petty jealousies—just tolerable, and sometimes finely drawn in *Salem Chapel*—become tedious and simply unkind when insisted on again in *Phoebe*.

The familiarity of this fictional zone is signalled by jokes about the 'flock' (Salem matrons are no 'lambs', even if 'of the flock'), and by Mr. Morgan, the Rector in *The Perpetual Curate*, thinking that Wentworth's 'impromptu chapel' by the canal is 'a little Bethel'.[2] Salem Chapel, seedy, sombre, red-brick, is a familiar fictional property; Dissenting commercialism—Tozer's concern not to 'let the steam go down' (Ch. 4)—had been done before. Vincent's impression of the 'miserable scene of trade . . . a preaching shop, where his success was to be measured by the seat-letting, and his soul decanted out into periodical issue under the seal of Tozer & Co.,' is a colourfully extravagant version of the usual kind of changes. At his most Shylockian, Tozer becomes a Gradgrind ('the Good Samaritan was a Bad Economist'): the Gospel cannot dictate charity in a business situation, business must not be interfered with. Copperhead senior is made abruptly to conform to utilitarian type (a patent device for extending *Phoebe*'s third volume); and his liking only industrial towns like Manchester, his notion that women should be exported like other surplus raw materials, his preference for railway stations against fifteenth-century chapels, his advocacy of political economy against the unwisdom of large clerical families, are stereotyped enough. (And his sinister 'we've had enough of Christianity' is curiously at odds with his faithful Dissent.)

---

[1] *Nonconformist*, 37 (5 July 1876), 675.
[2] *Salem*, Ch. 8; *The Perpetual Curate* (3 Vols., Edinburgh, 1864), Vol. I, Ch. 1.

The spirit of Matthew Arnold imbues Mrs. Oliphant's scorn for bacon and cheese merchants, for Copperhead's interest in his Turner only as an investment, for Clarence Copperhead's 'tendency towards those demonstrative and offensive whiskers which are the special inheritance of the British Philistine' (*Phoebe*, Vol. I, Ch. 2). The *Nonconformist* suspected animus, from the 'conspicuous absence of any attempt or desire to find a reality of religious conviction or feeling underlying the supposed defects of the system or the vulgar prejudices of its adherents. . . .' It recognized an old story: this was 'the aspect in which Dissent presents itself to a large class of minds possessing considerable influence in our day'.[1]

*Salem Chapel* and *Phoebe, Junior* outline the stock case against the Voluntary System: it enslaves its ministers, makes them men-pleasers, panderers in the pulpit and on pastoral visits to the congregation which pays them. The commonplace nature of the argument, which had, as the *Nonconformist* reviewer conceded, elements of truth in it,[2] can be gauged by noting the similarities between Mrs. Oliphant's charges and William Pitt Scargill's *Autobiography of a Dissenting Minister* (anonymously published, 1834), a bitter novel, posing as non-fiction, by an ex-Unitarian minister.[3] Scargill quotes from William Hull a passage which might serve epigraphically for Northcote and Vincent, describing the necessity for congregation-pleasing, and the possibility of maintaining greatest popularity only by being most anti-Establishment: the minister 'maintains his ascendancy . . . by cherishing the passions of sectarian bigotry and hate. . . .'[4] The decline of Northcote's and Vincent's popularity coincides with their waning sectarian fervour.

Mrs. Oliphant, like Scargill, notes the difference between country-town and metropolitan Dissent. In the small town the chapel's social range is limited: no upper-class members (Mrs. Hilyard is a freak member, imposed on Salem by the demands of the melodrama), the poor 'don't count', and the majority is 'in the way of business'. The

[1] *Nonconformist* (25 Feb. 1863), 157.

[2] Ibid., 158.

[3] There is no indication that Mrs. Oliphant read this book, and indeed, if my case that she is dealing merely in conventional ideas is true, it rather helps if she did not read it. But there is an odd resemblance between *Salem Chapel*'s Adelaide Tufton and the daughter of one of the grocer–draper members of Scargill's narrator's chapel: both are unmarried, sharp-eyed, quick-witted, outspoken girls of about thirty. Scargill, op. cit. (5th edn., 1835), Chs. 4 and 6; *Salem Chapel*, Chs. 3 and 41.

[4] Scargill, op. cit., Ch. 7. He is quoting Wm. Hull, *Ecclesiastical Establishments Not Inconsistent with Christianity: With a Particular View to some Leading Objections of Modern Dissenters* (1834), 58–9.

minister's style is cramped by the constricting demands and surveillance of the small-town shopocracy. Like Vincent, Scargill's narrator, a Dissenting minister, finds irksome the teas, the pastoral visits for little but gossip, the congregation's familiarity, inevitably breeding contempt. The congregation seeks to monopolize the pastor's time, interest, presence, to dictate his life-style, his choice of wife: friendships— particularly with gentry and Anglicans—and loves are closely super- vised. Any aloofness from the congregation generates disfavour ('To have people turn up their noses at you ain't pleasant . . .', 'And them getting their livin' off you all the time . . .' *Salem Chapel*, Ch. 1).

There are other pastures however. In 'the great towns of the North', '. . . Dissent attains its highest social elevation, and Chapel people are no longer to be distinguished from Church people except by the fact that they go to Chapel instead of Church.' Beecham (*Salem*'s Beecher) graduates from Carlingford, via northern pastorates, to a prosperous metropolitan congregation. Crescent Chapel people read newspapers, and sometimes magazines, and 'knew what was going on'; old Tozer reads only old sermons, the *Congregational Magazine*, and the *Carlingford Weekly Gazette*. His wife can only offer her granddaughter Phoebe (a new women who knows her John Stuart Mill) gossip about the chapel and her daughter-in-law. Anglicans are tolerated at Crescent Chapel; Copperhead's son is at Oxford; only a few members are 'hot Volun- taries'.[1] Scargill's narrator points to the same social gulf within Dissent: one night dining with a radical Houndsditch hardwareman, leader of his Chapel's democratic faction (opponent of Test and Corporation Acts), another night with a rich dry-salter in Portman Square, where the talk was of 'the price of stocks, Beethoven's music, forced strawberries, and Russian ambition. . . . I never saw such elegant people in my life, and I did not think that there had been such among the dissenters.'

But, whether in Crescent Park or Carlingford, the Voluntary System is equally tyrannous, the leading member equally to be feared. Phoebe's 'love' for Clarence Copperhead jeopardizes her father's position as a dependent on his father's goodwill. Tozer, the senior elder, must not be upset. A 'great deal', as Scargill claims (Ch. 3), 'depends on the influence of the leading people, who govern not by any express law, but by the mere force of circumstances, and the power of wealth'. Beecher and Vincent are in the pocket of their paymasters. Mrs. Oli- phant, like Scargill, derides: 'An additional fifty pounds of "salary"—a piece of plate—a congregational ovation—was it to be supposed that

---

[1] *Phoebe*, Vol. I, Chs. 1, 5, 12.

any Dissenting minister bred at Homerton could withstand such conciliatory overtures as these?' (*Salem Chapel*, Ch. 42.)

Political Dissent is regarded as irreligious (the *Nonconformist*, 'organ of the political Dissenter . . . can hardly be called a religious paper at all').[1] Mrs. Oliphant seems to approach, certainly in *Phoebe, Junior*, the Anglican fears of William Hull: if Congregationalists had their way, 'Radicalism would triumph; everything would be cut down to the level of republican meanness, and all that we love and revere as monuments of the ancient grandeur of our country would be disposed of by the voice of popular clamour.'[2]

Mrs. Oliphant's earlier sympathy for the 'preachers of the poor', shown in her rebuke to Dickens, has been eroded. She still talks, in *Phoebe*, of 'the little Salems and Bethesdas, with their humble flocks', a different species from Crescent Chapel, but we are never actually shown any of them. Salem Chapel certainly does not qualify: there the poor 'don't count'. We are told, indeed, that it is the parish churches that 'are like the nets in the Gospel, and take in all kinds of fish, bad and good'. But Dissenters who happen not to share the snobberies of Regent's Park and Mrs. Brown are actually discounted by the novelist: she referred contemptuously to the 'conversion of the heroes of the coal-pits and slums . . . chronicled in the literature presided over by General Booth', and to the bad English and impoliteness of the *War Cry*. Like Salem Chapel's, the life of the Salvation Army is deemed merely narrow and uncharitable.[3]

Mrs. Oliphant concentrates on the anomalies and difficulties on the surface of English Dissenting life, but fails to take account of 'the religious element', which might redeem and mellow the otherwise mean, harsh, and ungenial.[4] As her case stands, she has failed to explain Tozer's sturdy loyalty to Salem, or Copperhead's dogged allegiance ('obstinate as an old pig', according to his son; *Phoebe*, Vol. II, Ch. 11). She supports Dissenters in revolt, like Phoebe and Vincent, not realizing that they are unsympathetically disloyal. Vincent's instant feeling of 'dwindlement' in Carlingford makes one wonder why he ever went into the ministry, and his willingness to confess to Mrs. Hilyard, a fringe

---

[1] *Victorian Age of English Literature*, II. 339.

[2] William Hull, *Ecclesiastical Establishments . . . Second Part: Including Remarks on the Voluntary System, and, on the Baronial Functions of the Bishops* (1834), 7.

[3] 'The Sons of the Prophets: Two Representatives of the Catholic Faith', *Blackwood's* 135 (1884), 531.

[4] *Nonconformist* (25 Feb. 1863), 158.

member, how burdensome his officers were, is at least curious.[1] And
Phoebe could hardly have been 'so ready to tell strangers the quiet
contempt with which she viewed her own people, and yet have preserved their entire liking and respect'.[2] Support for Vincent leads to
absurdity: even if Mrs. Oliphant approved Vincent's shaking off the
congregational yoke ('I am either your servant, responsible to you, or
God's servant, responsible to Him' Ch. 42) it is unlikely that Homerton
College would endorse this rejection of Congregational polity as 'a
demonstration of the rightful claims of the preacher' (Ch. 43).

Mrs. Oliphant's acquaintance with Irving's life was clearly seminal.
Irving's long-faithful *aide*, William Hamilton, was, like Tozer, a chapel-
manager who loved to have the building full.[3] His final reluctant
opposition to Irving over the *charismata* is, as it were, the substance, of
which Tozer's rejection of Northcote and bright young ministers is a
vulgarized shadow. The Colbys have pointed out general similarities
between Vincent and Irving.[4] Both men achieve their most striking
effects in the pulpit by sincerity and truth to deep feelings. Vincent's
sermons on the Sunday when Susan's danger has brought him to
question Providence affect his audience, and revivalistically (there are
sobs, screams, fainting), because they have a relation to deeply felt
experience, as Irving's did: the heart is speaking. It was not, as Mrs.
Oliphant wrote of Irving,

. . . mere genius or eloquence, great as their magic is, but something infinitely
greater—a man, all visible in those hours of revelation, striving mightily with
every man he met, in an entire personal unity which is possible to very few, and
which never fails, where it appears, to exercise an influence superior to any
merely intellectual endowment.[5]

Both Vincent and Irving are challenged by lesser men, and both resist
the sanction of men as being less than God's. But Irving's principled
invoking of the Headship of Christ works in just that area of spirituality
that *Salem Chapel* avoids. Vincent's novelistic *crise* scarcely approximates
to the reality of Irving's spiritual struggles that Mrs. Oliphant conveys
in her *Life* of the preacher. Vincent's resistance to the regimen of
Independency on grounds vitiated by pride and his sense of 'dwindlement' is a long way from Irving's choosing to obey God rather than

[1] Even the *Spectator* thought his mind disagreeable, *Spectator*, 36 (14 Feb. 1863), 1640.
[2] *Nonconformist* (5 July 1876), 675.
[3] *Life of Irving*, I. 399–400; and cf. 356.
[4] See V. and R. A. Colby, op. cit., 46–7.
[5] *Life of Irving*, I. 161.

man. Vincent is scarcely an Irving: his treatment at the hands of his congregation does not raise the same questions about the power of the congregation as Irving's treatment by the presbytery raised about the function of presbyterian justice. Mrs. Oliphant seems, however, to think that it does, and *Salem Chapel* gloats excessively: Vincent 'took his way out of Salem with a sense of freedom, and a thrill of new power and vigour in his heart' (Ch. 42). But that echo of *Paradise Lost* ('They . . . through Eden took their solitary way') ironically serves rather to underline the reader's sense of something missing than to endorse the author's claim for a new freedom gained.

But then, she was never the best locater of the pluses and minuses in her work. Her indictment of the trade-spirit, of shopocratic scorn for the poor, of diaconal tyranny—the standard case against Dissent, the stereotyped points—in so far as it contacted the reality, could be taken, as the *Nonconformist* did take it.[1] But the most telling parts of *Salem Chapel* and *Phoebe, Junior* are where something of what Dissent meant to the chapel-member breaks through, despite the author. Mrs. Oliphant may find the odour of bacon and cheese uncongenial, even distasteful, but it claims and achieves for itself a certain validity in the novel. The tea-meetings, the congregation's relish for sitting in judgement on its pastors, Tozer's loyalty to his class and his chapel, may be from stock, a thin enough gruel, diluted further by repetition and dispensed with smug superiority (the mock heroic of 'fragrant lymph' locates Mrs. Oliphant's socially secured distance from a tea-meeting), but their value cannot be entirely suppressed. Vincent feels his ambition thwarted in a tea-meeting; the author notes that the enjoyment is that of 'humble girls and womankind who knew no pleasure more exciting'; but 'the schoolroom, with its blazing gas, its festoons, and its mottoes, its tables groaning with dark-complexioned plumcake and heavy buns' asserts its own warmth and attraction and brings home the legitimate role of a tea-meeting in the fellowship of a chapel community (*Salem Chapel*, Ch. 10). Such glimpses of the Dissenters' communal life from the inside, once admitted, effectively challenge any amount of outsiders' scorn:

The widow looked through her veil at the butterman and the poulterer with one keen pang of resentment, of which she repented instantly. She did not despise them as another might have done. They were the constituted authorities of the place, and her son's fate, his reputation, his young life, all that he had or could hope for in the world, was in their hands. The decision of the highest

[1] *Nonconformist* (25 Feb. 1863), 158.

authorities in the land was not so important to Arthur as that of the poulterer and butterman. . . . (Ch. 35)

Mr. Pigeon was a heavy orator; he was a tall man, badly put together, with a hollow crease across his waistcoat, which looked very much as if he might be folded in two, and so laid away out of mischief. His arms moved foolishly about in the agonies of oratory, as if they did not belong to him; but he did not look absurd through Mrs. Vincent's crape veil. . . . (Ch. 36)

# X.  WAS THERE A REVOLUTION IN TANNER'S LANE?

THE autobiographical reference is the most important aspect of William Hale White's writing. And here lies the single advantage he enjoyed over George Eliot—whom he admired, loved, imitated, but whom he could never match as a novelist: he at least was brought up in Nonconformity. In fact he never really escaped from a religious world to the literary coteries. Writing to his second-wife-to-be (in 1908) of a drawing-room talk by Caleb Morris on the Walk to Emmaus, he confided that 'This was the world in which I have lived, not the world of clever critics, or of literature or art for its own sake, nor yet the world of professedly dogmatic teachers, but a religious world.'[1]

His background was altogether of Dissent, and he writes with the assurance and bitterness of personal experience. His mother, Mary Ann Chignell, came from Colchester, where the families of the Hales and Chignells had, since their names began to appear in the membership book in the 1760s and '70s, established a complexly intermarried core of members of Lion Walk Congregational Church.[2] It was presumably through the chapel that William White, while he was an apprentice printer in Colchester, met his future wife.[3] Hale White's holidays with the Colchester relations were thus probably not so chapel-free as his biographer Catherine Maclean implies.[4] And his mother, a second- or even third-generation Dissenter, brought up among the prosperous commercial middle class of Lion Walk, then transposed to the similar

---

[1] D. V. White, *The Groombridge Diary* (1924), 14–15. For his hunger for notice from the literary world, see his engineering visits to Browning (C. M. Maclean, *Mark Rutherford: A Biography of William Hale White* (1955), 222–3), and his embarrassingly effusive response to William Dean Howell's favourable review of the *Autobiography* and *Deliverance* in *Harper's Monthly* (1886) (W. Stone, *Religion and Art of William Hale White* ('*Mark Rutherford*') (Stanford, Calif., 1954), 123–4).

[2] Lion Walk Congregational Church, Colchester, MSS., 'No. 1. Book: Members 1702–1839; Baptisms 1764–1785; Burials 1767–1840'; 'No. 2. Book: 1785–1828'.

[3] C. M. Maclean, op. cit., 36. She does not mention Lion Walk. The tip-off, for which I am very grateful, came from Clyde Binfield of Sheffield University. Of all the Mary Ann Chignells at Lion Walk, Mary Ann, daughter of Thomas and Mary Ann Chignell, born 28 Jan. 1799, baptized 20 Feb. 1799, is the most probable candidate ('No. 2. Book', p. 60, recto). Her brother Thomas, b. 23 Oct. 1800, baptized 3 Feb. 1801 ('No. 2. Book', p. 65, recto), would then be the Uncle Thomas C. M. Maclean refers to, op. cit., 23–4.

[4] C. M. Maclean, op. cit., 25.

circumstances of Bunyan Meeting, Bedford, was probably not unlike the aspiring *bourgeoises* of his novels, genteel and respectable chapel members in whom pure religious motive and character are clouded by habituation.[1]

His father, William White, was a Trustee of Bedford's Old Meeting, superintendent of the Sunday School work (1842–50), and an active lay preacher.[2] Hale White was initiated as a church member in 1848, when, having been scrutinized privately by 'messengers', he testified before the church to salvation.[3] He thus became a member of the 'elect', visibly demarcated by participation in the Lord's Supper from mere attenders (like Mr. Furze, who though a 'respectable member' of the congregation was 'not a member of the church': the distinction that applies to Nurse Barton in the *Revolution* and to George Eliot's Mrs. Holt).[4] He enjoyed full 'gospel privileges', and as a male member was part of the governing body of the chapel (women take no part in the business at Tanner's Lane, as in R. W. Dale's church at Carr's Lane, Birmingham, and presumably at Bedford).[5]

Hale White was educated at the Countess of Huntingdon's College at Cheshunt, and expelled for 'modernism' from the Congregational New College, St. John's Wood.[6] The accounts of decaying 'causes' in the *Autobiography of Mark Rutherford, Dissenting Minister* are based on White's experiences of preaching in villages as a student and heterodox ex-student. He identified 'D——' of the *Autobiography* as Ditchling, Sussex, where he 'supplied' the Unitarian Chapel for a year (1856–7).[7] Occasionally, in the 1850s, he preached at Friars Street Unitarian Chapel, Ipswich, where the member who entertained him lived in

---

[1] The prosperity of Lion Walk, as of so much eastern counties Congregationalism, is indicated by the cathedral-like 'Chapel' it was able to afford. See J. A. Tabor, *Nonconformist Protest Against the Popery of Modern Dissent: As Displayed in Architectural Imitations of Roman Catholic Churches* (Colchester, 1863).

[2] W. Stone, op. cit., 28. The Old Meeting was demolished and rebuilt as The Bunyan Meeting (opened 20 Feb. 1850), H. G. Tibbutt, *Bunyan Meeting Bedford 1650–1950* (Bedford, [1951]), 60–2.

[3] The messengers were Messrs. W. W. Kilpin and Ward; Hale was received into membership at the Church Meeting of February 1848. 'Act Book of the Church at Bunyan Meeting, Bedford, Vol. II. 1820– &c.', (MS), [44].

[4] *The Early Life of Mark Rutherford (W. Hale White)*, by Himself (1913), 18–19; *Catharine Furze*, Ch. 2; *The Revolution in Tanner's Lane*, Ch. 23; *Felix Holt*, Ch. 4.

[5] *Revolution in Tanner's Lane*, Ch. 27.

[6] C. M. Maclean, op. cit., 59–101 (Bk. II, 'The Divinity Student (1848–1852)').

[7] D. V. White, *Groombridge Diary*, footnote 1, 463. The date is disputed, but Hale's mother did record in her diary (15 Mar. 1857) that 'Hale went to Ditchling for the last time': Dr. W. Hale White, 'Notes About W. Hale White (Mark Rutherford)' (Bedford Public Library MS.), 11–12.

Tanner's Lane, a name that stuck.[1] In the 1850s (and into 1860) he seems also to have been a frequent preacher at Little Portland Street Unitarian Chapel, London.[2] White's Colchester cousin, William Chignell, who became a Unitarian pastor, introduced him to the Rev. Caleb Morris, the Congregationalist minister celebrated in *Catharine Furze*. There Mr. Cardew speaks on the Rich Young Ruler, and the novel gives a transcript of 'notes, made by one who was present' at the sermon. And,

> The writer of this history remembers when it was his privilege to listen continually to a man whose power over his audience was so great that he could sway them unanimously by a passion which was sufficient for any heroic deed. The noblest resolutions were formed under that burning oratory, and were kept, too, for the voice of the dead preacher still vibrates in the ears of those who heard him. (Ch. 6)

Baruch Cohen refers in *Clara Hopgood* (Ch. 22) to Morris, 'a young Welshman, with no education beyond that provided by a Welsh denominational college, who is a perfect orator and whose depth of insight is hardly to be matched, save by Thomas A. Kempis, whom he much resembles'. His intelligent mixture of modern freedom and traditional Biblicism guaranteed his appeal for White, and his sermons generated some of White's most potent images, like the Walk to Emmaus. White told his second wife, Dorothy, that 'He *made* me.'[3] And Morris's, leaving London (29 March 1856) for Wales, worn out by his labours, left a vacuum, but his impact helped keep White within the sphere of Christianity's influence.[4] Hale preached for Morris on 25 March 1856, the eve, as it were, of departure.[5]

Equally important, perhaps, was the influence of another Congregationalist minister, Thomas Binney: the man Dickens maligned. He may have been less eloquent than Morris, but he made the Bible relevant in his sermons at the King's Weigh House Chapel. He got his congregation (including 'hundreds of young men') '. . . to identify the Bible with genuine human experience. Abraham, Paul, and other Biblical heroes, whom he was never weary of depicting, were made to

[1] C. M. Maclean, op. cit., 140; Dr. W. Hale White, 'Notes', 11.

[2] Dr. W. H. White, 'Notes', 12.

[3] D. V. White, *Groombridge Diary*, 14–16, 27; C. M. Maclean, op. cit., 66–8, 71–2; William Hale White 'Caleb Morris', *BW* 31 (6 Mar. 1902), 532; 'Caleb Morris', in [James Grant], *The Metropolitan Pulpit; or Sketches of the Most Popular Preachers in London* (2 Vols., 1839), II. 197–206.

[4] C. M. Maclean, op. cit., 142–3; D. V. White, *Groombridge Diary*, 27–8.

[5] Dr. W. H. White, 'Notes', 12 and 23 (information from Mrs. White's diary).

stand in our place, and their experience became our own. That was the meaning of his almost miraculous influence.'[1] Thomas Bradshaw's sermon on Jephthah in *The Revolution in Tanner's Lane* (Ch. 7) is Thomas Binney's kind of subject.

White married his first wife, Harriet Arthur, in Kentish Town Congregational Church (22 December 1856), and one of Morris's 'best friends' officiated.[2] And though, after Morris left London, White 'went nowhere', it was with good Nonconformist cause—in old Dissent the sermon was the central act of worship—as he explained to his son:

> The reason why I do not go to church on Sunday is that I do not know anybody who can teach me anything at church which I want to know. When I lived in London I always went to Mr. Morris's. When I am in Exeter I always go to your cousin's [William Chignell] because I always learn something.[3]

Clearly, then, when he describes Dissent he speaks with the initiate's authority; if anyone could understand nineteenth-century Dissent it should be Hale White. According to his own dictum (and waiving the question momentarily about the sense in which he had been a 'believer'): 'We cannot really understand a religion unless we have believed it.'[4] The range of his references is always comprehensive (Wesley and the Methodists, Irving and the Irvingites, Plymouth Brethren, Joanna Southcott, Calvinism v. Arminianism) and indicates a continuing interest in the theological subtleties and sectarian varieties of Dissent.[5]

---

[1] W. H. W., in a tribute to Binney (who died Feb. 1874), *Norfolk News* (14 Mar. 1874), quoted by C. M. Maclean, op. cit., 192; and in 'Caleb Morris', *BW* 31 (6 Mar. 1902), 532.

[2] C. M. Maclean, op. cit., 144.

[3] (Mar. 1874), quoted by C. M. Maclean, op. cit., 194. Robertson Nicoll claimed that when he was in London White 'generally attended Spurgeon's ministry' (28 Mar. 1913), T. H. Darlow, *William Robertson Nicoll* (1925), 367.

[4] Mark Rutherford, *More Pages from a Journal* (1910), 240.

[5] Wesley: *Letters to Three Friends*, ed. D. V. White (1915), 93–4. Hale White's 'Black Notebook' shows he read Southey's *Life of Wesley*, and gives us his nice assessment of Methodist commercialism: 'Wesley gives amongst other instructions the following to his stewards. "You are to be men full of the Holy Ghost and wisdom"; "You are to produce your accounts the first Tuesday in every month, that they may be transcribed into the ledger." Characteristic of Methodism.' (I am grateful to Simon Nowell-Smith, nephew of the late Mrs. William Hale White (Dorothy Vernon Horace Smith) for access to MS. material, including Mrs. White's copies of the 'Black' and the 'White Notebook'.) Mr. Cardew reminds Catharine of a portrait of Edward Irving (*Catharine Furze*, Ch. 6). Clara and Madge sometimes attend A. J. Scott's lectures: he is now the heterodox ex-Irvingite (*Clara Hopgood*, Ch. 22). Because of Rutherford's objections to his fellow-clerks' language he is taken for a Plymouth Brother (*Mark Rutherford's Deliverance: being the Second Part of His Autobiography*, Ch. 8). In 1814, Zachariah Coleman's workmates class him with Joanna Southcott's followers (*Revolution*, Ch. 8). Calvinism v. Arminianism: *Revolution*, Ch. 9.

He is rather more than (in William Kent's phrase) 'a gifted war correspondent of sectarian strife', but he does keep us interested in that conflict.[1] His eye for the social stratification implied, and conditioned, by religious allegiances is sharp; his analysis of Cowfold's religious groups is justly famous.[2] He charts Anglican antagonisms: at one pole, evangelical Mrs. Fish in *Clara Hopgood* (Ch. 2), who concedes to her daughter that 'although Dissenters were to be pitied, and even to be condemned, many of them were undoubtedly among the redeemed . . .' (she allows into the fold Doddridge, Matthew Henry, and William Jay!); and at the other, the conceited young parson at Groombridge who

. . . divides the people in God's great world into two classes, Anglicans and all the rest. Anglicans are the Catholic Church. Those outside it, 'Romanists' as he calls them, Jews, Buddhists, Mahometans, Agnostics, Hindoos, Lutherans, Independents, Methodists, are all dissenting schismatics not worth differentiation.[3]

He had (by 1895) detached himself sufficiently from this conflict to be able to apply equal measures of scorn to Hastings Churchmen and Dissenters who raked over 'all the old, dead differences' in the local newspaper. But if compelled to choose, particularly between more attractive contestants than Hastings's 'most commonplace Dissent and equally commonplace Church-of-Englandism', he was always better disposed to Nonconformity.[4] Birds of passage, prosperous and bourgeois Nonconformists who slipped into Anglicanism for social prestige, he despised: like the 'retired mill-owner, who was a Wesleyan Methodist when he was in business in Manchester, but had become ostentatiously Anglican when he retired into the country', or Mrs. Furze, who exchanges chapel for church when the family moves to the smarter end of town.[5] White responded vigorously to a 'Churchwoman' who complained to a Church newspaper about uncultivated Dissenting ministers being received into the Church:

. . . she tells a story of a dissenting minister converted to the Establishment who, when he appeared in a drawing-room one evening, produced a pair of worked

---

[1] William Kent, 'Mark Rutherford', *Everyman*, 6 (Dec. 1931), 731, quoted by W. E. Davis, *ELT* 10 (1967), 108.

[2] *Revolution*, Ch. 16.

[3] ' "Mark Rutherford" 1831–1913: Extracts from letters written to his second son and his second son's wife', Typewritten extracts by his second son (Bodleian Library MS.), Letter 58 (4 Mar. 1904), 52.

[4] (10 Feb. 1895), *Letters to Three Friends*, 72.

[5] 'Kate Radcliffe', in Mark Rutherford, *More Pages from a Journal* (1910), 77; *Catharine Furze*, Ch. 2.

slippers and proceeded to change his boots there and then. When the boots were taken off they were stowed under a chair, and the owner resisted attempts on the part of the servant to remove them. All this is perfectly credible. A dissenting minister who is good enough to pervert himself to the Establishment would be likely to take off his boots, and for aught I know his coat or his shirt.[1]

Matthew Arnold's inept handling of 'Puritanism and Protestantism generally' confirmed White's suspicion that Anglicans were frequently unprepared to begin understanding Dissent ('It is to his *Culture and Anarchy* that we owe the celebrated inclusion of the whole of Luther in the phrase *a Philistine of Genius*'). Froude's description of Bunyan as the 'poet-apostle of the English middle-classes imperfectly educated like himself' was ignorant prejudice: the 'association of nonconformity with vulgarity, and of gentility with the church' was 'a curious characteristic of the English "imperfectly-educated" people. . . .'[2] White might have predicted one Anglican response to his own work:

Mark Rutherford has yet to overcome the handicap of the 'provincialism' of his themes. What are you to do about a writer who devotes an exquisite gift to recording the religious doubts and the pecuniary struggles of unsuccessful Non-conformist ministers, city clerks and country-town shopkeepers?[3]

Writing, for White, was a species of personal testimony. 'As far as Bunyan knew he spoke'; and as far as White knew he too was to speak.[4] The pervasively autobiographical character of his work clearly relates to the Puritan habit of keeping a journal, writing an autobiographical record. But there was an added responsibility, his conscience was the more strenuously alert to the temptation to untruth because under parental pressure, the pressure to conform to the ethos of Bedford's Old Meeting community, he had borne false witness. He often recalled the testimony that sealed his church membership: 'I was satisfied I understood what I did not in the least understand. This is very near lying'; 'I did not in the least know who God was, or what was salvation.' He allowed the implication to pass that he had experienced something similar to St. Paul on the Damascus Road, if not (and inevitably in view of his religious childhood) so great or so sudden. Undoubtedly the memory of this incident ('He remembers the scene vividly, standing

---

[1] Quoted by W. R. Nicoll, *Memories of Mark Rutherford* (1924), 58.

[2] *John Bunyan*, By the author of 'Mark Rutherford', etc. (1905), 234–5, and 239, footnote 1.

[3] E. H. Jeffs, 'Hale White', *Great Christians*, ed. R. S. Forman (1933), 608.

[4] *John Bunyan*, 248.

up there alone and beginning . . .') was made more painful in that it
initiated the chain of events that led to his abortive training for the
Independent ministry ('the great event and the great blunder of my life,
the mistake which well-nigh ruined it altogether'): to become a
theological student he had first to be a church member. The insistence
on truth to life in the novels is a kind of compensating for that youthful
hypocrisy.[1]

E. M. Forster labelled White's conscience a 'tiresome little recep-
tacle'.[2] Tiresome it may be: White's undeviatingly straightforward
manner can be tedious, he always means what he says, and says it simply
and directly. But objecting to his 'conscience' is not objecting to some
peripheral, easily disposable, nuisance without which he would be a
rather better novelist. Without it he would be quite different.

Ultimately, of course, this conscientiousness leads White to betray
his rights as a novelist. The criterion of excellence becomes almost
exclusively truth to personal experience. The essence of 'noble art' is
'Our actual *experience*, not what we can invent or dream: and no step a
hair's breadth beyond what is real and solid for us, proved and again
proved.'[3] Arnold Bennett was right in asserting that White had 'no
notion of fiction': novels for him were better the closer they approxi-
mated to life, and always occupied an inferior rank to life in validity and
seriousness.[4] Art was in the end a frivolity:

> Whenever Mrs. Caffyn talked about the labourers at Great Oakhurst, whom she
> knew so well, Clara always felt as if all her reading had been a farce, and, indeed,
> if we come into close contact with actual life, art, poetry and philosophy seem
> little better than trifling. When the mist hangs over the heavy clay land in
> January, and men and women shiver in the bitter cold and eat raw turnips, to
> indulge in fireside ecstasies over the divine Plato or Shakespeare is surely not
> such a virtue as we imagine it to be.[5]

Approving Byron's epistolary style ('There is not a single, baffling,
got-up sentence . . .') White noted the poet's rejection of fiction: 'I
hate things *all fiction*. . . . There should always be some foundation of

---

[1] *Early Life*, 55–9; D. V. White, *Groombridge Diary*, 71.

[2] *Aspects of the Novel* ([1927]; Pelican edn., 1962), 146.

[3] Letter to Jack Hale White (29 Aug. 1893), quoted by Irvin Stock, *William Hale White
(Mark Rutherford)* (1965), 14. (Hale White has been well served, and one sometimes feels
perhaps appropriately so, by Stock and Stone!).

[4] Arnold Bennett, Thur. 19 Feb. 1914, *Journals of Arnold Bennett*, ed. Newman Flower,
Vol. II, *1911–1921*, p. 83.

[5] *Clara Hopgood*, Ch. 26.

fact for the most airy fabric, and pure invention is but the talent of a liar.'[1]

Gide admired the 'honesty and integrity' of White's work as 'specifically Protestant' virtues.[2] And White's undoubtedly Protestant qualities are nourished on a characteristic respect for the Bible, a respect shaped by Caleb Morris.[3] Robertson Nicoll claimed that only Joseph Parker 'loved and studied' the Bible like White.[4] Textual criticism created for him no consternation, but the 'cold negativism' of the Chapman world led to his estrangement from the publisher whom he had assisted (1852–4), and he lamented that 'any fool' could buy a Bible, 'grin at it, and apparently get his folly printed'.[5] An Arnoldian ersatz religion of culture was a monstrosity: 'Better no chart whatever than one which shows no actually existing perils, but warns us against Scylla, Charybdis, and the Cyclops.'[6] Cardinal, in the *Deliverance* (Ch. 5), is held up for scorn because he bases his actions on fictional heroes; he was victim of 'the total chaos of a time without any moral guidance . . . Cardinal was adrift. . . .'[7] Any 'sweetness' in England derives from the Puritan distinction between right and wrong, hence from the Bible.[8]

White's fiction celebrates an age when the Bible's *mana* was still real. For a man like Zachariah Coleman, 'The mere opening of the sacred Book . . . always acted as a spell, and when its heavy lids fell down on either side the room cleared itself of all haunting, intrusive evil spirits . . .' (*Revolution*, Ch. 9)[9].

[1] 'Black Notebook': Byron's letter to Murray, 2 Apr. 1817: L. A. Marchand, *Byron: A Biography* (3 Vols., 1957), II. 687–8. Ruskin also admired Byron for his truthfulness, *Praeterita*, Intro. K. Clark (1949), 138–40.

[2] Irvin Stock, op. cit., 4–5, 23; and 'André Gide, William Hale White, and the Protestant Tradition', *Accent*, 12 (1952), 205–15.

[3] *Early Life*, 87.

[4] W. R. Nicoll, *Memories of Mark Rutherford* (1924), 126.

[5] D. V. White, *Groombridge Diary*, 411; 'Notes' by Jack White (Bodley MS.), 21; C. M. Maclean, op. cit., 118; W. R. Nicoll, op. cit., 62.

[6] *Pages from a Journal* (1900), 77.

[7] Cf. D. V. White, *Groombridge Diary*, 210: (12 Aug. 1909), 'Hale can never forgive Matthew Arnold and his "culture". . . .'

[8] *John Bunyan*, 246.

[9] See Letter to Miss Partridge (31 Dec. 1901), *Letters to Three Friends*, 222: '. . . you are almost the only friend I now possess who, having been brought up on the Bible, can feel what I feel about it, what is in my blood and can never by any chemistry be extracted, and who nevertheless does not treat the Bible as an idol.' And cf. John Wain, 'Strength and Isolation: Pessimistic Notes of a Miltonolater', *The Living Milton*, ed. Frank Kermode (Routledge paperback, 1963), 10–11, for an illustration, from Gide, of this Seventeenth-Century Biblicism in a Huguenot family.

White's own Family Bible had been a wedding present from Caleb Morris.[1] And his heroes, Luther and Bunyan, like his Biblicism, were distinctively Protestant. Luther's *Commentary* on Galatians was 'the text-book of a great religion'; *Pilgrim's Progress* was Everyman's journey.[2] John Bunyan was bred into his consciousness: 'Elstow and the Ouse and in a measure the temper of the man are in my blood.'[3] He had been not only a citizen of Bedford, but a member of Bunyan's church: the Old Meeting had been erected in 1707 on the site of the original barn that Bunyan had preached in from 1672. White was No. 1936 on the Church Roll on which John Bunyan was No. 27.[4] The pastors he knew, Samuel Hillyard and John Jukes, were only fourth and fifth in succession from Bunyan himself.[5]

And it is the Puritan's sense of individual responsibility to God and His Word—a matter of personal dignity and validation (Zachariah's treatment by employers as simply another unemployed worker contrasts bitterly with the divine favour of his 'calling and election') as well as a burden of conscience—that conditions White's reinterpretations of Scripture.

The effort—common enough in the period—was characteristically Protestant: unlike Graham Greene's novels, where the rejigging of orthodoxy is an alien habit imported from Protestantism and clashes almost daringly with the Catholic's duty towards immutable central authority. And it differs from George Eliot's revamping. She, one feels, is interested in humanist truth no matter what has to be jettisoned in the quest, and if that truth coincides with traditional Christian ideas, well and good; White is more pious, more concerned to revalidate the past for the present.

White seeks to do for his readers what Thomas Binney did for him: hence his essays on Gideon, Samuel, Saul, and Job.[6] And he will preserve

---

[1] C. M. Maclean, op. cit., 143–4.

[2] *John Bunyan*, 107, 120

[3] (23 Jan. 1905), *Letters to Three Friends*, 328.

[4] John Brown, *John Bunyan* (1885), 410; C. M. Maclean, op. cit., 54, footnote 1.

[5] In a guide to Westminster Abbey White's second wife Dorothy found a draft letter (probably written 1908) objecting to a Bunyan memorial window in the Abbey: 'For my own part I do not wish to have Bunyan in the Abbey nor do I think stained glass a suitable vehicle in which to honour him. He would not have cared either for the abbey or the glass.' MS. in pencil; property of Simon Nowell-Smith.

[6] 'Gideon', 'Samuel', 'Saul', in *Miriam's Schooling and Other Papers*; 'Notes on the Book of Job', appended to *The Deliverance* as among Mark Rutherford's papers. (The Bedford Public Library Collection includes White's copy (annotated by him) of Rev. J. M. Rodwell, *The Book of Job: translated from the Hebrew* (1868).)

for posterity certain Biblical events, particularly those Caleb Morris made meaningful. His second wife Dorothy became his companion on, so to say, the road to Emmaus late in life; his Damascus Road experience happened earlier, when the light from *Lyrical Ballads* shone on him, as it shines on Mark Rutherford. Wordsworth 're-created' his Supreme Divinity; the story of Genesis and the Gospels was 'rewritten'—he met God in the garden, and the Son of God drew him away from 'daily occupations into the divinest of dreams'.[1] Guilt about loving Catharine Furze instead of his rather ordinary wife smites the Evangelical Anglican minister Mr. Cardew 'as the light from heaven smote Saul of Tarsus journeying to Damascus' (*Catharine Furze*, Ch. 19). Miriam Tacchi decides to become a nurse, and White speculates on the cause of her decision: politicians and men of the world would resist any changing of old belief or character even though the Crucified One had spoken to them as He did to Paul on the Damascus Road, but,

There are some mortals on this earth to whom nothing more than a certain summer morning very early, or a certain chance idea in a lane ages ago, or a certain glance from a fellow-creature dead for years, has been the Incarnation, the Crucifixion, the Resurrection, or the Descent of the Holy Ghost.[2]

It is a measure of White's honesty, however, that he noted the persistence of conversions on the traditional model. The expectation was 'now altogether untrue' but, he conceded, the event was 'occasionally a reality' in Mark Rutherford's childhood.[3] This concession can be disconcertingly intrusive. In *Catharine Furze* (set in 1840), which reduces the Damascus Road to a guilty strengthening of the will to avoid hurting a sick wife's feelings, and the Atonement to renouncing an extra-marital alliance, Orkid Joe's sudden conversion from villainy, his becoming a preacher, 'by God's grace' bringing 'hundreds to a knowledge of their Saviour', disrupts the novel's smooth progress to post-Christian theology. White compares Joe with Bunyan's Mr. Tod, and assures his 'incredulous literary friends' that conversion was not uncommon and was very real 'years ago' (Ch. 20). But Joe's secure presence, an unprocessed gobbet of traditionalism, exposes as quite precarious and tentative the novel's assumption that in the 1840s, or even in the 1890s when the novel was published, diluted Paulinism was more common and relevant than the traditional evangelical experience.

[1] *The Autobiography*, Ch. 2.
[2] 'Miriam's Schooling', *Miriam's Schooling and Other Papers*, 118–19.
[3] *The Autobiography*, Ch. 1.

On another reading of the data evangelicalism might not appear so defunct as White on the whole strenuously insists.

The honesty that incorporated Orkid Joe undergirds White's intimate account of Dissenting life. He admired the nobility of aspects of the tradition of Calvinist Dissent, and was supremely capable of penetrating to the heart of the Calvinist character. *Michael Trevanion*, outstanding witness to that penetration, we have already praised. For once, White's narrow scope, his verbal astringency, find a perfect home: they become appropriately ascetic counterparts of the account of a narrow mentality. The story's ending is contrived and Michael's rescue from a suicide-attempt in the sea by Susan Shipton the girl he has maligned is conventional enough ('A hand was on him, firm but soft . . .'), but this weakness cannot displace the strength of the insight into the Calvinist temper.

But, White insists, the traditional phase is passing rapidly. Michael's son believes, but the doctrines 'failed to impress Robert with that depth and sharpness of cut with which they were wrought into his father'. Other children of religious parents share this dilution: Mark Rutherford himself; Frank Palmer in *Clara Hopgood*, whose faith has a partly second-hand air; Benjamin Cohen, 'indifferent to that religion by which his father lived' (*Clara Hopgood*, Chs. 4, 19). White is good at painting decrepit 'causes', like Cross Lanes Meeting House: its tombstones awry and overgrown, its congregation diminishing. Phoebe Crowhurst's father weeds her grave, 'but when he died, not long after, his wife had to go into the workhouse, and in one season the sorrel and dandelions took possession, and Phoebe's grave became like all the others—a scarcely distinguishable undulation in the tall, rank herbiage' (*Catharine Furze*, Ch. 18).

Likewise, the Calvinist system is in decay, untenable, advocated only by men like Dr. Harris of New College, archaically insisting on 'the scheme of redemption', or John Broad, concerned less about his son's moral education than his skill 'in systematic Theology, and more particularly the doctrine of the Comforter'.[1] Zachariah Coleman tries to show Major Maitland, Pauline, and Caillaud the 'way of salvation' but St. Paul's formulas, meaningful to him, mean nothing to them, and the system, Zachariah learns, is difficult to apply: Pauline and Caillaud are too good to be considered reprobate (*Revolution*, Ch. 6). Calvinism declines in usefulness: first it is found to be unworkable, then it is

[1] C. M. Maclean, op. cit., 60–1; *The Autobiography*, Ch. 2; *Revolution*, Ch. 18.

compromised—'Moderate Calvinism' is essentially dishonest for White;
only less so than using the terms of the Westminster Confession in
another than the original sense—and finally it is in practice abandoned.[1]
For the Rev. John Broad, his family and church, righteousness is a
secondary concern, and the drama of redemption a mere echo of a once
living reality. By 1902 White had come to regard Caleb Morris as 'the
last Christian'.[2]

On Sunday afternoons, in her Sunday best, Zachariah's wife would sit
at the window holding—but not to read, and not for long—Thomas
Boston's *Fourfold Estate*, a theological tome that was nothing if not
systematic.[3] The act is only a vestige of the Puritan past, both of the
practical godliness that is Boston's concern, and the tough intellectualism that generated his theological systematization: neither appealed to
decadent Dissenters like Mrs. Coleman. The intellectual glory of the
past is acknowledged: 'It may be questioned, indeed, whether any
religious body has ever stood so distinctly upon the understanding,
and has used its intellect with such rigorous activity, as the Puritans,
from whom Zachariah was a genuine descendant' (*Revolution*, Ch. 1).
Systematic theology, now a poor substitute among the Broads and at
Mark Rutherford's college for sturdy theological thought, was once the
expression and symbol of mental strength.

White's praise for Peter Bulkley, who left Odell, near Bedford, to
go to America in about 1635, for his *Gospel Covenant*, and his congregation of serious, thoughtful, deeply-experienced Odell farmers, reinforces
the sense of contemporary decadence. *The Gospel Covenant* displays 'a
masculine, powerful intellect . . . on a level with the best secular
intellects of that day'. It is 'a genuine religion', 'laboriously *mined* in

[1] '. . . a moderate Calvinist; that is to say, he held to Calvinism as his undoubted creed,
but when it came to the push in actual practice he modified it', *Revolution*, Ch. 1. Cf.
*Early Life*, 16–17, and *Autobiography*, Ch. 4.

[2] (22 Mar. 1902), *Letters to Three Friends*, 223.

[3] 'Thomas Boston, The Elder (1677–1732)', *DNB*. His very title-page indicates the
systematic nature of his theology:

*Human Nature in its Four-fold Estate*
*of*

| | | |
|---|---|---|
| *Primitive Integrity* | | *The Parents of Mankind in Paradise* |
| *Entire Deprivation* | *subsisting in* | *The Unregenerate* |
| *Begun Recovery* | | *The Regenerate* |
| *Consummate Happiness or Misery* | | *All Mankind in the future State* |

*in*
*Several Practical Discourses*
(1720; 12th edn., Edinburgh, 1761).

darkness, smelted in fire, and held as a precious possession'.[1] But in the generation after Caleb Morris serious business with God has ceased in orthodox Dissent; praying and preaching are not done by people who, in Baxter's phrase about George Herbert, 'really believe a God'.[2] James Harden's ardour and courage, the political radicalism of Thomas Bradshaw, have been transmuted into John Broad's moderation in all things: 'neither ultra-Calvinist, nor Arminian; not rigid upon Baptism, and certainly much unlike his lean and fervid predecessor' (*Revolution*, Ch. 17).

White admired the radicalism as well as the intellectualism of the tradition. Major Maitland is 'not surprised' that Zachariah is an Independent. 'Ever since Cromwell's day you have always been on the side of liberty' (*Revolution*, Ch. 2). White knew it was absurd to use the label 'political Dissenter' as though it denoted some absolutely new animal.[3] He thought the courage of the Cromwellian soldiers, 'who read Plato and Milton', likely to outlast that of the 'average French Catholic peasant, or the refuse of Paris'.[4] He could not actually claim descent from Cromwell's Major White, but he liked to think his ancestors were probably in 'Oliver's Army', and anyway he saw his father and grandfather as authentic Cromwellian survivors.[5]

In the best of all worlds, 'Culture' would not replace Puritanism— 'the most distinct, energetic and salutary movement in our history'— but incorporate it: 'We need Shakespeare as well as Bunyan.' But mid-century Dissent has betrayed the tradition and falls short of the ideal. Morally and politically decadent, it claims Bunyan, but does not really possess him, and it excludes Shakespeare. It has lost the strenuous righteousness, and the determined commitment to liberty, that might have made continuing narrowness tolerable.

The old shibboleths still obtain, but their vigour and meaning have drained away. Sunday observance is a farcical habit, stripped of sanctity. Mrs. Coleman's casuistry in 'giving' the water-cress man 2*d.* instead of paying him $1\frac{1}{2}d.$, becomes outright hypocrisy in Cowfold, where the

---

[1] 'Peter Bulkley', *Last Pages from a Journal*, ed. D. V. White (1924), 194–208. Originally published as 'An Ancestor of Emerson', *BW* 23 (17 Mar. 1898), 421–2. White also published an earlier article on Bulkley: 'What Mr. Emerson Owed to Bedfordshire', *Athenaeum*, No. 2846 (13 May 1882), 602–3.

[2] Quoted by Helen Gardner, in Intro. to *The Poems of George Herbert* (World's Classics, 1961), xvi.

[3] *Norfolk News* (1 July 1882): W. Stone, op. cit., 27–8.

[4] *Birmingham Daily Post* (23 Dec. 1871): W. Stone, op. cit., 27.

[5] D. V. White, *The Groombridge Diary*, 196 and footnote 1.

town-pump is chained on Sundays but to use a backyard pump is 'no breach of the Sabbath'.[1] Puritan objections to the world have become mere genteelism: according to Deacon Snale, Goldsmith will offend the 'young leedies' of the Dorcas meeting because he has not the 'requisite tone', and George Fox is not allowed because, though 'converted', he 'did not, you know, Mr. Rutherford, belong to us'.[2] The disappearance of Puritan intellectualism has left a vacuum to be filled by mean-mindedness and pursuits emphatically cut off from the wider cultural life: instead of Goldsmith and Fox, the small ads of denominational papers and 'religious novels'; in place of dancing and concerts, 'a travelling menagerie with a brass band' and 'religious picnics'—which provide more chances for Thomas Broad's sexual misdemeanours than dances ever would (*Revolution*, Ch. 18). White concedes this much to Arnold: the word for Cowfold, as for Water Lane, is *parochialism*.

White presumably knew that middle-class drapers like Snale, and sons of drapers like the Rev. John Broad, would tend towards the genteel, and that farmers like Water Lane's Deacon Catfield and some of the Bedford Elders could not, perhaps, be expected, as provincial townsmen or residents of country areas, to enjoy a particularly effervescent intellectual life. And, in this light, his blaming Dissent for their failings is perhaps unfair. But it was the comparison with Peter Bulkley's farmers and with Cromwell's soldiers who read Milton that irked. James Harden's wrestling 'even unto blood with the world, the flesh and the devil in Cowfold' is diminished into Broad's timid skirting of political controversy in order to conciliate as many factions as he can, but particularly the wealthier deacons, and into his retailing the simple gospel, a weak doctrine for congregations shaped by ministers from the retail-counter.[3] Intellectual rigour has been metamorphosed into the intellectual shoddiness of contemporary ministerial training and congregational expectation. Stern morality has become merely a concern for the proprieties: Mrs. Broad 'straightened her gown upon her knees, and pushed it forward over her feet so as to cover them altogether—a mute protest against the impropriety of the scenes she had partly described': her son had been flirting with Fanny Allen. The linguistic currency has been devalued into mere jargon: John Broad talks of the power of 'the Atoning Blood' to 'assuage' sin's might, but still unreasonably hates the Allens. God's name is invoked for personal credit: Mrs. Broad can

---

[1] *Revolution*, Chs. 6 and 16.
[2] *Autobiography*, Ch. 3.
[3] *Autobiography*, Ch. 2; *Revolution*, Ch. 17.

foil Mrs. Allen's response to her regretting that Priscilla will only be marrying George Allen instead of a metropolitan pastor, with 'professional unction' ('I am sure I pray that God will bless their union'). The only concession that Thomas Broad makes to his own lechery in preaching his stock sermon on the carnal mind is to add: 'The apostle did not merely state a fact that the carnal mind was not subject to the law of God; he said "Neither indeed *can* be." Mark, my brethren, the force of the *neither can*.'[1]

The *Revolution*'s curiously intense distaste for Thomas Broad is perhaps not unconnected with his similarities to his author:

. . . Thomas, your Samuel, who had been granted to the Lord, and who, to use his own words when his written religious autobiography was read at the church-meeting, being the child of pious parents, and of many prayers, had never been exposed to those assaults of the enemy of souls which beset ordinary young men, and consequently had not undergone a sudden conversion. . . .

There are, of course, indications that White's view of mid-century Congregationalism was more than merely personal. Basil Martin, a later alumnus of the Congregationalist New College, declared against the poverty of its education in a manner reminiscent of *The Autobiography*. And Kingsley Martin suggests parallels between Mark Rutherford and his father: both seekers for the relevance of old orthodoxies, both finding the work of ministering to the poor disappointing, both surrounded by the 'mean-minded' and the 'fanatically orthodox'.[2] Like White, Edward Miall (in *The British Churches in Relation to the British People*) lamented the substitution of gentility for Christian morality ('Christianity is dismissed as intrusive, and gentility is installed on its throne'). And Miall's complaints about the 'Aristocratic Sentiment' chime in with White's own. Dissenting mothers cherish caste: as Mrs. White pushed her son into ministerial training, so Mrs. Broad desires a metropolitan pulpit for Thomas. The daughter of the famous Dr. Flavel despises a mean position for her son.

The same pride of class, the same exclusiveness, the same deference to rank and wealth, the same depreciating view of poverty, the same struggle to keep up appearances, the same notions of respectability . . . proceeding from the same cause, and that cause having nothing whatever moral in its character, are to be found inside, as outside, the Christian Churches of our land.

The 'Professional Sentiment' has, according to Miall, generated a professional class of ministers, whose recruits have mixed motives, and

---

[1] *Revolution*, Chs. 17, 20, 21.     [2] Kingsley Martin, *Father Figures*, 30.

may well have no true calling: White's case against the theological, students of *The Autobiography*, against the Broads, against ambitious mothers, certainly finds general support from Miall. Hale White got out, where others might not manage to:

> . . . from a career so likely to be entered upon without calm calculation, with an incorrect estimate of their own powers, and, occasionally, with a delusive view of their own religious character, our sentiments have cut off the practicability of any but a difficult retreat. An education, in a great measure, technical, having consumed exactly that portion of life within which a choice of calling is feasible, leaves a young man, at the end of his preparatory course, even when he has discovered his original mistake, nearly precluded from altering his destination.[1]

But personal knowledge may sometimes generate very subjective estimates, and the more intense that personal experience the easier it is to feel sanctioned to generalize. *The Revolution in Tanner's Lane* makes a case about Dissent's divorce in mid-century from vital contact with the great social and political issues which may justly reflect aspects of White's Bedford experience, but is in fact wrong when applied, as White intends it to be applied, more widely.[2]

The forties are made to contrast with the immediate past. Zachariah's radicalism illustrates the traditional republicanism of Cromwellian Independency. James Harden (based on Samuel Hillyard, minister at Bedford, 1792–1839), was morally and socially committed, and had the Evangelical Revival's fervour (*Revolution*, Ch. 17).[3] Thomas Bradshaw, a tribute to Thomas Binney, was a Calvinist of Peter Bulkley's temper, who believed in predestination and final perseverance and preached 'a series of sermons on the Gospel Covenant' (*Revolution*, Ch. 2).[4] Like John Angell James he eschewed active politics but was 'republican through and through', never hesitating 'a moment in those degenerate days [1814] to say what he thought about any scandal'. He exemplified the learned ministry, was a classical scholar, knew Hebrew, and

[1] Edward Miall, *The British Churches in Relation to the British People* (1849), 165–6, 197, 246–67.

[2] White countered William Robertson Nicoll's identification (in *BW* 20 (9 July 1896), 185) of John Broad as John Jukes: '. . . I must deny altogether that the portraits of John Broad and Isaac Allen were taken from the gentlemen whom "Claudius Clear" has named. The type which Broad represents was so common at the time when the events in "Tanner's Lane" are supposed to have taken place that half-a-dozen persons whom my friend knew resembled it more or less.' Letter signed 'Reuben Shapcott', *BW* 20 (30 July 1896), 232.

[3] H. G. Tibbutt, *Bunyan Meeting Bedford 1650–1950*, 42. *The Bunyan Meeting Bedford: Constitution, History, and Rules* (Apr. 1958), 4, lists ministers.

[4] C. M. Maclean, 323–4.

preached mentally taxing sermons, 'unlike the simple stuff which became fashionable with the Evangelistic movement' (Ch. 7). (R. W. Dale made that same point.)[1]

Bradshaw claimed proudly to belong to the family of 'Bradshaw the regicide' (Ch. 7), and James Harden 'never scrupled to tell anybody what he thought, and would send an arrow sharp and swift through any iniquity, no matter where it might couch' (Ch. 17). By 1844–5, however, when the Cowfold section begins, the radicalism and the moral pointedness have been blunted. John Broad, based on John Jukes, Hillyard's successor at Bedford (1840), advises against disputed topics and particular reference in sermons.[2] The corollary of theological decline is a betrayal of Congregationalist radicalism: Broad remains neutral, in an election where he could have supported two Free-Trading Whigs, lest he offend his deacons—almost all farmers, or connected with agriculture, and Protectionists. Brother Bushel's annual £10 donation is the material factor for Broad. Isaac and George Allen are Free-Traders, and George complains to Priscilla about his father-in-law that Broad is betraying 'all the principles of the Independents', their traditional concern for 'Civil and Religious Liberty':

I cannot understand . . . how a Dissenting minister can make up his mind not to vote against a party which has been answerable for all the oppression and all the wrongs in English history, and for all our useless wars, and actually persecuted his predecessors in this very meeting-house in which he now preaches. . . . (Ch. 23)

The aged Mr. Bradshaw protests against 'taxing the poor for the sake of the rich', but Broad's, we are told, is the voice of the coming man ('. . . religion did not consist in vain strife upon earthly matters'): 'A sad falling-off,' notes Zachariah, 'from the days, even in my time, when the Dissenters were the insurrectionary class' (Ch. 24). Men like Zachariah and the Allens are driven out of Dissent, as the Whites were. The radical Dissenter finds a more congenial vehicle for political action in the overtly political pursuits of the secular radicals. Hale White focuses on the moment of transition, when Zachariah reluctantly attends a Manchester Hampden Club meeting at the traditional time for chapel on Sunday evening:

[1] e.g. *The Old Evangelicalism and the New* (1889), 19–22, 58; *History of English Congregationalism* (1907), 591.

[2] H. G. Tibbutt, op. cit., 53–66; John Brown, *John Bunyan* (1885), 424–5; *Revolution*, Ch. 24.

The reasons which induced him to alter his mind were, in the first place, the piety, methodistic most of it, which was then mixed up with politics; and secondly, a growing fierceness of temper, which made the cause of the people a religion. From 1816 downwards it may be questioned whether he would not have felt himself more akin with any of his democratic friends, who were really in earnest over the great struggle, than with a sleek half Tory professor of the gospel, however orthodox he might be. (Ch. 10)

In the 1840s Zachariah remains in Dissent because of traditional allegiance and inertia: and his sectarian allegiance is at odds with his politics. And the novel's view of the position of mid-century political Dissenters has, indeed, much in common with the Marxist model of A. L. Morton and E. J. Hobsbawm.[1]

The literary critics have, of course, chorused their endorsement of the novel's thesis that, in or around 1844, political Dissent ceased to be viable, that by then the 'Cromwellian Independent' was a defunct animal. White has himself been called 'One of the Last of the Historical Nonconformists'; 'The last Puritan', he lived, we are informed, 'just at the era of the passing of the old Nonconformity'.[2] And Broad and Snale

. . . need not be taken, however, simply as the portraits of two gross, venal men. They can equally well be taken as symbols of a creeping paralysis which manifested itself more and more obviously in the Nonconformist churches as the century wore on. The tendency to separate the affairs of the world from religion, so brilliantly advertised in Broad and Snale, was part of the heritage Dissent had received from the Revival. It had worked in subtle ways to render the Protestant Dissenters politically conservative.

"As their interest in theological polemics had cooled, they had lost their old taste for discussion, their former love of argument. And as their prejudices in favour of ecclesiastical autonomy weakened, their individualism in politics weakened simultaneously."[3]

. . . Hale White has undertaken to show us the disintegration of a religion. Part of his aim is to contrast a fading Puritanism with the fiery ardor of the earlier sect. This ardor is relit in a few isolated souls, like Mark Rutherford

[1] A. L. Morton, *Language of Men* (1945), 49–51; E. J. Hobsbawm, *Primitive Rebels* (Manchester, 1959), *passim*. (For Hobsbawm on Zachariah Coleman see *Primitive Rebels*, 146–8; and *Labouring Men* (1964), 25, 372–3.)

[2] Augustine Birrell, 'One of the Last of the Historical Nonconformists', *Nation and Athenaeum*, 34 (1 Mar. 1924), 767; 'The Last Puritan', A. L. Morton's chapter on White in *Language of Men* (1945), 49–57; A. E. Taylor, 'The Novels of Mark Rutherford', *ES* 5 (1914), 55.

[3] W. Stone, *Religion and Art of William Hale White* (1954), 24–5. The quotation is from Halévy.

and Zachariah Coleman, incarnations of pristine nonconformity in the nine-teenth century muddle. The fading is a symptom of prosperity and middle-class attitudes. Calvinism has climbed almost to the respectability of Anglicanism. It is this climb upon which the dominant note of irony in the novels centers.[1]

And as late as the 1830s, in Bedford, there were still Puritans who lived up to their noblest traditions, both religious and political. One example Hale White had . . . in his own home. Another was the minister in charge of his family's chapel . . . during his infancy. . . .

By the first decades of the nineteenth century, however, the Puritan doctrines had become for the majority a passively accepted legacy of phrases and rituals, a legacy which preserved their community but left the inner life largely un-touched. And it was a symptom of decay that Dissenters had changed in their political attitudes as well. 'We can watch', says Halevy [*sic*], 'between 1792 and 1815 an uninterrupted decline in the revolutionary spirit among the sects.'[2]

This a-historical mish-mash is what comes from reading novels as if they were history textbooks. White's historical model is accepted as read. The only external evidence adduced is Halévy's comments on the period of the war with France when, indeed, as we have seen, republi-can Dissenters' wings were clipped. The point is relevant, as historians know, only to the 1793–1815 period, and irrelevant when applied to the 1840s.[3]

White was in fact wrong; his model must be as it were inverted: radical Dissent increased in strength precisely when he suggested it was almost defunct. John Broad, who refused to commit himself to Free Trade and would not vote for the Whig-Liberal cause, is hardly the characteristic Victorian Dissenting or Congregationalist minister. 'No other occupation was so partisan, so militant, so unfloating, as the Dissenting ministers. They were a sort of Communist hard core to the Popular Front.'[4] Of Liberalism, of course. Victorian Congregationalism was 'the core of the genuine Liberal Party', 'the backbone of "the Liberal Party"'—the party, in other words, of the future, of freedom, progress and equal justice. . . .'[5]

Hale White cannot, perhaps, be expected to be aware of the resur-gence of Dissenting interest in Cromwell in the Victorian period, of the

[1] E. S. Merton, 'Mark Rutherford: the World of His Novels', *BNYPL* 67 (1963), 475. Cf. E. S. Merton, 'The Autobiographical Novels of Mark Rutherford', *NCF* 5 (1950–1), 190.

[2] Irvin Stock, *William Hale White (Mark Rutherford)* (1965), 31–2.

[3] E. J. Hobsbawm, *Labouring Men*, 25.

[4] J. R. Vincent, *Pollbooks: How the Victorians Voted* (Cambridge, 1967), 18.

[5] *Congregational Year Book* (1876), 106; ibid. (1874), 65–6: quoted by J. C. G. Binfield, thesis cit., 415–16, and 416, footnote 1.

fresh casting of Nonconformist radicals in the Cromwellian mould.[1] He assumed that Zachariah Coleman's glorying in Cromwellian Independency had become completely *passé*. Zachariah is indeed very reminiscent of Ebenezer Elliott's father, an ultra-Calvinist of the eighteenth century, with 'aquatint pictures' on the walls of incidents in the lives of his heroes Cromwell and Washington.[2] That enthusiasm however did not die, but increased, especially after Carlyle's heroizing of the Protector. White was himself enthusiastic for Carlyle. Clara Hopgood studies *Heroes and Hero Worship* at the bookshop where she works (Ch. 19). William White was seduced from orthodoxy by *Heroes* and *Sartor*. The visit of the Whites, father and son, to Carlyle in March 1868 was 'an event amongst the greatest in my life'.[3] Carlyle's was 'the voice which in our century came from the deepest depths'.[4] But loyal, as well as ex-Dissenters shared the enthusiasm. Howard Evans, reared on Cromwell, Milton, and Bunyan, who would not go to Oxford and betray his Nonconformity, whose father took him to hear radicals like Miall and Henry Vincent, 'revelled in Carlyle's "Letters and Speeches of Cromwell". . . .'[5]

Nonconformist radicals popularized Cromwell in lectures: Thomas Scales, at Leeds (1847); George Dawson, at Manchester (1846), and Hugh Stowell Brown, at Bradford (1853).[6] Nonconformist *Lives* of Cromwell proliferated: by Robert Vaughan (1838), John Forster (1839), Edwin Paxton Hood (1882), R. F. Horton (1897).[7] C. S. Horne's *A Popular History of the Free Churches* (1903) is full of the admiration for Cromwell that characterized his ministry and his career as Liberal M.P.[8] The gargoyles on Harrogate Congregational Church included Cromwell, as well as Wycliffe and William of Orange (*Congregational Year Book*,

[1] Much of the material for this section comes from contributions (some my own) to the *Past and Present* '19th Century Cromwell' project: typescript material in my possession.

[2] January Searle, *Memoirs of Ebenezer Elliott* (1852), 70–7.

[3] *Early Life*, 38.

[4] (18 Sept. 1900), to Mrs. Colenutt, *Letters to Three Friends*, 107.

[5] Howard Evans, *Radical Fights of Forty Years* (1913), 17–18.

[6] *Leeds Mercury* (15 May 1847); Alexander Ireland, 'Recollections of George Dawson and his Lectures in Manchester in 1846–7', *Manchester Quarterly*, 1 (1882), 181–204; *Bradford Observer* (5–19 May 1853).

[7] R. Vaughan, *The Protectorate of Oliver Cromwell* . . . (2 Vols., 1838); J. Forster, *Oliver Cromwell, 1599–1658* (2 Vols., 1839); E. Paxton Hood, *Oliver Cromwell* (1882); R. F. Horton, *Oliver Cromwell: A Study in Personal Religion* (1897).

[8] C. S. Horne, *Pulpit, Platform and Parliament* (1913), 75, 188 ff. His *Popular History* was an affirmation of 'Free Church principles and witness' in the midst of the struggle over the 1902 Education Act: W. B. Selbie, *The Life of Charles Silvester Horne M.A., M.P.* (1920), 136–7.

1863); the stained glass windows of Emmanual Congregational Church, Cambridge, dating from *c.* 1906, include one of Cromwell; a statue of Cromwell was erected outside the St. Ives, Hungtingdon, Free Church.[1] Radical and Liberal Dissenters affirmed a kind of Cromwellian status: James Maden assured Gladstone at the General Baptist Assembly that he would 'find his warmest friends and his best-disciplined troops, in the descendants of Cromwell's Ironsides—the Nonconformists of England'.[2] Nonconformists formed 'the Ironsides of the anti-Turkish army which marches under Mr. Gladstone's command'.[3] W. T. Henderson of Banbury supported Yates, an anti-State-Church parliamentary candidate (1857), as 'an admirer of the great Cromwell'.[4] At the 1902 Free Church Council Conference, fervent against the proposed Education Act, John Clifford declared resistance from 'the descendants of men like Oliver Cromwell'. In 1906 Lloyd George called Clifford 'the best fighting man the Free Churches had turned out since Oliver Cromwell'.[5] The catalogue could go on: Spurgeon modelled himself on Cromwell, who even as it were sanctioned his love of bowls; Basil Martin was upset when his children said they preferred Cavaliers to Roundheads.[6] Clearly Nonconformists projected themselves as Cromwellians for the whole period of the Liberal alliance.

But Hale White had cut himself off from the main streams of Dissenting life: expelled from the Congregationalist New College in 1852, in 1854 he allowed his membership of the Bedford Bunyan Meeting to lapse.[7] (It is true, though, that he returned to Ditchling in 1860 to marry a man, Macdougall, who had been minister there; and that his mother recorded in her diary hearing him preach at Little Portland Street on 1 April 1860.)[8] He can thus be excused some ignorance,

[1] Clyde Binfield, 'On Oliver Cromwell' (MS. '19th Century Cromwell').

[2] *General Baptist Year Book* (1880), 3.

[3] [W. T. Stead], *Northern Echo* (14 Nov. 1877).

[4] *Banbury Advertiser* (2 Apr. 1857).

[5] M. R. Watts, thesis cit., 321–2, 392.

[6] C. H. Spurgeon, *Autobiography*, compiled by Mrs. Spurgeon and his private secretary (4 Vols., 1897–1900), III. 46–7, 143, 189–90; [CHS], 'Puritan Names', *Sword and Trowel*, 24 (1888), 73–4; K. Martin, *Father Figures*, 21.

[7] At the Church Meeting, 4 May 1854, it was resolved 'That a short note be addressed to each of the following persons, requesting to know whether they are in connection with any Church, or if they desire to continue in fellowship with us . . .'—*inter al.*, William Hale White, London. The same meeting declared Mr. and Mrs. William White no longer members under Rule 8 of the church about lapse of membership after four months' absence from communion. 'Act Book of the Church at Bunyan Meeting, Bedford, Vol. II, 1820 &c.', (MS.), [60], 61, [62].

[8] MS. Letter from W. Robertson Nicoll to Dr. Hale White (White's son), 15 May 1914; and extracts from Mary Ann White's diaries, in Dr. W. Hale White, 'Notes About

but he is not entirely exculpated. He was perfectly well aware that radical Dissent had not faded out in the 1840s. He knew about Miall and the *Nonconformist*, which had (according to C. M. Maclean) declared against the 'spiritual tyranny' of his expulsion from New College, and had carried his own column (1872–3).[1] To some extent the *Nonconformist* had been a forum for the grievances of the three expelled students and their defenders.[2] White expressed disappointment that Miall lost at Bradford in 1868 (and blamed it on 'sleek little-Bethel bigotry').[3] He wrote an introduction to his father's collected *Illustrated Times* articles, one of which (7 June 1856), on 'Mr. Edward Miall and His Motion for an Inquiry into the Revenues of the State Church in Ireland and their Distribution', describes how Miall, at first widely despised by Dissenters, gradually pushed his radical principles into pre-eminence: 'and now his paper stands at the head of the dissenting press, and he is a Member of Parliament.'[4] The *Norfolk News*, which published White's articles (1872–3) was a Liberal–Nonconformist paper founded (1845) after a Church Rates case in Norwich.[5] It was John Bright himself who recommended White to the editor of the *Rochdale Observer*.[6] White's hero Thomas Binney, a virulent exponent of Dissenting grievances against the State Church, who pamphleteered against Church Rates, and celebrated the 1662 Bicentenary with *Farewell Sunday* and *St. Bartholomew's Day*, was much more characteristic of Congregationalism then Bedford's John Jukes: he was twice Chairman of the Congregational Union. He lived until 1874, did not preach his last sermon until 1873, and even (he was Chairman of its Council) lectured at New

W. Hale White (Mark Rutherford)', 26 (Bedford Public Library Collection). Geoffrey Best's statement, therefore (*The Revolution*, 'chapter 16 onwards, which although set in the forties reflects the author's later experience'), must be cautiously approached. The experience was hardly that much later. Geoffrey Best, *Mid-Victorian Britain 1851–1875* (1971), 293.

[1] C. M. Maclean, op. cit., 92–4, 197.

[2] See letters from Robert M. Theobald, William Hall [sic] White, Frederic M. White, *Nonconformist*, 12 (31 Mar. 1852), 240; from R. M. Theobald, ibid., 12 (14 July 1852), 539; from William White, ibid., 12 (15 Sept 1852), 722. (C. M. Maclean (see footnote 1 above) gives no reference for her quotation about 'spiritual tyranny', and I cannot find it; and Wilfred Stone refers, op. cit., p. 39, footnote 34, to a non-existent comment by Miall in the *Nonconformist*, 12 (28 Apr. 1852).)

[3] C. M. Maclean, op. cit., 182.

[4] W. White, *Illustrated Times* (7 June 1856): Ch. 3, of *The Inner Life of House of Commons*, ed. Justin McCarthy, Intro. W.H.W. (2 Vols., 1897), I. 19.

[5] W. Stone, op. cit., 133, lists papers which published White's journalism. J. C. G. Binfield, thesis cit., 441, discusses the origin of *Norfolk News*.

[6] C. M. Maclean, op. cit., 173.

College after 1869.[1] And the Rev. John Brown, grandfather of Keynes, likewise perpetuated the Dissenting and radical tradition. He came to Bedford in 1864, and became senior minister in 1866 when Jukes died.[2] In 1891 he was Chairman of the Congregational Union. His *John Bunyan* (1885) was used by White for his own *John Bunyan* (1905).[3] His *Bicentenary of the Revolution of 1688: An Appeal to the Congregational Churches for its Due Celebration* (1888), published by the Congregational Union, identifies Dissent with 'the great struggle for constitutional freedom', lauds Cromwell, anticipates Disestablishment, extols the radical tradition ('A brave ancestry beckons us on to a noble service'), and rejoices in 'a growingly-educated and newly-enfranchised democracy rising up around us'.[4]

John Brown's arrival in Bedford is acknowledged in *The Revolution*: he is presumably the London M.A., whose wife reads German. He lectures on secular subjects on weekdays, is a member of the County Archaeological Society, and a 'modernist' in theology. Older members complain that he does not preach the 'simple gospel'. Brown recognized himself in this new man who contrasts so strongly with John Broad ('I believe that I am the man referred to in the novel, who, after the revolution, was appointed as Mr. Broad's successor').[5] But the novel, while it thus honestly acknowledges that Broad is not the final word, refuses to concede that the new man's advent undercuts the use of Broad as a case against all of mid-century Dissent. Yet the London M.A. effectively destroys the novel's thesis. John Brown was far more like Zachariah Coleman and James Harden than like John Broad. Brown dissociated himself from Jukes: he was, Brown wrote, guilty in his 'conduct in public life' of 'erring on the side of caution'—like Broad.[6]

White may have exaggerated Broad's unpleasantness, though there are indications that Jukes provided plenty of ammunition. Even the Bunyan Meeting 'Act Book' records that 'His great defect was the utter absence of imagination and humour. This rendered his preaching somewhat heavy though it always aimed at that which was useful and im-

---

[1] *DNB*; Elaine Kaye, *The History of the King's Weigh House Church: A Chapter in the History of London* (1968), 81, 83; E. Paxton Hood, *Thomas Binney: His Mind, Life and Opinions* (1874).

[2] H. G. Tibbutt, *Bunyan Meeting Bedford 1650–1950*, 64–5.

[3] 'I am indebted to Dr. Brown's *John Bunyan* for my knowledge of many facts of Bunyan's Life', W.H.W., *John Bunyan* (1905), title-page, verso.

[4] *Bicentenary of the Revolution of 1688* (1888), 5, 9, 13–15.

[5] John Brown, in press cutting in Mrs. White's 'Scrapbook': W. Stone, op. cit., 21, footnote 33.

[6] John Brown, *John Bunyan* (1885), 424.

pressive.'[1] The impression his preaching left on Hale White is perhaps
not surprising if the boy was subjected to many sermons like the one
he probably heard (12 July 1846) on the death of Jukes's daughter.
Jukes has all of Broad's faith in his own child's piety:

> Turning to you, my young friends, I cannot but remark that you have had to-
> night a proof of the truth of his word who said, 'I love them that love me, and
> they that seek me early shall find me.' On opening the desk in which our dear
> child was accustomed to keep the objects she valued most, I found a little book
> which she had put aside with special care: it is entitled 'Early Piety'. . . .
>
> . . . I believe the three desires uppermost in her mind, when her fatal
> illness fell upon her were, that she might be allowed to sit down at the Lord's
> Table, to have a little class in the Sunday School, and a small district for the
> distribution of religious tracts. . . .[2]

It is easy to sympathize, after that, with the intent to prick the bubble
of pious fantasy enclosing Priscilla and Thomas Broad. And that Jukes
is the target is indicated by the correspondences: like Jukes, Broad is a
big man (actually he is described as 'a big, gross-feeding, heavy person
with heavy ox-face and large mouth'), has a son who goes into the
Congregational ministry, and trains young men as missionaries.[3]

But the insistence on Broad as the characteristic Congregationalist
minister must be put down to personal grievance. Zachariah Coleman
is a tribute to William White, who had his windows smashed for being
on Lord John Russell's committee at the Bedford election during the
time of the Reform Bill: on his seventy-eighth birthday Hale still
recalled how as a baby he had to be carried to the back of the house
for safety. Hale's grandfather too had been a radical, whose windows
were smashed for his not illuminating for British victories in the
Napoleonic wars.[4] William White was a stalwart for liberty: he
defended the Bedford Harpur Charity against Anglican domination,
supported the Liberal cause in politics, and protested against his son's
expulsion from New College in a pamphlet, *To Think, or, Not to Think?*
(1852).[5] Zachariah Coleman's love of Byron, and admiration for Cob-

---

[1] 'Act Book of the Church at Bunyan Meeting, Bedford, Vol. II, 1820 &c.', 1866, p. [92].

[2] *The Assurance of Hope: A Sermon Occasioned by the death of Susanna Clewin Jukes, Preached
July 12th, 1846, At the Old Meeting, Bedford, by John Jukes* (Bedford and London, 1846),
19, 23.

[3] *Revolution*, Ch. 17; H. G. Tibbutt, op. cit., 53–57. The caretaker of Bunyan Meeting
very kindly gave me a photograph of Jukes, who is indeed corpulent.

[4] D. V. White, *Groombridge Diary*, 196, 298.

[5] William White, *The Bedford Charity Not Sectarian* (Bedford, 1844), and *To Think or
Not to Think?: Remarks Upon the late Expulsions from New College, St. John's Wood,* by William
White (Father of One of the Expelled) (1852); C. M. Maclean, op. cit., 41–7, 92 ff.

bett, came from William White. 'Why that is old Cobbett again *minus* his vulgarity,' exclaimed Sir David Dundas of a speech White gave in honour of Lord John Russell.[1] When Jukes refused publicly to defend Hale White against New College's public allegations of incorrigible rejection of 'the Supreme Authority of the Sacred Scripture', William White's disaffection became complete. Before finally leaving Dissent, as William White and his son did, Isaac Allen of *The Revolution* leads a group of seceding members in Sunday worship: an incident based on White's being in charge of one of the two meetings the church was forced to hold while the Bunyan Meeting was being rebuilt, 1849–50. (In William White's case it was not, as C. M. Maclean tries to imply, a schism, or even half a schism.)[2] And though William White lapsed as a member of Bunyan Meeting in 1854, he seems to have remained a Trustee until he died: just as Isaac and George Allen 'are on the books till this day'.[3]

Jukes contrasted sadly, for the Whites, with his predecessor, Samuel Hillyard. Hillyard had been trained by Cowper's friend, William Bull of Olney. He had gone into the ministry during Samuel Sanderson's pastorate at Bedford (1737–66), and Sanderson was only separated from Bunyan's ministry there by one man, Ebenezer Chandler. The Whites admired Hillyard's hard work for home and foreign missions, for abolition of the slave-trade and extension of the franchise (he seconded Lord John Russell's nomination at Bedford, 1830). He was 'Passionately attached to the great principles of civil and religious freedom . . . urging his co-religionists to support Lord John and the House of Russell on the principle that your own friends and your father's friends you should forsake not. . . .'[4] And the White family was personally indebted to its pastor who did 'his best to protect' William White and his sister from their stepmother when Hale's grandfather died in 1815.[5]

Hillyard did them a personal service; Jukes refused to assist them. And so Jukes's fictional counterpart is loaded with all the resentment Hale White felt about his treatment at New College. His language on the subject could be hectic:

The Dissenters in England are always in trouble about their Colleges. They are constantly breaking out into heterodoxy. Not that there is ever any grand

[1] *Early Life.* 34.
[2] C. M. Maclean, op. cit., 83, 93, 96–8. See H. G. Tibbutt, op. cit., 62.
[3] C. M. Maclean, op. cit., 97, footnote 2.
[4] John Brown, *John Bunyan*, 415–16, 422–3.
[5] C. M. Maclean, op. cit., 35.

eruption to relieve the system of its foul humours once and for ever, but the disease is always coming up to the skin in pimples disfiguring the complexion exceedingly, and causing no small annoyance. Some years ago at New College. . . .[1]

Justice was not done to him, he claimed:

The Holy Office was never more scandalously indifferent to any pretence of justice or legality in its proceedings. We were not told what was the charge against us, nor what were the terms of the trust deed of the College, if such a document existed; neither were we informed what was the meaning of the indictment. . . .[2]

   In fact, the students *did* know that a creed was embodied in the college's trust deed, and had admitted this in a letter to the *Nonconformist*.[3] The picture given in the *Autobiography* of the college principal, Dr. Harris, as an ignorant and obscurantist theologian is, again, a distorted one: he was a good German scholar, familiar with continental theology, and in fact suspected of unorthodoxy himself. The evidence collected by William White in *To Think, or, Not to Think?* to show Harris's own unorthodoxy, and therefore hypocrisy in sacking his son, might also serve to indicate a progressive theologian.[4] Anger against the expulsion of students who were probably less progressive in theology than their teachers was understandable, but it does not altogether excuse the venom in the account of Tanner's Lane justice. George Allen commits no legal offence, but 'we', declares Broad, unconsciously ironic, 'as members, my dear brethren of Christ's body, have to be guided by other considerations.' Brother Bushel is not in favour even of telling the Allens the charges against them, nor of inviting them to the Church meeting to consider their case (Ch. 26). Broad's dislike of the Allens ('in his heart of hearts [Broad] bitterly hated them' (Ch. 19)) is unmotivated and inexplicable except by reference to White's assumptions about Jukes's attitude towards himself and his father in not coming to his aid at New College. And the novel's linking of Thomas Broad's exposure as a lecherous hypocrite with his father's sudden paralysis and disablement from ministry for the last two years of his life is the un-

[1] W.H.W., *Aberdeen Herald* (15 Jan. 1863): W. Stone, op. cit., 40.
[2] *Early Life*, 68–9.
[3] '. . . being aware that a creed exists in the deeds of the institution . . .' Letter signed by R. M. Theobald, F. M. White, and W. H. White, *Nonconformist*, 12 (31 Mar. 1852), 240. The Bedford Public Library Collection includes a copy in the hand of R. M. Theobald of the *Schedule* of Faith for tutors and students at New College.
[4] W. Stone, op. cit., 36 (and pp. 36–7, footnote 23).

kindest cut to Jukes's memory. Jukes suffered a paralytic stroke shortly after the death of his young assistant James Insull (1863) and never fully recovered before his own death (1866).[1] There is no hint, though, in the record to legitimate anything like Hale White's scurrilous suggestion.[2] But a victim might as well be properly victimized. What is more, Mrs. Broad is presented as yet another of the really irreligious Dissenting womenfolk, proper in chapel attendance, genteel in aspirations. She is made the target for White's resentment against his mother, who was 'a little weak in her preference for people who did not stand behind counters'. To keep up with the Chignell cousins Mrs. White had pushed her son into ministerial training, 'the great blunder of my life, the mistake which well-nigh ruined it altogether'.[3]

So personal resentments appear to have generated the picture of the Broads. They have also made Hale White play down the survival of the radical Dissenting tradition in men like Binney and John Brown. Binney was compromised. He was a member of the New College Council, but illness kept him from its meeting to examine Hale White, and, despite a plea from William White, from the meeting at which Hale appeared with his father. Jukes 'misrepresented' to Binney the events at New College when he visited Bedford, and perhaps for that reason White seems not to have attended his ministry after Morris had left London.[4] Thomas Bradshaw, White's fictional tribute to Binney, survives into the Broad era, but is much enfeebled, and already yesterday's man.

John Brown, too, was in a sense compromised by the spirit of Jukes. Hale protested in a letter to the *Bedfordshire Mercury* (18 March 1882) that Brown had misrepresented the late William White in a sermon:

[1] H. G. Tibbutt, op. cit., 64–5.
[2] '. . . a bitter feeling towards him [Jukes] is expressed in "Tanner's Lane", perhaps too bitter. Mr. Jukes, I have been told, was by no means a strong man intellectually, and his sympathies theologically were far from broad, but he was a worthy minister and thoroughly upright', 'Claudius Clear' [W. Robertson Nicoll], *BW* 20 (9 July 1896), 185. Sexual misdemeanours were not however unknown in eastern counties Congregationalism. Clyde Binfield has suggested to me that the plot of *Catharine Furze*, where Rev. Mr. Cardew, an evangelical Anglican, neglects his wife to pay court to Catharine, could have been generated by a scandal at St. Neots Congregational Church. The minister, W. Reuben Lewis, resigned (28 Feb. 1851), and admitted (2 Mar.) 'certain indiscretions'. A committee of inquiry, presided over by Jukes of Bedford, found a Mrs. Joyce guilty of receiving 'improper' letters from the Rev. Lewis. He subsequently went to Australia. In the novel, Mr. Cardew goes to a 'far distant' parish. 'St Neots Congregational Church, Minute Book No. 3. 1846–7' (MS.). Reginald Denness Cooper, *The History of the 'Old Meeting House'*, *St. Neots, 1691–1890* (St. Neots, 1890), 40, suppresses the reason for Lewis's emigration.
[3] *Early Life*, 55–6.     [4] C. M. Maclean, op. cit., 85–6, 97.

Mr. Brown says that my father left Bunyan Meeting because the church did not support him in his controversy with one of the dissenting colleges. I am anxious that it should be known that his separation from the chapel was due, not to any personal and insufficient cause such as that assigned, but to a conviction, the gradual growth of years, that what he heard in the chapel in those days taught him nothing and satisfied no want. . . .

   Mr. Brown furthermore thinks that my father's noblest, best, and happiest days were those in which he was 'in loyal allegiance to the Christian Church' . . . my father certainly was never happier than during the last thirty years of his life. The implication that he was not in communion with the Christian Church may perhaps mislead some who are not aware of the technical sense in which the word Church is used by Dissenters. With the Church, giving the term a wider signification and one which, I believe, would have been sanctioned by its Founder, my father was in fullest communion up to the hour when Death laid his hand on him.[1]

Whether or not Brown would be able to appreciate this rather tendentious point, it is clear that in White's mind Brown had joined Jukes in not appreciating the family's worth. Furthermore, of course, Cromwellian Independent or not, Brown threatened Hale White's confidence in a post-Dissenting righteousness ('there are many things in which I am far more strict than churchgoing people').[2]

   The three strongly anti-Dissenting novels, *The Autobiography*, *Deliverance*, and *Revolution*, are all products of the 1880s, when White was very conscious of the passing of a generation. Important political and literary figures who had shaped his world died in a short space: Earl Russell (May 1878), George Eliot (December 1880), Carlyle (February 1881). When his father died (26 February 1882), the great break was made between the present and the past.[3] Dissent partook of that sense of final loss. When the King's Weigh House Chapel was threatened with demolition, Hale wrote: 'Is it really true, that the Weigh House Chapel is about to be demolished, and that a district train will run over or under the spot on which Mr. Binney preached? If so, then one more spot is to be desecrated which to a number of middle-aged persons like myself is sacred with a thousand memories.'[4] This

---

   [1] C. M. Maclean, op. cit., 227. John Brown was presumably *not* using the church *v.* congregation distinction in his sermon.
   [2] Letter to his son (Mar. 1874): C. M. Maclean, op. cit., 195.
   [3] Ibid., 225.
   [4] C. M. Maclean, op. cit., 224. The Metropolitan Railway first sought the site in Fish Street Hill of the old King's Weigh House Chapel in 1864, and after much delay the congregation had to leave it in 1883. The new home was the Duke Street Chapel (1891). Elaine Kaye, *The History of the King's Weigh House Church*, 96, 97, 100.

luxuriating in epochal gloom might have been less intense, however, as
the historical model of the *Revolution* might have been more accurate,
had he conceded that Hillyard's and Binney's work was perpetuated in
the Browns and Cliffords, the Hortons and Hornes; and that Jukes/Broad
was not Congregationalism's, nor Dissent's, last word.[1]

---

[1] *The Revolution in Tanner's Lane* is the only English novel I have read that illustrates
George Steiner's thesis that nineteenth-century European literature is characterized by
ennui arising from a sense that nothing can match the revolutionary excitements of the
1798–1815 period. Mid-century Dissent is presented by Hale White as boringly complacent, smugly bourgeois, in comparison with the radicalism of the Blanketeers, the
excitement of Peterloo. See George Steiner, 'In Bluebeard's Castle: Some Notes Towards
the Re-Definition of Culture', *Listener*, 85 (18 Mar. 1971), 327–32.

# XI. THE SENSE OF AN ENDING

Hallilujah! should now be the watch-word through-out Verdopolis, but alas, some there be who scruple not to cry 'ICHABOD! ICHABOD! the glory is departed'.

Charlotte Brontë, 'My Angria and the Angrians'.

It seems, as one becomes older,
That the past has another pattern, and ceases to be a mere sequence—
Or even development: the latter a partial fallacy
Encouraged by superficial notions of evolution,
Which becomes, in the popular mind, a means of disowning the past.

T. S. Eliot, 'The Dry Salvages'.

A SENSE of the end of Dissent lies heavily on many Victorian novelists. 'I feel increasingly that the race to which I belonged is fast passing, and that the Dissenting minister of the present day is a different being altogether from the Dissenting minister of forty years ago', laments Mark Rutherford in *The Autobiography* (Ch. 1). And the obsolescence of Nonconformity, as of Calvinism, or Christian orthodoxy, or of Christianity itself, is continually and widely affirmed. What the novelists envisage as viable alternatives are offered instead. George Eliot replaces a supernaturally sanctioned Christianity by its humanist 'essence'. The original Methodist spirit fades; Dinah abandons preaching, in acknowledgement perhaps that the saving factor in Hetty's case was less God's grace than Dinah's humanity, which will henceforth be perpetuated in family circumstances, not in the redundant formulas of Methodism. In *Felix Holt* the humanist point is clearer still: Rufus Lyon's efforts and words are inefficacious, and it is Felix Holt who converts Esther to seriousness and maturity.[1] Rufus is made to acknowledge the change ('Surely the work of grace is begun in her . . .' Ch. 26) and nothing is said of his continuing as a Dissenting pastor when he leaves Treby to live with Esther and Felix. Felix, the preacher of humane politics, has matched and surpassed him point for point. They are both serious, unworldly, ascetic.[2] But Felix is the new Saviour (he

[1] See George McCrie, *The Religion of Our Literature* (1875), 292–4; and Laurence Lerner, *The Truthtellers* (1967), 40–52.
[2] *Felix Holt*, Chs. 10, 27.

takes a child on his knee, and will 'set' a little child 'in the midst' of the Sproxton miners; Chs. 22, 13), and the new Apostle: like St. Paul, 'necessity is laid upon' him to preach his gospel (Ch. 27). And his political evangelism at least contacts the Sproxton miners where Rufus's Gospel fails to attract more than the infirm and the women (Ch. 13).[1] George Eliot was writing early enough in the post-Christian phase to be able to maintain this high debree of optimism about the possibilities for men like Felix. Hale White and Hardy are much more subdued about their humanist preachers of righteousness: Mark Rutherford fails to convert Drury Lane, and Clym Yeobright, a sort of post-Methodist itinerant, though 'kindly received', earns a mixed response: 'Some believed him, and some believed not; some said that his words were commonplace, others complained of his want of theological doctrine; while others again remarked that it was well enough for a man to take to preaching who could not see to do anything else' (*The Return of the Native*, Bk. 6, Ch. 4). Even before the end of the century George Eliot's Feuerbachian enthusiasm was clearly difficult to sustain.

But, whatever the alternatives might be, a consensus of the novelists who were not practising Nonconformists agreed that there was little possibility of a vital connection being maintained between Dissent—or evangelicalism in general—and modern life. Nonconformist novelists, however, continued to assume that Dissenting life was a vital and continuing possibility, even though under attack. To be sure, Joseph Hocking's *Jabez Easterbrook* (1890) acknowledges what Hardy might call 'the ache of modernism' (*Tess*, Ch. 19). Easterbrook, a Methodist preacher, comes to believe that all scientific discovery stems from God, and is expelled from the ministry. He marries the woman who was sceptical about his Biblical literalism, 'and sets up in a neighbouring town as a Dissenters' Robert Elsmere'.[2] But Methodism, the life of the chapel, the preaching 'plan', the preachers, the prayer-meetings, are firmly established in the life of the community in stories set in Methodist regions, like the Cornwall of Silas Hocking's *Tales of a Tin Mine* (1898), the North-East of Ramsay Guthrie's *The Canny Folks O' Coal-Vale* (1910), and the Lancashire of John Ackworth's *Clog Shop Chronicles* (1896). Mark Guy Pearse, in his Preface to *Daniel Quorm, and His Religious Notions* (First Series), adverts to complaints of Methodist decline ('Daniel's beloved mother Methodism is much troubled just now by a

---

[1] See D. R. Carroll, ' *Felix Holt*; Society as Protagonist', *NCF* 17 (1962–3), 243–6.
[2] See L. J. Henkin, *Darwinism in the English Novel 1860–1910* (New York, 1940), 129–30.

host of physicians who would persuade her that she is ill') but nevertheless feels justified in offering Daniel Quorm, Penwinnin's shoemaker, 'Class-leader', and 'Society-steward', as a late-century example of the acknowledged power of the Methodist system 'to develop the gifts of her lowliest members'. It is not yet too late, the novelist feels, to add Quorm to the already legendary list of thoughtful miners, prayerful ploughmen, and godly labourers.[1]

But elsewhere Dissenters tended to be regarded as having become, or as rapidly becoming, anachronistic, and the old-fashioned appearance of their theology and way of life was reinforced by their being set back in the past. Thus one can see that for some novelists at least there was an ideological, a doctrinaire point, behind the historical perspective, the extension in time, which Kathleen Tillotson has noticed and discussed.[2] Dinah Morris, Adam Bede, Rufus Lyon, and Zachariah Coleman are distanced in time as a ready way of manifesting their mere historicity. Even a Nonconformist like Mrs. Gaskell invests her most memorable Dissenting scene (the evening psalm-singing in *Cousin Phillis*) with an elegiac quality as of something now, or about to be, lost. Novelists antagonistic towards contemporary Nonconformity can afford generosity for, or even enthusiasm about, Dissent in the past: it is a way of pretending that Dissent has no present relevance, and insulates them from any challenge, any possibility of its speaking to their present condition. Charles Kingsley notably combines strong reservations about modern Dissenters with enthusiasm for their fathers. *Westward Ho!* pays open-handed tribute to Salvation Yeo, the Anabaptist, and his heroic blend of valour and godliness; it presents straightforwardly his Calvinist, orthodox conversion. But the Baptists in *Alton Locke* are on the whole odious: where you might expect a Puritan divine you get a Baptist missionary—'squat, red-faced, pig-eyed, low-browed'. The Major in *Two Years Ago* is as manly as Wesley or the Covenanters, but so little connection is allowed between Wesley and the Bryanites that they are only his '*soi-disant* disciples'.

Some Victorian novelists, especially George Eliot and Hardy, are committed to an over-simplified linear model of evolutionary progress, according to which Christianity has become simply anachronistic. Man

---

[1] Mark Guy Pearse, *Daniel Quorm, and His Religious Notions*, First Series [1875], (One Hundredth Thousand, 1895), Preface, vii–ix.

[2] Kathleen Tillotson, *Novels of the Eighteen-Forties*, 'Introductory', section 15 (Oxford, paperback reprint, 1962), 91–115. See Maurice Hussey, 'Structure and Imagery in "Adam Bede" ', *NCF* 10 (1955), 122; and Thomas Pinney, 'The Authority of the Past in George Eliot's Novels', *NCF* 21 (1966–7), 131–47.

has progressed, and the once-valuable Christian faith has become redundant. For George Eliot, Darwin's *Origin of Species*, published at the end of 1859, 'makes an epoch'; a Comtean faith in human amelioration had paved the way for this enthusiasm.[1] But already by the 90s her dated commitment to Darwinism was sufficient explanation for her loss of popularity:

It is difficult for those who have not lived through it to understand the influence that George Eliot had upon those of us who came to our intellectual majority in the 'seventies'. Darwinism was in the air, and promised, in the suave accents of Professor Huxley and in the more strident voice of Professor Clifford, to solve all the problems of humanity. George Eliot's novels were regarded by us not so much as novels, but rather as applications of Darwinism to life and art. They were to us *Tendenz-Romane*, and we studied them as much for the *Tendenz* as for the *Roman*. Nowadays, when their *Tendenz* is discredited, their artistic qualities have been depreciated far below their just value. . . .[2]

Hardy lived long enough into the twentieth century to see the absolute discrediting of simplistic evolutionary optimism on the battlefields of the First World War. He had been one of 'the earliest acclaimers of the *Origin of Species*', and had attended Darwin's funeral in Westminster Abbey (26 April 1882). But:

. . . the war destroyed all Hardy's belief in the gradual ennoblement of man, a belief he had held for many years, as is shown by poems like 'The Sick Battle-God', and others. He said he would probably not have ended *The Dynasts* as he did end it if he could have foreseen what was going to happen within a few years.[3]

[1] *GE Letters*, III. 214 (25 Nov. [1859]). For Comte and progress, see, e.g. Basil Willey, *Nineteenth-Century Studies* (1949; Penguin edn., 1964), 204. For the linear model of history, see Humphry House's essays 'The Mood of Doubt' and 'Qualities of George Eliot's Belief', in *All in Due Time* (1955), particularly 94–5, 111.

[2] Joseph Jacobs, *Jewish Ideals and Other Essays* (1896), xii. 'George Eliot is, in fact, the peculiar product of this particular age, of this age and no other. She is the crown and blossom of the evolution philosophy', John A. Bellows, 'The Religious Tendencies of George Eliot's Writings', *Unitarian Review*, 16 (1881), 130. She 'has heralded in the pages of imaginative literature the new Religion of Humanity, by far the most popular substitute for the Gospel which has yet been offered to our age . . . has voiced in artistic form and won an audience in the novel-reading community for some of the leading ideas of Comte, Mazzini, and Darwin', Rev. S. Law Wilson, *The Theology of Modern Literature* (Edinburgh, 1899), 231.

[3] 'Florence Emily Hardy', *The Early Life of Thomas Hardy 1840–1891* (1928), 198, and *The Later Years of Thomas Hardy 1892–1928* (1930), 165 (see also p. 162). (McLuhan has suggested that Darwinian lineality was dissolved by the discovery in 1905 of curved space: *The Gutenberg Galaxy: The Making of Typographic Man* (Routledge paperback, 1967 reprint), 251, 253. I offer the reference for what it might be worth.)

The emphatic *fin de siècle* tone of Hardy's dismissals of evangelicalism in *Tess* (the text-painter represented the 'last grotesque phase of a creed which had served mankind well in its time'; 'old Mr. Clare was a clergyman of a type which, within the last twenty years, has well nigh dropped out of contemporary life') seems curiously threatened by his remembering at the end of his life the Baptist friends of his youth. The precision of Hardy's note about them reveals the sharpness of the memory of what he might have been (the Baptist Chapel was 'at the eastern end of town'; he recalled his youthful respect for the Baptist minister, and the circus which distracted the Baptists from the 'prayer-meeting'). And the reiteration, a few days before his death, of his un-belief, seems defensively, shakily assertive: 'On December 26 he said that he had been thinking of the Nativity and of the Massacre of the Innocents, and his wife read to him the gospel accounts, and also articles in the *Encyclopaedia Biblica*. He remarked that there was not a grain of evidence that the gospel story was true in any detail.' [1]

The lineality of a Darwinian model for history is difficult to apply to the progress of Christianity. Sects do have a habit of renewing themselves, or of recrudescing in new forms. The appropriate model for sectarian and Dissenting history is, rather, a cyclic one. [2] Nonconformity since the eighteenth-century Evangelical Revival illustrates the point that though sects and denominations may decline, their spirit may be perpetuated elsewhere in a slightly variant but recognizably similar form. Primitive and other revivalist Methodists saw themselves as continuing the true spirit of Wesley; Maximin Piette pointed out that the Salvation Army did the same in the latter part of the nineteenth century and into the twentieth; and late nineteenth-century and twentieth-century Holiness and Pentecostalist movements are emphatically in the Methodist tradition. [3] By a not uninteresting coincidence, 1859 was not only the year of *Adam Bede* and the *Origin of Species*, but the year of the Ulster Revival (which has been seen as initiating the massive evangelical effort of the second half of the century) and of the birth of Smith Wiggles-

---

[1] *The Later Years*, 237, 264. Hardy died on 11 January 1928 (ibid., 265–6).

[2] See John Walford, *Life and Labours of Hugh Bourne*, II (1856), 439–41; R. A. Knox, *Enthusiasm*, Ch. 1, 'The Nature of Enthusiasm'; R. E. Davies, *Methodism*, Ch. 1, 'The Methodist Element in Church History'; and cf. K. S. Latourette: Christianity 'has gone forward by a series of pulsations of advance, retreat, and advance', *Christianity in a Revolutionary Age: A History of Christianity in the Nineteenth and Twentieth Centuries* (5 Vols., 1959–63), V. 534.

[3] John Walford, op. cit., II. (1856), 439; Samuel Coley, *The Life of the Rev. Thomas Collins* (2nd edn., 1869), 52; Maximin Piette, *John Wesley in the Evolution of Protestantism* (1937), 470–1.

worth, prophet of the twentieth-century Pentecostal Movement. And in 1859 William Booth's dissatisfaction with the restricted ministry of the Methodist New Connection was growing and was to lead to his becoming a freelance evangelist and later founding the Salvation Army.[1]

The Darwinian myth, however, predisposed George Eliot and others to a failure to perceive that the sects and movements over which they readily wrote 'Ichabod' might survive, or recrudesce. They extrapolated from the personal loss of faith; and the intensity of the personal experience of loss that informs the extrapolation guarantees, for them, its validity.

Of course Dissent, like other forms of Christianity, declined sharply in size at the beginning of the twentieth century. Counting heads had occasioned concern from 1851 onwards.[2] The working classes—it is a familiar burden—evaded evangelism, even in the northern cities where the strength of Nonconformity was impressive.[3] In London, according to Charles Booth at the beginning of the twentieth century, the working classes were 'outside of all the religious bodies, whether organised as churches or as missions. . . .'[4] All the evangelistic energy had failed to convert England.[5] Instead of creating the just city, Dissenters, like all Christians, had inherited the secular city.

In M. R. Watt's phrases, the apogee of Liberalism in 1906 was also the zenith of Nonconformity: there were then 2,201,848 Free Church members (nearly 100,000 more than Anglican Easter communicants). And this period of numerical and political might was the eve of significant decline for Dissent, as well as for the Liberal party with which it had become largely identified. After their peak years, the Wesleyans (1905), Congregationalists (1906), Baptists (1906), Primitive Methodists (1910), fell in numbers. Radical 'Cromwellian' Dissenters, like John Clifford, lived on into the post-war period when Nonconformity's political allegiance fragmented—divided between support of Coalition

---

[1] Michael Harper, *As at the Beginning* (1965), 43; J. Edwin Orr, *The Second Evangelical Awakening in Britain* (1949), 9; Stanley H. Frodsham, *Smith Wigglesworth: Apostle of Faith* [1949] (1968 reprint), 1; Harold Begbie, *Life of William Booth* (2 Vols., Abridged, 1926), I. 248–54. Booth did not leave 'Wesleyanism' in 1859 however: Michael Harper, loc. cit., repeats Frodsham's mistake.

[2] See e.g. Geoffrey Best, *Mid-Victorian Britain, 1851–75* (1971), 176–7.

[3] E. R. Wickham, *Church and People in an Industrial Society* (1957), 148–50.

[4] Charles Booth, *Life and Labour of the People in London* (ser. iii, 7 Vols., 1902), VII. 399. See *Christianity and the Working Classes* (1906), ed. George Haw.

[5] G. Kitson Clark, *The Making of Victorian England* (1968 paperback edn.), 284–5; Geoffrey Best, op. cit., 191–2.

Liberals, Independent Liberals, and the Labour Party—and its congregations dwindled.[1] A social gospel, to lack of which R. Mudie-Smith ascribed shrinking attendances, did not seem to guarantee continuing support: Methodism's numerical decline was only temporarily evaded by Hugh Price Hughes's Forward Movement, and the creation of Central Halls. Even socialism in the pulpit, whose absence was assumed by many radicals to be the stumbling block to workers joining chapels, did not necessarily succeed in attracting labour. Indeed, secularization in pulpit and chapel merely paved the way for the secular society, when the people would look for social and political benefits to the state, or to entirely political and social agencies.[2] The habit of attending church for respectable custom's sake gradually died; that penumbra of attenders who were not actually members faded away: only the truly committed would continue to go to church in the twentieth century.[3] And the First World War made a quite decisive *terminus ad quem*, not only disrupting traditional patterns and styles, emancipating women, but killing a whole generation of men. After the slaughter the only reminder of the Sunday afternoon men's meetings, that were often astonishingly well attended, would be the lists of the dead on memorial tablets.[4] During the war Joseph Ashby, though he was an old-ish man (born in 1859), had to continue his local preaching since so many young men were at the front. For those who returned, the old rootedness in chapels, friendly societies, and in their work had been permanently dislocated.[5]

But the decline of orthodoxy, the explosion of secularism, the falling population of church attenders, do not mean the death of Christianity, nor of Nonconformity itself—vigorously perpetuated if only in its sects. There has been decline, but not the fall anticipated by the Victorian novelists and confirmed by their successors like D. H. Lawrence. There were still chapels in 1935 in the eastern counties

[1] M. R. Watts, thesis cit. 391, 426–8. 'But hypertrophy is the mark of obsolescence, as we shall see again and again', Marshall McLuhan, *The Gutenberg Galaxy*, 44.

[2] P. d'A. Jones, *The Christian Socialist Revival, 1877–1914*, 65; my note above, p. 100, footnote 1; M. R. Watts, thesis cit., 480–5; Bryan Wilson, *Religion in Secular Society*, Chs. 3 and 4.

[3] E. E. Kellett, *As I Remember* (1936), 105–7; see discussion of 'respectability' in Geoffrey Best, op. cit., 260–3.

[4] See E. R. Wickham, *Church and People in an Industrial City*, 157–8; and photograph of the Whitefield's Memorial Church's Men's Meeting, in C. S. Horne, *Pulpit, Platform and Parliament* (1913), facing p. 65.

[5] M. K. Ashby, *Joseph Ashby of Tysoe*, 293–4.

whose mid-week attenders listened to addresses on nineteen scriptural proofs of final perseverance; the Strict Baptists of 'Akenfield' still operate the 'messenger system' for examining converts which Hale White had to submit to; Pentecostalists have a theology of the *charismata* identical to Edward Irving's, and would be recognized by Charles Wesley as spiritual descendants of the Mr. Hollis (a disciple of the French Prophets) he exorcized for 'gobbling like a turkey-cock' (presumably some form of *glossalalia*); and W. E. Bacon can suggest plausibly that the twentieth-century 'Fellowship of Independent Evangelical Churches' perpetuates the spirit and theology of Spurgeon.[1]

The novelists assumed too readily that because *their* account had been closed, Christianity itself was bankrupt. And, of course, the manipulation and illogic that inform the pretence that Nonconformity is defunct show through in the novels. Hale White's Orkid Joe is 'orkid' in more senses than one: what he represents cannot simply be willed away. We have seen how George Eliot tried to push back into the past her aunt and uncle to legitimate her discussion of 'old fashioned' Methodists and noted how difficult it was to present Rufus Lyon as both a Puritan fossil and a modern 'political dissenter'. Seth's comment at the end of *Adam Bede* ('. . . and if Dinah had been as I did, we'd ha' left the Wesleyans and joined a body that 'ud put no bonds on Christian liberty') is lame indeed, but it does hint a possibility to the reader that the novel has done its best to suppress: that Dinah's primitive Methodism might have been perpetuated elsewhere after the Wesleyan Conference forbade 'the women preaching'. And the conflict between an author's personal designs on history and the historical facts themselves is nowhere more clearly illustrated than in the gap between Dissent in *A Laodicean* and *Tess*. *A Laodicean* (1881) was sub-titled *A Story of Today*, and Hardy did not declare any change of mind about its theme in the Preface of January 1896 or the Postscript of October 1912. Whereas he insists elsewhere on the defunct nature of Nonconformity, here Dissent is very much of the present, indeed of the future. In the novel's symbolic antithesis between past and present, the Baptists (with their brick and iron chapel) and Paula's Baptist father, the railway-builder, stand for modernity. Symbolically Dissent belongs to the age of the telegraph, to

[1] Bryan Wilson, *Religion in Secular Society* (Penguin edn., 1969), 254; J. C. G. Binfield, thesis cit., 464–5; Ronald Blythe, *Akenfield: Portrait of an English Village* (1969), 65; Charles Wesley's *Journal*, ed. T. Jackson (2 Vols., 1849), I. 138: 'While we were undressing, he fell into violent agitations, and gobbled like a turkey-cock. I was frightened, and began exorcising him . . .' (Monday 11 Dec. 1739); E. W. Bacon, *Spurgeon: Heir of the Puritans* (1967), 144.

the era of Smiles's *Lives of the Engineers* (1874) and of 'the march of mind —the steamship, and the railway, and the thoughts that shake mankind'. Intrusively, but emphatically, Nonconformity insists on its survival, despite the author.[1]

---

[1] *A Laodicean* (1881), Bk. 1, Ch. 11.

# APPENDIX

Extract from Charlotte Brontë's MS. 'Julia' (29 June 1837) (property of the Miriam Lutcher Stark Library, University of Texas): her parody of the *Methodist Magazine.*[1]

[18] In the vicinity of Evesham, about three miles, out of the town, stands a remarkably pretty little building quite new, with its pointed front turned towards the road and in the centre a large window—It rises against the sky from a group of old trees, a monument of the successful labours of Mr. Bromley—[Pro] That great apostle of methodism, committing the superintendence of the Verdopolitan circuits to his fellow-labourers in the Gospel— Messr Simpson, Barlow and Chadwick—set out \about ten months ago/ on a mission to that benighted district lying immediately east on the borders of Sinegambia[?] For a full detail—of all his persecutions trials, temptations &c. as well \as/ of his successes and conquests I refer the reader to the last six numbers of [The] our Magazine from December to June inclusive.—Truly he suffered much—the sword of the flesh was unsheathed against him—yet in spite of almost universal opposition [the bles] his endeavours finally prevailed for the blessing of the Lord was upon them. I would [refer] particularly direct the reader's attention. to the last letter received from him by our Superintendent—In the case of the late William Rhodes Esq^r of Orchard-Gate. it gives an awful instance of God's judgement upon the wicked. That Gentleman was one of the most [ ] \determined/ opposers of Methodism in the whole country—The following extract from Mr. Barlow's Journal will sufficiently testify the violence of his persecuting spirit.

'Twelve o'clock. midnight. May 18^th—I have had a day of conflicts—but he that brought the three children unharmed out of the fiery furnace, and delivered David [sic] safe from the Lions- Den, hath likewise rescued me, his darling from the power of the Dog.', This morning Thomas Dun came to me with the intelligence

---

[1] The numbers in square brackets are the notebook page numbers. Square brackets indicate illegible deletions or contain legible ones. Caret marks contain insertions.

that we should never be able to hold [the camp] \our/ meeting
—for that Mr Rhodes had threatened Jones who was his tenant
with expulsion if he [   ] \lent/ his wharehouse for the purpose
—direct inspiration from heaven furnished me with an answer to
this difficulty—'Thomas, said I fetch the steward & three of the
class-leaders—and we will go up to Orchard-Gate & try the power of
the word upon that man. of sin. Thomas sent away and soon returned
[19] with John Butler, Reuben Ash, Charles Whitehall and Samuel
Clay—After we had sung an hymn & prayed we set out—I think
it might be about two o'clock when we arrived at the house
knocking civilly at the back-door  I asked of the servant who
opened it if Mr Rhodes were at home—he replied 'Yes'. 'Then'
said I 'Go tell your master that six men stand without desiring to
speak with him'  The man stared but did as I desired—ere long he
returned with the answer that Mr. Rhodes was at dinner and
could not for the present be inter[fered with] \rupted/—'We
can wait' said & I each of us taking a chair we sat in a circle round
the hall—It was the [second course] servant's hall, and they were
arranging dinner upon the table—as I watched them bringing in
first a tureen of soup & then a leg of pork & then a pie, vegetables
&c. a voice came unto me 'arise and eat'—'Thy will be done' I
answered aloud & getting up I came towards the table. 'With your
leave said I to a maid who was standing by' 'I will take a bason of
that broth'—She made no attempt to help me so I took the ladle
and served myself—I had no sooner finished this than the voice I
had heard before came again & I felt I stood in the situation of
Elijah who as he lay under the juniper tree was again & again
bidden to arise & eat—obeying the Supernatural impulse I cut in
to the pie, & helping myself to greens, took such sustenance as
the body needed—Then whispered my inward monitor 'Give unto
the men that are with [th] thee, So shaving a few slices off the leg
of pork and adding [greens] \turnips/ I passed it round. The
maid, the only person who stood in the hall looked greedily at the
servants'—'I made her no answer but falling on my knees went
to prayer—. It was a time of peculiar freedom. I felt priviledged to
wrestle with God and to cry out importunately and insist upon the
acceptance of my petitions—O! Lord!' said I 'I will have what I
want—I will take the gates of thy favour by storm—thy great
cause shall prosper, it [h] must—Ride on thou most Mighty &
crush thine enemies before thee—the great oppressor shall be

trodden underfoot, the proud man shall be brought down and choked in his swollen insolence—I spoke loud—my words were fervent & so were the groans & responses of my friends, we drank of the living-waters flowing from above as we had (which I forgot to mention) a few minutes before, drank two Gallons of mellow old ale which stood on the table. Whilst we thus strove with God in the midst of the footmen & maids who had flocked in from the kitchen & stood staring at us as if we were wild beasts, a bell rung violently just above us. a footman ran to answer it as he opened an [20] inner voice [sic] we heard rough & angry voice exlaim—'what the d——l is that d——d noise. Who is making it?' The Methodist Preachers Sir' answered the man 'They've eat up all our dinner & drank eights quarts of ale & now they're praying— 'Praying! be hanged to them' was the answer. 'Kick them every one out this minute James   Kick them out I say or I'll send you after them'. These brutal words were scarcely out of Mr Rhodes' mouth when we were set upon by three great, strong men who I'll take my oath before any magistrate attempted to stick us with the [kniVes] knives they snatched off the table—the steward & the three class-leaders were hustled out of the house speedily—but I escaping rushed towards the dining-room—I burst open the door and dashed in leaning upon the rod & staff which even in this hour of trial continued to comfort me. There I saw one of the dens [?] which Satan in this world often gives to his worshippers—pampering them with magnificence here, ere he sends them [hereafter] to lament in the burning vaults of hell \hereafter/— It was a long room & there were pictures in gold-frames all down the walls—the side-board groaned under plate & glass & the large table in the centre glittered with decanters of cut crystal, full of wine & plates of gilt china heaped with fruit—There was Mrs Rhodes at the [at the head] \at the head/, in silks & satins & jewels & feathers [at the foot]—& down the sides were their sons & daughters with several guests all dressed in the worldlings flare & frippery. Blessed be my maker I was not shaken either by the multitude or the Sodomitish appearance of my adversaries—I calmly advanced & taking out my pocket-bible & holding it forth in my right hand—I commenced with a loud clear voice—Go to now Ye rich men! Howl & cry for your miseries that are come upon you—' Mr Rhodes broke \out/ violently [upon me] with a profane oath 'Sacriligeous scoundrel.' cried he 'How dare you come here the arrogant insolence of your craft is not unknown to me, but it won't tell sir—it won't tell—I'll have you washed like wool under the pump before you leave my house' I opposed his brutality by a mild and steady demeanour—'William Rhodes' said I 'You call yourself a magistrate, a guardian of the morals of the land—I fine you five shillings for that oath you have uttered. I shall lay information against you'—He answered me by some abuse which I do not think it worth my while to repeat—' I [   ] quietly proceeded 'You will not live long I know you will not—you have nearly filled the measure of your iniquity—repent then while it is yet day—even at the eleventh hour there may be hope—I [warn] exhort you in all brotherly kindness, my bowels yearn toward you —the [cri] crimes you have committed are black, are double-dyed but the Lord's mercy knoweth no limits—' Mrs Rhodes started up trembling & livid with rage 'I cannot bear it' she said 'What emboldens this wretch to speak so to my husband—? 'Woman!' I [21] answered part of my mission is also to you—Cover your head with ashes & sit down & weep—you shall oppress the Lord's saints no longer—& you young women the daughters of them that have grown grey in wickedness—put of that immodest dress & those neck-chains, & those love-tokens & those rings for the ears & for the hands—& clothe yourselves with sackcloth & seek the Ditch & the out-house for your home'—Mr Rhodes hand was now on my mouth, he was as white as a sheet, he called as if frantic for his servants—they came open-mouthed like bulls of Bashan, I was delivered into their hands, & what I suffered after it baffles language to descripe [sic] I was scourged   I was dragged through a horse-pond   I was drowned under a deluge from the pump—Nay I have good reason to believe that [pistols] more than one \pistol/ [were] was discharged at my \head/—but I survived all & by the blessing of God was \that/ night able to make a hearty supper & to sleep as soundly as ever I did in my life. My master avenged me in his own good time about a fortnight after I saw the dead body of Rhodes dragged out of his house & with the rope that he had been hung with still round his neck—I beheld him flung into that very horse-pond where by his orders I had \been/ nearly [? run] murdered.

But this digression has led me away from the subject with which I commenced—I was speaking of a little chapel, whose white front

looks upon a lowly part of the road [between] leading from Evesham—west-wards as I said before—this little sanctuary had
sprung up in the wilderness—the first shrine of a new religion and
the first monument to the labours of our great-Apostle—It was
Tuesday evening, on the next day four sermons were to be preached
within its walls & four collections to be made to defray the expenses
of its erection—Mr Broadbent our Steward had requested—me to
walk up & see that all was right—I had just completed my survey—
seen that the \penitential/ benches were properly placed & that
the \hamper of/ wine, spirits cold meat & bread & cheese &c
had been conveyed into the vestry according to directions given
in the morning—for our preachers proposed to work hard the
next day & it was necessary that [ ] support should be provided
for the flesh I had just I say looked to these little matters an [sic]
was locking the chapel door—when a voice said to me 'Townshend
how are you'. . . .[1]

[1] Cf. Winifred Gérin's astonishingly inaccurate transcription of parts of this manuscript story in her *Charlotte Brontë, The Evolution of Genius* (Oxford, 1967; paperback
reprint, 1969), 121–3.

# BIBLIOGRAPHICAL NOTES

The footnotes reveal the sources—of all kinds—of my information. The following are, however, indications of the more important primary materials.

## MANUSCRIPT MATERIALS

Charlotte's manuscript story 'Julia' is in the Miriam Lutcher Stark Library of the University of Texas. The British Museum has George Eliot's fair copy of *Adam Bede* (B.M. Addit. MSS. 34,020–34,022): valuable to the researcher only for the dedicatory fly-leaf note to George Henry Lewes. George Eliot's notebook for *Felix Holt* (known as the 'Quarry') and her Journal for 1854–61 are in the Beinecke Library of Yale University. The Brotherton Library, Leeds, has diaries of Edmund Gosse (for 1857) and of his mother (1849–55, and 1854)

I used the copy of the *Household Words* Contributors' Book typed and indexed by K. J. Fielding and deposited in the English Faculty Library, Oxford. Much of the information about the reaction to Cromwell in the nineteenth century came from a mass of duplicated typescript material, collected by several researchers, for the abortive Oxford *Past and Present* nineteenth-century Cromwell project (I own a set of this material). Details about William Hale White's family at Colchester came from the record books of the Lion Walk Congregational Church, Colchester ('No. 1 Book: Members 1702–1839; Baptisms 1764–1785; Burials 1767–1840'; 'No. 2 Book: Baptisms 1785–1828'—both deposited at the church), and details about the White family at Bedford from the 'Act Book of the Bunyan Meeting, Bedford, Vol II, 1820, &c' (kept at the church).

Simon Nowell-Smith let me see the Hale White material in his possession: letters and notes of William Hale White, and the copies made by the second Mrs. Hale White of letters and notes, and of her husband's 'Black Notebook' and 'White Notebook'. The very large cache of unclassified Hale White materials deposited in two suitcases in the Bedford Public Library includes the following MS. material relevant to my topic:

Letters to and from W. H. W.

Letter from W. H. W. to William White *re* meeting with New College Committee (6 Mar. 1852).

Letters from and to William White, and one to W. H. W., *re* the expulsions (including W. White to Thomas Binney, and Mrs. Binney's apology for her sick husband's non-intervention (16 Feb. 1852)).

Books and articles annotated in hand of W. H. W., including Rev. J. M. Rodwell, *The Book of Job: translated from the Hebrew* (2nd ed., 1868).

Letters to W. White, concerning *To Think or Not to Think?*, including one from John Jukes (8 Apr. 1853).

Copy by D. V. White of W. H. W's draft of letter to Dr. Harris, Principal of New College (23 Feb. 1852).

Copy of Schedule of Faith for Tutors and Students of New College: in hand of R. M. Theobald.

Letter from W. R. Nicoll to Dr. W. Hale White (15 May 1914).

Notes by Dr. W. H. White for Massingham's entry in *DNB*. on W.H.W.

Dr. W. Hale White, *Notes about W. Hale White* (*Mark Rutherford*), includes extracts from the novelist's mother's diaries, made by W.H.W., 1932): two typewritten copies (top-copy and carbon-copy) and the manuscript (in Red Notebook and in Private Notes).

(Typescript) *Comments made upon Sir James Fitzjames Stephen's Book 'Liberty, Fraternity', by William Hale White (Mark Rutherford),* annotated by his second son.

(Typescript) *William Hale White: 'Mark Rutherford' 1831–1931: Extracts from Letters written to his second son and his second son's wife.*

The Bodleian Library has (MSS. Eng. Misc. c. 445–447):
(Typescript) *William Hale White: 'Mark Rutherford', 1831–1931, Notes by His Second Son* (Geneva, Feb. 1931).

(Typescript) *William Hale White: 'Mark Rutherford', 1831–1931, Extracts from Letters written to his second son and his second son's wife.*

(Typescript) *William Hale White (Mark Rutherford). Correspondence with Thomas Hutchinson. Notes by His Second Son* [1934].

SPECIAL COLLECTIONS OF PRINTED MATERIALS

The two suitcases of Hale White material in Bedford Public Library mentioned above also contain the following:

Several *Scrapbooks* of newspaper cuttings, collected by W.H.W.
*Press Cuttings 1931–2*
Pamphlets, including: White, William. *The Bedford Charity Not Sectarian* (Bedford, 1844).
>    White, William, *To Think or Not to Think?* (1852).
>    Theobald, R. M., *Expulsion of Students* (Paris, Oct. 1852).
>    Morris, Caleb, *The Bible and the Poor* (6th Thousand, 1849).
>    Coombs, Alderman, M.D., J. P., *Recollections, Personal and Political* (Bedford, 1899).
3 paste-up volumes of the *Illustrated Times* articles that constitute W. White, *The Inner Life of the House of Commons*, ed. J. McCarthy (2 vols., 1897).
Klinke, Hans, *William Hale White (Mark Rutherford): Versuch einer Biographie* (Frankfurt am Oder, 1930).

Bodley's John Johnson Collection includes several boxes and folders of enormously interesting religious material: in boxes ('Religion': 13, 14, 15, 17, 17a, 19, 19a, 20, 27); in small folders ('Salvation Army'; 'Pietistic', I.II.III; 'Religious'; and 'Ecclesiastical', I.II.III); in a large folder ('Pietistic Large'). Bodley's Pettingell Collection of (uncatalogued) popular nineteenth-century fiction has several of the Dickens parodies in it. The Coventry City Reference Library has material relevant to George Eliot, namely: The Lowe Collection of Newscuttings; *George Eliot, 1818–1919: A Record of the Centenary Celebrations Held at Coventry, November 1919*, Collected, Mounted and Arranged by Joseph Sidwell (Coventry, 1920); and an interleaved and annotated copy of John Sibree and M. Caston, *Independency in Warwickshire: A Brief History of the Independent or Congregational Churches in the County* (Coventry, 1855). The Nottingham City Public Libraries also have material relating to George Eliot, most important of which is the Methodist broadsheet tract by Henry Taft: *An Account of the Experience and Happy Death of Mary Voce, who was Executed on Nottingham Gallows, on Tuesday, March 16, 1802, for the Murder of Her Own Child*.

A number of relevant Methodist documents (including Z. Taft, *Biographical Sketches . . . of Various Holy Women* (2 vols., 1825–8), which George Eliot thought not to exist) are in the Methodist Archives and

Research Centre, Epworth House, 25–35 City Road, London, E.C.1.
I have found other useful sectarian books, periodicals, and records in
the Oxford libraries of Regent's Park College (the Angus Library),
Mansfield College, and Manchester College.

BIBLIOGRAPHIES

Apart from the usual, and of course extremely valuable, *New Cambridge
Bibliography*, I have found the following bibliographies very helpful:

ANDERSON, J. P., GE Bibliography, Appendix to BROWNING,
    OSCAR, *Life of George Eliot* (1890).
COGHILL, MRS. HARRY, List of Mrs. Oliphant's articles in *Black-
    wood's*, appended to the 2nd ed. of *The Autobiography and Letters of
    M. O. W. Oliphant* (Edinburgh, 1899), 441–51.
DAVIS, W. E., 'William Hale White ("Mark Rutherford"): An Anno-
    tated Bibliography of Writings About Him', *ELT*, 10 (1967),
    97–117; 150–60.
KITTON, F. G., *Dickensiana: a Bibliography of the Literature Relating to
    Charles Dickens and His Writings* (1886).
——, *The Novels of Charles Dickens* (1897).
——, *The Minor Writings of Charles Dickens* (1900).
MILLER, W., *The Dickens Student and Collector: a List of Writings
    Relating to Charles Dickens and His Works 1836–1945* (1946).
NORTHUP, C. S., Bibliography for Mrs. Gaskell, in SANDERS, G. DE
    W., *Elizabeth Gaskell* (New Haven, 1929), 163–262.
RIVLIN, J. B., 'Harriet Martineau: a bibliography of the separately
    printed books' *BNYPL.*, 50 (May–July, Oct. 1946); 51 (Jan.
    1947).
SMITH, SIMON NOWELL, *Mark Rutherford: Short Bibliography of the First
    Editions* (1930).
SPIELMANN, M. H., *The Hitherto Unidentified Contributions of W. M.
    Thackeray to 'Punch'* (1899).
STONE, W. H., Bibliography for W. Hale White, *Religion and Art of
    William Hale White ('Mark Rutherford')* (Stanford, Calif., 1954).
STONEHOUSE, J. H. (ed.), *Reprints of the Catalogues of the Libraries of
    Charles Dickens and W. M. Thackeray* (1935).
WHITFIELD, A. S., Bibliography for Mrs. Gaskell (to 1928): *Mrs.
    Gaskell: Her Life and Works* (1929), Appendix III, 228–53.

NOVELS

The following is a list of the Victorian novels that are discussed or mentioned in this book (the list excludes earlier and later novels):

ACKWORTH, JOHN (FREDERICK R. SMITH), *Clogshop Chronicles* (1896).

AINSWORTH, WILLIAM HARRISON, *December Tales* (1823).

——, *Mervyn Clitheroe* (1858). Originally published as *Life and Adventures of Mervyn Clitheroe* (1851–8).

ANON, *Rosa Fielding, Or, A Victim of Lust* (1876).

BANKS, MRS. G. LINNAEUS, *The Manchester Man* (3 vols., 1876).

BARR, AMELIA, *The Hallam Succession: A Tale of Methodist Life in Two Counties* (1885).

——, *Friend Olivia* (1890).

BORROW, GEORGE, *Lavengro: the Scholar, The Gypsy, the Priest* (3 vols., 1851).

BRONTË, ANNE, *Agnes Grey: a novel*, by Acton Bell (published as vol. 3 with *Wuthering Heights*, 1847).

BRONTË, CHARLOTTE, *Jane Eyre: an autobiography*, edited by Currer Bell (3 vols., 1847); with Dedication and Preface (1848); ed. and introduced by Q. D. Leavis (Penguin, 1966); ed. Jane Jack and Margaret Smith (Oxford, 1969).

——, *Shirley: a tale*, by Currer Bell (3 vols., 1849).

——, *Villette*, by Currer Bell (3 vols., 1853).

——, *The Professor: a tale*, by Currer Bell (2 vols., 1857).

——, *The Twelve Adventures and other stories*, ed. C. W. Hatfield (1925).

——, *Legends of Angria: compiled from the early writings of Charlotte Brontë*, ed. F. E. Ratchford and W. C. De Vane (New Haven, 1933).

——, *The Miscellaneous and Unpublished Writings of Charlotte and Patrick Branwell Brontë*, ed. T. J. Wise and J. A. Symington (2 vols., Oxford, 1936–8).

——, [J. R. Geer], 'An Unpublished Manuscript by Charlotte Brontë', *BST*. 15 (1966), 20–7.

BRONTË, EMILY JANE, *Wuthering Heights: a novel*, by Ellis Bell (2 vols., 1847); Foreword by Geoffrey Moore (Signet, 1959); ed. T. C. Moser (New York, 1962).

——, *The Tenant of Wildfell Hall*, by Acton Bell (3 Vols., 1848).

BRONTË, CHARLOTTE, EMILY, and ANNE, *Wuthering Heights* and *Agnes Grey*, by Ellis and Acton Bell: A new edition revised, with A

Biographical Notice of the Authors, A Selection from their literary remains, and a Preface, by Currer Bell (1850).

——, *Life and Works of Charlotte Brontë and Her Sisters*, Illustrated Edition, 7 vols., 1872–3.

CLIFFORD, JOHN, *George Mostyn: the Story of a Young Pilgrim Warrior* (1874). Originally published as 'Familiar Talks with Young Christians', *General Baptist Magazine* (1872).

COLLINS, WILLIAM WILKIE, *The Woman in White* (*All the Year Round*, from 26 Nov. 1859; 3 vols., 1860; corrected, 1861).

CROCKETT, S. R., *The Stickit Minister, and Some Common Men* (1893).

DAWSON, REV. WILLIAM JAMES, *The Redemption of Edward Strachan: a Social Story* (1891).

DICKENS, CHARLES, *The Posthumous Papers of the Pickwick Club* (Apr. 1836–Nov. 1837).

——, *The Life and Adventures of Nicholas Nickleby* (Apr. 1838–Oct. 1839).

——, *The Old Curiosity Shop* (25 Apr. 1840–6 Feb. 1841).

——, *Barnaby Rudge* (13 Feb. 1841–27 Nov. 1841).

——, *Dombey and Son* (Oct. 1846–Apr. 1848).

——, *David Copperfield* (May 1849–Nov. 1850).

——, *Bleak House* (Mar. 1852–Sept. 1853).

——, *Hard Times, for These Times* (*Household Words*, 1 Apr.–12 Aug. 1854).

——, *Little Dorrit* (Dec. 1855–June 1857).

——, *A Tale of Two Cities* (*All the Year Round*, 30 Apr.–26 Nov. 1859; and in parts June–Dec. 1859).

——, *Great Expectations* (*All the Year Round*, 1 Dec. 1860–3 Aug. 1861).

——, *Our Mutual Friend* (May 1864–Nov. 1865).

——, 'The Lazy Tour of Two Idle Apprentices' (with Wilkie Collins), *Household Words*, 3–31 Oct. 1857).

——, 'The Haunted House' (Extra Christmas No., 1859, *All the Year Round*, 2 (1860).

——, *The Uncommercial Traveller* (1861).

——, 'George Silverman's Explanation', *Atlantic Monthly*, Jan.–Mar. 1867; reprinted in *All the Year Round*, 19 (1867–8), Nos. 458, 460, 462 (1, 15, 29 Feb. 1868).

DISRAELI, BENJAMIN, *Contarini Fleming: a Psychological Autobigraphy* (4 vols., 1832).

——, *Coningsby: or The New Generation* (3 vols., 1844); Foreword, Asa Briggs (Signet, 1962).

——, *Sybil: or The Two Nations* (3 vols., 1845).

——, *Tancred: or The New Crusade* (3 vols., 1847).

ELIOT, GEORGE (Marian Evans), *Scenes of Clerical Life* (2 vols., Edinburgh, 1858). Originally published in *Blackwood's* ('Janet's Repentance', *Blackwood's* July–Nov. 1857).

——, *Adam Bede* (3 vols., Edinburgh, 1859).

——, *Silas Marner: the Weaver of Raveloe* (Edinburgh, 1861).

——, *Felix Holt, the Radical* (3 vols., Edinburgh, 1866); introduced by F. R. Leavis (Everyman, 1966).

——, *Middlemarch: a Study of Provincial Life* (4 vols., Edinburgh, 1872).

EVANS, HOWARD, *From Serfdom to Manhood: a Story of Agricultural Life* (Leamington [1875]). Reprinted from the *Labourer's Union Chronicle*.

FLETCHER, ELIZABETH SOPHIA (Mrs. Robert Watson), *Building Her House: (A Religious Tale)* (1881).

GASKELL, (MRS.) ELIZABETH CLEGHORN, 'Life in Manchester', by Cotton Mather Mills, Esq., *Howitt's Journal of Literature and Popular Progress* (5, 12, 19 June, 1847).

——, *Mary Barton: a tale of Manchester Life* (2 vols., 1848); edited and introduced by Stephen Gill (Penguin, 1970).

——, *Ruth: a novel* (3 vols., 1853).

——, *Cranford* (*Household Words*, 13 Dec.–21 May 1853).

——, *North and South* (*Household Words*, 2 Sep. 1854–27 Jan. 1855).

——, 'My Lady Ludlow', *Household Words* (19 June–25 Sept. 1858).

——, *Round the Sofa* (1859), includes 'My Lady Ludlow', and 'An Accursed Race' (*Household Words*, 25 Aug. 1855).

——, *Right at Last and Other Tales* (1860), includes 'A Manchester Marriage' (*Household Words*, Christmas No., 1858) and 'Lois the Witch' (*All the Year Round*, Oct. 8–22, 1859).

——, *Sylvia's Lovers* (3 vols., 1863).

——, *Cousin Phillis: a tale*, *Cornhill Magazine* (Nov. 1863–Feb. 1864); *Cousin Phillis and other tales* (1865).

——, *Wives and Daughters: An Every-day Story*, *Cornhill Magazine* (Aug. 1864–Jan. 1866). Last part completed by F. Greenwood. 2 vols. (1866); ed. F. G. Smith, introduced by Laurence Lerner (Penguin, 1969).

GOSSE, WILLIAM EDMUND, *The Unequal Yoke* (anon., *The English Illustrated Magazine*, Nos. 31–3, Apr.–June 1886).

HARDY, THOMAS, *Far from the Madding Crowd* (*Cornhill Magazine*, Jan.–Dec. 1874).

——, *The Return of the Native* (*Belgravia*, Jan.–Dec. 1878).

——, *A Laodicean* (*Harper's New Monthly Mag.*, Dec. 1880–Dec. 1881).

——, *Wessex Tales: strange, lively, and commonplace* (2 vols., 1888), including 'The Distracted Preacher' (*New Quarterly Magazine*, N.S. 1, 1879).

——, *Tess of the d'Urbervilles: a Pure Woman Faithfully Presented* (*Graphic*, 4 July–26 Dec. 1891, omitting some chapters: for details see *New Cambridge Biblio.*, III, Cols. 982–3); (3 vols., 1891; revised, 1892).

HOCKING, JOSEPH, *Harry Penhale: the Trial of His Faith* (1887).

——, *Jabez Easterbrook: a religious novel* (1890).

HOCKING, SILAS KITTO, *Her Benny: a tale of Street Life* (*United Methodist Free Churches' Magazine*, 22, 1879).

——, *Tales of a Tin Mine* (1898).

HUGHES, THOMAS, *Tom Brown at Oxford* (3 vols., Cambridge, 1861).

KEELING, ANNIE E., *The Oakhurst Chronicles: a tale of the times of Wesley* (1883).

KINGSLEY, CHARLES, *Yeast: a Problem* (*Fraser's Magazine* (July–Dec. 1848); 1851).

——, *Alton Locke, tailor and poet: an autobiography* (2 vols., 1850; with Preface addressed to the working-men of Great Britain, 1856; with a new Preface To the Undergraduates of Cambridge, 1862; with a Prefatory Memoir by Thomas Hughes, 1876).

——, *Westward Ho!* (3 vols., Cambridge, 1855).

——, *Two Years Ago: a Novel* (3 vols., Cambridge, 1857).

MACDONALD, GEORGE, *David Elginbrod* (3 vols., 1863).

MACLAREN, IAN (Rev. Dr. John Watson), *Beside the Bonnie Brier Bush* (1894).

MARTINEAU, HARRIET, *Principle and Practice: or the orphan family. A tale* (Wellington, Salop., 1827).

MOORE, GEORGE, *Esther Waters: a novel* (1894; revised 1889; revised, 1920; revised, 1926).

NEWMAN, J. H., *Loss and Gain* (1848; 1853).

OLIPHANT, (MRS.) MARGARET OLIPHANT [Wilson], *Passages in the Life of Mrs. Margaret Maitland of Sunnyside*, Written by Herself (3 vols., 1849).

——, *Magdalen Hepburn: a Story of the Scottish Reformation* (3 vols., 1854).

——, *Lilliesleaf: being a Concluding Series of Passages in the Life of Mrs. Margaret Maitland of Sunnyside* (3 vols., 1855).

——, *Salem Chapel* (*Blackwood's* Feb. 1862–Jan. 1863; 2 vols., Edinburgh, 1863; new ed., 1 vol., 1863); introduced by W. R. Nicoll (Everyman, 1907): drawing heavily on *The Nonconformist*, 23 (Feb. 25, 1863).

——, *The Perpetual Curate* (*Blackwood's* June 1863–Sept. 1864; 3 vols., Edinburgh, 1864).

——, *A Son of the Soil* (2 vols., 1866).

——, *The Minister's Wife* (3 vols., 1869).

——, *Phoebe, Junior: a Last Chronicle of Carlingford* (3 vols., 1876).

PARKER, JOSEPH, *Springdale Abbey: extracts from the Diaries and Letters of an English Preacher* (1868).

PEARSE, MARK GUY, *Daniel Quorm, and His Religious Notions. First Series* (1875).

RANDS, WILLIAM BRIGHTY, *The Frost Upon the Pane: a Christmas Story* (1854).

——, *Henry Holbeach, Student in Life and Philosophy: a Narrative and a Discussion*, by Henry Holbeach (2 vols., 1865).

REYNOLDS, HENRY ROBERT & JOHN RUSSELL, *Yes and No: or, Glimpses of the Great Conflict* (3 vols., 1860).

ROBINSON, FREDERICK WILLIAM, *Church and Chapel* (3 vols., 1863).

SCARGILL, WILLIAM PITT, *The Autobiography of a Dissenting Minister* (1834).

STICKNEY, SARAH (later Mrs. Sarah Stickney Ellis), *Pictures of Private Life* (1833).

THACKERAY, WILLIAM MAKEPEACE, *Vanity Fair: Pen and Pencil Sketches of English Society* (Jan. 1847–July 1848); *Vanity Fair: a novel without a Hero* (1848).

——, *The Newcomes: Memoirs of a Most Respectable Family*, edited by Arthur Pendennis, Esqre (Oct. 1853—Aug. 1855; 2 vols., 1854–5).

THOMPSON, JEMIMA (Mrs. Samuel Luke), *The Female Jesuit: or, the the Spy in the Family* (1851).

——, *A Sequel to the Female Jesuit* (1852).

TROLLOPE, ANTHONY, *The Warden* (1855).

——, *The Small House at Allington* (*Cornhill Magazine*, Sept. 1862–Apr. 1864; 2 vols., 1864).

——, *Miss Mackenzie* (2 vols., 1865).

——, *The Vicar of Bullhampton* (July 1869–May 1870; 1870).

——, *John Caldigate* (*Blackwood's*, Apr. 1878–June 1879; 3 vols., 1879).

TROLLOPE, MRS. FRANCES, *The Vicar of Wrexhill* (3 vols., 1837).

WHITE, WILLIAM HALE ('Mark Rutherford'; all six novels are 'by Mark Rutherford, edited by his friend Reuben Shapcott'), *The Autobiography of Mark Rutherford, Dissenting Minister* (1881).

——, *Mark Rutherford's Deliverance: being the Second Part of His Autobiography* (1885).

WHITE, WILLIAM HALE, *The Autobiography of Mark Rutherford and Mark Rutherford's Deliverance* (1888), second edn., corrected and with additions; introduced by Basil Willey (Leicester, 1969).

——, *The Revolution in Tanner's Lane* (1887).

——, *Miriam's Schooling and Other Papers* (1890).

——, *Catharine Furze* (2 vols., 1893). (The cheap one-vol. copy issued by T. Fisher Unwin has on title-page and cover *Catherine Furze*: the contents, from original plates, have *Catharine*.)

——, *Clara Hopgood* (1896). (*Pages from a Journal* (1900), *More Pages* (1910), and *Last Pages* (1915), also contain fictional material.)

WOOD, MRS. HENRY, *East Lynne* (3 vols., 1861).

# INDEX

Ackworth, John, 61, 74, 279
Addison, Joseph, 221
Ainsworth, William Harrison, 57 f., 74, 172 (n. 2), 194
*All the Year Round*, 14 (n. 4), 34, 195
Alleyne, Joseph, 175, 177
Anstey, Christopher, 220 f.
Arch, Joseph, 11–12, 73 (n. 2), 92 f., 99
*Aris's Birmingham Gazette*, 77
*Arminian Magazine*, 163 (See also *Methodist Magazine*)
Arminian Methodists (Derby Faith Folk), 26, 44, 72, 145
Arminianism, 6, 44, 47, 63 ff., 91, 124, 149, 155, 165, 184, 219, 252, 261
Arnold, Matthew, 21, 53 f., 58, 67, 84, 108, 130, 178 ff., 200 f., 207 f., 239, 243, 254, 256 (n. 7), 262; *Culture and Anarchy*, 13, 21, 54, 178, 180 ff., 204, 254
Arnold, Thomas, 84
Ashby, Joseph, 284
Ashton, Thomas, 132
Ashworth, Edmund, 89
*Athenaeum*, 76, 199, 222 f., 261 (n. 1)
Austen, Jane, 142
Aykroyd, Tabitha ('Tabby'), 107 f., 116, 120 f.

Bagehot, Walter, 207
Baines, Edward, 67, 76, 103, 104 (n. 3)
Bamford, Samuel, 2
Band Room Methodists, 26
*Baptist Handbook*, 230
*Baptist Magazine*, 57 (n. 1), 93
Baptist Missionary Society, 12, 184
Baptists, 12, 28, 31, 39, 43, 45 ff., 52, 54, 60, 71, 74 f., 77, 84, 86, 88, 92 ff., 97, 101 ff., 108 ff., 115, 123, 146, 183 ff., 192, 197, 200 ff., 209 f., 224 f., 226 (n. 3), 230, 280, 282 f., 285 (See also: General Baptists; General Baptist New Connexion; Particular Baptists; Scotch Baptists; Seventh-Day Baptists; Strict and Particular Baptists; Suffolk and Norfolk New Association of Strict Baptists)

Barker, Joseph, 38, 42, 44 (n. 1), 94 f.
Barr, Amelia, 42, 61, 63, 73
Bastow, Henry Robert, 110–12
Baxter, Richard, 163, 177, 185, 188, 208, 261
Bayley, J. O., 5 f., 8
Beadnell, Maria, 197
Bennett, Arnold, 56 (n. 4), 255
Betjeman, John, 87
*Bible Christian Magazine*, 60
Bible Christians (See Bryanites)
Bickerstaffe, Isaac, 15, 220 ff., 224
Binney, Thomas, 18, 58 (n. 1), 211 ff., 251 f., 257, 264, 270, 275 ff.
Birch, A. S. O., 81
*Birmingham Journal*, 11
Birrell, Augustine, 214, 266
*Bitter Cry of Outcast London*, 81
Black Bartholomew's Day: 1862 Bicentenary, 33, 182 f., 239, 270
Black, William Henry, 177, 188, 209 (See also Seventh-Day Baptists)
*Blackwood's Magazine*, 2, 23, 178 f., 196, 225 (n. 2), 231 ff., 245
Booth, Catherine, 99
Booth, Charles, 19, 54, 71, 81, 202, 283
Booth, Mrs. Charles (née Mary Macaulay), 132
Booth, William, 40, 72, 81, 226 (n. 3), 245, 283
Borrow, George, 59, 101
Bosanquet, Mary (See Fletcher, Mrs. John)
Boston, Thomas, 49, 56, 260
Bourne, Hugh, v, 26, 44, 92
Branwell, Elizabeth, 48, 107, 116
Branwell, Maria (See Brontë, Mrs. Patrick)
Bray, Billy, 40, 61
Bray, Charles, 146 f., 156
Brethren (See Plymouth Brethren)
Brianites (See Bryanites),
Bright, John, 20, 89, 92, 270
Bristol Tent Methodists, 26
British and Foreign Unitarian Association, 40 (n. 1), 141
British Anti-State-Church Association, 182, 187 (See also Liberation Society)

British Israelites, 32
*British Quarterly Review*, 18, 52 f., 58 f., 133 f., 171 (n. 1), 178, 181, 210, 213, 230
*British Weekly*, 33, 41 (n. 1), 54 (n. 5), 62, 201 (n. 1), 236, 251 (n. 3), 252 (n. 1), 261 (n. 1), 264 (n. 2), 275 (n. 2)
Brontë, Anne, 114 ff.; *Agnes Grey*, 125; *Tenant of Wildfell Hall*, 118
Brontë Branwell, 105, 115 ff., 215–17, 223
Brontë, Charlotte, 50, 105, 114 ff., 138, 165, 216 f., 278; *Jane Eyre*, 15, 58, 108, 119, 125, 191, 235 f.; *Shirley*, 14, 41, 50, 63, 74, 86, 98, 105, 109, 116 ff., 203 f., 207, 209 ff., 215 ff.; *Villette*, 124; *The Professor*, 125 (n. 5), 210; MS. 'Julia', 116 f.; 287–91; other juvenilia, 116 ff., 203 f., 215–17, 278
Brontë children, 59, 63, 73, 105, 112, 113–26, 215
Brontë, Emily, 114 ff., 138; *Wuthering Heights*, 11, 23, 63, 115, 119 f., 123 ff., 217
Brontë, Patrick, 105, 107 f., 109, 113 ff.
Brontë, Mrs. Patrick (née Maria Branwell), 107, 114 ff.
Brook Street Unitarian Chapel, Knutsford, 127 f.
Brooke, Henry, 52
Brotherton, Joseph, 90
Brown, Hugh Stowell, 268
Brown, James Baldwin, 46
Brown, John, 271, 273, 275 ff.
Brown, William, 91
Browning, Robert, 2, 194, 206 f.; 'Christmas Eve', 74 f., 210
Brownists, 172 f.
Bryanites (or Brianites, or Bible Christians), 23, 26, 36 f., 40, 43 f., 66, 70, 74, 76, 90, 98, 210, 226 (n. 3), 280
Bulkley, Peter, 260 ff., 264
Bunting, Jabez, 92, 95 ff., 105, 114, 119, 159
Bunyan, John, 10, 71, 254, 257, 261, 268; *Pilgrim's Progress*, 52, 54, 80, 160, 163, 185
Burdsall, Dicky, 42
Burnett, Henry, 191 ff.
Burnett, Mrs. Henry (née Fanny Dickens), 108, 191 ff.
Burns, Robert, 220, 223
Butler, Samuel, 144 (n. 5)

Byron, Lord George Gordon, 255 f., 272
Cadman, Elijah, 40
Calvinism, 6, 22, 28, 44 ff., 63 ff., 91, 108 f., 113, 144, 149, 155, 175, 182 ff., 219, 252, 259 ff., 264, 267 f., 278, 280
Calvinistic Methodists, 47, 219 (See also Whitefield, George, and Countess of Huntingdon's Connexion—under Huntingdon)
Cambridge University, 20
Campbell, J., 52 f.
Campbell, R. J., 100
Capper, Joseph, 97
Carlyle, Thomas, 2, 11, 29, 76, 79, 178 ff., 233, 268, 276
Catholic Apostolic Church (See Irvingites)
Cazamian, Louis, 109 (n. 7), 134
Censuses of Religious allegiance, 1851: 18, 67, 69 ff., 75, 81, 106; 1881 (survey of cities): 75, 82; 1902 (*Daily News*): 71 f. (n. 3), 101, 225, 284
Channing, William E., 38, 194
Chapman, John, 34, 37, 95, 146 (n. 8), 256
Chartism, 38, 92, 96 f., 99, 102, 186, 188
Chignell, Mary Ann (See White, Mrs. William)
Chignell, Thomas, 249 (n. 3)
Chignell, William, 251 f.
Children's Employment Commission, 1842, 67 f., 103 f., 133
Christadelphians, 32, 76
Church Rates, 20, 78, 91, 93, 109, 182, 186 ff., 200, 270
Cibber, Colley, 220
Clifford, John, 20, 54, 60, 81, 92, 100, 207 (n. 1), 230, 269, 277, 283
Clough, Arthur Hugh, 83
Cobbett, William, 75, 95, 272 f.
Cogan, Eliezer (or Eli), 108
Colenso, Bishop John William, 47
Coleridge, Samuel Taylor, 91, 93, 95
Collins, Wilkie, 41 (n. 4), 232, 240
Complete Suffrage Union, 92
Comte, Auguste, 143, 281
Conder, E. R., 71
*Congregational Magazine*, 244
Congregational Union of Scotland, 62
*Congregational Year Book*, 267 ff.
Congregationalism (or Independents), 6, 13, 19, 25, 31, 33, 38 ff., 44 ff., 49, 52 f., 57 f., 59 f., 71 f., 74 f., 77, 79,

81, 88, 92 ff., 97, 106 ff., 112, 141 (n. 2), 146, 172 ff., 186 ff., 191 f., 201, 239, 241, 245 f., 251 ff., 263 ff., 267 ff., 275 (n. 2), 277, 283

Congregationalist, 187 (n. 4)

Congregationalist New College, St John's Wood, 250, 263, 269 ff., 272 ff.

Connoisseur, 221

Contemporary Pulpit, 146

Cooper, Thomas, 38, 94, 109

Corn Laws, 78, 89, 91, 104, 186, 236

Cornhill Magazine, 178 f.

Cowper, William, 144 f., 273

Crabbe, George, 16, 25 f., 30, 34, 63

Craigie, Pearl (See Hobbes, John Oliver)

Crockett, S. R., 62

Cromwell, Oliver, 21, 177, 261 f., 266 ff.

Crosby, Sarah, 158 f., 162

Cross, John, 146 (nn. 1, 6), 185

Cross Street Unitarian Chapel, Manchester, 48, 77, 129, 131 ff., 140 ff., 193

Crosskey, H. W., 78

Cruikshank, George, 211 ff.

Cumberland, Richard, 219 f.

Cumming, Dr. John, 178

Daily News Religious Census (See Censuses, and Mudie-Smith, R.)

Dale, R. W., 25 (n. 3), 45 f., 48 (n. 3), 56 (n. 4), 78, 178 f., 187 f., 203 (n. 1), 250, 265

Darby, J. N. 29, 51

Darbyites (See Plymouth Brethren (Exclusive))

Darwin, Charles, 281 ff.

d'Aubigné, Merle, 22, 53

Davidson, Samuel, 46

Dawson, Coningsby William, 61

Dawson, George, 78, 146, 268

Dawson, William James, 61

Defoe, Daniel, 9, 161 (n. 4), 164, 166 f.

Delamere Forest 'Mystic' or 'Magic' Methodists, 26

Denney, James, 23, 214

de Tocqueville, Alexis, 25, 84

Dickens, Charles, 3, 7, 10, 15 f., 27 f., 30, 41, 57 ff., 63, 65 f., 83 ff., 87 f., 91, 108 f., 142, 190–230, 241 f.; Pickwick, 11, 13 ff., 63, 65 f., 85, 117, 142, 190, 192, 195 f., 203 f., 207 ff., 214, 218, 222 f., 226 ff.; Nicholas Nickleby, 192; Old Curiosity Shop, 85, 191, 195 ff., 207, 209, 211, 228, 230; Barnaby

Rudge, 85, 222; Dombey and Son, 28, 41, 86, 190, 211 f.; Bleak House, 3, 11, 14, 35, 41, 63, 66, 69, 117, 190 f., 196, 198, 204, 209, 211 f., 215 ff., 218, 222 f., 226 ff., 241 f., Hard Times, 5, 11, 69, 74, 84 f., 91, 134, 198 f., 204, 242; A Tale of Two Cities, 229; Great Expectations, 170; Our Mutual Friend, 191; 'The Lazy Tour of Two Idle Apprentices', 41 (n. 4); 'The Haunted House', 203; Uncommercial Traveller, 191 ff., 197 f.; 'George Silverman's Explanation', 14, 35, 41, 43 f., 63, 203, 209; Sunday Under Three Heads, 35 f., 85, 195, 211, 218; American Notes, 35, 223; imitations and parodies, 226 ff.

Dickens, Fanny (See Burnett, Mrs. Henry)

Dickens, John and Mrs., 193

Dickens, Sydney Smith Haldimand, 225

Disraeli, Benjamin, 83, 102 f., 108; Contarini Fleming, 108; Coningsby, 18 (n. 3), 68, 79; Sybil, 2, 86, 98, 101 ff., 105; Tancred, 205; Lothair, 102 (n. 5)

Doddridge, Philip, 177, 208, 253

Donne, John, 166

'Down-Grade' debate, 46, 50

Dyer, John, 12, 184 f.

Dyer, Rebekah, 184

Eclectic Review, 54, 58, 195, 222 f., 239

Edinburgh Review, 58, 127, 134 f., 224 f.

Education Acts, 1843: 20, 67 f., 200; 1902: 20

Edwards, George, 92, 94, 100

Eliot, George, 3, 9 f., 12, 23, 34, 37 f., 59, 63 ff., 87, 91, 108, 143–89, 190, 231, 257, 276, 278 ff., 285; Scenes of Clerical Life, 154 f., 231; 'Janet's Repentance', 17, 86, 119 (n. 2), 145, 230; Adam Bede, 2, 12, 17, 37, 43, 63 ff., 68 f., 72 ff., 86, 101, 122, 145, 147–71, 185, 189, 203, 205, 231, 249, 278, 280, 282, 285; Silas Marner, 6, 30, 31 f., 69, 80, 101, 174, 198; Felix Holt, 2, 17, 69, 143 f., 171–89, 204 f., 231, 250, 278, 280, 285; Middlemarch, 2, 9, 16 ff., 64, 69 (n. 5), 127, 169, 171, 177, 180 f., 189, 204; Romola, 171; 'Address to Working Men, by Felix Holt', 2, 178 f.

Eliot, T. S., 1, 229 (n. 3), 278

Elliott, Ebenezer, 268

Ellis, William, 59
Engels, Friedrich, 89, 95, 103
*English Illustrated Magazine* (See under Gosse, Edmund)
Essex Peculiar People, 27, 28 (n. 6), 72, 197
Evans, Howard, 99, 268
Evans, Marian (See Eliot, George)
Evans, Samuel (or 'Seth'), 149 (n. 6), 153, 156 f., 170 (See also *Seth Bede*, '*The Methody*')
Evans, Mrs. Samuel (née Elizabeth Tomlinson), 44, 145 f., 149 f., 152–7, 158 f., 162, 164, 168 –71, 185
Exclusive Brethren (See Plymouth Brethren)
Exeter Free Spiritual Research Society, 32
Exeter Hall, 211

Factory Reform, 89 f., 93, 132, 200
Farrar, Frederick William (*Eric*), 59
Faucher, Léon, 88
Felton, C. C., 194, 211 f.
Fennell, John, 114
Feuerbach, Ludwig, 143 ff., 146 (n. 7), 169 ff.
Fielden, John, 89 f., 132
Fielding, Henry, 214, 219, 221
Fields, J. T., 211, 213 (n. 1)
Fletcher, Elizabeth Sophia, 60 f.
Fletcher, John, 114 f., 149, 161, 163
Fletcher, Mrs. John (née Mary Bosanquet), 114, 157–62, 164
Foote, Samuel, 220 ff.
Forster, E. M., 1, 7, 255
Forster, John, 57 f. (n. 3), 191, 194, 212 f., 268
Forster, W. E., 108
*Fortnightly Review*, 179
Foster, John, 10 f.
*Fountain*, 60
Fowler, Ellen Thorneycroft, 60
Fowler, Henry, 60
Fox, George, 41, 207, 262
Fox, W. J., 146, 194
Franklin, Francis, 12, 146, 183 ff.
Franklin, Mary and Rebecca, 12, 146, 185
*Fraser's Magazine*, 29, 51, 226
Free Church Council, 62, 269
Free Church of Scotland, 62 f., 107, 234, 236 f.
Fuller, Andrew, 45, 184

Gadsby, William, 94
Galsworthy, John, 201
Gaskell, William, 48, 127, 129 f., 141 f., 193
Gaskell, Mrs. William (née Elizabeth Cleghorn Stevenson), 13, 30, 58, 73, 79 f., 83, 90 f., 95 f., 105 (nn. 1, 2), 107, 112, 125, 127–42, 154, 194; *Mary Barton*, 74, 90, 95 f., 101, 132 ff., *Ruth*, 2, 13 ff., 17, 63, 101, 127 f., 131, 134, 138 ff., 202 f., 205, 210; *Cranford*, 141 f.; *North and South*, 74, 91, 95 f., 136 ff., 207; 'My Lady Ludlow', 79 f., 138, 203; 'Lois The Witch', 139; *Sylvia's Lovers*, 64, 139, 203; *Cousin Phillis*, 15, 17, 43, 63, 140, 142, 280; *Wives and Daughters*, 13, 139, 141 (n. 2); 141 f.
*General Baptist Magazine*, 60
General Baptist New Connexion, 28, 38, 92 ff., 115
General Baptists, 28, 184, 269
George, David Lloyd, 28, 230, 269
Gide, André, 256
Gilbert, W. S., 201
Giles, Rev. William, 192 f.
Giles, Rev. William, Jr., 192 f.
Gissing, George, 65, 195, 232
Gladstone, W. E., 20, 269
Golding, William, 67
Goldsmith, Oliver, 221 f., 262
Gosse, Edmund, 51, 54 (n. 5), 55, 107, 126, 191, 196; *The Unequal Yoke* (*English Illustrated Magazine*), 19, 74, 101, 206
Gosse, Emily, 49, 51, 54 f.
Gosse, Philip Henry, 33, 54 ff., 109
Gosse, Mrs. Philip Henry (See Emily Gosse)
Gosse, Thomas, 33 (n. 7)
Graham, Sir James, 67 f., 200 (See also Education Acts)
Graves, Richard, 218 f.
Greene, Graham, 257
Greg, Robert Hyde, 133
Greg, Samuel, 133, 135 ff., 141
Greg, William Rathbone, 133 ff.
Griffin, James, 191
Grimshaw, William, 42, 113, 115 f., 120 f.
Gurney family, 201
Guthrie, Ramsay, 74, 279
Guthrie, Thomas, 82
Guyon, Madame, 160, 162

Halévy, Élie, 266 f.
Halifax Psychological Society, 32
Hall, Robert, 187
Hardy, Thomas, 34, 37, 73, 110 ff., 126, 279 ff.; *Far from the Madding Crowd*, 44 (n. 3); *Return of the Native*, 279; *A Laodicean*, 15 f., 18, 39, 43, 69, 80, 86 f., 101, 110 f., 200 ff., 210, 285 f.; 'The Distracted Preacher', 13, 24, 74, 107; *Tess*, 24, 37, 47, 63, 74, 111, 204, 279, 282, 285; *The Dynasts*, 281
Harrison, Frederic, 172, 179
Harvey, William Edwin, 100
Hazlitt, William, 223 f.
Henderson, W. T., 92, 188, 269
Hennell, Charles Christian, 146
Henry, Matthew, 127 f., 133, 137, 177, 253
Henry, Philip, 128, 133, 137
Herbert, George, 10, 144, 261
Higginson, Henry (The Roving Ranter), 40
Hillyard, Samuel, 257, 264 f., 273, 277
Hinton, James, 184, 186 f.
Hinton, Dr. James, 185
Hinton, John Howard, 146, 185, 187
Hobbes, John Oliver, 60
Hocking, Joseph, 49, 56, 61, 74, 279
Hocking, Silas, 30, 44 (n. 1), 47, 57, 60, 62, 74, 92, 101, 208, 230, 279
Holiness Movements, 27, 282
Hone, William, 190, 211 ff.
Hood, Edwin Paxton, 268
Hood, Thomas, 222
Hopkins, G. M., 207 (n. 1)
Horne, C. S., 268, 277
Horne, R. H., 103 f.
Horton, R. F., 268, 277
*Household Words*, 23, 27, 79 (n. 5), 88 (n. 2), 91, 134, 190 f., 195, 197, 199, 207, 211, 222
Howe, John, 177, 188
Howells, William Dean, 249
Howitt, Mary, 133
Howitt, William, 27, 94, 133
Hughes, Hugh Price, 22, 284
Hughes, Thomas, 206 f.; *Tom Brown's Schooldays*, 59; *Tom Brown at Oxford*, 21
Hull, William, 243, 245
Hunt, Leigh, 223
Huntingdon, Selina Countess of, 5, 113, 115, 117 f.; Countess of Huntingdon's Connexion, 47, 117 f.; Countess of Huntingdon's College, Cheshunt, 250

Hymns, 40, 42 f., 47, 57, 86 f., 96, 99, 105, 112, 116, 119, 122 ff., 149, 164–7, 185

Independents (See Congregationalism)
Independent Methodists (Scarborough), 26
Independent Methodists (Singing Quakers), 26, 42, 43
Independent Religious Reformers, 32
Independent Wesleyans (North Wales), 26
Irving, Edward, 29 f., 32, 51, 232, 235, 246 f., 252, 285
Irvingites (Catholic Apostolic Church), 29, 32, 34, 76, 93, 197, 252

Jackson, William, 93
James, Henry, 6, 147, 170, 231 f., 234
James, John Angell, 48, 56, 187 f., 264
Johnson, Samuel, 5, 142, 160
Jones, Ernest, 98
Jonson, Ben, 220, 222
Jukes, John, 257, 264 f., 270 ff.
Jukes, Susanna Clewin, 272

Keats, John, 25, 215
Kilham, Alexander, 26 (for Kilhamites, see Methodist New Connexion)
Kingsley, Charles, 22, 36 ff., 54, 59, 63, 66, 73 f., 108 ff., 119 (n. 2), 206 f., 210; *Yeast*, 74, 102, 201 f.; *Alton Locke*, 14 f., 22 f., 43, 45, 52, 63, 74, 102, 108 f., 202, 210, 280; *Westward Ho!*, 280; *Two Years Ago*, 23, 36 f., 52, 63 f., 66, 74, 102, 107, 109, 207, 210, 230, 280

Labour Church, 100
Labour Party, 284
Lamb, Charles, 221
Lancashire Independent College, 46, 58
Lansbury, George, 90
Lavington, Bishop George, 215, 221
Lawrence, D. H., 8, 284; *Sons and Lovers*, 181; 'Daughters of the Vicar', 14; 'St. Mawr', 23; 'Hymns in a Man's Life', 40, 112, 128
Lay preachers, 43 f., 52
'Learned Ministry', 176 f., 264
Leavis, F. R., 83, 149 (n. 1), 170 (n. 3), 174 (n. 3), 178 (n. 1), 198
Leavis, Q. D., 3, 83, 120, 126 (n. 1)
Lee, Bishop James Prince, 138, 141
*Leeds Intelligencer*, 105

*Leeds Mercury*, 67, 77
Lewes, G. H., 12, 18 (n. 3), 59 (n. 4), 125, 143, 146 (n. 8), 147, 154, 157, 170, 185, 231
Liberal Party, 33, 92 f., 134, 182, 183 (n. 2), 267 ff., 283 f.
Liberation Society (The Society for the Liberation of Religion from State Control), 92, 182 f., 187, 238 f. (See also British Anti-State-Church Association)
Liddon, Canon Henry, 47
*Life and Labour of the People in London* (See Booth, Charles)
Liggins, Joseph, 155 f., 164
Lion Walk Congregationalist Church, Colchester, 249 f.
London Missionary Society, 59
*London Quarterly Review*, 36
Luther, Martin, 254, 257
Lytton, Bulwer, 53, 170, 232

Macdonald, George, 30, 59, 202 f., 212 (n. 1), 230
Maclaren, Ian, 62
Macleod, Norman, 48
McLuhan, Marshall, 281 (n. 3), 284 (n. 1)
*Macmillan's Magazine*, 178, 180
Madge, Travers, 31, 76, 131
Maes, Nicolas, 145 (n. 2)
*Manchester Guardian*, 77, 130 (n. 1), 133
*Manchester Times*, 77
Mann, Horace (See Censuses, 1851)
Martin, Basil, 39, 81, 92, 202, 263, 269
Martineau, Harriet, 57, 88, 126, 143
Martineau, James, 141, 147
Martyn, Henry, 108, 113, 119
Marx, Karl, 79, 89 f., 143
Maurice, F. D., 37, 109
Maxwell, Gavin, 34, 93 (n. 2)
Maxwell, Sir Herbert, 34 (n. 3), 93 (n. 2)
Mayhew, Henry, 82 f.
Methodism, 6, 25, 28, 31, 38 f., 43 f., 47, 52, 60 f., 63 ff., 66, 68 ff., 70, 72 ff., 76, 88, 92 ff., 100 f., 107, 113 ff., 139, 145, 147 ff., 190, 207, 210, 215 ff., 239, 252 f., 278 ff., 284 f. (See also Arminian Methodists (Derby Faith Folk); Band Room Methodists; Bristol Tent Methodists; Bryanites (Bible Christians); Calvinistic Methodists; Countess of Huntingdon's Connexion— under Huntingdon; Delamere Forest 'Magic' or 'Mystic' Methodists; Inde-

pendent Methodists (Singing Quakers); Independent Methodists (Scarborough); Independent Wesleyans (North Wales); Methodist New Connexion; Primitive Methodism; Protestant Methodists (Leeds); Revivalist Methodists of Leeds; Scottish United Methodist Churches; Teetotal Methodists; United Methodist Free Churches; Welsh Methodists; Wesleyan (Methodist) Association; Wesleyan Reform Union)
*Methodist Magazine*, 37 (n. 3), 116 f., 151 (n. 6), 152 (n. 1), 159, 161 f. (n. 4), 164, 168. (See also *Arminian Magazine*)
Methodist New Connexion, 26 f., 29, 37 (n. 4), 38, 50, 70, 91, 97, 121, 283
*Methodist New Connexion Magazine*, 60 f.
*Methodist Times*, 56
Miall, Edward, 53, 58, 75 (n. 1), 79, 92, 98, 106, 182, 183 (n. 1), 187 f., 204 f., 207 (n. 1), 263 f., 268, 270
Milnes, Monckton, 89, 201
Milton, John, 175, 208, 247, 262, 268
Molière, Jean Baptiste de, 220, 223
Moody, D. L., 34, 41 (n. 4), 45, 83
Moore, George, 231; *Esther Waters*, 52, 74
Moravians, 25, 40, 75, 125
More, Hannah, 225
Morison, James, 62
Morisonian Evangelical Union, 62
Mormons, 76, 217
Morris, Caleb, 41, 249, 251 f., 256 ff., 260 f., 275
Mudie, Charles Edward, 59
Mudie-Smith, R., 225, 284. (See also Censuses, 1902)
Muir, Edwin, 52
Murdoch, Iris, 3, 6, 8 f., 216
Mursell, J. P., 92, 187

Nasmyth, James, 136
*National Temperance Magazine*, 53
Neal (or Neale), Daniel, 172 ff., 177 f.
Nelson, John, 55, 148, 151
Newman, Francis W., 51
Newman, J. H., 14, 25
Nicoll, William Roberton, 23 (n. 2), 62, 194, 201, 213 (n. 1), 214, 236, 252 (n. 3), 254 (n. 1), 256, 264 (n. 2), 269 (n. 8), 275 (n. 2)
Niebuhr, H. Richard, 33
*Nonconformist*, 21, 31, 53, 58, 67, 78 f.,

92, 147, 174, 178, 182, 187, 237 ff.,
241 (n. 1), 242 f., 245 ff., 270, 274
'Nonconformist Conscience', 56
*North of England Magazine,* 76
Nussey, Ellen, 121 f.

Oakley, John, 20
Oastler, Richard, 89
Oliphant, F. R., 233 (n. 1), 236 f.
Oliphant, M. O. W., 10, 23, 107, 175,
189, 196, 225, 230, 231–48; *Passages in
the Life of Mrs. Margaret Maitland,* 234;
*Magdalen Hepburn,* 234 f.; *Lilliesleaf,*
234; *Salem Chapel,* 13, 65, 109, 202 f.,
231 ff.; *Perpetual Curate,* 241 (n. 1), 242;
*A Son of the Soil,* 239; *The Minister's Wife,*
232 f., 235, 241; *Phoebe, Junior,* 65, 69,
200 ff., 231 ff.
Orwell, George, 84, 112 (n. 2), 171, 197,
212
Oxford University, 19 ff., 85

Parker, Joseph, 47, 50, 59 f., 62, 256
Particular Baptists, 28, 45, 146, 184,
201
*Patriot,* 182, 211, 239
Payne, John Burnell, 12, 185
Payne, Joseph Frank, 12, 185
Peake, A. S., 47
Pearse, Mark Guy, 61, 73 f., 279 f.
Pease, Joseph, 89
Pentecostalism, 101, 282 f., 285
*People's Paper,* 98
Perkins family, 110 f.
Peto, Sir Samuel Morton, 201 f.
Philips, Mark, 133
Phillips, R. N., 141
Philpotts, Bishop Henry, 177
*Physiologist of the Sects,* 41, 60, 188, 202
(n. 4)
Plymouth Brethren, 19, 29, 31, 33, 38 f.,
44, 51 ff., 72, 74, 81, 93, 107 f., 252;
Exclusive Brethren, 33, 47, 211
'Political Dissent', 176, 183, 185 ff., 245,
261
Positivists, 32
Potter, Beatrix, 132
Potter, Edmund, 132
Potter, John, 133
Potter, Sir John, 77, 132 f.
Potter, Richard, 132
Potter, Sidney, 132
Potter, Thomas, 77, 132

Potter, Thomas Bayley, 132
Pound, Ezra, 229
Presbyterian Church of England, 62
Presbyterians, 25, 48, 88, 236
Primitive Methodism, 13 (n. 3), 19, 26,
32, 37 (n. 4), 38, 40 f., 43, 46, 52, 70,
72, 81, 85, 92 ff., 96 ff., 101, 103 f.,
109, 112, 145, 153, 155, 169, 171, 202,
282 f.
*Primitive Methodist Magazine,* 60
Pritchett, V. S., 94, 197, 211 (n. 1)
Protestant Methodists (Leeds), 26
Pugin, Augustus Welby, 84, 86 f., 205 f.
*Punch,* 229
*Puritan,* 22 (n. 2), 23 (n. 5), 43 (n. 4), 49
(n. 2), 56, 62, 106
*Putnam's Magazine,* 222 f.

Quakers, 20, 25, 29, 34, 38, 40 f., 44, 53,
59, 63 f., 75, 77, 84, 88 f., 92 f., 108,
122, 127 (n. 2), 140, 149, 201 ff.,
205
*Quarterly Review,* 58, 76

Ragged School Union, 83
*Ragged School Union Magazine,* 228
Ramsbottom, Samuel, 61
Ramus, Peter, 176
Rands, William Brighty, 59
Ranters, 26, 40 ff., 97 f., 122, 176
Reade, Charles, 232 f.
Reed, Joseph, 220 ff.
Revivalism, 29, 34 ff., 150 f., 235
Revivalist Methodists of Leeds, 26
Reynolds, Henry Robert, 59
Reynolds, John Russell, 59
Richardson, Samuel, 218
Riehl, Wilhelm Heinrich von, 143
Rigg, J. H., 36 f., 66, 108 (n. 2), 109
*Rivulet* controversy, 46
Robbe-Grillet, Alain, 7 f.
Robberds, John Gooch, 129, 193
Roberson, Hammond, 105
Robinson, Frederick William (*Church and
Chapel*), 238
Rosevear, W. T., 156
Roth, Philip, 229
Rowse, A. L., 33, 41, 226 (n. 3)
Ruskin, John, 84, 107, 109, 256 (n. 1)
Russell, Lord John, 272 f., 276
Rutherford, Mark (See White, William
Hale)
Ryland, John, 184

Sadler, Michael, 89, 93
Salvation Army, 27, 34, 39 ff., 72, 74, 81, 99, 101, 226 (n. 3), 229, 245, 282 f.
Sankey, Ira D., 34, 83
Scales, Thomas, 268
Scargill, William Pitt, 175, 243
Scotch Baptists, 28
Scott, Walter, 48 f., 166, 177, 231
Scottish United Methodist Churches, 26
Selkirk, Alexander (*The Country and Church of the Cheeryble Brothers*), 5
Senior, Nassau, 56
Sergeant, Adeline, 60
*Seth Bede*, 'The Methody', 5, 156, 170 (n. 4) (See also Evans, Samuel)
Seventh-Day Baptists, 28, 176 f., 188, 209, 230 (See also Black, W. H.)
Shaftesbury, Anthony Ashley, Earl of, 34, 68, 89 f., 224
*Sheffield Independent*, 77
Sibree, John, 146, 185 (n. 4), 186, 188
Simeon, Charles, 108, 113
Skevington, John, 97
Smiles, Samuel, 82, 286
Smith, Frederick R. (See Ackworth, John)
Smith, Gipsy Rodney, 94
Smith, J. Pye, 58
Smith, Sidney, 10, 224 f.
Smith, W. H., 59
Smollett, Tobias, 218, 221
Society for the Liberation of Religion from State Control (See Liberation Society)
Southcott, Joanna, 252
Southey, Robert, 101 (n. 3), 125 (n. 2), 148–52, 153, 164, 252 (n. 5)
Sparks, Tryphena, 111
*Spectator*, 221 f., 231, 241, 246 (n. 1)
Spencer, Herbert, 143
Spicer, Albert, 202
Spiritualists, 32, 76
Spurgeon, C. H., 19, 34, 41 ff., 45 ff., 50, 55, 71, 144, 208, 252 (n. 3), 269, 285
Steele, Richard, 221
Steiner, George, 277 (n. 1)
Stephens, Joseph Rayner, 97
Stevenson, Elizabeth Cleghorn (See Gaskell, Mrs. William)
Stevenson, William, 127, 129
Stickney, Sarah, 59
Stoughton, John, 49
Stowe, Harriet Beecher, 144; *Minister's Wooing*, 59; *Uncle Tom's Cabin*, 48, 56

Strict and Particular Baptists, 28, 45, 94, 121, 285 (See also Suffolk and Norfolk New Association of Strict Baptists)
Sturge, Joseph, 92
Suffolk and Norfolk New Association of Strict Baptists, 28, 72
Swan, Annie S., 62
Swift, Jonathan, 222
*Sword and Trowel*, 50, 55 (n. 4), 269 (n. 6)

Tagart, Edward, 193 f., 197
*Tait's Edinburgh Magazine*, 59 (n. 4)
Tayler, John James, 130, 141
Taylor, Dan, 45, 93, 115
Taylor, Joshua, 50, 121 f.
Taylor, Mary, 121 f.
Teetotal Methodists, 27
Teetotal movement, 36, 38, 53, 78, 83, 85, 92, 99, 204, 206, 211, 218
*Teetotaler*, 53
Thackeray, W. M., 3, 10, 22, 28 (n. 3), 59, 63 f., 108, 214, 226, 228 f.; *Vanity Fair*, 22, 203, 205, 207, 211, 222; *The Newcomers*, 63, 206
Thompson, E. P., 44, 55 (n. 1), 90 (n. 3), 93 (n. 6), 95 (n. 5), 97 f., 100 (n. 1)
Thompson, Flora, 32, 44
Thompson, Jemima, 57
Thomson, James, 28, 38
Told, Silas, 167 f.
Tom Paine Methodists (See Methodist New Connexion)
Tomlinson, Elizabeth (See Evans, Mrs. Samuel)
Trevor, John, 100
Troeltsch, Ernst, 141
Trollope, Anthony, 10, 48 f., 56, 59, 104, 110, 220, 223, 225, 232, 234, 238; *The Warden*, 14, 226; *Small House at Allington*, 41 f. (n. 4); *Miss Mackenzie*, 210; *Vicar of Bullhampton*, 14, 19, 22, 24, 73, 85 f., 101, 207 f., 230; *John Caldigate*, 16, 207 f.
Trollope, Frances, 10, 22, 35, 109, 219 f., 223, 225 f.; *Domestic Manners of the Americans*, 35, 223, 226; *Vicar of Wrexhill*, 22, 223, 225 f.
Tuckniss, William, 82 f.
Turner, William, 2, 127, 129

*Unitarian Review*, 281 (n. 2)
Unitarianism, 25, 28, 31 f., 34, 38 ff., 48,

57 ff., 71, 73, 75, 77 f., 84, 88, 90, 93, 107, 127 ff., 146 ff., 193 ff., 197, 250 f.
United Methodist Free Churches, 27, 38, 47, 57
*United Methodist Free Churches Magazine*, 47 (n. 5), 60
United Secession Church, 62

Vaughan, Robert, 58, 76, 268
Vince, Charles, 78
Vincent, Henry, 268
Voce, Mary, 146, 154, 167–9
Voluntary Church Society, 187
Voluntaryism, 174 f., 182, 186, 200, 243 f.

Walworth Jumpers, 28, 75 f., 229
*War Cry*, 245
Watson, John (See Maclaren, Ian)
Watts, John, 186
Waugh, Evelyn, 5
Webb, Beatrice, 10, 95 f., 109, 132, 208
Weber, Max, 150
Welsh Methodists, 76
Wesley, Charles, 115, 165, 167, 285
Wesley, John, 5, 52, 70, 91, 101, 103, 113, 115 f., 121 ff., 148 ff., 157 ff., 167 (n. 2), 207, 219, 232, 252, 280, 282 (See also Southey, Robert)
Wesleyan (Methodist) Association, 26. (See also United Methodist Free Churches)
*Wesleyan Methodist Magazine*, 60
Wesleyan Reform Union, 27, 70
Wesleyanism, 23, 33, 36 ff., 44, 52, 60 f., 68, 70, 72 ff., 75, 84, 92 f., 96 f., 99 f., 100 (n. 1), 103 f., 108, 115 ff., 145, 157, 159 f., 163 f., 170, 201, 206 f., 253, 283, 285
*Westminster Review*, 34 (n. 5), 143 ff., 146 (n. 8), 147, 162

*Whitaker's Almanack*, 25, 32 (n. 1)
White, Edward, 46
White, William, 249 f., 265, 268, 270, 272 ff.
White, Mrs. William (née Mary Ann Chignell), 249, 275
White, William Hale (Mark Rutherford), 10, 23, 34, 38 f., 41, 73, 107, 175, 189, 199, 249–77, 279, 285; *Autobiography of Mark Rutherford*, 44, 63, 249 f., 258 f., 262, 264, 274, 276, 278; *Mark Rutherford's Deliverance*, 80, 205, 249, 252 (n. 5), 256, 257 (n. 6), 276, 279; *Revolution in Tanner's Lane*, 2, 18, 63 ff., 74, 249–77, 280; *Miriam's Schooling and Other Papers*, 257 (n. 6), 258; 'Michael Trevanion', 16, 259; *Catharine Furze*, 202, 250 f., 252 (n. 5), 253, 258 f., 275; *Clara Hopgood*, 251, 252 (n. 5), 253, 255, 259, 268
White, Mrs. W. H. (née Harriet Arthur), 252
White, Mrs. W. H. (née Dorothy Vernon Horace Smith), 249, 251, 257 (n. 5), 258
Whitefield (or Whitfield), George, 17, 47, 113, 115, 151, 159, 183, 188, 215, 218–22 (See also Calvinistic Methodists)
Wigglesworth, Smith, 282 f.
Wilberforce, Samuel, 18
Willenhall, Staffordshire, 103 f.
Wilson, Carus, 49
Winkworth, Susanna and Catherine, 130
*Woman at Home* (or *Annie Swan's Magazine*), 62
Wood, Mrs. Henry, 233, 240
Woodhouse Grove Wesleyan Academy, 114, 119
Woolf, Virginia, 6
Woolmer, Theophilus, 61
Wordsworth, William, 258